ADROS VERSE EDUCATION S.R.L.

Learn & Retain

Spanish

with Spaced Repetition

5,000+ Vocabulary, Grammar, & Audio Pronunciation with Anki

Bucharest - 2022

Table of Contents

I. Introduction to Spaced Repetition

Remember all the times that you learned something just to forget it when you get rusty after not practicing for a while? Now imagine that there is some way to remind yourself of only the things that you are about to forget before you forget them, without boring yourself with the ones that you have already memorized. You may think that this would be convenient but also impossible, when in fact, it is possible using *spaced repetition*. Spaced repetition is a method of learning new material and then reviewing and memorizing that material over *spaced* intervals. Spaced repetition is often carried out using *flashcards*. The cards that you memorize successfully (i.e., *easy* material) will be reviewed less often, whereas the cards that you stumble over and struggle to memorize (i.e., *hard* material) will be shown more often.

In essence, spaced repetition is an enhancement of the old technique of learning by flashcards. Flashcards rely on cramming the material into the learner's memory regardless of how many times the learner successfully memorizes the material. This makes the learning process inefficient and exhausting. Spaced repetition addresses this flaw by presenting the material to the learner with a frequency that is inversely proportional to his or her ability to memorize it. This way, the learner will ideally be presented with the learned material right before he or she is about to forget it. As you can guess, this technique comes in handy when used to learn new vocabulary.

There has been a lot of research on the usefulness of the spaced repetition of learned material since its first proposal by C. A. Mace in 1932. Since then, it has remained a subject of interest for many researchers and people who seek to improve their memory. In any case, we believe that the improvement that spaced repetition adds to old flashcard techniques, especially in the context of learning a new language, is substantial.

ANKI: THE MOST POPULAR SPACED REPETITION SOFTWARE

To apply spaced repetition to flashcards, we need to decide on many parameters, such as the interval between reviews and whether the interval is fixed or graduated. Many software programs use algorithms to implement spaced-repetition learning. We will not delve into the details of each software and the algorithms they use. Instead, we will pick the most popular software among students and language learners, and that is *Anki*. The word "Anki" in Japanese means "memorization." It is an application developed by Damien Elmes in 2006 that uses an algorithm called SM-2, developed by SuperMemo. The software seems to offer many features while maintaining a reasonable level of simplicity.

In the next chapter, we will walk you briefly through the basics of Anki, how to install it, and how to use the basic features. The Anki software can be used on a desktop device (AnkiWeb) or a smartphone using Android (AnkiDroid) or iOS (AnkiMobile). The use of AnkiWeb and AnkiDroid is free. AnkiMobile, unfortunately, is paid and can be purchased from the Apple Store. Alternatively, if you use an iPhone or iPad, you could install AnkiWeb on your computer and test it for a few days. If you like it, you can continue to use AnkiWeb or purchase AnkiMobile—if you deem it worthwhile. If you create an account using your Anki software, you can synchronize your account on different devices, including multiple desktops and mobile phones.

USING ANKI FOR LANGUAGE LEARNING

There are many studies out there that try to answer the question: "How many words do I need to know to understand X% of a language?" Stuart Webb, professor of linguistics at the University of Western Ontario, asserts that a typical native speaker knows 15,000 to 20,000 word families. A word family is the base form, or root, of a word (e.g., break, breaker, broken, broke, etc., all count as one word family). A language learner who learns only 800 of the most common words in English can understand 75% of the daily-spoken language.

Research done by Francis and Kucera in 1982 found that having a vocabulary size of 2,000 word families is sufficient to cover nearly 80% of a written English text.

To understand dialogue in a movie or on TV, Professor Webb asserts that you need to know 3,000 of the most common word families. A similar assertion has been made by famous linguist Paul Nation, who defines 3,000 as the reasonable threshold of high-frequency words needed by a second-language learner.

With over 5,000 flashcards of verbs, nouns, and adjectives, as well as detailed grammar lessons, this book aims at getting you to that level where you can converse, understand, and speak Spanish in everyday settings.

A lot of Anki cards are available online. Some are free, and many others are on the costlier side. However, the issue with many of the available products is that they simply do not have progressive guidelines that go hand-in-hand with the cards. After all, memorization is different from knowledge acquisition, which requires an understanding of the material you are learning. We attempt to solve this missing piece of the puzzle by providing the proper introduction, learning progression, and grammar knowledge to make sense of the information you are trying to memorize.

We would like to clarify that although Spanish in Spain and Spanish in Latin America have their differences, most of the grammar and vocabulary remain unchanged. Thus, this book is useful for learners of both variations of the language. When it comes to regional differences in vocabulary and pronunciation, we generally focus on Latin American Spanish without limiting ourselves to a specific country or region.

We truly hope that many learners will find this technique and this book useful and that learning Spanish and other languages will find its way to as many people as possible to help us understand and recognize each other in a way that serves humanity as a whole.

HOW TO USE THIS BOOK

First and foremost, make sure that you read Chapter II of this book following this introduction. This chapter will help you set up Anki on your desktop computer and mobile device(s). It is essential that you do that successfully to gain the maximum benefit of this book. The coupon code to obtain the flashcards, available for free for a limited time, can be found in **Appendix A**. Once you download the cards and back them up with the Anki account you create, the cards do not expire.

As you go through each level's introductory topics and grammar, we recommend that you use this book to read the levels and lessons in the order that they are presented. You can, of course, go quickly over the lessons that you find familiar. Nevertheless, we do not recommend that you skip any lesson. The best way to study using this book is to start with reading Level I, Lesson 1 in the book, then go to your Anki app and activate the cards of that lesson. If the lesson is easy compared to your level, you will be able to answer most of the cards as *easy*. As a result, you will see these cards less often in the future as they *fade away* in the memory of the app.

There may be some lessons that you find useful to return to for further review or reference. We try to point these out throughout the book. The appendix also contains some cheat sheets that summarize some of these rules. You can use those if you find them useful. The Anki app will help you through this process because it will keep repeating the concepts that slip your memory.

In the vocabulary-building section, we cover basic verbs and adjectives; then, we go over nouns from different categories. The vocabulary-building section of each level in this book is meant to serve as a reference rather than be used to read and memorize the content by rote. The Anki flashcards are intended to take away the dull and boring part of that process. We recommend that you take a look at the vocabulary section of the book for an overview of the topics and use the Anki flashcards to learn the new vocabulary.

In case you want to look up a word, you will find a Spanish index, followed by an English index at the end of the book.

Finally, in the appendix, you will find two useful cheat sheets that give you an overall perspective of most moods and verb tenses in Spanish. The first cheat sheet is the Verb Conjugation Chart, which is structured as a comprehensive reference for the reader. The second sheet dives deeper into the irregular verbs of each tense where necessary.

We recommend that you keep these two sheets handy by printing them out or having them available separately on your desk or electronic device.

II. Setting Up Anki

This is an important chapter that you should NOT skip if you want to use the Anki flashcards that accompany the book, which is highly recommended for your maximum benefit.

In this chapter, we cover how to download the Anki software, import the ADROS VERSE EDUCATION Spanish Anki package, and activate the cards associated with the lessons in the book as you read through it.

If you prefer video instructions, go to our YouTube page at https://youtu.be/s53C0vcQPLc or simply search for **ADROS VERSE EDUCATION** channel on YouTube and look for the title: **Setting up Anki and Importing the ADROS VERSE Package**.

The video in the link above goes through the same steps explained in this chapter.

DOWNLOAD ANKI SOFTWARE

The first step is to download the latest version of Anki compatible with your desktop, Android, or iOS device(s). You can download Anki on different devices and synchronize all of them to the latest study review that you have completed. It is highly recommended that you download a desktop version first to use it as a master copy and then synchronize any other mobile devices you have. However, you can choose to use Anki on your mobile device only.

Windows Desktop

1. Go to https://apps.ankiweb.net/ and download the latest Anki version for Windows. The procedure is similar for Mac and Linux if you use a different operating system.
2. Run the ".exe" file, and open the program by double-clicking on the Anki icon.

3. A default window will open under the username **"User 1**." It is recommended that you create an account to have a backup of your data in the cloud and synchronize it with other devices. To create an account, click on **"Sync**." A window that says **"Account Required"** will pop up. Click on **"Sign Up**." This will take you to a web page where you can complete the signup process.

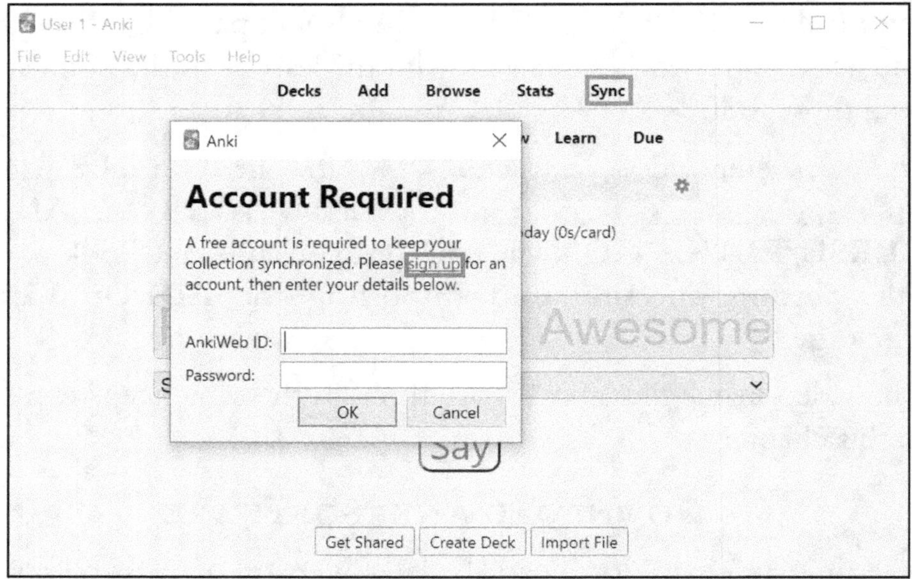

Android or iOS

1. If you have an Android device, go to **"Google Play"** and download **"AnkiDroid Flashcards**," available for free. If you have an iOS device, go to **"Apple Store"** and download **"AnkiMobile Flashcards**." Unfortunately, at the time of writing this book, the app is not free and is sold by **"Apple Store"** for $24.99. Alternatively, you can choose to use the desktop version for free.

2. Open the app from your mobile device.

3. If you have created an account on desktop Anki, you can simply synchronize to your account.

- ❖ On Android: Tap the three horizontal lines at the top left of the screen. Then, select **Settings** > **General Settings** > **AnkiWeb** account. Enter the same email from the account you created on desktop Anki.
- ❖ On iOS: Tap "**Synchronize**" at the bottom right of the screen and enter the same email from the account you created on desktop Anki.

4. If you have not created an account on desktop Anki, you can continue to use Anki on your mobile device without creating an account. However, you will not have any backup online if you lose the data on your phone.

DOWNLOAD & IMPORT THE SPANISH ANKI PACKAGE

After downloading the Anki software on your device, you need to download the Anki package (.apkg) created specifically for this book.

Windows Desktop

1. Go to https://www.adrosverse.com/books-and-flashcards/, and download the "**Spanish: All-Levels Complete Course**" package. At the check-out, use the discount code provided to you in **Appendix A**. If you purchased the book, you should get the Anki package for FREE for a limited time. Once you download the cards, the cards do not expire.
2. After downloading the package, take note of the folder in which it was downloaded.
3. Go to your Anki app, and in the menu bar, go to "**File**," then select "**Import**" from the list of options and navigate to where the package was downloaded.

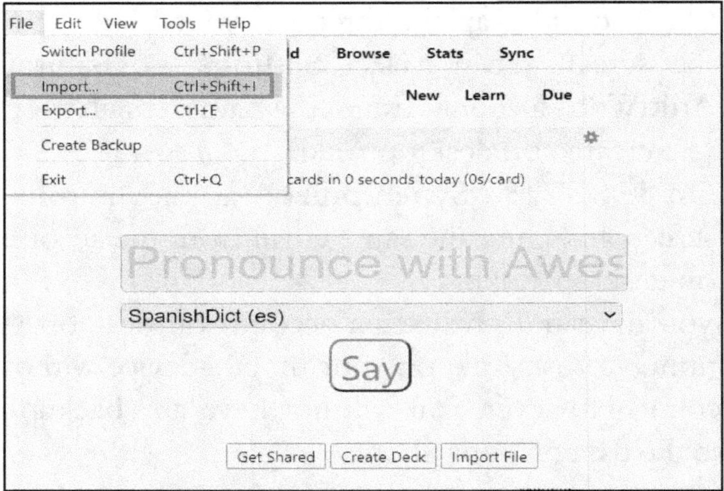

4. If you have not done so already, you can still create an account to save a backup copy online and synchronize it with other devices by clicking on the **"Sync"** button; this is highly recommended.

Android or iOS

If you have created an account on a desktop device, you only need to log in to your account on the mobile Anki app and synchronize it with the backup copy online.

If you want to continue without creating an account, you can still download and import the package on Android. This is a little more difficult on iOS because you may need to create a download link.

ACTIVATE CARDS

As you successfully import the Anki package with all the lessons, you may realize that all the cards are suspended. This is done intentionally because you do not want to be presented with cards from all levels before you even start reading the book.

You are expected to start reading Level 1, Lesson 1. After you finish, you want to activate or *unsuspend* the cards associated with that lesson. To do this, follow the simple steps described here.

Windows Desktop

1. On the main Anki page where decks are presented, click on "**Browse.**"

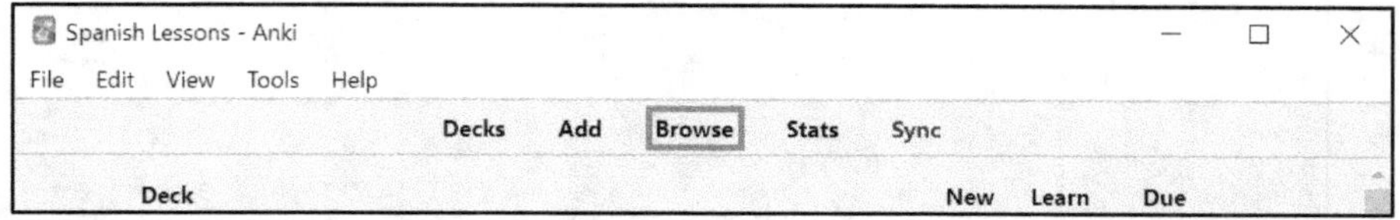

2. Highlight Lesson 1 from the menu on the left.

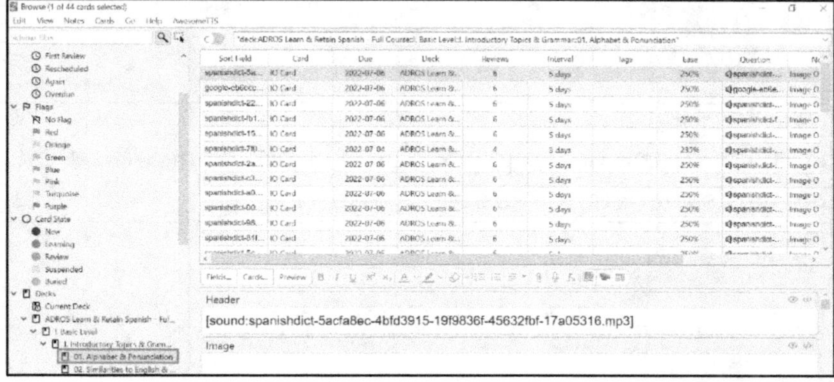

3. Highlight all the cards (shown on the right) in Lesson 1 using CTRL+A. Alternatively, you can click on **Edit > Select All**.

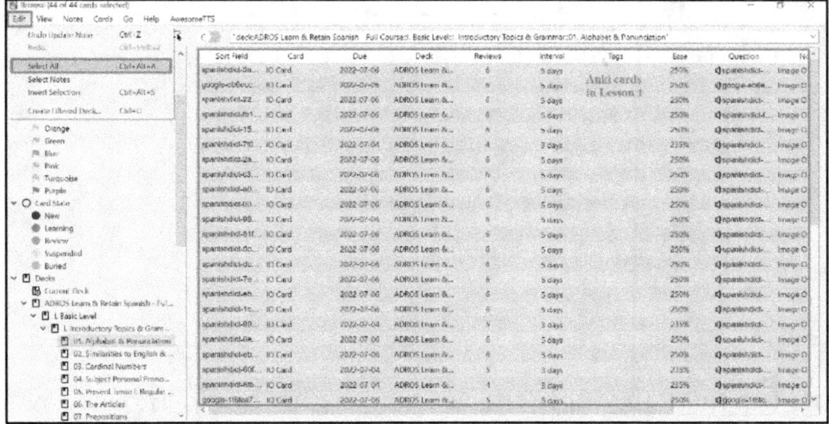

4. After highlighting all the cards from Lesson 1, activate them by clicking on **Cards > Toggle Suspend** to unsuspend the cards.

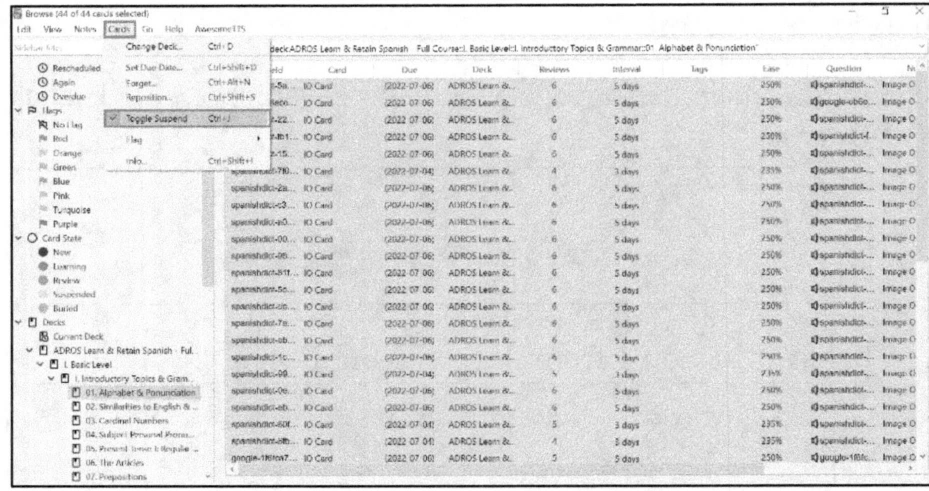

5. Go back to the decks page. You will notice now that there are a few cards that are due from Lesson 1.

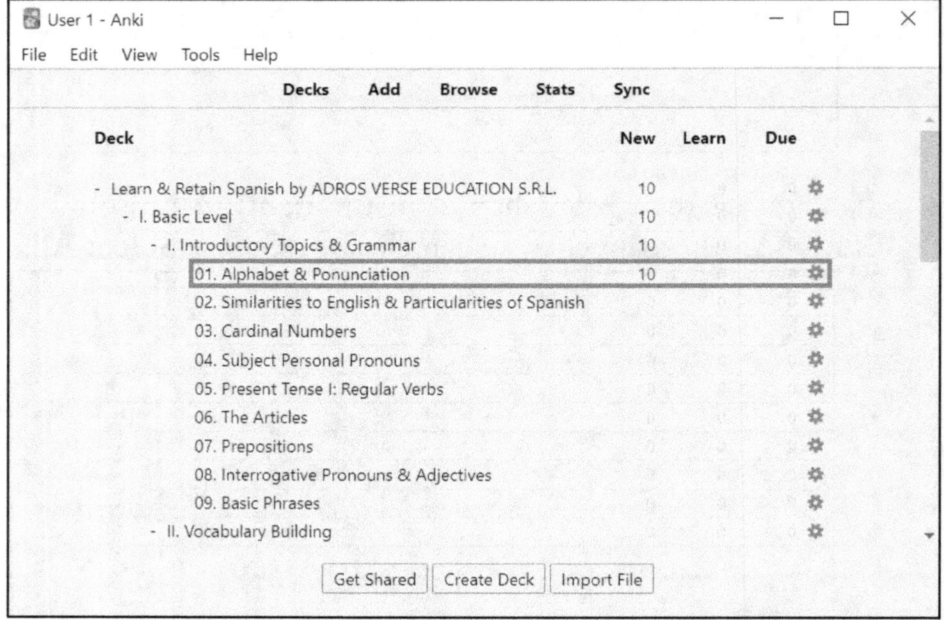

6. If you read through the lesson in the book and are ready, you can start studying and reviewing the cards by clicking on the deck, as highlighted above.

7. On the next page, click on the **"Study Now"** button.

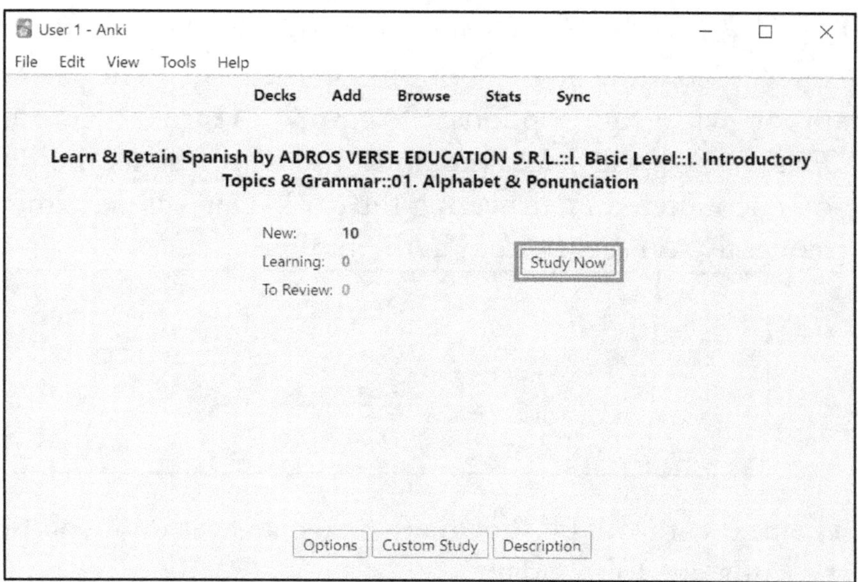

8. The first card will appear, and you will test your knowledge of the information presented on the card. Notice that you may see a different card than the one shown below. That is okay.

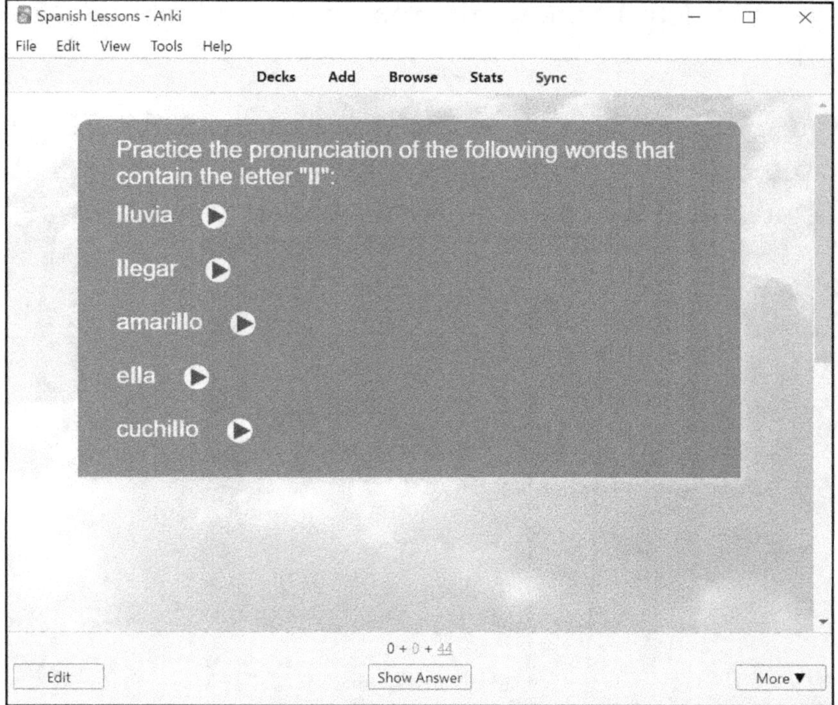

9. Once you are satisfied with your answer, click on the **"Show Answer"** button at the bottom of the page. The answer will appear with four options: **"Again," "Hard," "Good,"** and **"Easy."** You will select the button that represents the difficulty you encountered in answering the card. This will determine how frequently you see the card in the future.

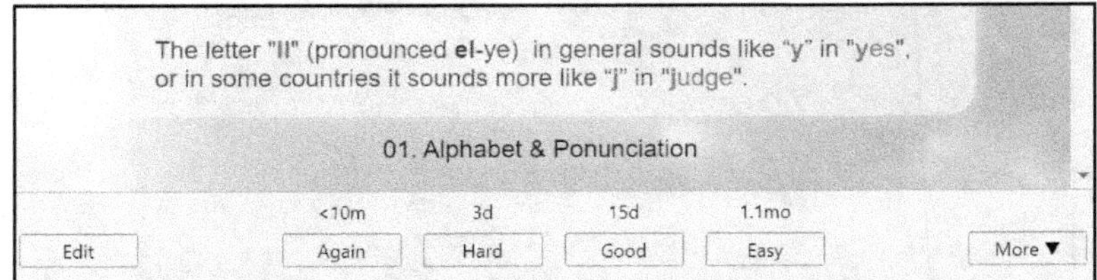

10. The next card will be shown after each answer until you finish all the cards due for the day.

Android

If you have activated the cards from the desktop app, you simply need to synchronize your phone version to see them activated. If you want to activate the cards from your mobile device, follow the steps below:

1. On the main AnkiDroid app page, where decks are presented, tap the three horizontal lines at the top left of the page. You will be presented with a list of options. Select **"Card browser."**

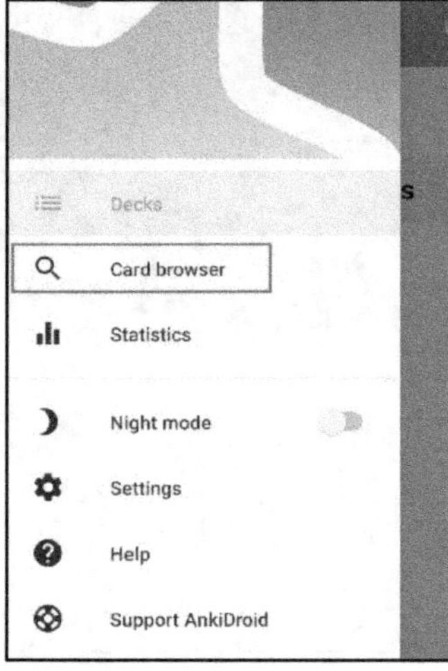

2. Tap the drop-down menu at the top and select Lesson 1 of Level I.

3. A list of cards will appear. Tap the three dots at the top right corner and select "**Select all**" to highlight all the cards.

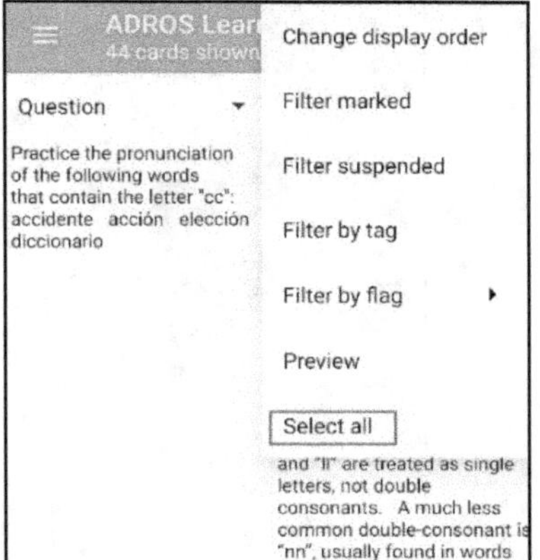

4. Tap the three dots at the top right corner again and select "**Unsuspend cards**" to activate all the cards in the lesson. If you make a mistake, go back to step 2, select all decks, select all cards, and suspend them. Then unsuspend only Lesson 1 of Level I.

5. Go back to the main page where the decks are presented. You will notice now that there are a few cards that are due from Lesson 1.

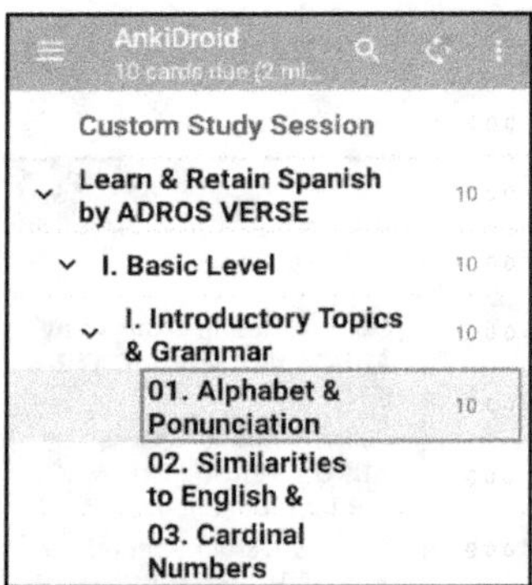

6. If you read through the lesson in the book and are ready, you can start studying and reviewing the cards by tapping on the deck, as highlighted above.

7. The first card will appear, and you will test your knowledge of the information presented on the card. Notice that you may see a different card than the one shown below. That is okay.

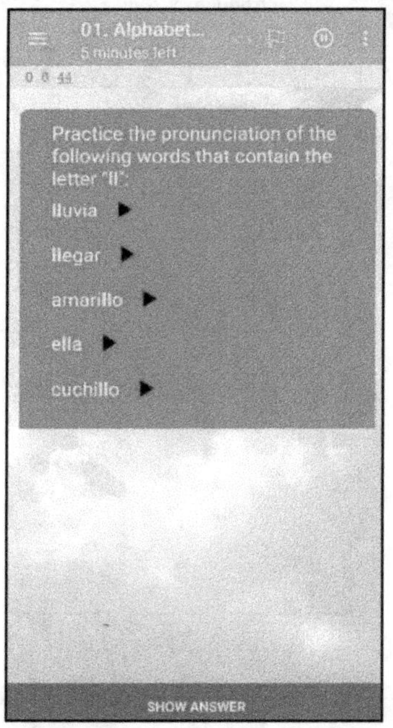

8. Once you have thought your answer through, tap the "**Show Answer**" button at the bottom of the page. The answer will appear with four options: "**Again**," "**Hard**," "**Good**," and "**Easy**." You will select the button that represents the difficulty you encountered in answering the card. This will determine how frequently you see the card in the future.

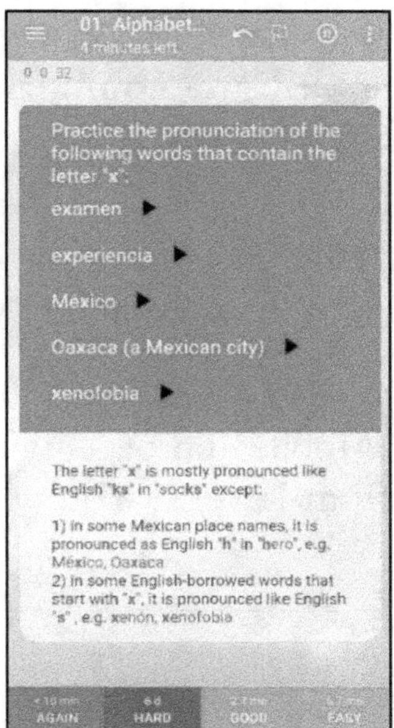

9. The next card will be shown after each answer until you finish all the cards due for today.

IMPORTANT:

If the cards appear too small or too large on your mobile device, as shown below, for example:

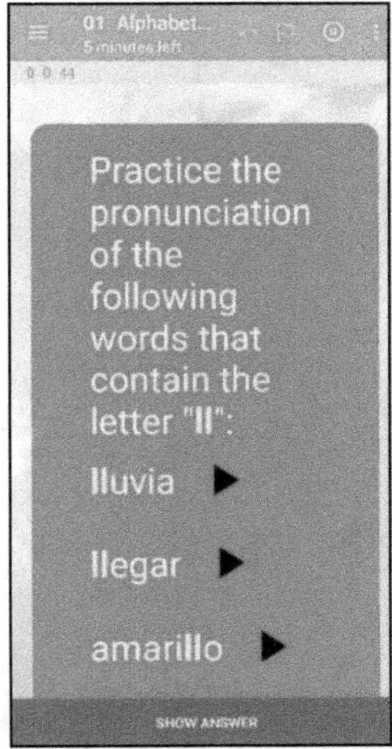

Tap on the three horizontal lines on the top left, then tap on: **Settings** > **Reviewing** > **Card Zoom**, and adjust the zoom until the font and card size fit your needs.

iOS

For iOS, replace the first four steps in the Android instructions with the following:

1. On the main AnkiMobile app page, where decks are presented, tap on Lesson 1 from Level I. You will be presented with the first card.

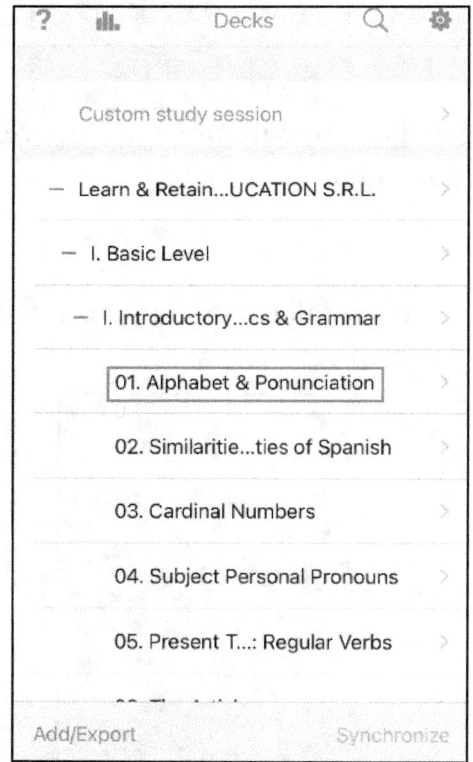

2. Tap on "**Browse**" at the top right of the screen.

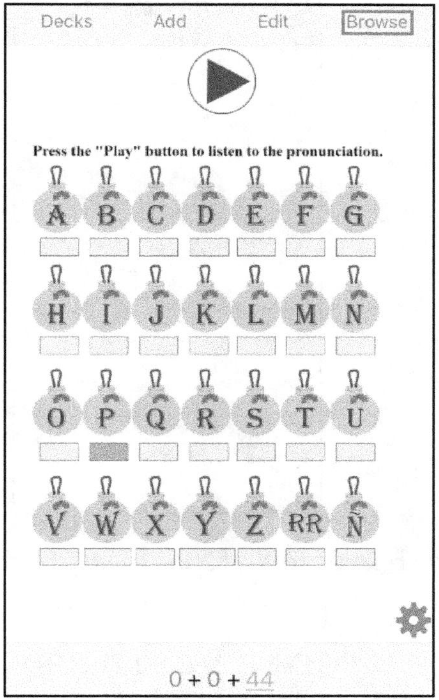

3. Tap on **"Select"** at the top right of the screen, then tap on **"Select All."**

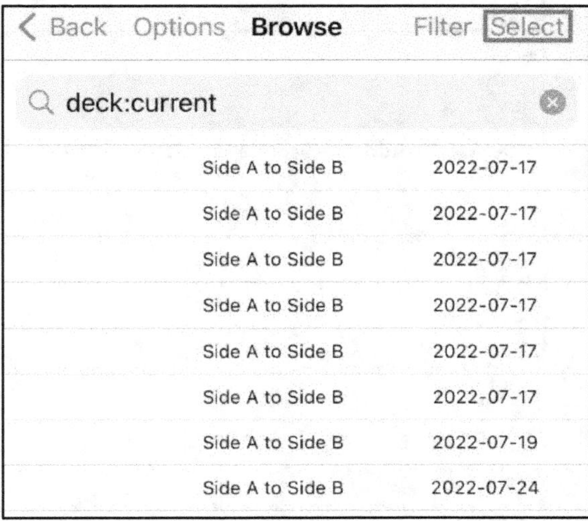

4. Tap on **"Actions,"** and from the drop-down menu, tap on **"Toggle Suspend"** to activate the cards in this lesson.

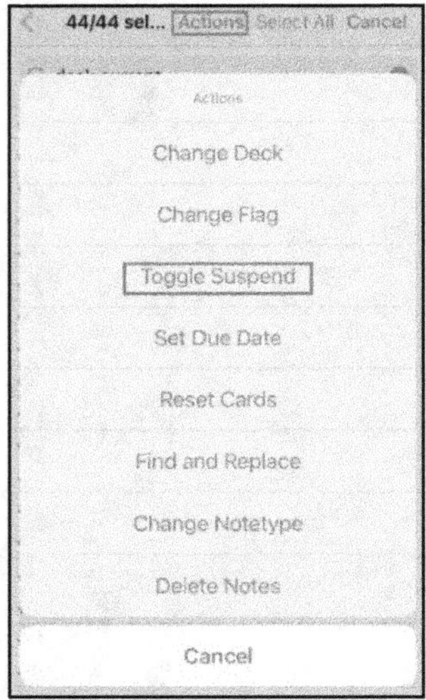

Follow the same remaining steps from 5 to 9 in the Android instructions.

MORE SETTINGS

You can always tweak your Anki settings based on how often you forget your cards. These settings can be accessed by clicking on the settings icon on your deck page, as shown below.

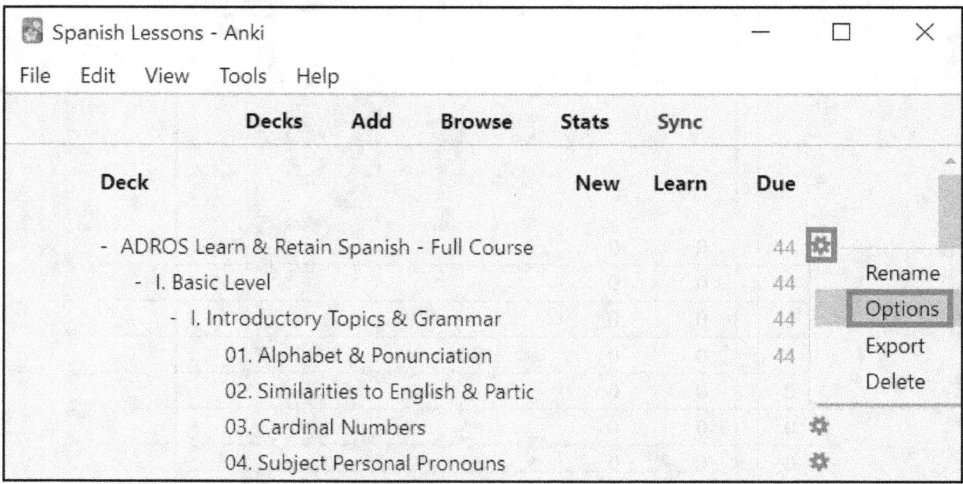

We recommend that you switch off the automatic audio play and keep the other default settings. However, feel free to experiment with the settings for a better personal experience.

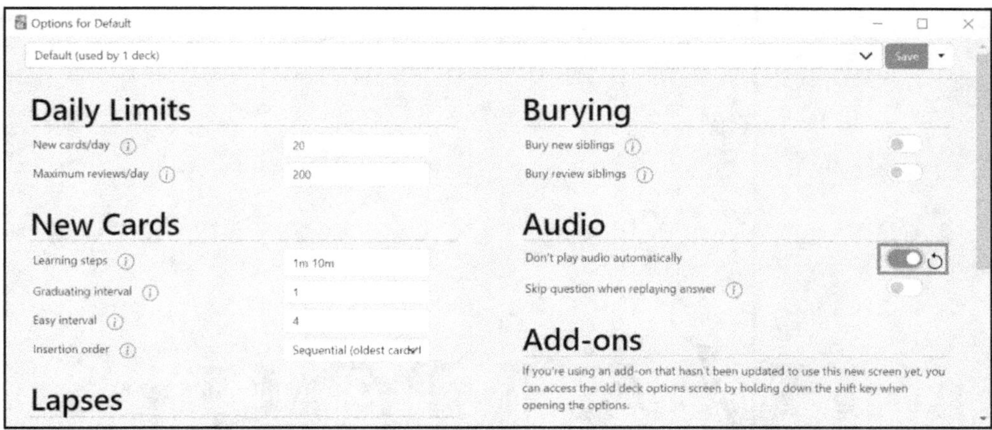

You can add your custom cards and even decks. To add a note (that is an Anki card), go to your **"Browse"** page and click on **Notes > Add Notes**.

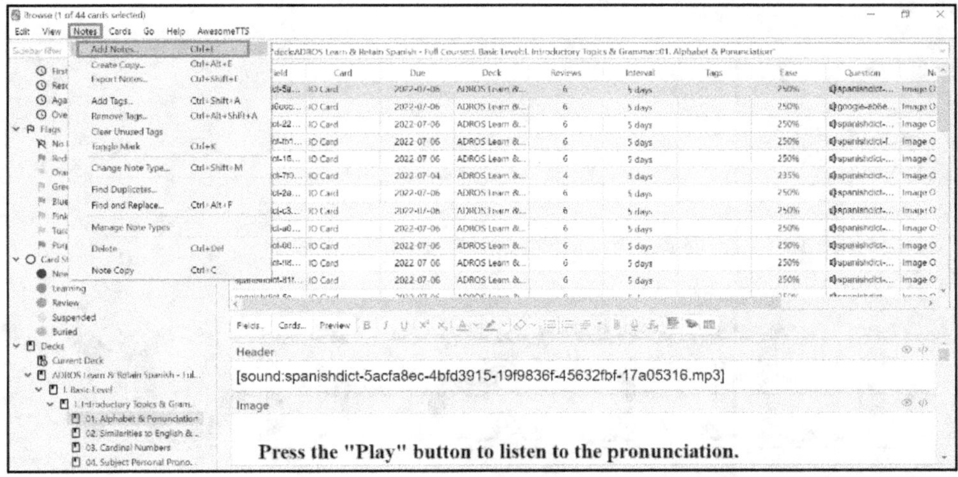

You can choose your preferred note type and add it to your learning deck.

It is not a requirement to know how to use Anki beyond the basics that we have covered in this introduction. However, if you are interested, we encourage you to learn from the plethora of resources online that teach you how to create and edit decks and notes on Anki.

¡VAMOS!

LET'S GO!

I. Introductory Topics & Grammar

Start your journey with Spanish by familiarizing yourself with the introductory topics in this section. We will cover grammar and basic knowledge that you need to equip yourself with to make the learning process easier, such as the alphabet, numbers, etc.

Do not worry if you do not absorb all the information. Your Anki cards will help you memorize the material in a non-boring way until you master what you have learned. Ensure that you did not skip the introductory Chapter II of this book on setting up Anki.

1. ALPHABET & PRONUNCIATION

Luckily, Spanish uses the Latin letters used in English with only a few differences in pronunciation. Spanish, unlike English, is a phonetic language, meaning that you should be able to pronounce any written word without the need for a dictionary.

Start with the Spanish alphabet in the table below and use your Anki cards to anchor what you learned via spaced-repetition exercises.

Spanish Letter		English Pronunciation[1]	Notes
A	a	ah	like "a" in "father"
B	b	be	equivalent to English "b" but softer
C	c	se	sounds like English "k" and like English "s" only before "e" or "i"[2]
CH	ch	che	like "ch" in **ch**eese
D	d	de	equivalent to English "d" with tongue slightly forward like "th" in "then"
E	e	e	like "e" in "bet" or "a" in "say" (without the final "y")
F	f	ef-e	equivalent to English "f"
G	g	he	sounds like "g" in "get," and like "h" in "hero" only before "e" or "i"

H	h	**ach**-e	silent letter like "**h**" in "**h**our"
I	i	ee	like "**ee**" in "s**ee**" or "**i**" in "mar**i**ne"
J	j	**ho**-ta	like "**h**" in "**h**ero" but may sound harsher by some Spanish speakers
K	k	ka	equivalent to English "**k**"
L	l	**el**-e	equivalent to English "**l**" but softer
LL	ll	**ely**-e	like "**y**" in "**y**es," or in some countries, it sounds more like "**j**" in "**j**udge"
M	m	**em**-e	equivalent to English "**m**"
N	n	**en**-e	equivalent to English "**n**"
Ñ	ñ	**eny**-e	like "**ni**" in "o**ni**on" or "**ny**" in "ca**ny**on"
O	o	o	equivalent to English "**o**," but can be shorter when not stressed
P	p	pe	equivalent to English "**p**"
Q	q	koo	always followed by "**u**" to form "**qu**" which sounds like English "**k**"
R	r	**er**-e	like English "**r**" but rolled with a single flap against the upper palate
RR	rr	**er**-re	strongly trilled "**r**" sound with multiple flaps against the upper palate
S	s	**es**-e	equivalent to English "**s**"
T	t	te	like "**t**" in "**t**able"
U	u	oo	like "**oo**" in "f**oo**d"
V	v	**oo**-be[3]	pronounced exactly like the letter "**b**"
W	w	**dob**-le oo[4]	only exists in loan words, mostly pronounced as English "**w**"
X	x	**ek**-ees	like "**ks**" in "so**cks**," and in a few exceptions pronounced like "**h**" in "**h**ero," e.g., "Mé**x**ico"
Y	y	ee-gree-**ye**-ga[5]	like "**y**" in "**y**es," or in some countries, it sounds more like "**j**" in "**j**udge," with two exceptions: 1. At the end of a word, it is considered a vowel, e.g., "**rey**" *(king)* and pronounced as English "**y**" in "sa**y**." 2. If used as a vowel meaning *"and,"* it is then pronounced like "**ee**" in "s**ee**."
Z	z	**se**-ta[6]	pronounced exactly like the letter "**s**"

[1] The stressed syllable in the English pronunciation is in bold.

[2] In Spain, "**c**" before "**e**" or "**i**" is pronounced like "**th**" in "**th**eta."

[3] Also called "**ve corta**," "**ve chica**," or "**ve pequeña**."

[4] Also called "**doble ve**" or "**doble uve**" in some parts of Latin America, and "**uve doble**" in Spain.

[5] Alternatively, the synonym "**ye**" has been recommended by the Real Academia Española (RAE), but adoption has been slow.

[6] In Spain, "**z**" is called "**the**-ta," and is always pronounced like "**th**" in "**th**eater."

Further Notes on Alphabet Pronunciation

❖ In the table above, "**ch**," "**ll**," and "**rr**" are treated as single letters.

❖ The Real Academia Española (RAE), the institution that sets the standard for the Spanish language, decided in 2010 that "**ch**" and "**ll**" should no longer be considered distinct letters.

❖ The letters "**k**" and "**w**" are only found in foreign words used in Spanish.

❖ The letters "**b**" and "**v**" have identical sounds in Spanish, which are close to the English "**b**" but with less pressure on the lips and with less aspiration. The letter "**v**" is called "**uve**" (pronounced "**oo**-be") or "**ve corta**" (pronounced "**be cor**-ta").

❖ The letter "**r**" sounds like a strongly trilled "**r**" (identical to "**rr**") when it is at the beginning of a word or after "**l**," "**n**," or "**s**," e.g., "**rojo**" *(red)* sounds like "**rro**-ho" and "**deshonra**" *(dishonor)* sounds like "des-**on**-rra," where the stressed syllable in the pronunciation script is in bold.

❖ The vowels in Spanish are "**a**," "**e**," "**i**," "**o**," and "**u**." The letter "**y**" is considered a vowel when used as a conjunction meaning *"and,"* e.g., "**Adán y Eva**" (*Adam and Eve*) where "**y**" is pronounced *"ee"* as in *"beef."* The letter "**y**" is also considered a vowel at the end of a word, e.g., "**rey**" *(king)*, where it is pronounced as English *"y"* in *"ray"* or *"say."*

❖ Every vowel is pronounced separately, and each with its alphabetical sound. Thus, there are no diphthongs in the English sense.

❖ Every letter is pronounced. There are no silent letters such as *"b"* in *"lamb"* or *"l"* in *"walk."* There are only two exceptions to this rule:

1. The letter "**h**" is silent, e.g., "**hola**" pronounced "o-la," unless it is combined with "**c**" to form the sound "**ch**" as in *"cheese."*

2. The letter "**u**" is silent in two cases:

   a. The letter "**u**" is always silent after "**q**," e.g., "**querer**" *(to want)*, pronounced "ke-**rer**" and not "kwe-**rer**."

   b. The letter "**u**" is silent after "**g**" if it is followed by "**e**" or "**i**," e.g., "**guitarra**" *(guitar)* is pronounced "gee-**ta**-rra" and not "gwee-**ta**-rra." An exception is made when the "**u**" in "**gue**" or "**gui**" has a dieresis "**ü**," in which case the "**güe**" and "**güi**" sounds are pronounced as "**gwe**" and "**gwee**," respectively, e.g., "**argüir**" *(to argue)*. If the "**gu**" is not followed by "**e**" or "**i**," it is then pronounced as "**gw**," e.g., "**guardar**" *(to keep)* is pronounced "gwar-**dar**."

❖ The only case of a double consonant that one must be aware of is "**cc**," as in words like "**accidente**" *(accident)*. In such cases, one "**c**" is hard *(k-sound)* and the other soft *(s-sound)*, in a similar fashion to the English pronunciation. Note that "**rr**" and "**ll**" are treated as single letters, not double consonants.

❖ A much less common double-consonant is "**nn**," usually found in words having the prefix "**in-**," as in "**innavegable**" *(unnavigable)*, "**perenne**" *(perennial)*, and very few more words.

❖ Throughout this book and the audio accompanying the Anki cards associated with the lessons in the book, we will focus on Latin American Spanish pronunciation, in general, rather than Spanish from Spain.

Syllable Stress in Spanish Words

As mentioned earlier, Spanish is a phonetic language. If you practice enough, you should eventually be able to pronounce any Spanish word without listening to an audio transcription or referring to a dictionary. At the start, some beginner Spanish learners complain that most Spanish learning books do not have a phonetic transcription. They, hopefully then, realize that once you learn some basic rules, you will be able to figure it out more easily with sufficient practice.

Knowing which syllable to stress in Spanish is critical to speaking comprehensibly and achieving fluency. The good news is that, unlike in English, where syllable stress seems more arbitrary, there are well-established rules in Spanish that eliminate the need for guessing. It is important to ensure that you master these rules early on as you build your vocabulary. The three main rules are:

1. If the last syllable is a vowel (**a, o, u, i**), "**s**," or "**n**," the stress falls on the second-to-last syllable, also called the penultimate syllable. For example, "**factura**" *(invoice)*: fak-**too**-ra, "**joven**" *(young)*: **ho**-ben, and "**lunes**" *(Monday)*: **loo**-nes, where the stressed syllable in the pronunciation script is in bold.

2. If the last syllable is *not* a vowel (**a, o, u, i**), "**s**," or "**n**," the stress falls on the last syllable. For example, "**azul**" *(blue)*: a-**sool**, "**abril**" *(April)*: ab-**reel**, "**hablar**" *(to speak)*: hab-**lar**.

3. If the word has a written accent (´), this overrides the two previous rules, and we simply stress the syllable that contains the accent. For example, the word "**inglés**" *(English)*, if not marked by an accent, following the first rule, would be pronounced as "**een**-gles." However, the accent on the second syllable overrides that rule and necessitates that we pronounce it correctly as "een-**gles**." Other examples include "**útil**" *(useful)*: **oo**-teel, "**habló**" *(spoke)*: ab-**lo**, and "**jóvenes**" *(youth)*: **ho**-be-nes.

The above three rules constitute the basic guidelines that should be practiced frequently as you read Spanish text. In addition to these rules, here are two less important rules to remove any confusion:

1. Spanish vowels are classified as strong (**a, e**, and **o**) and weak (**i** and **u**).

- o If the stressed syllable contains two vowels, one is strong and the other is weak, the stress falls on the strong vowel, e.g., **"reina"** (*queen*): rr<u>ey</u>-na, **"igual"** *(equal)*: ee-<u>gwa</u>l, **"cielo"** (*sky*): c<u>ye</u>-lo.
- o If the stressed syllable contains two weak vowels, the stress falls on the last of the two vowels, e.g., **"viuda"** (*widow*): by<u>oo</u>-da, **"ruido"** (*noise*): rr<u>wee</u>-do.
- o If the stressed syllable contains two strong vowels, the two vowels are pronounced as two distinct syllables, also known as *hiatus*, and normal stress rules apply, e.g., **"europeo"** (*European*): eyoo-ro-**pe**-o, **"maestro"** (*teacher*): ma-**es**-tro, **"empleado"** (*employee*): em-ple-**a**-do.

2. A word in its plural form stresses the same syllable as in its singular form. A written accent may be added or removed to enforce this rule. For example, **"joven"** *(young)*: **ho**-ben becomes **"jóvenes"**: **ho**-be-nes, **"inglés"** *(Englishman)*: een-**gles** becomes **"ingleses"**: een-**gles**-es.

2. SIMILARITIES TO ENGLISH & PARTICULARITIES OF THE SPANISH LANGUAGE

English is considered a Germanic language, whereas Spanish is a Romance language. Yet, they share a substantial amount of vocabulary. The main reason is attributed to the Norman Conquest of England in the eleventh century, as a result of which the English language borrowed a lot of French words. French Prime Minister Georges Clemenceau (1841-1929) famously claimed that "English is just badly pronounced French." French, like Spanish, is a Romance language and shares Latin roots, and thus a lot of vocabulary, with Spanish. You can see the connection here between Spanish and English via the French language. This is why the US Foreign Service Institute (FSI), which provides language training to diplomats and government employees, ranks Spanish in the easiest language learning category for English speakers.

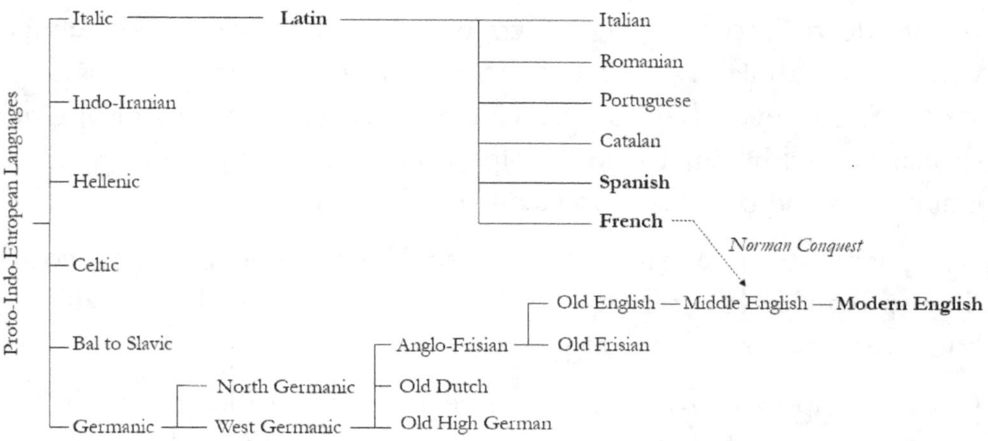

English Cognates in Spanish

History aside, we can definitely capitalize on this connection. There are a lot of English cognates in the Spanish language. English cognates are words that are directly descended from a common ancestor language, in this case, mostly the French language. Moreover, since English has become a universal language, some English words have obviously found their way directly into many languages, including Spanish.

Although cognates will often have the same meaning in Spanish and English, it is important to note that this is not always the case, as languages have evolved separately. For example, the Spanish word **"embarazada"** may appear to mean *"embarrassed."* However, if you want to express your embarrassment in Spanish, you should use the word **"avergonzado"** (masculine) or **"avergonzada"** (feminine). The word **"embarazada"** in Spanish means *"pregnant."* Chances are that using the word **"embarazada"** instead would add to your embarrassment. Similarly, the word **"fábrica"** in Spanish means *"factory"* and not *"fabric,"* as you may have guessed. That being said, recognizing English cognates is a powerful tool that can enhance the Spanish vocabulary of any English-speaking learner. We will include some English cognates in our vocabulary-building section at the end of each level to help give your Spanish vocabulary a jump start.

As we delve into the English cognates, do not feel overwhelmed with the vocabulary. You are not expected to memorize all cognates at this basic level. It is only meant to give you an idea about the similarities with English and help provide a sense of the Spanish language based on prior knowledge of English.

Here, we list some parallels between English and Spanish words that will make you realize how many Spanish words you already know or perhaps are able to guess correctly.

It is also important to note that these are not considered strict rules, but rather useful guidelines to make learning Spanish easier for English speakers.

1. Many English words ending in *"-or," "-ble,"* and *"-al"* are (almost) the same in Spanish, e.g., **"col<u>or</u>," "doct<u>or</u>," "horri<u>ble</u>," "posi<u>ble</u>," "anim<u>al</u>," "loc<u>al</u>."**

2. Some English words ending in *"-cal"* break the above *"-al"* ending rule and end in **"-co"** (masculine) or **"-ca"** (feminine) in Spanish, e.g., **"lógi<u>co</u>," "políti<u>co</u>," "físi<u>co</u>."**

3. Many English words ending in *"-ic"* end in **"-ico"** (masculine) or **"-ica"** (feminine) in Spanish, e.g., **"públi<u>co</u>," "democráti<u>co</u>," "mecáni<u>co</u>."**

4. Many English words ending in *"-ant"* or *"-ent"* end in **"-ante"** or **"-ente"** in Spanish, respectively, e.g., **"restaur<u>ante</u>," "import<u>ante</u>," "accid<u>ente</u>," "difer<u>ente</u>."**

5. Many English words ending in *"-ment"* end in **"-mento"** in Spanish, e.g., **"instru<u>mento</u>," "suple<u>mento</u>," "monu<u>mento</u>."**

6. Many English words ending in *"-ist"* end in **"-ista"** in Spanish, e.g., **"pian<u>ista</u>," "art<u>ista</u>," "dent<u>ista</u>."**

7. Many English words ending in *"-am"* or *"-em"* end in **"-ama"** or **"-ema"** in Spanish, respectively, e.g., **"progr<u>ama</u>," "diagr<u>ama</u>," "probl<u>ema</u>," "sist<u>ema</u>."**

8. Many English words ending in *"-ous"* end in **"-oso"** (masculine) or **"-osa"** (feminine) in Spanish, e.g., **"fam<u>oso</u>,"** **"religi<u>oso</u>,"** **"curi<u>osa</u>,"** **"delici<u>osa</u>."**

9. Many English words ending in *"-ry"* end in **"-rio"** (masculine) or **"-ria"** (feminine) in Spanish, e.g., **"aniversa<u>rio</u>,"** **"adversa<u>ria</u>,"** **"imagina<u>ria</u>,"** **"itinera<u>rio</u>."**

10. Many English words ending in *"-tion"* end in **"-ción"** in Spanish, e.g., **"condi<u>ción</u>,"** **"descrip<u>ción</u>,"** **"institu<u>ción</u>,"** **"civiliza<u>ción</u>."**

11. Many English words ending in *"-tional"* end in **"-cional"** in Spanish, e.g., **"condi<u>cional</u>,"** **"institu<u>cional</u>,"** **"tradi<u>cional</u>."**

12. Many English words ending in *"-tial"* end in **"-cial"** in Spanish, e.g., **"ini<u>cial</u>,"** **"poten<u>cial</u>,"** **"par<u>cial</u>."**

13. Many English words ending in *"-ce"* or *"-cy"* end in **"-cia"** in Spanish, e.g., **"justi<u>cia</u>,"** **"diferen<u>cia</u>,"** **"democra<u>cia</u>,"** **"agen<u>cia</u>."**

14. Many English words ending in *"-ty"* end in **"-dad"** in Spanish, e.g., **"electrici<u>dad</u>,"** **"universi<u>dad</u>,"** **"posibili<u>dad</u>."**

15. Some English words that end *"-tor"* end in **"-dor"** in Spanish, e.g., **"genera<u>dor</u>,"** **"eleva<u>dor</u>,"** **"ventila<u>dor</u>."** There are many exceptions, such as **"doc<u>tor</u>,"** **"tu<u>tor</u>,"** and **"au<u>tor</u>"** (*author*).

16. Some English words ending in *"-ly"* end in **"-mente"** in Spanish, e.g., **"normal<u>mente</u>,"** **"natural<u>mente</u>,"** **"exacta<u>mente</u>."**

17. Many English nouns ending in *"-phy"* end in **"-fía"** in Spanish, e.g., **"geogra<u>fía</u>,"** **"fotogra<u>fía</u>"** *(photography)*, **"filoso<u>fía</u>"** *(philosophy)*.

18. Many English words ending in *"-ct"* end in **"-cto"** (masculine) or **"-cta"** (feminine) in Spanish, e.g., **"a<u>cto</u>,"** **"dire<u>cto</u>,"** **"corre<u>cto</u>."** In some exceptions, the **"c"** is dropped, e.g., **"respe<u>to</u>"** *(respect)*, **"contra<u>to</u>"** *(contract)*, **"obje<u>to</u>"** *(object)*, **"suje<u>to</u>"** *(subject)*.

19. Many English words ending in *"-sion"* end in "**-sión**" in Spanish, e.g., "**conversión**," "**expresión**," "**conclusión**." The accent on the "**o**" signifies stress on the last syllable, as discussed in **Lesson 1** of this level.

20. Many English words ending in *"-ism"* end in "**-ismo**" in Spanish, e.g., "**organismo**," "**patriotismo**," "**comunismo**."

21. Many English verbs ending in *"-fy"* end in "**-ficar**" in Spanish, e.g., "**clarificar**," "**clasificar**," "**verificar**."

22. Many English words ending in *"-id"* end in "**-ido**" (masculine) or "**-ida**" (feminine) in Spanish, e.g., "**fluido**," "**líquido**," "**tímido**."

23. Many English words ending in *"-ile"* end in "**-il**" in Spanish, e.g., "**juvenil**," "**hostil**," "**frágil**."

24. Many English words ending in *"-ive"* end in "**-ivo**" (masculine) or "**-iva**" (feminine) in Spanish, e.g., "**activo**," "**atractivo**," "**nativo**."

In addition to the above notes, some extra minor spelling notes can be useful:

1. Many English words change *"ph"* to "**f**" in Spanish, e.g., "**foto**," "**elefante**," "**teléfono**."

2. Many English words change *"th"* to "**t**" in Spanish, e.g., "**catedral**," "**autor**," "**católico**."

3. Many English words that have the beginning *"st-"* or *"sp-"* change to "**est-**" or "**esp-**," respectively, in Spanish, e.g., "**estudiante**" *(student)*, "**estable**," "**especial**," "**espiritual**."

A summary of the above rules is given in the table below. An extended list is available in **Appendix C**.

English	Spanish	Examples
-or	-or	actor, color, conductor, doctor, error, exterior, favor, horror, interior, inventor, superior, tractor

-ble	-ble	cable, flexible, horrible, inevitable, noble, notable, posible, probable, terrible, variable
-al	-al	animal, canal, central, criminal, final, industrial, legal, local, social, musical, personal
-al	-co -ca	crítico, eléctrico, físico, lógico, mágico, mecánico, óptico, político
-ic	-ico -ica	básico, democrático, diabético, fantástico, mecánico, plástico, público, romántico, tóxico
-ant	-ante	abundante, constante, elegante, ignorante, importante, restaurante, significante, tolerante
-ent	-ente	accidente, agente, cliente, competente, continente, diferente, excelente, inteligente, prudente, urgente
-ment	-mento	documento, elemento, experimento, instrumento, monumento, parlamento, suplemento, testamento
-ist	-ista	artista, comunista, dentista, especialista, lista, novelista, pianista, turista (tourist)
-am	-ama	caligrama, diagrama, programa, radiograma, telegrama
-em	-ema	emblema, poema, problema, sistema
-ous	-oso -osa	curioso, delicioso, fabuloso, famoso, furioso, misterioso, nervioso, religioso, victorioso
-ry	-rio -ria	adversario, aniversario, contrario, culinario, diccionario, imaginario, itinerario, notario, salario
-tion	-ción	acción, civilización, concepción, condición, descripción, edición, institución, nación, noción
-tional	-cional	adicional (additional), condicional, institucional, nacional, operacional, racional, tradicional
-tial	-cial	confidencial, esencial, inicial, parcial, potencial, presidencial, residencial
-ce -cy	-cia	agencia, Alicia, democracia, diferencia, evidencia, Francia, justicia, licencia, urgencia, violencia
-ty	-dad	autoridad , cavidad, dignidad, electricidad, hospitalidad, identidad, posibilidad, unidad
-tor	-dor	colaborador, creador, dictador, elevador, investigador, generador, operador, orador, ventilador
-ly	-mente	exactamente, finalmente, naturalmente, normalmente, personalmente, probablemente, totalmente
-phy	-fía	cinematografía, filosofía, fotografía, geografía
-ct	-cto -cta	acto, conflicto, correcto, directo, efecto, exacto, impacto, insecto, perfecto, producto
-sion	-sión	admisión, compasión, conclusión, conversión, decisión, discusión, expresión, ocasión, versión

-ism	-ismo	astigmatismo, comunismo, despotismo, electromagnetismo, idealismo, organismo
-fy	-ficar	certificar, clarificar, clasificar, dignificar, glorificar, gratificar, justificar, modificar, notificar, verificar
-id	-ido -ida	ávido, espléndido, fluido, líquido, lúcido, plácido, rápido, sólido, tímido, válido, vívido
-ile	-il	ágil, automóvil, facsímil, frágil, hostil, juvenil
-iv	-ivo -iva	activo, adhesivo, aditivo, atractivo, decisivo, definitivo, efectivo, festivo, nativo, negativo
ph	f	elefante, filosofía, fonético, foto, teléfono
th	t	auténtico (authentic), autor, catedral, católico
st-	est-	estable, estación, estricto, estudiante, estúpido
sp-	esp-	especial, específico, espiritual, esposo (spouse)

As mentioned earlier, there are some *false cognates*. It can be useful to be familiar with these false friends so that you can avoid some embarrassing errors. Below is a list of some of the most common ones. For an extended list, refer to **Appendix C** at the end of the book.

Spanish Word	Meaning in English	English Cognate	Meaning of cognate in Spanish
éxito	*success*	exit	**salida**
largo	*long*	large	**grande**
molestar	*to annoy*	molest	**abusar sexualmente**
constipado	*cold (illness)*	constipated	**estreñido**
recordar	*to remind or remember*	record	**grabar**
actual	*current*	actual	**real**
red	*network*	red	**rojo**
enviar	*to send*	envy	**envidiar**
carpeta	*folder*	carpet	**alfombra**
grosería	*rudeness*	groceries	**comestibles**

Plural and Negation in Spanish

Luckily, forming the plural and the negation in Spanish are simple procedures, without many exceptions.

Forming the plural in Spanish is similar to forming a regular plural in English. To form the plural, the letter **"s"** is added if the noun or adjective ends with a vowel[1], e.g., "**casa**" *(house)*, "**casa̲s**" *(houses)*, and "**es**" is added if the noun or adjective ends with a consonant, e.g., "**mujer**" *(woman)*, "**mujer̲e̲s**" *(women)*. Notice that Spanish adjectives can also be plural, e.g., "**mujer̲e̲s jóven̲e̲s**" *(young women)*. We will encounter some minor orthographic changes in the plural form of some words, but the vast majority are regular.

Forming the negation in Spanish is even easier than in English. We simply add "**no**" in front of the verb (and before any object pronoun before the verb), e.g., "**No juego al fútbol**" *(I don't play soccer)*, "**No lo quiero**" *(I don't want it)*. We can have a double negative in Spanish without changing the meaning to affirmative, e.g., "**N̲o lo hago n̲u̲n̲c̲a̲**" *(I never do it)*.

Uses of the Written Accent in Spanish

In addition to marking the exceptions to the syllable stress rules, the written acute accent in Spanish (´) has the following two uses:

❖ To distinguish between the meaning of words that would otherwise be written in the same manner. For example, "**el**" is the masculine definite article *"the,"* whereas "**él**" is the personal pronoun *"he,"* "**mas**" (formal use only) is a conjunction meaning *"but,"* whereas "**más**" means *"more."*

❖ To distinguish between interrogative and relative pronouns, e.g., "**¿Dónde vives?**" *(Where do you live?)* vs. "**No hay transporte donde vivo**" *(There is no transportation where I live)*. Notice that the interrogative pronoun "**dónde**" *(where)* has an accent on the vowel of the first syllable in the first example. The same concept applies to some other interrogative pronouns, such as "**¿Quién?**" *(who?)*, "**¿Qué?**" *(what?)*, "**¿Cuál?**" *(which?)*, "**¿Dónde?**" *(where?)*.

---

[1] Although the letter "**y**" at the end of a word is considered a vowel, the "**es**" ending is used to form the plural in such words, e.g., "**rey**" (plural "**reyes**").

Punctuation in Spanish

In general, Spanish punctuation marks are used the same way as in English. One notable exception is the following:

❖ Interrogation and exclamation marks are used in Spanish both at the beginning and at the end of the question or exclamation with the inverted sign at the beginning, such as "**¿Cómo estás?**" *(How are you?)* and "**¡Qué lástima!**" *(What a pity!).*

Notice that this rule is not always enforced in many countries except in formal and legal documents.

Punctuation is also important to distinguish a question from a statement. For instance, the sentence "**El café está caliente**" *(The coffee is hot)* is a statement. Adding question marks to the beginning and end of the sentence "**¿El café está caliente?**" makes it a question. This is how questions are formed in Spanish. Unlike in English, we do not use any auxiliary or reorder the sentence to form a question. Saying "**¿Está el café caliente?**" is grammatically incorrect.

Abbreviations in Spanish

The concepts behind the formation of acronyms and abbreviations in Spanish are very similar to those in English. One notable exception is the doubling of the letters in the abbreviation of some plural nouns, e.g., "**Estados Unidos**" *(United States)* is abbreviated as "**EE. UU.**" For more detail on this rule and a list of common abbreviations in Spanish, interested readers can refer to **Appendix G** at the end of this book.

Capitalization in Spanish

The words are capitalized in cases almost identical to those in English, with a few notable exceptions that are not capitalized in Spanish, mainly:

❖ Adjectives of nationality and languages, e.g., **"italiano"** (*Italian*), **"canadiense"** (*Canadian*), **"español"** (*Spanish*).

❖ Days and months, e.g., **"martes"** (*Tuesday*), **"enero"** (*January*), **"julio"** (*July*).

It is also worth noting that all alphabet letters are feminine in Spanish. For example, when referring to a letter in Spanish, one may say: **la "a" in "padre"** (*the "a" in "father"*), referring to the letter "a" using the feminine article "**la**." We will learn more about masculine and feminine nouns and adjectives in **Level II, Lesson 1**.

3. CARDINAL NUMBERS

uno, una	1	veintiuno	21	doscientos/-as	200
dos	2	veintidós	22	trescientos/-as	300
tres	3	veintitrés	23	cuatrocientos/-as	400
cuatro	4	treinta	30	quinientos/-as	500
cinco	5	treinta y uno	31	seiscientos/-as	600
seis	6	treinta y dos	32	setecientos/-as	700
siete	7	treinta y tres	33	ochocientos/-as	800
ocho	8	cuarenta	40	novecientos/-as	900
nueve	9	cuarenta y uno	41	mil	1.000
diez	10	cuarenta y dos	42	dos mil	2.000
once	11	cincuenta	50	tres mil	3.000
doce	12	cincuenta y uno	51	diez mil	10.000
trece	13	cincuenta y dos	52	cien mil	100.000
catorce	14	sesenta	60	cien mil uno	100.001
quince	15	setenta	70	cien mil diez	100.010
dieciséis	16	ochenta	80	un millón	1.000.000
diecisiete	17	noventa	90	dos millones	2.000.000
dieciocho	18	cien	100	diez millones	10.000.000
diecinueve	19	ciento uno	101	mil millones	1.000.000.000
veinte	20	ciento dos	102	dos mil millones	2.000.000.000

❖ The number "**0**" in Spanish is "**cero**," pronounced as "**se**-ro."

❖ Before a masculine noun, "**uno**" becomes "**un**," e.g., "**un perro**" (*a dog*), "**un carro**" (*a car*).

❖ You will encounter a similar dropping of the final "**o**" with a few other words in Spanish, such as "**bueno**" *(good)*, "**malo**" *(bad)*, and "**alguno**" *(some)*, e.g., "**Este restaurante es buen<u>o</u>**" *(This restaurant is good)*, "**Este es un buen restaurante**" *(This is a good restaurant)*.

❖ Numbers 16-19 are formed by contracting the combination of the tens and the units (**diez** + **y** + "**seis, siete, … etc.**") into (**dieciséis, diecisiete, … etc.**), and converting "**z**" in "**diez**" into "**c**," and "**y**" into "**i**."

❖ The multiples of hundred (200-900) are formed by combining (**dos, tres, … etc.**) and "**cientos**" to form (**doscientos, trescientos, … etc.**), except for "**quinientos**" (500).

❖ The multiples of hundred (200-900) can have a masculine "**-os**" or a feminine "**-as**" ending depending on the nouns they describe, e.g., "**doscientos libros**" *(200 books)*, "**doscientas manzanas**" *(200 apples)*.

❖ The word "**cien**" does not have a "**-to**" or "**-tos**" ending when referring to the number 100 or thousand multiples of the number 100, e.g., "**cien**" (100), "**cien mil**" (100.000), "**cien millones**" (100.000.000).

Otherwise, if preceded or followed by a number, "**ciento**" or "**cientos**" must be used instead, e.g., "**cien<u>to</u> uno**" (101), "**trescien<u>tos</u>**" (300).

❖ Most, but not all, Spanish-speaking countries use a *comma* to separate *decimals* and a *period* to separate *thousands* in Spanish. For instance, the number **2.155,25** in Spanish is equivalent to *2,155.25* in English.

❖ The conjunction "**y**" meaning *"and"* is used between tens and units, either *explicitly* as in "**treinta y cuatro**" (34) or in *contracted* form as in "**veintitrés**" (23), i.e., "**veinte + y + tres**."

❖ The conjunction "**y**" is not used between hundreds and tens or between thousands and hundreds, e.g., "**cuatrocientos cincuenta y uno**" (451), "**mil novecientos**" (1900).

❖ In plural form, "**mil**" remains the same, e.g., "**tres mil**" (3.000), whereas "**millón**" becomes "**millones,**" e.g., "**ocho millones**" (8.000.000), "**cien millones**" (100.000.000).

❖ When describing items in millions, one must add "**de**" after "**millón**" or "**millones,**" e.g., "**un millón de estudiantes**" *(a million students)*, "**dos millones de habitantes**" *(two million inhabitants)*.

❖ To say *a billion* in Spanish, we use "**mil millones,**" that is, *a thousand million*. The word "**billón,**" in Spanish, is *a trillion* in English.

❖ Notice that in Spanish, we cannot use the English way of expressing years, as in *"nineteen eighty-three"* (1983); that is, saying "**diecinueve, ochenta y tres**" is incorrect. The correct way is to say "**mil novecientos ochenta y tres.**"

4. SUBJECT PERSONAL PRONOUNS

Subject personal pronouns in Spanish serve the same function as their English counterparts by pointing out who carries out the action described by the verb.

yo	*I*	1st person singular
tú	*you (informal)*	2nd person singular
usted	*you (formal)*	2nd person singular
él/ella	*he/she/it*	3rd person singular
nosotros/nosotras	*we*	1st person plural
vosotros/vosotras	*you (informal)*	2nd person plural
ustedes	*you (formal)*	2nd person plural
ellos/ellas	*they*	3rd person plural

❖ More often than not, the subject personal pronoun is dropped because the verb endings can be sufficient to refer to the subject, as you will learn in **Lesson 5** of this level.

❖ There are two forms of singular *"you"* in Spanish; the first is the informal **"tú"** and is used with familiar people (e.g., child, relative, friend, peer, etc.), and the second is the formal **"usted"** which is used with older people and with people we are not familiar with or to show respect.

❖ In writing, you can abbreviate **"usted"** as **"Ud."** and **"ustedes"** as **"Uds."** where the abbreviation forms are always capitalized.

❖ In some Spanish-speaking countries like Argentina, Uruguay, Paraguay, El Salvador, and Nicaragua, the informal **"tú"** is replaced with **"vos"** and has different verb conjugations that you will find in this book in **Level VI, Lesson 9**.

❖ The accent on the **"u"** in **"tú"** is to distinguish it from the possessive pronoun **"tu,"** meaning *"your,"* and does not affect the pronunciation. Similarly, the accent is used to distinguish **"él,"** meaning *"he"* or *"it,"* from the definite article **"el,"** meaning *"the."*

❖ The masculine pronouns **"nosotros"** and **"vosotros"** have the feminine forms **"nosotras"** and **"vosotras,"** respectively. The feminine forms are used for groups that consist exclusively of feminine-gender members. Even if one masculine-gender member of that group exists, we must use **"nosotros"** and **"vosotros."** The same gender rules apply to **"ellos"** and **"ellas,"** both meaning *"they."*

❖ In Latin America, **"vosotros"** is not used; instead, **"ustedes"** is used for both the formal and informal plural versions of *"you."* Throughout the book, we keep the **"vosotros"** conjugation for reference only. However, feel free to ignore it if you want to focus exclusively on Latin American Spanish, as this book is intended.

❖ There is no direct equivalent to the English subject pronoun *"it."* Since all nouns in Spanish are either masculine or feminine, we use **"él"** or **"ella"** to refer to an object depending on whether it is masculine or feminine.

❖ There is also the neuter personal pronoun **"ello,"** often translated as *"it,"* which refers to a statement or a situation. This is usually used in writing but seldom in spoken Spanish, e.g., **"Ello no significa mucho"** *(It does not mean much)*. In spoken Spanish, you would use the masculine demonstrative article **"esto,"** meaning *"this,"* e.g., **"Esto no significa mucho."** More detail on this will be discussed in **Level II, Lesson 6**.

5. PRESENT TENSE I: REGULAR VERBS

Verbs in their infinitive form in Spanish have one of three endings: **-ar**, **-er**, **-ir**. When conjugated, these endings are replaced with different endings based on the subject. In English, verb conjugation in the present tense is quite simple. For example, the verb *"to break"* is conjugated as follows: *I/you/we/they break, he/she/it breaks*. Thus, there are only two conjugation forms of the verb *"to break"* in the present tense, which are *"break"* and *"breaks."* In Spanish, it is a little more complicated. Regular verbs in the present indicative tense follow the conjugation rules shown below, with an example from each verb group: **-ar**, **-er**, **-ir**.

	-ar ending hablar (to speak)	-er ending comer (to eat)	-ir ending vivir (to live)
yo	hablo	como	vivo
tú	hablas	comes	vives
él/ella/usted	habla	come	vive
nosotros/-as	hablamos	comemos	vivimos
vosotros/-as	habláis	coméis	vivís
ellos/ellas/ustedes	hablan	comen	viven

In Spanish, unlike in English, we can drop the subject pronoun because the conjugation is usually sufficient to indicate the subject. For instance, we could say **"Yo vivo en España"** or **"Vivo en**

España" *(I live in Spain)*. Both are considered perfect speech and grammatically correct. It even sounds more native to drop the subject pronoun in informal speech. Opting to use the subject pronoun can sound less natural in some contexts, as it can indicate an emphasis on the subject rather than the verb.

Remember that the "**vosotros**" conjugation is included in the table above for reference only. You can ignore it if you want to use your Spanish only in a Latin American country.

It is important to note that the present tense we have discussed so far is also called the present *indicative* tense, to distinguish it from the present *subjunctive* tense. The indicative and the subjunctive are two different moods. You do not have to worry about the difference for now. We will cover the subjunctive mood in more advanced lessons starting in **Level IV, Lesson 7**. As we progress with more advanced tenses in the levels to come, refer to **Appendix B** to use the provided verb conjugation chart as a cheat sheet and gain perspective on the different moods and tenses in Spanish.

6. THE ARTICLES

In Spanish, all nouns are either masculine or feminine. There are no neuter nouns in Spanish.

Definite Articles

Below are the four definite articles (equivalent to *"the"* in English). We have four definite articles in Spanish because the definite article has to agree with the noun in both gender and number.

el	Before a **singular masculine** noun	e.g., el hombre *(the man)*
la	Before a **singular feminine** noun	e.g., la casa *(the house)*
los	Before a **plural masculine** noun	e.g., los hombres *(the men)*
las	Before a **plural feminine** noun	e.g., las casas *(the houses)*

❖ There are only two contractions in Spanish that involve the singular masculine definite article "**el**," and, unlike in English, these contractions are not optional and must be applied:

1	a + el = **al**	e.g., "Yo voy **al** restaurante" (*I go to the restaurant*).
2	de + el = **del**	e.g., "Yo vengo **del** café" (*I come from the café*).

❖ Before a singular feminine noun that starts with "**a**" or "**ha**," "**el**" is used instead of "**la**." For instance, both nouns "**agua**" (*water*) and "**águila**" (*eagle*) are feminine. When singular, we use "**el**," i.e., "**el agua**" (*the water*), "**el águila**" (*the eagle*). However, the plural is regular; thus, "**las**" is used, e.g., "**las águilas**" (*the eagles*).

❖ There are cases in which Spanish uses the definite article when in English, it would be omitted, such as:

1. Abstract concepts or speaking in a general sense, e.g., "**La ciencia es importante**" (*Science is important*), "**Los animales son inteligentes**" (*Animals are intelligent*).

2. Languages and nationalities, e.g., "**el español**" (*Spanish*), "**los alemanes**" (*Germans*). Exceptionally, we drop the definite article in Spanish when the language name is an object of a verb, e.g., "**Yo hablo y enseño español**" (*I speak and teach Spanish*), "**Me gustaría aprender árabe**" (*I would like to learn Arabic*), or after the preposition "**en**," e.g., "**escrito en italiano**" (*written in Italian*).

3. Days of the week, e.g., "**Yo trabajo el lunes**" (*I work on Monday*), "**Yo voy al gimnasio los jueves**" (*I go to the gym on Thursdays*). An exception is when the day name comes after the verb "*to be*," e.g., "**Hoy es viernes**" (*Today is Friday*).

4. Body parts and clothes, e.g., "**Levanta la mano**" (*Raise your hand*), "**Ponte los zapatos**" (*Put on your shoes*).

5. Telling time, e.g., "**Son las dos**" (*It's two o'clock*), "**Nos encontramos a la una**" (*We meet at one o'clock*).

6. Before a personal title, such as "**señor**" (*Mr.*), "**señora**" (*Mrs.*), "**doctor**" (*doctor*), "**presidente**" (*president*), etc., e.g., "**el presidente Kennedy**," "**la señora Hernández**," "**el doctor Davids**." An exception is when addressing the person directly, e.g., "**Señor Adams, ¿cómo está?**" (*Mr. Adams, how are you?*).

7. Before each noun in the case of multiple nouns, e.g., **"el padre y la madre"** (*the father and mother*), **"los perros y los gatos"** (*the cats and dogs*). Although you can use one definite article in English to refer to all nouns, the grammatically correct way in Spanish is to repeat the definite article for each noun.

❖ In the following cases, the definite article, unlike in English, is omitted in Spanish:
1. Before the ordinal number describing a king or a queen, e.g., **"Luis catorce"** (*Luis the Fourteenth*), **"Isabel primera"** (*Elizabeth the First*).
2. Although optional, it is common to omit the definite article before the seasons of the year, e.g., **"en verano"** (*in the summer*), **"en invierno"** (*in winter*), **en otoño** (*in the fall*).

Indefinite Articles

The indefinite articles in Spanish are **"un"** (for singular masculine) and **"una"** (for singular feminine). These are equivalent to *"a"* or *"an"* in English.

un	Before a **singular masculine** noun	e.g., un hombre (*a man*)
una	Before a **singular feminine** noun	e.g., una casa (*a house*)

❖ The plural forms **"unos"** and **"unas"** are used to mean *"some,"* e.g., **"unos momentos"** (*some moments*), **"unas palabras"** (*some words*).

❖ Before a singular feminine noun that starts with **"a"** or **"ha,"** **"un"** is used instead of **"una,"** e.g., **"un águila."** The plural is regular, thus **"unas"** is used, e.g., **"unas águilas."**

7. PREPOSITIONS

Here are some of the most used prepositions in Spanish that will help you construct basic sentences.

Prep.	Meaning	Examples	
a	*to*	Voy **a** la escuela por la mañana.	*I go **to** school in the morning.*
	at	Nos juntamos **a** las dos.	*We meet **at** 2 o'clock.*
	by	Hecho **a** mano.	*Made **by** hand (handmade).*
	on	Volveré a casa **a** pie.	*I will come back home **on** foot.*
al lado de	*beside*	Hay un gato **al lado de** la silla.	*There is a cat **beside** the chair.*
a lo largo de	*along*	Hay casas **a lo largo de**l lago.	*There are houses **along** the lake.*
antes de	*before*	Te voy a llamar **antes de** irme.	*I will call you **before** leaving.*
a través de	*across* *through*	Viajamos **a través de**l país.	*We travel **across** the country.*
bajo debajo de	*under*	El gato está **bajo** la silla.	*The cat is **under** the chair.*
cerca de	*near*	Vivo **cerca de** la ciudad.	*I live **near** the city.*
con	*with*	Él habla **con** su amigo.	*He speaks **with** his friend.*
contra en contra de	*against*	Estoy **en contra de** la injusticia.	*I am **against** injustice.*
de	*of*	El color **de** mi auto es azul.	*The color **of** my car is blue.*
	from	Ella es **de** España.	*She is **from** Spain.*
	about	Hablan **de** él.	*They talk **about** him.*
delante de	*in front of*	Estoy **delante de** la escuela.	*I am **in front of** the school.*
dentro de	*inside*	La bola está **dentro de** la caja.	*The ball is **inside** the box.*
desde	*since*	No he fumado **desde** abril.	*I haven't smoked **since** April.*
	from	Viajé **desde** Egipto a Corea.	*I traveled **from** Egypt to Korea.*
después de	*after*	Hoy dormí **después de**l almuerzo.	*I slept **after** lunch today.*
detrás de	*behind*	El árbol está **detrás de** la casa.	*The tree is **behind** the house.*
durante	*during*	Podemos salir **durante** el día.	*We can go out **during** the day.*
en	*in*	El gato está **en** la caja.	*The cat is **in** the box.*
	on	La comida está **en** la mesa.	*The food is **on** the table.*
encima de	*on top of*	Las llaves están **encima de**l armario.	*The keys are **on top of** the cupboard.*
en frente de frente a	*in front of*	Esperaré **en frente de** la puerta.	*I will wait **in front of** the door.*

entre	*between*	El pájaro está atrapado **entre** las ramas.	*The bird is stuck **between** the branches.*
	among	Soy el más alto **entre** mis amigos.	*I am the tallest **among** my friends.*
fuera de	*outside*	El garaje está **fuera de** la casa.	*The garage is **outside** the house.*
hacia	*toward*	Ella corrió **hacia** la salida.	*She ran **toward** the exit.*
hasta	*until*	Trabajé **hasta** las 9 de la noche.	*I worked **until** 9 at night.*
	as far as	La luz alcanza **hasta** el parque.	*The light reaches **as far as** the park.*
para	*for*	Salgo **para** Barcelona mañana.	*I will leave **for** Barcelona tomorrow.*
	in order to	Estudiamos **para** aprender.	*We study **in order to** learn.*
por	*for*	Ayer dormí **por** 10 horas.	*I slept **for** 10 hours yesterday.*
	by	Te contacté **por** teléfono.	*I contacted you **by** phone.*
	per	Cuesta 20 dólares **por** día.	*It costs 20 dollars **per** day.*
	because of	Sufrieron **por** falta de agua.	*They suffered **because of** the lack of water.*
según	*according to*	**Según** la ley, está prohibido.	***According to** the law, it is prohibited.*
sin	*without*	Un pez no puede vivir **sin** agua.	*A fish can't live **without** water.*
sobre	*over*	La mosca está **sobre** la mesa.	*The fly is **over** the table.*
	about	Hablan **sobre** el origen de la vida.	*They talk **about** the origin of life.*
tras	*behind*	La escoba está **tras** la puerta.	*The broom is **behind** the door.*
	after	**Tras** mucho tiempo, quiero jubilarme.	***After** a long time, I want to retire.*

❖ The preposition "**hasta**" can also be an adverb, meaning *"even,"* e.g., "**Hace calor hasta con el ventilador**" (*It's hot even with the fan*).

❖ Both "**para**" and "**por**" can be used to mean *"for."* Differences between the two with examples will be explained in **Level III, Lesson 2.**

❖ Both "**tras**" and "**detrás**" mean *"behind."* However, "**detrás**" is more widely used in daily conversations, whereas "**tras**" is found mostly in formal writing. Also, "**detrás**" can be used as an adverb, e.g., "**Mira detrás**" *(Look behind)*, whereas "**tras**" cannot be used as an adverb. For instance, we can say "**Mira tras la silla**" (*Look behind the chair*), but we cannot say "**Mira tras**" without it being followed by a noun.

❖ To express the meaning of *"about"* (e.g., to talk *about* someone or watch a documentary *about* something), we often use "**sobre**" or "**acerca de**." For example:

Vi un documental **sobre** la guerra.	*I watched a documentary **about** the war.*
Leí un libro **acerca de** la vida en Japón.	*I read a book **about** life in Japan.*

In some contexts, we could use "**de**" to mean *"about."* For example:

Ellos hablan **de** él.	*They talk **about** him.*
Quiero leer un libro **de** ciencia.	*I want to read a book **about** science.*

8. INTERROGATIVE PRONOUNS & ADJECTIVES

Interrogative pronouns are the tools we use to ask questions. If the interrogative pronoun is followed by a noun, it becomes an interrogative adjective, e.g., "**¿Qué libro te gusta leer?**" *(What book do you like to read?)*. In this case, the interrogative "**qué**" is considered an interrogative adjective. If the noun is dropped, "**qué**" becomes an interrogative pronoun, e.g., "**¿Qué te gusta leer?**" *(What do you like to read?)*.

Interrogative pronoun	English meaning	Examples
¿Qué?	*What?*	**¿Qué estás haciendo?** *What are you doing?*
¿Quién(es)?	*Who/Whom?*	**¿Quién hizo esto?** *Who did this?*
¿De quién(es)?	*Whose?*	**¿De quién es este libro?** *To whom does this book belong?*
¿Cuál(es)?	*Which?*	**¿Cuál es tu auto?** *Which one is your car?*

¿Cuánto(-a,-os,-as)?	How much? How many?	**¿Cuánto cuesta este abrigo?** *How much does this coat cost?*
¿Cuándo?	When?	**¿Cuándo quieres venir?** *When do you want to come?*
¿Dónde?	Where?	**¿Dónde has estado?** *Where have you been?*
¿Cómo?	How?	**¿Cómo hiciste eso?** *How did you do that?*
¿Por qué? **¿Para qué?**	Why?	**¿Por qué no quieres comer?** *Why don't you want to eat?* **¿Para qué fuiste allá?** *Why did you go there?*

❖ The interrogative pronoun "**¿por qué?**" means *"Why?"* If written without the accent and the space, i.e., "**porque,**" it means *"because."*

❖ Both "**¿por qué?**" and "**¿para qué?**" are often translated as *"Why?"* However, there is a subtle difference. Whereas "**¿por qué?**" enquires about the reason, "**¿para qué?**" enquires about the purpose and can be better translated as *"What for?"*, e.g., "**¿Para qué necesitas eso?**" *(What do you need this for?).*

❖ The interrogative pronouns "**cuál**" and "**quién**" have the plural forms "**cuáles**" and "**quiénes,**" respectively, whereas "**cuánto**" has four plural forms based on gender and number.

9. BASIC PHRASES

Learning greetings and short conversations is essential for taking the first steps to communicate in any language. Take some time to practice the following formal and informal basic phrases.

Hola	*Hi*
Buenos días.	*Good morning.*
Buenas tardes.	*Good afternoon.*
Buenas noches.	*Good evening.*
¿Cómo está?	*How are you? (formal, singular)*
¿Cómo estás?	*How are you? (informal, singular)*
Muy bien.	*Very good.*

No tan bien.	*Not so good.*
Así así. Regular.	*So-so.*
Gracias.	*Thank you.*
De nada.	*You're welcome. It's nothing.*
Por favor.	*Please.*
No mucho.	*Nothing much.*
Disculpa. Perdón. Lo siento.	*Sorry.*
Permiso. Con permiso.	*"If I may," or "Excuse me."*
Perdóneme. Disculpe.	*Excuse me.*
¡Oye!	*Hey, listen! (informal)*
Mucho gusto.	*It's a pleasure. (formal/informal)*
Encantado/-a de conocerte.	*Nice to meet you. (informal, singular)*
Encantado/-a de conocerlo/-a.	*Nice to meet you. (formal, singular)*
Hasta luego.	*See you later.*
Hasta pronto.	*See you soon.*
Hasta mañana.	*See you tomorrow.*
Bienvenido. (addressing a male) Bienvenida. (addressing a female)	*Welcome.*
Gusto en verlo.	*It's a pleasure to see you.*
¿Cuál es tu nombre?	*What is your name? (informal, singular)*
¿Cómo te llamas?	*What is your name? (informal, singular)*
¿Cómo se llama (usted)?	*What is your name? (formal, singular)*
Me llamo… Mi nombre es…	*My name is …*
Soy …	*I am …*
¿Cuántos años tienes?	*How old are you? (informal, singular)*
¿Cuántos años tiene?	*How old are you? (formal, singular)*
Tengo 20 años.	*I am 20 years old.*
¿De dónde es usted?	*Where are you from? (formal, singular)*
¿De dónde eres?	*Where are you from? (informal, singular)*
¿De qué parte?	*From which part?*
Soy de …	*I am from …*
¿Dónde has estado?	*Where have you been?*
¡Hace mucho tiempo que no te veo!	*It's been a while since I've seen you!*
¿Hablas inglés?	*Do you speak English? (informal, singular)*
¿Habla inglés?	*Do you speak English? (formal, singular)*

¿Dónde está …?	*Where is …?*
¿Dónde vives?	*Where do you live? (informal, singular)*
¿Dónde vive?	*Where do you live? (formal, singular)*
Vivo en …	*I live in …*
¿Cuánto cuesta eso?	*How much does that cost?*
La cuenta, por favor.	*The bill, please.*
¿Puede ayudarme?	*Can you help me? (formal)*
¿Puedes hablar más despacio?	*Can you speak more slowly?*
¿Cómo puedo llegar hasta allí?	*How can I get there?*
Adiós.	*Goodbye.*

There are many ways to say *"What's up?"* or *"What's going on?"* that range from less formal to very informal and vary in popularity from one Spanish-speaking country to another, such as:

¿Qué pasa?	¿Qué onda?	¿En qué andas?
¿Qué hay de nuevo?	¿Cómo te va?	¿Cómo vas?
¿Quiubo?	¿Cómo van las cosas?	¿Qué tal?

II. Vocabulary Building

This section contains some vocabulary that you will need to get you going at this basic level. As you go over it in the book, we recommend that you use the Anki flashcards to study and memorize the new vocabulary as a more efficient and less boring way of learning and reviewing the material.

1. VERBS I

Below is a list of the most common 40 verbs in Spanish. You can start by adding them to your vocabulary to improve your comprehension of Spanish speech and writing. Use the Anki flashcards created for this section to help you memorize the meaning of each verb in its proper context. We limit verb conjugation here to the infinitive and the regular present tense which are what we have learned so far.

English	Spanish	Examples
arrive	llegar	Voy a **llegar** tarde mañana. *I am going to **arrive** late tomorrow.*

believe	creer	**Creo** que mis padres no van a venir hoy. *I **believe** that my parents won't come today.*
call	llamar	Mi mamá siempre me **llama** por la noche. *My mom always **calls** me at night.*
can **be able to**	poder	Necesito mis zapatos para **poder** correr. *I need my shoes to **be able to** run.*
change	cambiar	Tienes que **cambiar** tu rutina diaria. *You have to **change** your daily routine.*
close **lock**	cerrar	No me gusta **cerrar** las ventanas por la tarde. *I don't like to **close** the windows in the afternoon.*
come	venir	Pienso que mi hermano no quiere **venir**. *I think that my brother doesn't want to **come**.*
create	crear	Los científicos siempre **crean** nuevos métodos. *Scientists always **create** new methods.*
do **make**	hacer	No vamos a **hacer** todo hoy. *We are not going to **do** everything today.*
drink	beber tomar [1]	¿Quieres **beber/tomar** agua? *Do you want to **drink** water?*
eat	comer	Los viernes **comemos** a las cuatro. *On Fridays, we **eat** at four o'clock.*
exit **leave** **go out**	salir	Nos gusta **salir** los fines de semana. *We like to **go out** on the weekend.*
explain	explicar	Este profesor **explica** las lecciones muy bien. *This teacher **explains** the lessons very well.*
finish **end**	terminar	Voy a **terminar** la novela muy pronto. *I am going to **finish** the novel very soon.*
give	dar	Te voy a **dar** un regalo mañana. *I am going to **give** you a gift tomorrow.*
go	ir	No quiero **ir** a la escuela mañana. *I don't want to **go** to school tomorrow.*
have	tener	Quiero **tener** un buen trabajo. *I want to **have** a good job.*
learn	aprender	Quiero **aprender** sobre la historia de Turquía. *I want to **learn** about the history of Turkey.*
live	vivir	María **vive** en un barrio pequeño. *Maria **lives** in a small neighborhood.*
look **watch**	mirar	Me gusta **mirar** escenas hermosas. *I like to **look at** beautiful scenes.*

---

[1] Depending on the context, the verb "**tomar**" can mean *"to take"* or *"to drink."*

love	amar	**Amo** el sonido de los pájaros. I **love** the sound of birds.
open	abrir	Las panaderías no **abren** muy tarde. Bakeries don't **open** very late.
put	poner	Debes **poner** la ropa en el armario. You must **put** the clothes in the wardrobe.
read	leer	Yo **leo** italiano, pero no lo hablo bien. I **read** Italian, but I don't speak it well.
receive	recibir	Siempre **recibimos** invitados en verano. We always **receive** guests in the summer.
say **tell**	decir	Él tiene que **decir** la verdad. He must **tell** the truth.
see	ver	Puedo **ver** que no hay servicios aquí. I can **see** that there are no services here.
sleep	dormir	Es más saludable **dormir** temprano. It is healthier to **sleep** early.
speak **talk**	hablar	Ella **habla** tres idiomas con fluidez. She **speaks** three languages fluently.
start	empezar comenzar	Podemos **comenzar** las clases a las 8 a.m. We can **start** classes at 8 a.m.
study	estudiar	Los chicos **estudian** con sus amigos. The boys **study** with their friends.
take	tomar[1]	Prefiero **tomar** el autobús la próxima vez. I'd prefer to **take** the bus next time.
think	pensar	No quiero **pensar** en el futuro ahora. I don't want to **think** of the future now.
travel	viajar	Me gustaría **viajar** a China este año. I would like to **travel** to China this year.
understand	entender comprender	No puedo **entender** lo que dice. I can't **understand** what he's saying.
use	usar utilizar	No **usamos** el tren en esta parte del mundo. We don't **use** the train in this part of the world.
walk	caminar andar[2]	Siempre **camino** después de cenar. I always **walk** after having dinner.
want to	querer	Me hace **querer** ser una mejor persona. He makes me **want to** be a better person.

[1] Depending on the context, the verb "**tomar**" can mean *"to take"* or *"to drink."*

[2] The literal meaning of the verb "**andar**" is *"to walk."* However, depending on the context and the local Spanish it can also mean *"to function," "to go," "to travel," "to be,"* as well as some other usages. For example, "**¿Cómo andás?**" is the common way to say "**¿Cómo estás?**" *(How are you?)* in Argentina.

| work | trabajar | **Trabajo** como contador.
*I **work** as an accountant.* |
| write | escribir | Este autor **escribe** novelas entretenidas.
*This author **writes** entertaining novels.* |

In addition to the above new verbs, we add 20 English cognates that are easy to memorize.

English	Spanish	Examples
accept	aceptar	Gracias por **aceptar** mi invitación. *Thank you for **accepting** my invitation.*
calm	calmar	Me gusta leer para **calmar** mis nervios. *I like to read to **calm** my nerves.*
cancel	cancelar	Me siento mal por **cancelar** mi visita. *I feel bad for **canceling** my visit.*
circulate	circular	El aire debe **circular** por la habitación. *The air should **circulate** through the room.*
compensate	compensar	Debo **compensar** por llegar tarde. *I have to **compensate** for arriving late.*
confirm	confirmar	¿Puedes **confirmar** el número? *Can you **confirm** the number?*
continue	continuar	La calle **continúa** hasta el río. *The street **continues** to the river.*
copy	copiar	En el pasado, era difícil **copiar** libros. *In the past, it was hard to **copy** books.*
decide	decidir	Hoy **decidimos** si vamos a viajar. *Today we **decide** if we are going to travel.*
depend	depender	Los resultados **dependen** de muchas variables. *The results **depend** on many variables.*
describe	describir	No sé cómo **describir** esa ciudad. *I don't know how to **describe** that city.*
enter	entrar[1] a/en	Debemos **entrar** al edificio temprano. *We must **enter** the building early.*
exist	existir	**Existen** muchos idiomas en el mundo. *A lot of languages **exist** in the world.*
form	formar	Los cuatro países **forman** una alianza. *The four countries **form** an alliance.*
insult	insultar	No es educado **insultar** a otras personas. *It is not polite to **insult** other people.*

---

[1] Whereas the verb *"enter"* is not followed by a preposition in English, the verb **"entrar"** in Spanish is followed by either **"a"** (more common in Latin America) or **"en"** (more common in Spain).

interfere	interferir	No debes **interferir** en su relación. *You shouldn't **interfere** in their relationship.*
observe	observar	La policía **observa** sus movimientos. *The police **observe** his movements.*
organize	organizar	Quiero **organizar** un viaje este mes. *I want to **organize** a trip this month.*
resolve	resolver	Quiero **resolver** este problema matemático. *I want to **resolve** this math problem.*
rob **steal**	robar	Hay ladrones que solo **roban** autos. *There are thieves who only **steal/rob** cars.*

2. ADJECTIVES I

Below is a list of the most common 50 adjectives in Spanish. Use the Anki cards created for this section to help you memorize the meaning of each word in proper contexts. Notice that an adjective must agree with the noun in number and gender. For example, "**feo**" means *"ugly,"* "an ugly house" is "**una fea casa**" because "casa" is feminine singular, and *"ugly houses"* is "**feas casas**" because "**casas**" is feminine plural. Do not worry if you are struggling to figure it out now. We will cover masculine and feminine nouns and adjectives in detail in **Level II, Lesson 1**.

English	Spanish	Examples
bad	malo [1]	El servicio es **malo** aquí. *The service is **bad** here.*
beautiful	hermoso	La vista allí es **hermosa**. *The view there is **beautiful**.*
better	mejor	Es **mejor** tomar la ruta más corta. *It's **better** to take the shortest route.*
big	grande	Nuestros vecinos tienen una casa **grande**. *Our neighbors have a **large** house.*
boring	aburrido	Esta clase es muy **aburrida**. *This class is very **boring**.*
busy	ocupado	Estoy muy **ocupado** este fin de semana. *I'm very **busy** this weekend.*
cheap	barato	Busco un vuelo **barato**. *I'm looking for a **cheap** flight.*

---

[1] Before a masculine noun, the final "o" is dropped, e.g., "**Este restaurante es malo**" *(This restaurant is bad)*, "**Este es un mal restaurante**" *(This is a bad restaurant)*.

clean	limpio	Mi baño siempre debe estar **limpio**. *My bathroom must always be **clean**.*
closed	cerrado	El cine está **cerrado** hoy. *The cinema is **closed** today.*
cold	frío	Me gusta el café **frío**. *I like **cold** coffee.*
crazy	loco	Este chico está **loco**. *This boy is **crazy**.*
difficult	difícil	Calcular los impuestos puede ser **difícil**. *Calculating taxes can be **hard**.*
dirty	sucio	Este es el cesto de la ropa **sucia**. *This is the **dirty** laundry basket.*
dry	seco	Esta región tiene un clima **seco**. *This region has a **dry** climate.*
easy	fácil	Este rompecabezas es muy **fácil**. *This puzzle is very **easy**.*
expensive	caro	Ese vestido es muy **caro**. *That dress is very **expensive**.*
fast	rápido	Este auto es muy **rápido**. *This car is very **fast**.*
fun	divertido	El viaje de mañana va a ser **divertido**. *Tomorrow's trip is going to be **fun**.*
good	bueno [1]	Este es un **buen** libro. *This is a **good** book.*
happy	feliz	El dinero solo no te hace **feliz**. *Money alone doesn't make you **happy**.*
hard (inflexible)	duro	Este yeso no me parece **duro**. *This plaster doesn't seem **hard** to me.*
high tall	alto	Este árbol es muy **alto**. *This tree is very **tall**.*
hot	caliente [2] caluroso [2]	El té está muy **caliente**. *The tea is very **hot**.*
long	largo	En verano los días son **largos**. *In the summer, the days are **long**.*
many much	mucho	Hay **muchas** casas aquí. *There are **many** houses here.*

---

[1] Before a masculine noun, the final "o" is dropped, e.g., "**Este restaurante es bueno**" *(This restaurant is good)*, "**Este es un buen restaurante**" *(This is a good restaurant)*.

[2] Whereas "**caluroso**" is used to describe the weather, e.g., "**Es un día caluroso**" *(It is a hot day)*, "**caliente**" is used for most other purposes to mean *"hot,"* e.g., "**El café está caliente**" *(The coffee is hot)*.

new	nuevo	Este es mi auto **nuevo**. *This is my **new** car.*
old	viejo	La casa de mi abuela es muy **vieja**. *My grandmother's house is very **old**.*
open	abierto	El supermercado ya está **abierto**. *The supermarket is already **open**.*
poor	pobre	Este hombre es **pobre**. *This man is **poor**.*
pretty	lindo bonito	¡Qué casa tan **linda**! *What a **pretty** house!*
quiet	tranquilo	Me gusta leer en un lugar **tranquilo**. *I like to read in a **quiet** place.*
ready	listo	Estoy **listo** para las vacaciones. *I am **ready** for vacation.*
rich	rico[1]	Las personas **ricas** tienen mucho dinero. ***Rich** people have a lot of money.*
sad	triste	Es un hombre muy **triste**. *He is a very **sad** man.*
same	mismo	Tengo dos camisetas del **mismo** color. *I have two shirts of the **same** color.*
short	bajo[2] corto[2]	Mi hermano es **bajo**. *My brother is **short**.*
sick	enfermo	Voy a visitar a mi abuelo **enfermo**. *I'm going to visit my **sick** grandfather.*
slow	lento	Es más saludable comer a paso **lento**. *It's healthier to eat at a **slow** pace.*
small	pequeño	Carlos tiene una nariz **pequeña**. *Carlos has a **small** nose.*
soft	suave blando	Este pan es muy **suave**. *This bread is very **soft**.*
strong	fuerte	Mi caballo es muy **fuerte**. *My horse is very **strong**.*
sure **certain**	seguro	Siempre intento responder si estoy **seguro**. *I always try to answer if I'm **certain**.*
sweet	dulce	Este refresco me parece muy **dulce**. *This refreshment seems too **sweet** to me.*

---

[1] When describing food, **"rico"** means *"delicious"* or *"tasty,"* e.g., **"¡Qué rico pastel!"** *(What a delicious cake!).*

[2] The direct translation of **"bajo"** is *"low,"* and the direct translation of **"corto"** is *"short."* However, only when we refer to the height of a person or an object, we use **"bajo"** to mean *"short,"* and we do not use **"corto."*

tired	cansado	Luego del trabajo, llego a casa **cansado**. *After work, I get home **tired**.*
too much	demasiado	No quiero comer **demasiado** azúcar hoy. *I don't want to eat **too much** sugar today.*
ugly	feo	Esta es una noticia **fea**. *This is **ugly** news.*
weak	débil	Tiene un cuerpo **débil** porque casi no come. *He has a **weak** body because he hardly eats.*
wet	mojado	No me gusta acostarme con el cabello **mojado**. *I don't like going to bed with my hair **wet**.*
worse	peor	En el **peor** de los casos, cancelas. *In the **worst** case, you cancel.*
young	joven	No es posible ser **joven** para siempre. *It is not possible to be **young** forever.*

In addition to the above new adjectives, we add 30 more English cognates that are easy to memorize.

English	Spanish	Examples
additional	adicional	Necesito un sobre **adicional**. *I need an **additional** envelope.*
adult	adulto	Este medicamento es solo para **adultos**. *This medication is for **adults** only.*
aggressive	agresivo	El gato de mi amiga es muy **agresivo**. *My friend's cat is very **aggressive**.*
basic	básico	Debes saber las reglas **básicas**. *You should know the **basic** rules.*
common	común	Esa marca es muy **común** aquí. *That brand is very **common** here.*
complete	completo	El proceso **completo** es complejo. *The **complete** process is complex.*
convenient	conveniente	Es **conveniente** guardar la ropa aquí. *It is **convenient** to store the clothes here.*
correct **right**	correcto	Debes seleccionar la opción **correcta**. *You must select the **right** option.*
diverse	diverso	Me gusta comer comida **diversa**. *I like to eat **diverse** foods.*
excellent	excelente	Sus calificaciones son **excelentes**. *His grades are **excellent**.*
familiar	familiar	Su cara me resulta **familiar**. *His face seems **familiar** to me.*
frank	franco	Intenta ser **franco** con su padre. *He tries to be **frank** with his father.*
global	global	Internet facilita la comunicación **global**. *The internet facilitates **global** communication.*

honest	honesto	Necesito tu opinión **honesta**. *I need your **honest** opinion.*
impatient	impaciente	Es una persona **impaciente**. *He is an **impatient** person.*
important	importante	Guardo los archivos **importantes** aquí. *I store **important** files here.*
incorrect	incorrecto	No hay un modo **incorrecto** de hacerlo. *There is no **incorrect** way to do it.*
intelligent	inteligente	Mi madre es muy **inteligente**. *My mom is very **intelligent**.*
interesting	interesante	Este libro es muy **interesante**. *This book is very **interesting**.*
necessary	necesario	Es **necesario** ir al médico periódicamente. *It's **necessary** to go to the doctor periodically.*
obvious	obvio	Es **obvio** que la puerta está abierta. *It is **obvious** that the door is open.*
patient	paciente	Las mamás son **pacientes** con sus hijos. *Mothers are **patient** with their children.*
personal	personal	Este es mi diario **personal**. *This is my **personal** diary.*
practical	práctico	Es **práctico** tener las cosas organizadas. *It's **practical** to have things organized.*
rare	raro [1]	Es muy **raro** hallar piedras preciosas allí. *It's very **rare** to find precious stones there.*
real	real	Obviamente, los monstruos no son **reales**. *Obviously, monsters aren't **real**.*
remote	remoto	Tengo una oficina **remota**. *I have a **remote** office.*
sincere	sincero	Es mejor ser **sincero** con esto. *It is better to be **sincere** with this.*
special	especial	Voy a preparar una receta **especial** para ti. *I am going to prepare a **special** recipe for you.*
stupid	estúpido	Estos errores me hacen sentir **estúpido**. *These errors make me feel **stupid**.*

---

[1] In addition to meaning *"rare,"* the adjective **"raro"** has another common use, meaning *"weird"* or *"strange,"* e.g., **"Es raro que no hay nadie acá"** *(It is weird that there is nobody here)*, **"¡Qué raro que es todo esto!"** *(How strange this all is!)*.

3. COUNTRIES & NATIONALITIES I

A *country* in Spanish is **"un país"** and a *nationality* is **"una nacionalidad."** The following are some countries and nationalities (or demonyms) in Spanish:

Africa	**África**[f]	*African*	**africano/-a**
Argentina	**Argentina**[f]	*Argentinian*	**argentino/-a**
Asia	**Asia**[f]	*Asian*	**asiático/-a**
Australia	**Australia**[f]	*Australian*	**australiano/-a**
Brazil	**Brasil**[m]	*Brazilian*	**brasileño/-a** **brasilero/-a**
Canada	**Canadá**[m]	*Canadian*	**canadiense**
China	**China**[f]	*Chinese*	**chino/-a**
Colombia	**Colombia**[f]	*Colombian*	**colombiano/-a**
Croatia	**Croacia**[f]	*Croatian*	**croata**
Cuba	**Cuba**[f]	*Cuban*	**cubano/-a**
Egypt	**Egipto**[m]	*Egyptian*	**egipcio/-a**
England	**Inglaterra**[f]	*English*	**inglés/-esa**
Europe	**Europa**[f]	*European*	**europeo/-a**
France	**Francia**[f]	*French*	**francés/-esa**
Germany	**Alemania**[f]	*German*	**alemán/-ana**
Iran	**Irán**[m]	*Iranian*	**iraní**
Iraq	**Irak**[m]	*Iraqi*	**iraquí**
Italy	**Italia**[f]	*Italian*	**italiano/-a**
Japan	**Japón**[m]	*Japanese*	**japonés/-esa**
Jordan	**Jordania**[f]	*Jordanian*	**jordano/-a**
Latin America	**América Latina**[f]	*Latin American*	**latinoamericano/-a**
Mexico	**México**[m]	*Mexican*	**mexicano/-a**
Morocco	**Marruecos**[m]	*Moroccan*	**marroquí**
Palestine	**Palestina**[f]	*Palestinian*	**palestino/-a**
Panama	**Panamá**[f]	*Panamanian*	**panameño/-a**
Poland	**Polonia**[f]	*Polish*	**polaco/-a**
Russia	**Rusia**[f]	*Russian*	**ruso/-a**
South America	**Sudamérica**[f] **América del Sur**	*South American*	**sudamericano/-a**
Spain	**España**[f]	*Spanish*	**español/-la**
Turkey	**Turquía**[f]	*Turkish*	**turco/-a**
Uruguay	**Uruguay**[m]	*Uruguayan*	**uruguayo/-a**

Notice that most countries ending with "**-a**" are feminine. A notable exception in the table above is "**Canadá**" which is masculine.

4. COLORS I

The word *"color"* has the same spelling in Spanish, that is, **"color"** (pronounced co-**lor**). Some of the basic colors in Spanish are:

black	**negro/-a**	*orange*	**naranja**[m,f]
blue	**azul**[m,f]	*purple*	**morado/-a** **púrpura**[m,f]
brown	**marrón**[m,f]	*red*	**rojo/-a**
gray	**gris**[m,f]	*white*	**blanco/-a**
green	**verde**[m,f]	*yellow*	**amarillo/-a**

5. TIMES & SEASONS

A *day* in Spanish is **"un día,"** and a *week* is **"una semana."** The *days of the week* or **"los días de la semana"** are:

Monday	**lunes**	*Friday*	**viernes**
Tuesday	**martes**	*Saturday*	**sábado**
Wednesday	**miércoles**	*Sunday*	**domingo**
Thursday	**jueves**	*weekend*	**fin**[m] **de semana**

Today is **"hoy,"** and *tomorrow* is **"mañana,"** followed by **"pasado mañana"** *(the day after tomorrow)*. *Yesterday* is **"ayer,"** preceded by **"anteayer"** *(the day before yesterday)*.

Tonight is **"esta noche"** (literally *this night*), *last night* is **"anoche,"** and *tomorrow night* is **"mañana por la noche"** (literally *tomorrow at night*).

The main periods of the day are **"la mañana"** *(morning)*, **"la tarde"** *(afternoon)*, and **"la noche"** *(night)*. We generally use the preposition **"por"** to say **"por la mañana/tarde/noche"** *(in the morning/afternoon or at night)*, although in Latin America the use of **"en"** is also common, and in some regions **"a"** is used instead.

Notice also that **"mañana"** can mean *tomorrow* or *morning*. For example, *"tomorrow morning"* is **"mañana por la mañana,"** where the first **"mañana"** is translated as *"tomorrow,"* and **"por la mañana"** means *"in the morning."*

A *month* in Spanish is "**un mes**" and a *year* is "**un año**." A *decade* is "**una década**," and a *century* is "**un siglo**."

The *months of the year* or "**los meses del año**" are:

January	enero	July	julio
February	febrero	August	agosto
March	marzo	September	septiembre
April	abril	October	octubre
May	mayo	November	noviembre
June	junio	December	diciembre

Notice from the two tables above that the days and months are not capitalized in Spanish, and they are all masculine.

Finally, a *season* in Spanish is "**una estación**." The *seasons of the year* or "**las estaciones del año**" are:

autumn, fall	otoño[m]	summer	verano[m]
spring	primavera[f]	winter	invierno[m]

Notice that only "**la primavera**" is feminine, while the other three seasons are masculine.

6. DIRECTIONS I

A *direction* in Spanish is "**una dirección**." The word "**una dirección**" is used also to refer to an *address* of a house or a store. A *map* is "**un mapa**," and a *street* is "**una calle**."

The four geographical directions of a *compass* or "**una brújula**" are:

east	este[m]	south	sur[m] sud[m]
north	norte[m]	west	oeste[m]

And the four main directions *right*, *left*, *up*, and *down* are:

right	derecha	up	arriba
left	izquierda	down	abajo

To describe the location of an object with respect to another, one can use:

above on top (of)	sobre encima (de)	there	ahí allá allí
here	acá aquí	to the left of	a la izquierda de
inside	dentro (de)	to the right of	a la derecha de
near	cerca (de)	far (from)	lejos (de)
outside	fuera (de)	toward	hacia
straight ahead	derecho recto	under beneath	bajo debajo (de)

There is a subtle difference between **"aquí"** and **"acá,"** both translated as *"here,"* as **"aquí"** tends to be less specific about the location. However, this subtle difference is not often respected, and **"acá"** tends to be used more often in Latin America.

While **"ahí,"** **"allí,"** and **"allá"** all mean *"there,"* **"ahí"** is used more often for things that are within reach whereas **"allí"** and **"allá"** are sometimes better translated as *"over there,"* with **"allá"** being more popular than **"allí"** in Latin America.

7. FAMILY I

A *family* in Spanish is **"una familia."** The status of being *single* is **"soltero"** or **"soltera,"** and *married* is **"casado"** or **"casada."** Some *members of the family,* or **"miembros de la familia,"** are:

aunt	**tía**[f]	grandmother	**abuela**[f]
couple	**pareja**[f]	grandson	**nieto**[m]
cousin	**primo/-a**	husband	**marido**[m]
daughter	**hija**[f]	mother	**madre**[f] **mamá**[f]
daughter-in-law	**nuera**[f]	relatives	**parientes**[m] **familiares**[m]
father	**padre**[m] **papá**[m]	son	**hijo**[m]

fiancé *boyfriend* *groom*	**novio**^m 1	*son-in-law*	**yerno**^m
fiancée *girlfriend* *bride*	**novia**^f 2	*spouse*	**esposo/-a**
granddaughter	**nieta**^f	*uncle*	**tío**^m
grandfather	**abuelo**^m	*wife*	**mujer**^f

[1] The word "**prometido**" can also be used for *"fiancé."*
[2] The word "**prometida**" can also be used for *"fiancée."*

8. ANATOMY I

Body in Spanish is "**el cuerpo**," and some *body parts*, or "**las partes del cuerpo**," are:

arm	**brazo**^m	*hand*	**mano**^f
back	**espalda**^f	*head*	**cabeza**^f
blood	**sangre**^f	*heart*	**corazón**^m
brain	**cerebro**^m	*leg*	**pierna**^f
ear	**oreja**^f	*lip*	**labio**^m
eye	**ojo**^m	*mouth*	**boca**^f
face	**cara**^f	*nose*	**nariz**^f
finger	**dedo**^m	*shoulder*	**hombro**^m
foot	**pie**^f	*stomach*	**estómago**^m
hair	**pelo**^m	*toe*	**dedo**^m **del pie**

Notice that in the above table all words ending with "**a**" are feminine, whereas all words ending with "**o**" are masculine with the notable exception of "**mano**" *(hand)* which is feminine despite ending with "**o**."

In Spanish, there are two words for *"ear."* The outer part of the ear is referred to as "**oreja**^f" whereas the inner ear is "**oído**^m," which is the same word used to refer to the sense of *"hearing."*

9. PEOPLE I

The following is some vocabulary that we use to describe *people*, "**la gente**" in Spanish. Notice how the word "**gente**" is singular in Spanish whereas the word *"people"* is plural in English.

baby	**bebé**^m	*most people*	**la mayoría de la gente**
boss	**jefe**^m **patrón**^m	*neighbor*	**vecino/-a**
boy	**chico**^m **muchacho**^m	*nobody*	**nadie**^{m,f}
businessman	**empresario**^m	*person*	**persona**^f
child	**niño/-a**	*pilot*	**piloto**^{m,f}
criminal	**criminal**^m	*player*	**jugador/-a**
date appointment	**cita**^f	*president*	**presidente**^{m,f}
everyone everybody	**todos todo el mundo**	*queen*	**reina**^f
friend	**amigo/-a**	*roommate*	**compañero/-a de piso**
girl	**chica**^f **muchacha**^f	*some people*	**algunas personas**^f
human	**humano**^m	*someone*	**alguien**^{m,f}
king	**rey**^m	*student*	**estudiante**^{m,f}
man	**hombre**^m	*thief*	**ladrón**^m**/-ona**^f
minor	**menor**^{m,f}	*woman*	**mujer**^f

10. ANIMALS I

The word *"animal"* in Spanish is also written **"animal"** (pronounced ani-**mal**). Below are some animal names in Spanish:

bird	**pájaro**^m	*hen*	**gallina**^f
bull	**toro**^m	*horse*	**caballo**^m
cat	**gato/-a**	*mouse*	**ratón**^m
chicken	**pollo**^m	*pet*	**mascota**^f
cow	**vaca**^f	*pig*	**cerdo**^m **cochino**^m
dog	**perro/-a**	*rabbit*	**conejo**^m
donkey	**burro**^m **asno**^m	*rat*	**rata**^f
duck	**pato**^m	*rooster*	**gallo**^m
fish	**pescado**^m **pez**^m	*sheep*	**oveja**^f
fly	**mosca**^f	*turkey*	**pavo**^m

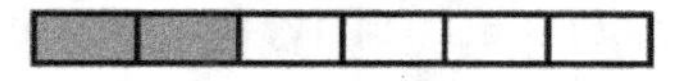

I. Introductory Topics & Grammar

At this level, you will continue to familiarize yourself with some of the fundamental grammar rules and basic topics that will enhance your Spanish-language knowledge.

1. MASCULINE & FEMININE NOUNS & ADJECTIVES

As a general rule, adjectives in Spanish, unlike in English, come after the noun they describe, e.g., **"edificio alto"** *(tall building)*. There are some exceptions to this rule, e.g., **"gran mercado"** *(big market)*. Many adjectives that tend to come before the noun are *indefinite adjectives*, which will be covered in **Level III, Lesson 4**.

Nouns and adjectives in Spanish have only two genders: *masculine* and *feminine*. There is no neuter gender. The gender of an adjective follows the gender of the noun it describes.

There are general rules that help determine the gender of a noun or adjective in Spanish. However, there remain many exceptions that can only be learned by practice.

As a very loose and general rule, words ending in "**o**" are likely to be masculine, and most words ending in "**a**" are likely to be feminine. However, this rule—if it is even reasonable to consider it a rule—has many exceptions. Thus, we will have sub-rules that are more specific.

As we attempt to encompass most of the gender rules in Spanish, try not to feel overwhelmed with the vocabulary in this lesson. You can use it as a reference and revisit this lesson whenever in doubt. We find this to be a better approach than cluttering the book with rules on determining the gender of different words. The Anki cards designed specifically for this lesson will help you retain most of the information presented here. We strongly advise that you practice them.

Although not a universal rule, many feminine words can be formed from masculine words that end with a consonant by adding an "**a**" at the end, e.g., "**jugador**" *(player)* (feminine "**jugadora**"), "**juez**" *(judge)* (feminine "**jueza**"), and from masculine words that end with an "**o**" by replacing the last "**o**" with an "**a**," e.g., "**ingeniero**" *(engineer)* (feminine "**ingeniera**"), "**alto**" *(tall)* (feminine "**alta**"). As we shall see, there are exceptions, as some words deviate from this simple rule to form the feminine. In addition, there are many words that do not change form based on gender. For example, "**artista**" *(artist)*, "**piloto**" *(pilot)*, and "**estudiante**" *(student)* all have the same form in both masculine and feminine.

For the purpose of brevity throughout the book, if a noun or an adjective has both a masculine and a feminine form, we may often only refer to the masculine form. We trust that by learning the following basic rules, you will be able to guess the feminine form most of the time.

Feminine Nouns

❖ Most words ending in "**-a**" are feminine. The following are some exceptions:

   1. Words that end in "**-ma**," "**-pa**," or "**-ta**" and originate from *Greek*. These are masculine. Examples are: "**el idioma**" *(language)*, "**el problema**" *(problem)*, "**el sistema**" *(system)*, "**el clima**" *(climate)*, "**el tema**" *(topic)*, "**el diploma**" *(diploma)*, "**el drama**" *(drama)*, "**el dilema**" *(dilemma)*, "**el diagrama**" *(diagram)*, "**el mapa**" *(map)*, "**el planeta**" *(planet)*, "**el cometa**" *(comet)*, etc. This exception does not apply to words that did *not* originate from *Greek*, such as "**la forma**" *(form)* and "**la plataforma**" *(platform)*.

   2. Words that end in "**-ista**" and refer to masculine or feminine people performing a profession, such as: "**el taxista**" *(taxi*

driver), "**el artista**" *(artist)*, "**el analista**" *(analyst)*, "**el pianista**" *(pianist)*, etc.

3. Words that end in "**-a**" and refer to professions with the same masculine and feminine forms. For example, "**atleta**" can refer to a male or female *"athlete,"* and "**espía**" can refer to a male or female *"spy."*

4. A few other words that are learned by practice, such as "**el día**" *(day)*, "**el Buda**" *(Buddha)*, and "**el panda**" *(panda)*.

❖ Most words ending in "**-d**," "**-z**," and "**-ión**" are feminine, e.g., "**la ciudad**" *(city)*, "**la escasez**" *(shortage)*, "**la religión**" *(religion)*, etc. The following are some exceptions:

1. Some masculine words with a "**-d**" ending are: "**el huésped**" *(guest)*, "**el césped**" *(grass)*, "**el récord**" *(record)*, "**el ataúd**" *(coffin)*, "**el abad**" *(abbot)*, "**el milord**" *(milord)*, and "**el lord**" *(lord)*.

2. Some masculine words with a "**-z**" ending are: "**el aprendiz**" *(apprentice)*, "**el pez**" *(fish)*, "**el arroz**" *(rice)*, "**el lápiz**" *(pencil)*, "**el ajedrez**" *(chess)*, "**el antifaz**" *(mask)*, "**el maíz**" *(corn)*, "**el disfraz**" *(costume)*, "**el haz**" *(beam)*, "**el albornoz**" *(bathrobe)*, and "**el altavoz**" *(speaker)*.

3. Some masculine words with "**-ión**" ending are: "**el avión**" *(plane)*, "**el camión**" *(truck)*, and "**el embrión**" *(embryo)*.

Masculine Nouns

❖ Most words ending in "**-o**" are masculine, with a few exceptions that are feminine, such as: "**la mano**" *(hand)*, "**la radio**[1]" *(radio)*, "**la foto**" *(photo)*, "**la moto**" *(motorcycle)*, and "**la libido**" *(libido)*, in addition to words that end with "**-o**" used to refer to professions that have the same masculine and feminine forms,

---

[1] According to the Real Academia Española (RAE), the word "**radio**" is *feminine* when referring to the broadcast or programming of the radio, e.g., "**Lo escuché en la radio**" *(I heard it on the radio)*. When referring to the radio set or device, the word "**radio**" is *feminine* in Spain and the southern cone of South America, but *masculine* in most of the rest of Latin America.

e.g., "**piloto**" can refer to a male or female *pilot*, where "**el piloto**" is masculine and "**la piloto**" is feminine.

❖ Words ending with an accented vowel (**á, é, í, ó, ú**) are generally masculine, e.g., "**el maní**" *(peanut)*, "**el ají**" *(chili pepper)*, "**el ñandú**" *(rhea)*, "**el colibrí**" *(hummingbird)*, "**el bambú**" *(bamboo)*, etc.

❖ Most words ending with a consonant other than "**d**" or "**z**" are masculine, with some exceptions, such as: "**la miel**" *(honey)*, "**la piel**" *(skin)*, "**la sal**" *(salt)*, "**la hiel**" *(gall)*, "**la flor**" *(flower)*, "**la coliflor**" *(cauliflower)*, and "**la labor**" *(labor)*.

❖ Words ending with "**-e**" tend to be masculine, especially those ending in "**-aje**" or "**-ambre**," but with a lot of exceptions that are feminine, such as: "**la calle**" *(street)*, "**la carne**" *(meat)*, "**la gente**" *(people)*, "**la llave**" *(key)*, "**la fiebre**" *(fever)*, "**la noche**" *(night)*, "**la nube**" *(cloud)*, "**la sangre**" *(blood)*, "**la suerte**" *(luck)*, "**la tarde**" *(afternoon* or *evening)*, "**la fuente**" *(source* or *fountain)*, "**la torre**" *(tower)*, "**la sede**" *(headquarters)*, "**la serpiente**" *(snake)*, "**la corriente**" *(current)*, "**la clave**" *(key code)*, "**la clase**" *(class)*, "**la base**" *(base)*, "**la madre**" *(mother)*, "**la muerte**" *(death)*, "**la nieve**" *(snow)*, and "**la frase**" *(phrase)*.

As you can see, it is not always easy to determine the gender of a noun in Spanish, and practice remains the best tool. However, these examples can serve as a good reference to help establish some rules and memorize them. Do not let this minor difficulty discourage you from learning Spanish. Most Spanish speakers are forgiving of errors in gender made by foreigners learning Spanish.

2. PRESENT TENSE II: IRREGULAR VERBS

Some verbs deviate from the general conjugation rules in the present indicative tense. Some of these deviations are simple and easy to apply, while others may require some practice. Nevertheless, do not give up because conjugation in other tenses tends to be more straightforward with fewer irregularities. Use your Anki cards to practice more examples until you master this lesson. In addition, you can use the summary in the cheat sheets in **Appendix B** as a quick reference.

Let us start with the easier irregularities. In the *first* group, the following four sets of irregular verbs are only irregular in the first-person singular form, that is, with the subject "**yo.**"

1. The verbs "**estar**" *(to be)* and "**dar**" *(to give)* are conjugated with "**-oy**" ending in the first-person "**yo**" form as "**estoy**" and "**doy**," respectively, e.g., "**Yo estoy aquí**" (*I am here*), "**Yo le doy dinero a mi hermano**" (*I give money to my brother*).

2. The verbs "**hacer**" *(to do)*, "**poner**" *(to put)*, "**valer**" *(to be worth)*, "**salir**" *(to go out or to exit)*, "**traer**" *(to bring)*, and "**caer**" *(to drop)* are conjugated with "**-go**" ending in the first-person "**yo**" as "**hago**," "**pongo**," "**valgo**," "**salgo**," "**traigo**," and "**caigo**," respectively, e.g., "**Yo salgo con mis amigos**" (*I go out with my friends*).

3. The verbs ending in a vowel followed by "**-cer**" or "**-cir**" are conjugated with "**-zco**" in the first-person "**yo.**" Examples are "**conocer**" *(to know)*, "**ofrecer**" *(to offer)*, "**conducir**" *(to drive)*, and "**traducir**" *(to translate)*.

4. The verbs "**saber**" *(to know)*, "**caber**" *(to fit)*, and "**ver**" *(to see)* do not follow any rules and are conjugated in first-person "**yo**" form as "**sé**," "**quepo**," and "**veo**," respectively.

Remember that these three sets of irregular verbs are only irregular in their first-person "**yo**" form. In other forms, they are conjugated as regular verbs.

	estar	dar	hacer	salir	conocer	saber
yo	es**toy**	**doy**	ha**go**	sal**go**	cono**zco**	s**é**
tú	est**ás**	d**as**	hac**es**	sal**es**	conoc**es**	sab**es**
él/ella/usted	est**á**	d**a**	hac**e**	sal**e**	conoc**e**	sab**e**
nosotros/-as	est**amos**	d**amos**	hac**emos**	sal**imos**	conoc**emos**	sab**emos**
vosotros/-as	est**áis**	d**ais**	hac**éis**	sal**ís**	conoc**éis**	sab**éis**
ellos/-as/ustedes	est**án**	d**an**	hac**en**	sal**en**	conoc**en**	sab**en**

Added to these four sets are three more sets of verbs that are regular in essence but change spelling when conjugated in first-person "**yo**" form. These are the verbs ending in "**-guir**," "**-ger**," "**-gir**," and "**-quir**."

1. Verbs ending in "**-guir**" in first-person "**yo**" form end in "**-go**," e.g., "**extinguir**" *(to extinguish)* becomes "**yo extingo**."

2. Verbs ending in "**-ger**" and "**-gir**" in first-person "**yo**" form end in "**-jo**," e.g., "**escoger**" *(to choose)* becomes "**yo escojo**," and "**exigir**" *(to demand)* becomes "**yo exijo**."

3. Verbs ending in "**-quir**" in first-person "**yo**" form end in "**-co**," e.g., "**delinquir**" *(to commit an offense or a crime)* becomes "**yo delinco**."

	-guir ending extinguir	-ger ending proteger	-gir ending exigir
yo	exting**o**	prote**jo**	exi**jo**
tú	extingu**es**	proteg**es**	exig**es**
él/ella/usted	extingu**e**	proteg**e**	exig**e**
nosotros/-as	extingu**imos**	proteg**emos**	exig**imos**
vosotros/-as	extingu**ís**	proteg**éis**	exig**ís**
ellos/ellas/ustedes	extingu**en**	proteg**en**	exig**en**

The justification for such a spelling change is to maintain the pronunciation rules. For instance, the letter "**g**" sounds like the *"g"* in *"get,"* except when it is followed by "**e**" or "**i**," in which case it is pronounced like the *"h"* in *"hero."* Similarly, the letter "**c**" sounds like *"c"* in *"car,"* except when it is followed by "**e**" or "**i**," in which case it is pronounced like the *"c"* in *"city."*

The *second* group of irregular verbs includes verbs with stem changes. In these verbs, the irregular conjugation is applied to all forms except with the subject pronouns "**nosotros/-as**" and "**vosotros/-as**." The verbs in this group are divided into five categories:

1. Verbs that change stem from "**e**" to "**i**," e.g., "**corregir**" *(to correct)*, "**elegir**" *(to choose* or *to elect)*, "**medir**" *(to measure)*, "**pedir**"

(to ask for or *to request)*, **"reír"** *(to laugh)*, **"repetir"** *(to repeat)*, **"seguir"** *(to follow)*, **"servir"** *(to serve)*.

2. Verbs that change stem from "**e**" to "**ie**," e.g., **"advertir"** *(to warn)*, **"atender"** *(to attend to)*, **"atravesar"** *(to cross)*, **"calentar"** *(to heat)*, **"cerrar"** *(to close)*, **"comenzar"** *(to commence* or *to start)*, **"confesar"** *(to confess)*, **"convertir"** *(to convert)*, **"defender"** *(to defend)*, **"divertir"** *(to amuse)*, **"empezar"** *(to begin)*, **"encender"** *(to light)*, **"entender"** *(to understand)*, **"enterrar"** *(to bury)*, **"fregar"** *(to scrub)*, **"herir"** *(to injure)*, **"hervir"** *(to boil)*, **"mentir"** *(to lie)*, **"negar"** *(to deny)*, **"pensar"** *(to think)*, **"perder"** *(to lose)*, **"preferir"** *(to prefer)*, **"querer"** *(to want)*, **"regar"** *(to water)*, **"sugerir"** *(to suggest)*, **"temblar"** *(to tremble)*, **"tropezar"** *(to trip* or *to stumble)*, **"verter"** *(to pour)*.

3. Verbs that change stem from "**o**" to "**ue**," e.g., **"acordar"** *(to agree)*, **"almorzar"** *(to have lunch)*, **"aprobar"** *(to approve)*, **"contar"** *(to count)*, **"costar"** *(to cost)*, **"dormir"** *(to sleep)*, **"encontrar"** *(to find)*, **"forzar"** *(to force)*, **"morder"** *(to bite)*, **"mostrar"** *(to show)*, **"poder"** *(to be able to)*, **"probar"** *(to test* or *to taste)*, **"volar"** *(to fly)*, **"volver"** *(to return)*.

4. Verbs that change stem from "**u**" to "**ue**" include only one verb, which happens to be commonly used, that is, **"jugar"** *(to play)*.

5. Verbs that change stem from "**i**" to "**ie**" include only two verbs **"adquirir"** *(to acquire)* and **"inquirir"** *(to inquire)*.

The table below summarizes the stem change rules with examples.

	pedir e→i	pensar e→ie	dormir o→ue	jugar u→ue	adquirir i→ie
yo	pido	pienso	duermo	juego	adquiero
tú	pides	piensas	duermes	juegas	adquieres
él/ella/usted	pide	piensa	duerme	juega	adquiere
nosotros/-as	pedimos	pensamos	dormimos	jugamos	adquirimos
vosotros/-as	pedís	pensáis	dormís	jugáis	adquirís
ellos/ellas/ustedes	piden	piensan	duermen	juegan	adquieren

Notice again how the conjugation remains regular with the subject pronouns "**nosotros/-as**" and "**vosotros/-as**."

The first three groups are the most encountered, whereas the last two groups contain only three verbs, which can be memorized easily.

The rules about verbs ending in "-**guir**," "-**ger**," and "-**gir**" should be respected in the first-person "**yo**" form if a verb happens to belong to one of the abovementioned categories. For example, the verb "**seguir**" changes stem from "**e**" to "**i**." In the first-person "**yo**" form, in addition to the stem change, the "**gu**" is replaced with "**g**," while the other forms only change the stem. Similarly, the verb "**elegir**" changes stem from "**e**" to "**i**." In the first-person "**yo**" form, in addition to stem change, the "**g**" is replaced with "**j**," while the other forms only change the stem.

	"-**guir**" ending e.g., seguir	"-**gir**" ending e.g., elegir
yo	si**go**	eli**jo**
tú	sigu**es**	elig**es**
él/ella/usted	sigu**e**	elig**e**
nosotros/-as	segu**imos**	eleg**imos**
vosotros/-as	segu**ís**	eleg**ís**
ellos/ellas/ustedes	sigu**en**	elig**en**

The *third* group of verbs includes the verbs that are irregular in the first-person "**yo**" form with a "-**go**" ending and have a stem change in all other forms except the "**nosotros/-as**" and "**vosotros/-as**" forms. This group includes the commonly used verbs "**decir**" (*to say*), "**venir**" (*to come*), and "**tener**" (*to have*).

	decir	venir	tener
yo	di**go**	ven**go**	ten**go**
tú	dic**es**	vien**es**	tien**es**
él/ella/usted	dic**e**	vien**e**	tien**e**
nosotros/-as	dec**imos**	ven**imos**	ten**emos**
vosotros/-as	dec**ís**	ven**ís**	ten**éis**
ellos/ellas/ustedes	dic**en**	vien**en**	tien**en**

The *fourth* group of verbs includes completely irregular verbs. These must be practiced until memorized. Verbs in this group include **"ser"** (*to be*), **"ir"** (*to go*), **"oler"** (*to smell*), and **oír** (*to hear*). Note that **"ser"** and **"estar"** both mean *"to be."* Differences between the two will be explained in **Lesson 3** of this level.

	ser	**ir**	**oler**	**oír**
yo	soy	voy	huelo	oigo
tú	eres	vas	hueles	oyes
él/ella/usted	es	va	huele	oye
nosotros/-as	somos	vamos	olemos	oímos
vosotros/-as	sois	vais	oléis	oís
ellos/ellas/ustedes	son	van	huelen	oyen

The *fifth* group includes verbs that undergo some other orthographic changes when conjugated. We have already encountered the verbs with **"-guir,"** **"-ger,"** and **"-gir"** endings, which undergo some orthographic change when conjugated in the first-person **"yo"** form. We have also encountered verbs that end in a vowel followed by **"-cer"** or **"-cir,"** whose conjugation in the first-person **"yo"** form ends in **"-zco."** Here we discuss two more orthographic changes:

1. Verbs ending in **"-uir"** (excluding **"-guir"**) add **"y"** between the stem and the conjugation suffix in all forms except with **"nosotros/-as"** and **"vosotros/-as,"** e.g., **"atribuir"** (*to attribute*), **"construir"** (*to construct*), **"contribuir"** (*to contribute*), **"disminuir"** (*to diminish* or *to decrease*), **"distribuir"** (*to distribute*), **"huir"** (*to escape* or *to run away*), **"incluir"** (*to include*), **"sustituir"** (*to substitute*).

	construir	**incluir**	**huir**
yo	construyo	incluyo	huyo
tú	construyes	incluyes	huyes
él/ella/usted	construye	incluye	huye
nosotros/-as	construimos	incluimos	huimos
vosotros/-as	construís	incluís	huís
ellos/ellas/ustedes	construyen	incluyen	huyen

2. Some verbs ending in "**-iar**" or "**-uar**" add an accent to the "**i**" or "**u**" before the conjugation suffix in all forms except with "**nosotros/-as**" and "**vosotros/-as**," e.g., "**enviar**" *(to send)*, "**fiar**" *(to trust* or *to believe in)*, "**liar**" *(to bundle* or *to bind)*, "**variar**" *(to vary)*, "**actuar**" *(to act)*, "**continuar**" *(to continue)*, "**habituar**" *(to get used to)*, "**situar**" *(to position* or *to situate)*.

	enviar	**actuar**	**continuar**
yo	env**ío**	act**úo**	contin**úo**
tú	env**ías**	act**úas**	contin**úas**
él/ella/usted	env**ía**	act**úa**	contin**úa**
nosotros/-as	envi**amos**	actu**amos**	continu**amos**
vosotros/-as	envi**áis**	actu**áis**	continu**áis**
ellos/ellas/ustedes	env**ían**	act**úan**	contin**úan**

3. THE VERB "TO BE": "SER" VS. "ESTAR"

There are two verbs in Spanish that are translated as the verb *"to be"* in English. The two verbs are: "**ser**" and "**estar**." It is often tricky for English speakers to wrap their heads around the difference, but we will explain the difference in a simple manner. Before we do that, you need to recognize the two verbs in their present tense indicative conjugated forms.

	ser	**estar**
yo	soy	estoy
tú	eres	estás
él/ella/usted	es	está
nosotros/-as	somos	estamos
vosotros/-as	sois	estáis
ellos/ellas/ustedes	son	están

We have encountered the verbs "**ser**" and "**estar**" in **Lesson 2** of this level. We have seen that the verb "**estar**" is irregular only in the first-person "**yo**" form and is regular in all other forms. On the other hand, the verb "**ser**" is irregular in all its forms. Thus, it must be memorized because it is a very important verb that you will encounter frequently.

Now, let us look at the difference in meaning between "**ser**" and "**estar**." The easiest way to distinguish between the two is to remember the uses of "**estar**." These tend to be more limited than the uses of "**ser**." If you remember the uses of "**estar**," you can safely assume that everything else should take the verb "**ser**."

Uses of the Verb "estar"

1. To describe location, e.g., "**¿Dónde está el estadio?**" (*Where is the stadium?*), "**Yo estoy aquí**" (*I am here*), "**No sé donde están las llaves**" (*I don't know where the keys are*).

   o There is one notable exception when we describe where an event (and not a physical thing) is taking place. In that case, we use "**ser**," e.g., "**El partido es en el estadio**" (*The match is in the stadium*), "**¿Dónde es la reunión?**" (*Where is the meeting?*).

2. To describe a *temporary* state, condition, or emotion, e.g., "**Estoy acostado**" (*I am lying down*), "**Mi amigo está enfermo**" (*My friend is sick*), "**Ellos están felices**" (*They are happy*).

   As you can observe, lying down, being sick, and being happy are temporary states. Therefore, we use the verb "**estar**." There are a few exceptions:

   o Occupation, religion, nationality, and political affiliation: Although one may change any of those, we use the verb "**ser**" to describe these states, e.g., "**Soy ingeniero**" (*I am an engineer*), "**Ella es católica**" (*She is Catholic*), "**Él es portugués**" (*He is Portuguese*), "**Ellos son socialistas**" (*They are socialists*).

   o Time: Although time changes, we use the verb "**ser**" to describe it, e.g., "**¿Qué hora es?**" (*What time is it?*), "**Son las 9**" (*It is 9 o'clock*), "**Hoy es viernes**" (*Today is Friday*).

o   Physical description: Although one may grow up taller, lose, or gain weight, we still use the verb "**ser**," e.g., "**Él es alto y delgado**" (*He is tall and thin*).
o   Relationships: whether they are unchangeable, e.g., "**Ella es mi madre**" (*She is my mother*), or changeable, e.g., "**Él es mi jefe**" (*He is my boss*), "**Ella es mi esposa**" (*She is my spouse*).

Uses of the Verb "ser"

Most other cases use the verb "**ser**," especially if they describe the essence, origin, or characteristics of something or someone, e.g., "**Soy Diego**" (*I am Diego*), "**Ella es de Chile**" (*She is from Chile*), "**Esta silla es de madera**" (*This chair is made of wood*), "**Él es amigable**" (*He is friendly*), "**Ella es inteligente**" (*She is intelligent*).

In some cases, using "**ser**" or "**estar**" can convey a different meaning. For example, "**Él es celoso**" and "**Él está celoso**" both are translated as *"He is jealous."* However, "**Él es celoso**" conveys that someone is jealous by *nature* and that this is a *characteristic* of him, whereas "**Él está celoso**" conveys that he is *feeling* jealous in response to a certain *condition* or event.

The statement "**El helado es rico**" (*Ice cream is delicious*) means that ice cream, in general, has the characteristic of being delicious, whereas "**El helado está rico**" likely refers to a specific ice cream that tastes delicious because of its ingredients, flavor, preparation, etc.

Similarly, "**La manzana es verde**" and "**La manzana está verde**" both are translated as *"The apple is green."* However, "**La manzana es verde**" describes the color of the apple as an *intrinsic characteristic* of the apple, whereas "**La manzana está verde**" refers more to the *state* of the apple being unripe.

Another more common example is when we describe the climate of a place versus the weather at a particular time, e.g., "**Canadá es muy frío**" (*Canada is very cold*) describes Canada as a cold place, indicating that being cold is a permanent trait of the place. On the other hand, "**Está frío hoy**" *(It is cold today)* simply means that the weather is cold at a specific time, that is, today.

One notable exception is to describe a dead person. We say "**está muerto**," referring to a male, or "**está muerta**," referring to a female. We do not use "**ser**" in this case.

To describe your marital status, we could use either "**ser**" or "**estar**." Although legal documents may use "**ser**," you may hear "**estar**" more often by Spanish speakers, e.g., "**Estoy/Soy casado**" *(I am married)*, "**Está/Es soltera**" *(She is single)*, etc.

4. FUTURE TENSE

One informal but common way to express the future tense in the indicative mood is by using the auxiliary verb "**ir**" *(to go)* to form "**ir + a + infinitive**." For example, "**Yo voy a viajar**," literally means *"I go to travel,"* but it is similar in purpose to the English expression *"I am going to travel."* To form the informal future tense, "**ir**" can be used only in the simple present tense.

		-ar ending **e.g., hablar**	**-er ending** **e.g., comer**	**-ir ending** **e.g., vivir**
yo	voy a			
tú	vas a			
él/ella/usted	va a	hablar	comer	vivir
nosotros/-as	vamos a			
vosotros/-as	vais a			
ellos/ellas/ustedes	van a			

The formal simple future tense is also used to express events in the future and is more common in written literature. The regular verb conjugation is the same for all verb endings. Different endings must only agree with the subject pronoun.

	-ar ending **hablar (to speak)**	**-er ending** **comer (to eat)**	**-ir ending** **vivir (to live)**
yo	hablar**é**	comer**é**	vivir**é**
tú	hablar**ás**	comer**ás**	vivir**ás**

él/ella/usted	hablará	comerá	vivirá
nosotros/-as	hablar**emos**	comer**emos**	vivir**emos**
vosotros/-as	hablar**éis**	comer**éis**	vivir**éis**
ellos/ellas/ustedes	hablar**án**	comer**án**	vivir**án**

❖ In addition to expressing events in the future, the simple future tense can also be used to express conjecture or possibility, e.g., "**La chica tendrá 15 años**" (*The girl might be 15 years old*), "**¿Dónde estará mi celular?**" (*Where could my cell phone be?*).

❖ Another less common use of the simple future tense is giving commands, e.g., "**No mentirás**" (*You shall/will not lie*), "**Te sentarás acá**" (*You shall/will sit here*).

Irregular Verbs

There are a few irregular verbs in the simple future tense, but only twelve are commonly used and will be discussed here.

1. Some verbs ending in "**-er**" and "**-ir**" drop the "**e**" or "**i**" from the infinitive and add a "**d**." There are five common verbs in this category: "**tener**" (*to have*), "**poner**" (*to put*), "**valer**" (*to value or be worth*), "**venir**" (*to come*), and "**salir**" (*to go out* or *to exit*).

	tener **tendr-**	poner **pondr-**	valer **valdr-**	venir **vendr-**	salir **saldr-**
yo	tendr**é**	pondr**é**	valdr**é**	vendr**é**	saldr**é**
tú	tendr**ás**	pondr**ás**	valdr**ás**	vendr**ás**	saldr**ás**
él/ella/usted	tendr**á**	pondr**á**	valdr**á**	vendr**á**	saldr**á**
nosotros/-as	tendr**emos**	pondr**emos**	valdr**emos**	vendr**emos**	saldr**emos**
vosotros/-as	tendr**éis**	pondr**éis**	valdr**éis**	vendr**éis**	saldr**éis**
ellos/ellas/ustedes	tendr**án**	pondr**án**	valdr**án**	vendr**án**	saldr**án**

2. Some verbs ending in "**-er**" drop the "**e**" from the infinitive. There are also five common verbs in this category: "**saber**" (*to know*), "**poder**" (*can*), "**caber**" (*to fit*), "**querer**" (*to want*), and "**haber**," which is an auxiliary verb equivalent to the English auxiliary verb *"have."*

	saber sabr-	poder podr-	caber cabr-	querer querr-	haber habr-
yo	sabré	podré	cabré	querré	habré
tú	sabrás	podrás	cabrás	querrás	habrás
él/ella/usted	sabrá	podrá	cabrá	querrá	habrá
nosotros/-as	sabremos	podremos	cabremos	querremos	habremos
vosotros/-as	sabréis	podréis	cabréis	querréis	habréis
ellos/ellas/ustedes	sabrán	podrán	cabrán	querrán	habrán

3. The verbs "**decir**" (*to say*) and "**hacer**" (*to do* or *to make*) change their stem to "**dir-**" and "**har-**" to form the simple future tense conjugation. These two verbs are irregular and must be memorized.

	decir dir-	hacer har-
yo	diré	haré
tú	dirás	harás
él/ella/usted	dirá	hará
nosotros/-as	diremos	haremos
vosotros/-as	diréis	haréis
ellos/ellas/ustedes	dirán	harán

5. POSSESSIVE ADJECTIVES & PRONOUNS

Possessive adjectives (*my, your, his/her, our, their*) come before a noun, e.g., "*This is my house*," while possessive pronouns (*mine, yours, his/hers, ours, theirs*) are used to replace a noun and its possessive adjective, e.g., "*This house is mine.*"

In Spanish, possessive adjectives and pronouns must agree in gender and number with the noun they describe. Fortunately, only "**nosotros/-as**" and "**vosotros/-as**" have distinct masculine and feminine possessive adjective forms.

	Singular	Plural
my	mi	mis

your (informal singular)	tu	tus
his/her/your (formal singular)	su	sus
our	nuestro/-a	nuestros/-as
your (informal plural)	vuestro/-a	vuestros/-as
their/your (formal plural)	su	sus

❖ Note that, unlike in English, the possessive adjective agrees in number and gender with the noun it describes and not the subject, e.g., **"mis hermanos"** (*my brothers*). Note that we use **"mis"** because the *noun* we describe is *plural*, although the subject is singular. Similarly, in the example **"nuestras madres"** (*our mothers*), the possessive adjective **"nuestras"** agrees in gender and number with the noun it describes, i.e., **"madres."**

❖ Notice the lack of accent on the vowel in the possessive adjectives **"mi"** and **"tu"** to distinguish them from the prepositional object pronoun **"mí"** meaning *"me,"* and the subject pronoun for second-person singular informal **"tú"** meaning *"you,"* respectively. This is inconsequential in spoken Spanish and does not affect pronunciation.

Let us now examine the *possessive pronouns* in Spanish. Unlike possessive adjectives, all possessive pronouns have masculine and feminine forms as well as singular and plural forms. One must use the correct form that agrees in gender and number with the noun being described.

	Masc. Sing.	Masc. Plural	Fem. Sing.	Fem. Plural
mine	mío	míos	mía	mías
yours (informal singular)	tuyo	tuyos	tuya	tuyas
his/hers/yours (formal singular)	suyo	suyos	suya	suyas
ours	nuestro	nuestros	nuestra	nuestras
yours (informal plural)	vuestro	vuestros	vuestra	vuestras
theirs/yours (formal plural)	suyo	suyos	suya	suyas

❖ Possessive pronouns are normally preceded with a definite article "**el, la, los**, or **las**" that agrees in gender and number with the possessive pronoun, e.g., "**Tu celular es mejor que el <u>mío</u>**" (*Your cell phone is better than <u>mine</u>*), "**Esa casa es la <u>nuestra</u>**" (*That house is <u>ours</u>*). The only exception is after the verb "**ser**," where it is *optional* and can be dropped, e.g., "**No es <u>tuyo</u>, es <u>mío</u>**" (*It is not <u>yours</u>, it's <u>mine</u>*), "**Esa casa es <u>nuestra</u>**" (*That house is <u>ours</u>*).

❖ The possessive pronoun can come after the noun if the emphasis is placed on the possessor, e.g., "**un amigo <u>mío</u>**" (*a friend of <u>mine</u>*), "**la casa <u>tuya</u>**" (*<u>your</u> house*), etc.

❖ In another special case, the possessive pronoun can be preceded by the neuter article "**lo**" to denote property, e.g., "**lo <u>mío</u>**" (*that which is <u>mine</u>*), "**lo <u>nuestro</u>**" (*that which is <u>ours</u>*), "**lo <u>suyo</u>/lo propio</u>**" (*one's own property*), "**lo <u>ajeno</u>**" (*that which belongs to <u>others</u>*).

6. DEMONSTRATIVE ADJECTIVES & PRONOUNS

Demonstrative adjectives (*this, that, these, those*) come before a noun, e.g., "*I want <u>this</u> book*," while possessive pronouns (same as demonstrative adjectives: *this, that, these, those*) are used to replace a noun and its possessive adjective, e.g., "*I want <u>this</u>.*"

Demonstrative adjectives and pronouns must agree in gender and number with the noun being described.

The following are the demonstrative adjectives in Spanish:

	Masc. Singular	Masc. Plural	Feminine Singular	Feminine Plural
this/these	este	estos	esta	estas
that/those	ese	esos	esa	esas
that/those (over there)	aquel	aquellos	aquella	aquellas

In general, "**este**," "**esta**," "**estos**," and "**estas**" are used to refer to nouns close to the speaker and listener. On the other hand, "**ese**," "**esa**," "**esos**," and "**esas**" are used to refer to nouns close to the listener but far away from the speaker, whereas "**aquel**," "**aquella**," "**aquellos**," and "**aquellas**" are used to refer to nouns far away from both the speaker and the listener.

Demonstrative pronouns are the same as demonstrative adjectives in addition to the set of neuter demonstrative pronouns "**esto**," "**eso**," and "**aquello**," which mean *"this," "that,"* and *"that over there,"* respectively. These are used to refer to a whole sentence or concept, e.g., "**Esto no es aceptable**" (*This is not acceptable*), or to point at something without mentioning it, e.g., "**¿Qué es eso?**" *(What is that?)*.

The following are the demonstrative pronouns in Spanish:

	Masc. Sing.	Masc. Plural	Fem. Sing.	Fem. Plural	Neuter
this/these	este	estos	esta	estas	esto
that/those	ese	esos	esa	esas	eso
that/those (over there)	aquel	aquellos	aquella	aquellas	aquello

7. OBJECT PERSONAL PRONOUNS

Object pronouns can be divided into three classes: prepositional, direct, and indirect object pronouns.

Prepositional Object Pronouns

Prepositional object pronouns come after a preposition, such as "**de**" *(of, from,* or *about)*, "**con**" *(with)*, "**en**" *(in* or *on)*, "**sin**" *(without)*, etc. Prepositional object pronouns are the same as subject pronouns except in the first- and second-person singular cases.

Personal Subject Pronoun	Prepositional Object Pronoun	Examples
yo	mí	Ellos hablan de **mí**. *They talk about **me**.*
tú	ti	Este regalo es para **ti**. *This gift is for **you**.*
él/ella/usted	él/ella/usted	Saldré con **él**. *I will go out with **him**.*
nosotros/-as	nosotros/-as	No está contra **nosotros**. *He is not against **us**.*

| vosotros/-as | vosotros/-as | Yo confío en **vosotros**.
 I trust in ***you***. |
| ellos/ellas/ustedes | ellos/ellas/ustedes | No voy sin **ellos**.
 I won't go without ***them***. |

❖ One notable exception is when using the preposition "**con**" with "**mí**" and "**ti**," one should use "**conmigo**" and "**contigo**" instead of "**con mí**" and "**con ti**," which do not exist, e.g., "**Ven conmigo**" (*Come with me*), "**Quiero salir contigo**" (*I want to go out with you*), etc.

❖ The subject pronouns "**yo**" and "**tú**" are used instead of "**mí**" and "**ti**," respectively, following these prepositions: "**entre**" (*between* or *among*), "**excepto/salvo/menos**" (*except*), "**incluso/hasta**" (*including*), and "**según**" (*according to*). For example, "**Mucha gente, incluso yo, no lee el periódico**" (*Many people, including myself, do not read the newspaper*), "**Lo mantenemos entre tú y yo**" (*We keep it between you and me*), "**Es la verdad según tú**" (*It is the truth according to you*), etc.

The reflexive prepositional pronouns are a special case of the prepositional object pronouns, such as *"myself," "yourself," "himself,"* etc. This is used when the subject and the object pronoun refer to the same person.

Subject Pronoun	Reflexive Prepositional Object Pronoun	Examples
yo	<u>mí</u>	Yo no hablo de **mí**. *I don't talk about* ***myself***.
tú	<u>ti</u>	Compraste un regalo para **ti**. *You bought a gift for* ***yourself***.
él/ella/usted	<u>sí</u>	Ella se alaba a **sí** misma. *She praises* ***herself***.
nosotros/-as	nosotros/-as	Lo hacemos para **nosotros**. *We do it for* ***ourselves***.
vosotros/-as	vosotros/-as	Pensáis solo en **vosotros**. *You only think of* ***yourselves***.
ellos/ellas/ustedes	<u>sí</u>	Quieren todo para **sí**. *They want everything for* ***themselves***.

❖ The reflexive prepositional pronoun "**sí**" becomes "**consigo**" when combined with the preposition "**con**." For example, "**Él está feliz consigo**" *(He is happy with himself)*, "**Ellos siempre llevan dinero consigo mismos**" *(They always carry money with themselves)*.

❖ More often than not, the reflexive prepositional object pronoun is followed by the adjective "**mismo**," "**misma**," "**mismos**," or "**mismas**," meaning *"same"* for emphasis. For example, in the expression "**Yo hablo de mí mismo**," meaning *"I speak about myself,"* the adjective "**mismo**" is added to emphasize that one is speaking about himself. The expression "**Yo hablo de mí**" has the same meaning but without emphasis.

❖ Note that "**sí**" can mean *"himself," "herself," "itself," "yourself"* (formal singular), *"themselves,"* or *"yourselves,"* depending on the subject it refers to.

Direct and Indirect Object Pronouns

The second and third classes of object pronouns are direct and indirect object pronouns. This tends to be one of the most challenging grammar lessons for English-speaking students. Nevertheless, the use of direct and indirect objects is so ubiquitous that we feel obliged to cover it at this beginner level. Feel free to return to this lesson at times of confusion if you do not fully grasp all the details.

Before we delve into the details, let us first define the difference between the two classes, since the distinction in English is not always clear. The direct object is the noun directly acted upon, whereas the indirect object is usually the noun (or person) receiving the direct object. For example, in the expressions *"He gives it to us"* and *"I give it to you,"* the *"it"* is the direct object acted upon, whereas *"us"* is the indirect object in the first example and *"you"* in the second. In English, we use *"me," "you," "him," "her," "us,"* and *"them,"* regardless of whether we are referring to a direct or indirect object. In Spanish, there are some differences.

❖ The direct and indirect object pronouns generally come before the verb, e.g., "**nos lo** da" (*He gives it to us*). Attachment to the end of the verb will be discussed as an exception.

❖ The indirect object always comes before the direct object when both are in the same sentence.

❖ Unlike in English, we do not add the equivalent of *"to"* before the indirect object, e.g., *"I give it to you"* becomes "**te lo doy**" where "**te**" means *"to you"* in this context.

Now, let us learn the direct and indirect object pronouns and their equivalents in English.

Direct Object Pronoun	Indirect Object Pronoun	English Equivalent
me	me	me
te	te	you (informal singular)
lo/la	le	him/her/it/you (formal singular)
nos	nos	us
os	os	you (informal plural)
los/las	les	them/you (formal plural)

Notice that the direct and the indirect object pronouns are only different in the third-person singular and plural forms.

Attaching Object Pronouns to Verb Ends

Now, let us look at the three cases in which the direct or indirect object pronoun attaches to the end of the verb. Object pronouns attach to the infinitive, gerund (ending with "**-ando**" or "**-endo**," equivalent to "*-ing*" in English), or affirmative imperative.

Quiero **hacerlo**.	*I want to do it.*	obj. pron. + infinitive
Voy a **preguntarle**.	*I'm going to ask him.*	indirect obj. pron. + inf.
Estoy **haciéndolo**.	*I am doing it.*	direct obj. pron. + gerund
Estaba **preguntándole**.	*I was asking him.*	indirect obj. pron. + gerund
Ábrelo.	*Open it.*	dir. obj. pron. + imperative
Pídele dinero.	*Ask him for money.*	ind. obj. pron. + imperative

Keep in mind that attachment is optional in some of the cases above. The sentences in the first and the second columns are equivalent.

Quiero **hacerlo**.	**Lo** quiero **hacer**.	*I want to do it.*
Estoy **haciéndolo**.	**Lo** estoy **haciendo**.	*I am doing it.*
Estaba **preguntándole**.	**Le** estaba **preguntando**.	*I was asking him.*

Combining Direct and Indirect Object Pronouns

We will examine how to combine direct and indirect objects in the same sentence through the following two examples:

❖ Let us take the example: *"She sells <u>me</u> the house."* This translates to:

Ella <u>me</u> vende la casa.

In the above example, we recognize that **"la casa"** *(the house)* is the direct object being acted upon, i.e., being sold, whereas **"me"** *(me)* is the indirect object that receives the direct object, i.e., the house is being sold *to me*.

Let us first focus on the direct object in **"Ella vende la casa"** *(She sells the house.* If we remove the direct object **"la casa"** *(the house)* to say *"She sells <u>it</u>,"* we must use **"lo"** or **"la"** to refer to the direct object pronoun *"it."* Since **"la casa"** is feminine, we must use **"la"**:

Ella <u>la</u> vende.

Next, we add the indirect object **"me"** *before* the direct object **"la"** to say *"She sells <u>it</u> <u>to me</u>"*:

Ella <u>me</u> <u>la</u> vende.

❖ Let us take another example: *"I give <u>him</u> a gift."* This translates to:

Yo <u>le</u> doy un regalo.

Here, "**un regalo**" *(a gift)* is the direct object, whereas "**le**" *(him)* is the indirect object.

Let us first focus on the direct object in "**Yo doy un regalo** …" *(I give a gift …)*. If we remove the direct object "**un regalo**" *(a gift)* to say *"I give it …,"* we must use "**lo**" or "**la**" to refer to the direct object pronoun *"it."* Since "**un regalo**" is masculine, we must use "**lo**":

Yo lo doy …

Now, we add the indirect object "**le**" *before* the direct object "**lo**" to say *"I give it to him"*:

Yo le lo doy. (This would be wrong)

To avoid alliteration when saying "**le lo**" in this case, one must replace the indirect object with "**se**." Thus, we instead say:

Yo se lo doy.

As a general rule to avoid *alliteration*:

(le/les) + (lo/la/los/las) = **se** (lo/la/los/las)

| *I give **them to her**.* | Yo **se los** doy. | *le + los = se los* |
| *I give **it to them**.* | Yo **se lo** doy. | *les + lo = se lo* |

Notice also that Spanish speakers maintain the indirect object pronoun even when the indirect object itself exists in the sentence, which may seem redundant to English speakers, for example:

Ella **me** la vende **a mí**.	*She sells it **to me**.*
Yo **le** doy un regalo **a mi amigo**.	*I give a gift **to my friend**.*
Yo **se lo** doy **a mi amigo**.	*I give **it to my friend**.*

8. RELATIVE PRONOUNS

Relative pronouns are the same as interrogative pronouns, but without the written accent to distinguish the two groups. The most common relative pronouns used in Spanish are **"que"** *(that)* and **"quien(es)"** *(who/whom)*. Other relative pronouns that you may encounter less frequently are **"cuyo"** *(whose)* and **"el cual"** *(who/whom/which)*. The two relative pronouns, **"cuyo"** and **"el cual,"** have four forms based on gender and number.

Relative pronoun	English meaning	Examples
que	*that/which*	El té **que** te gusta está acá. *The tea **that** you like is here.*
quien (singular) **quienes** (plural)	*who/whom*	Es la persona con **quien** hablé. *This is the person with **whom** I talked.*
cuyo (sing. masc.) **cuya** (sing. fem.) **cuyos** (pl. masc.) **cuyas** (pl. fem.)	*whose*	Es el hombre **cuyos** dos hijos son médicos. *This is the man **whose** two sons are doctors.*
el cual (sing. masc.) **la cual** (sing. fem.) **los cuales** (pl. masc.) **las cuales** (pl. fem.)	*who/whom/which*	Ellos discuten sobre un tema importante, **el cual** te afecta. *They are discussing an important topic, one **which** affects you.*

❖ The relative pronoun **"que,"** meaning *"that"* or *"which,"* can refer to a thing, a place, or a person.

❖ The relative pronoun **"quien"** can only refer to a person. The plural form **"quienes"** can be used when referring to more than one person. In general, **"quien"** and **"quienes"** cannot refer to a thing or a place.

❖ Since both **"que"** and **"quien"** can refer to a person, it is important to understand when to use each. As a general rule, if the person(s) you are referring to is(are) separated from the relative pronoun by a preposition or comma, **"quien(es)"** must be used. Otherwise, if there is no such separation, and the relative pronoun is to be used right after the person it describes, **"que"** must be used.

"quien (es)" and "que" examples	Explanation
Es el chico _de_ quien estaba hablando. *This is the guy* **whom** *I was talking about.*	Referring to a person, and the preposition **"de"** is used before the relative pronoun, use **"quien."**
Ellos son los jugadores _con_ quienes yo jugaba. *They are the players with* **whom** *I used to play.*	Referring to multiple persons, and the preposition **"con"** is used before the relative pronoun, use **"quienes."**
Mi amigo, **quien** es ingeniero, me dijo esto. *My friend,* **who** *is an engineer, told me this.*	Referring to a person, and a comma that introduces a new idea or information is used before the relative pronoun, use **"quien."**
Este es el restaurante **que** abrió la semana pasada. *This is the restaurant* **that** *opened last week.*	Referring to a place, we always use **"que."** **"Quien"** can only refer to a person. Thus, use **"que."**
Es el profesor **que** me enseñó. *This is the teacher* **who** *taught me.*	Referring to a person, and the relative pronoun is used right after without a preposition or comma, use **"que."**

❖ Another case that requires using **"quien"** instead of **"que"** is after the verb **"ser,"** e.g., **"Ella es quien me dijo esto"** (*She is the one who told me this*).

❖ The relative pronoun **"cuyo"** (and its variants in gender and number) has a similar use to the English *"whose,"* e.g., **"Este es el hombre cuyo hijo es médico"** (*This is the man whose son is a doctor*).

❖ Instead of **"cuyo,"** one can use **"de quien," "de que,"** or **"del cual,"** e.g., **"Este es el hombre de quien su hijo es médico"** (*This is the man whose son is a doctor*).

❖ The relative pronoun **"el cual"** (and its gender and number variants) is not commonly heard in spoken Spanish but is used more frequently in written Spanish. It is used when the noun described by the relative pronoun is separated by a preposition or a comma, e.g., **"Yo voy a leer el libro, el cual estaba en el garaje"** (*I am going to read the book, the one that was in the garage*),

"Limpiaré la silla, detrás de la cual se escondía el gato" *(I will clean the chair behind which the cat was hiding).*

❖ The relative pronouns **"el que,"** **"la que,"** **"los que,"** and **"las que"** can also be used in a similar way to **"el cual,"** **"la cual,"** **"los cuales,"** and **"las cuales,"** respectively.

9. ORDINAL NUMBERS I

Ordinal numbers describe the order of a noun. Thus, it is considered an adjective and must agree in gender and number with the noun. Here are the ordinal numbers from 1 to 10.

uno, una	1	primer(o), primera	1.º / 1.ª
dos	2	segundo, segunda	2.º / 2.ª
tres	3	tercer(o), tercera	3.º / 3.ª
cuatro	4	cuarto, cuarta	4.º / 4.ª
cinco	5	quinto, quinta	5.º / 5.ª
seis	6	sexto, sexta	6.º / 6.ª
siete	7	séptimo, séptima	7.º / 7.ª
ocho	8	octavo, octava	8.º / 8.ª
nueve	9	noveno, novena	9.º / 9.ª
diez	10	décimo, décima	10.º / 10.ª

❖ When the masculine form **"primero"** or **"tercero"** is placed before a noun, the **"o"** is dropped, e.g., **"Es el primero"** *(He is the first)* versus **"Es el primer atleta"** *(He is the first athlete).*

❖ The ordinal numbers are abbreviated as follows:

1. Feminine: cardinal number + " . " + " ª ," e.g., **"primera"** (1.ª), **"cuarta"** (4.ª), **"novena"** (9.ª).

2. Masculine: cardinal number + " . " + " º ," e.g., **"primero"** (1.º), **"cuarto"** (4.º), **"noveno"** (9.º), except for **"primer"** (1.ᵉʳ), and **"tercer"** (3.ᵉʳ), which use the superscript **"er"** instead of **"o."**

❖ Unlike in English, where dates are described using ordinal numbers, e.g., *"the 24th of October,"* in Spanish, dates are expressed using cardinal numbers, e.g., **"el 24 de octubre."** A notable exception is the first day of the month, in which case the ordinal or the cardinal number can be used, e.g., **"el primero de noviembre"** or **"el uno de noviembre."** The use of the ordinal number **"primero"** is more common in Latin America, whereas the use of the cardinal number **"uno"** is more common in Spain.

Fractional Numbers

❖ Fractional numbers from *fourth* to *tenth* are the same as the ordinal number, e.g., **"un cuarto de los jugadores"** (*a fourth of the players*), **"un quinto de los recursos"** (*a fifth of the resources*).

❖ To describe the fractional number 1/2 *(half)*, we use the adjective **"medio"** (masculine) or **"media"** (feminine), e.g., **"medio kilo"** *(half a kilo)*, **"media hora"** *(half an hour)*, **"medio camino"** *(half way)*.

❖ We also use the feminine noun **"mitad"** to describe half the quantity of something, and it is often followed by **"de,"** e.g., **"la mitad de la tierra"** *(half of the land)*.

❖ The main difference that you need to remember to distinguish between **"medio"** and **"mitad"** is that the former is often an adjective, and in a few cases, can be an adverb, e.g., **"a medias"** *(halfway* or *half-finished)*. In contrast, the latter is always a noun, e.g., **"la mitad de la clase"** *(half of the class)*.

❖ The fractional number 1/3 *(third)* is **"tercio"** (not **tercero**), e.g., **"un tercio de la población"** (*a third of the population*).

❖ The **"un"** can be dropped before 1/2, 1/3, and 1/4 if preceded by an integer, e.g., 1 ½ (**uno y medio**), 5 ¼ (**cinco y cuarto**).

We will cover higher ordinal numbers and fractions in **Level VI, Lesson 1**.

II. Vocabulary Building

Go over the vocabulary in this section and use the provided Anki flashcards to study and memorize the new vocabulary efficiently. Here, we cover basic verbs and adjectives in the first two sections, then we go over nouns from different categories.

1. Verbs II

Below is a list of the next most common 60 verbs in Spanish. Use the Anki flashcards created for this section to help you memorize the meaning of each verb in proper contexts.

English	Spanish	Examples
allow	permitir dejar [1]	Mi mamá no me **permite** comer dulces. *My mom doesn't **allow** me to eat candy.*
answer	contestar responder	No podré **contestar** el teléfono. *I won't be able to **answer** the phone.*
appear	aparecer	**Aparecerá** una celebridad hoy en el programa. *A celebrity **will appear** today on the show.*
ask (question)	preguntar [2]	Puedes **preguntar**me lo que quieras. *You can **ask** me whatever you want.*
ask (request)	pedir [2]	No necesitas esperar para **pedir** ayuda. *You don't need to wait to **ask** for help.*
bother upset	molestar	Me **molestan** los olores fuertes. *Strong scents **bother** me.*
build	construir	Quiero **construir** un portón aquí. *I want to **build** a fence here.*
buy	comprar	Carlos **compra** pan todos los días. *Carlos **buys** bread every day.*
choose	elegir escoger	A menudo **escojo** sabores frutales. *I often **choose** fruit flavors.*
clean	limpiar	**Limpiaré** el baño más tarde. *I **will clean** the bathroom later.*
cook	cocinar	Mi hermano **cocina** todos los días. *My brother **cooks** every day.*

[1] The verb **"dejar"** also means *"to let"* or *"to leave (something or someone),"* e.g, **"Voy a dejar las llaves aquí"** *(I am going to leave the keys here).*

[2] We use **"preguntar"** *(to ask)* when we refer to asking questions. On the other hand, we use **"pedir"** *(to ask for)* when we refer to requesting something or ordering from a restaurant.

cover	cubrir	**Cubriré** la masa con un trapo. *I **will cover** the dough with a cloth.*
cry	llorar	No me gusta ver a la gente **llorar**. *I don't like to see people **cry**.*
dance	bailar	No **bailo** muy bien. *I don't **dance** very well.*
die	morir fallecer	Quiere escribir un testamento antes de **morir**. *He wants to write a will before **dying**.*
dine	cenar	Iremos a **cenar** al restaurante italiano. *We'll go **dine** at the Italian restaurant.*
disappear	desaparecer	Los mosquitos **desaparecen** en invierno. *Mosquitoes **disappear** in winter.*
discover	descubrir	Quiero **descubrir** un café cerca de casa. *I want to **discover** a café close to home.*
draw	dibujar	**Dibujaré** este paisaje para mi nueva pintura. *I **will draw** this landscape for my new painting.*
drive	conducir	Quiero aprender a **conducir**. *I want to learn how to **drive**.*
find	encontrar hallar	Debo **encontrar** mis llaves. *I must **find** my keys.*
forget	olvidar	Siempre **olvido** mi contraseña. *I always **forget** my password.*
get	conseguir	¿Dónde puedo **conseguir** comida? *Where can I **get** food?*
go shopping	ir de compras	**Iremos de compras** este fin de semana. *We **will go shopping** this weekend.*
grow	crecer	Este árbol **crecerá** muy rápido. *This tree **will grow** very fast.*
hear	oír	**Oigo** una voz que viene de lejos. *I **hear** a voice coming from afar.*
help	ayudar	Mi hijo **ayuda** siempre en el jardín. *My son always **helps** in the garden.*
joke	bromear	**Bromeo** mucho con mis primos. *I **joke** a lot with my cousins.*
kiss	besar	**Beso** a mi gato en la nariz todos los días. *I **kiss** my cat on its nose every day.*
laugh	reír	Es bueno **reír** de vez en cuando. *It's good to **laugh** from time to time.*
lie	mentir	Mi hijo **miente** acerca de su edad. *My son **lies** about his age.*
listen to hear	escuchar	Debes **escuchar** otras opiniones. *You must **listen to** other opinions.*
lose	perder	Siempre **pierdo** las monedas más pequeñas. *I always **lose** the smaller coins.*

mean	significar querer decir	¿Qué **quieres decir**? *What do you **mean**?*
need	necesitar	**Necesito** cuidar a mis niños. *I **need** to take care of my children.*
pay	pagar	**Pago** todas las cuentas a principios de mes. *I **pay** all my bills at the start of the month.*
plan	planear	Siempre **planeo** lo que comeré en la semana. *I always **plan** what I'll eat during the week.*
play (sports)	jugar	Mi primo **juega** al fútbol los sábados. *My cousin **plays** football on Saturdays.*
rain	llover	Creen que **lloverá** este miércoles. *They believe it **will rain** this Wednesday.*
relax	relajar	Es bueno **relajar** las piernas. *It's good to **relax** your legs.*
repair	reparar arreglar	Debes **reparar** ese auto. *You have to **repair** that car.*
reply **respond**	responder	Él nunca **responde** a mis mensajes. *He never **responds** to my messages.*
rest	descansar	Me gusta **descansar** al lado de la piscina. *I like to **rest** by the pool.*
run	correr	Es peligroso **correr** rápido en la calle. *It is dangerous to **run** fast in the street.*
search for **look for**	buscar	Ella quiere **buscar** las llaves para salir. *She wants to **search for** the keys to go out.*
sell	vender	Esta tienda se dedica a **vender** postres. *This store is dedicated to **selling** desserts.*
send	enviar mandar	Le **enviaré** un mensaje para avisarle. *I **will send** him a message to let him know.*
share	compartir	Debes **compartir** con tu hermano. *You have to **share** with your brother.*
show	mostrar	Te **mostraré** la cocina. *I **will show** you the kitchen.*
sing	cantar	Ese joven **canta** hermoso. *That young man **sings** beautifully.*
smile	sonreír	Siempre **sonrío** para las fotos. *I always **smile** for photos.*
smoke	fumar	No está permitido **fumar** aquí. ***Smoking** is not allowed here.*
snow	nevar	**Nevará** mucho este invierno. *It **will snow** a lot this winter.*
swim	nadar	Voy a **nadar** en el río. *I go **swimming** in the river.*
teach	enseñar	Te **enseñaré** cómo se hace. *I **will teach** you how it's done.*

translate	traducir	¿Puedes **traducir** este archivo? *Can you **translate** this file?*
try	intentar tratar de	Siempre **intento** llegar temprano. *I always **try** to arrive early.*
wait (for) **hope**	esperar	Tiene que **esperar** el autobús. *He has to **wait for** the bus.*
wash	lavar	Debes **lavar** los platos después de la cena. *You must **wash** the dishes after dinner.*
win **earn**	ganar	**Ganaré** la carrera. *I **will win** the race.*

In addition to the above new verbs, let us take advantage of English cognates to memorize the following verbs.

English	**Spanish**	**Examples**
abandon	abandonar	Algunas personas **abandonan** sus pasatiempos. *Some people **abandon** their hobbies.*
accuse	acusar	No está bien **acusar** sin fundamentos. *It's not okay to **accuse** without grounds.*
appreciate	apreciar	**Aprecio** mucho lo que hacen mis padres. *I really **appreciate** what my parents do.*
comprehend	comprender	No **comprendo** estas instrucciones. *I can't **comprehend** these instructions.*
confess	confesar	**Confieso** que me comí todas las galletas. *I **confess** I ate all the cookies.*
consider	considerar	Debes **considerar** lo que sienten los demás. *You must **consider** how others feel.*
consist	consistir	La obra **consiste** en tres partes. *The play **consists** of three parts.*
consult	consultar	**Consultaré** a un profesional. *I **will consult** a professional.*
count	contar	Mi hijo pequeño sabe **contar** hasta diez. *My little son knows how to **count** to ten.*
differentiate	diferenciar	No puedo **diferenciar** entre los gatos. *I am unable **to differentiate** between the cats.*
distribute	distribuir	El cartero **distribuye** el correo por la mañana. *The postman **distributes** the mail in the morning.*
divide	dividir	Esta calle **divide** las dos ciudades. *This street **divides** the two cities.*
edit	editar	**Editaré** este manuscrito. *I **will edit** this manuscript.*
estimate	estimar	**Estimo** que estará listo en 30 minutos. *I **estimate** it'll be done in 30 minutes.*

explore	explorar	Amo **explorar** ciudades que no conozco. *I love **exploring** cities I don't know.*
express	expresar	Es bueno **expresar** las emociones. *It's good to **express** emotions.*
extend	extender	Queremos **extender** nuestra estadía aquí. *We want to **extend** our stay here.*
float	flotar	El patito **flota** en la bañera. *The duckling **floats** in the bathtub.*
force	forzar	No debes **forzar** la cerradura. *You shouldn't **force** the lock.*
ignore	ignorar	No es fácil **ignorar** los ruidos fuertes. *It's not easy to **ignore** loud noises.*
imitate	imitar	Mi hermano menor siempre me **imita**. *My little brother always **imitates** me.*
inform	informar	Debes **informar**me si planeas salir. *You have to **inform** me if you plan on going out.*
limit	limitar	**Limito** mis golosinas a una por semana. *I **limit** my candies to one per week.*
manipulate	manipular	No es agradable **manipular** a la gente. *It's not nice **to manipulate** people.*
mention	mencionar	Este libro no **menciona** todos los detalles. *This book doesn't **mention** all the details.*
minimize	minimizar	No debemos **minimizar** la situación. *We shouldn't **minimize** the situation.*
pass	pasar [1]	Voy a **pasar** por tu casa más tarde. *I'm going to **pass** by your house later.*
prefer	preferir	**Prefiero** las verduras al pan. *I **prefer** vegetables to bread.*
pronounce	pronunciar	No es fácil **pronunciar** mi nombre en inglés. *It's not easy to **pronounce** my name in English.*
prosper	prosperar	Los negocios **prosperan** en verano. *Businesses **prosper** in the summer.*
recommend	recomendar	**Recomiendo** más esta marca. *I **recommend** this brand more.*
regulate	regular	El gobierno quiere **regular** el mercado. *The government wants to **regulate** the market.*
reside	residir	**Reside** cerca de la capital. *She **resides** near the capital.*
revise **check**	revisar	Debo **revisar** este proyecto. *I have to **revise** this project.*

---

[1] Depending on the context, the verb **"pasar"** can have other meanings, such as *"to happen,"* e.g., **"¿Qué pasa?"** *(What's happening?)*, and *"to spend (time),"* e.g., **"Me gusta pasar tiempo en el parque"** *(I like spending time in the park).*

suffer	sufrir	A nadie le gusta **sufrir** enfermedades. *No one likes to **suffer** from illnesses.*
validate	validar	Tiene que **validar** su diploma. *She has to **validate** her diploma.*
verify	verificar	Los médicos van a **verificar** los resultados. *The doctors are going to **verify** the results.*

2. ADJECTIVES II

Below is a list of 40 adjectives that we need at this level. Notice that an adjective must agree with the noun in number and gender.

English	Spanish	Examples
any	cualquier	Me gusta el helado de **cualquier** sabor. *I like ice cream of **any** flavor.*
available	disponible	El asiento del acompañante está **disponible**. *The passenger's seat is **available**.*
awake	despierto	Trato de mantenerme **despierto** en clase. *I try to remain **awake** in class.*
blond	rubio	El cabello de mi vecino es **rubio**. *My neighbor's hair is **blond**.*
both	ambos	**Ambos** padres están invitados. ***Both** parents are invited.*
comfortable	cómodo	Este sillón es muy **cómodo**. *This armchair is very **comfortable**.*
complex	complejo	Esta estructura es muy **compleja**. *This structure is very **complex**.*
each	cada	**Cada** persona es diferente. ***Each** person is different.*
empty	vacío	El asiento está **vacío**. *The seat is **empty**.*
equal	igual	Las dos paredes son **iguales**. *Both walls are **equals**.*
fair just	justo	Siempre intento ser **justo** con mis hijos. *I always try to be **fair** with my children.*
faraway distant	lejano	Mis abuelos viven en un país **lejano**. *My grandparents live in a **faraway** country.*
fresh	fresco	El agua con pepino tiene un sabor **fresco**. *Water with cucumber has a **fresh** taste.*
friendly	amigable	Mi gato es muy **amigable**. *My cat is very **friendly**.*
full	lleno	Quiero el tanque **lleno**. *I want the tank to be **full**.*

funny	gracioso chistoso	Este hombre es muy **chistoso**. *This man is very **funny**.*
healthy	sano saludable	Comer verduras a diario es **saludable**. *Eating vegetables every day is **healthy**.*
light (weight)	ligero	Cuando viajo, empaco una maleta **ligera**. *When I travel, I pack a **light** suitcase.*
lonely	solitario	Mi gato es un animal **solitario**. *My cat is a **lonely** animal.*
loud noisy	ruidoso	Mi hijo es muy **ruidoso**. *My son is very **loud**.*
lucky	afortunado	Eres muy **afortunado** si ganas hoy. *You are very **lucky** if you win today.*
nearby close	cercano	La universidad está en un barrio **cercano**. *The university is in a **nearby** neighborhood.*
nice pretty (object)	bonito	Me compraré un vestido muy **bonito**. *I'll buy myself a very **nice** dress.*
older oldest (age)	mayor	Soy el **mayor** de mis hermanos. *I am the **oldest** of my siblings.*
pleasant nice (person)	agradable amable simpático	Mi tío es una persona **agradable**. *My uncle is a **pleasant** person.*
polite	educado cortés	Mi sobrino es un niño muy **cortés**. *My nephew is a very **polite** child.*
reasonable	razonable	Mi jefe es muy **razonable**. *My boss is very **reasonable**.*
salty	salado	Me gustan las palomitas de maíz **saladas**. *I like **salty** popcorn.*
shy	tímido	Disculpa, es muy **tímido**. *I'm sorry, he's very **shy**.*
silly	tonto	Es **tonto** preocuparse sin razón. *It's **silly** to worry without a reason.*
simple	sencillo simple	El examen es muy **sencillo**. *The exam is very **simple**.*
true	verdadero	Un **verdadero** amigo no te miente. *A **true** friend doesn't lie to you.*
unfair	injusto	Ese árbitro es muy **injusto**. *That referee is very **unfair**.*
unlucky	desafortunado	Mi primo es una persona **desafortunada**. *My cousin is an **unlucky** person.*
useful	útil	Las tijeras son una herramienta **útil**. *Scissors are a **useful** tool.*

useless	inútil	Sin combustible, mi encendedor es **inútil**. *Without gas, my lighter is **useless**.*
weird **strange**	extraño raro	Sé que esto parece **extraño**. *I know this looks **strange**.*
worried	preocupado	¡Estoy muy **preocupado** por ti! *I am very **worried** about you!*
wrong	equivocado	No quiero tomar el camino **equivocado**. *I don't want to take the **wrong** road.*
younger **youngest**	menor	Mi padre es el **menor** de sus hermanos. *My father is the **youngest** of his brothers.*

In addition to the above new adjectives, we add a few more English cognates that are easy to memorize.

English	Spanish	Examples
brilliant	brillante	La hija de mi prima es **brillante**. *My cousin's daughter is **brilliant**.*
complicated	complicado	Hacer tu propia pasta es **complicado**. *Making your own pasta is **complicated**.*
delicious	delicioso	Este pastel de bodas está **delicioso**. *This wedding cake is **delicious**.*
dishonest	deshonesto	No confío en él porque es **deshonesto**. *I don't trust him because he's **dishonest**.*
educational	educativo	Mirar videos **educativos** es útil. *Watching **educational** videos is helpful.*
false **fake**	falso	Esa planta es **falsa**. *That plant is **fake**.*
famous	famoso	Mi primo quiere ser un escritor **famoso**. *My cousin wants to be a **famous** writer.*
favorite	favorito	¿Cuál es tu película **favorita**? *What is your **favorite** movie?*
feminine **female**	femenino	Su estilo es bastante **femenino**. *Her style is pretty **feminine**.*
festive	festivo	El verano es una época **festiva**. *Summer is a **festive** time.*
firm **steady**	firme	Esta mesa me parece **firme**. *This table seems **steady** to me.*
generous	generoso	Quieren hacer un donativo **generoso** al hospital. *They want to make a **generous** donation to the hospital.*
genius	genio	Einstein fue un **genio**. *Einstein was a **genius**.*
historical	histórico	Esa fecha conmemora un evento **histórico**. *That date commemorates a **historical** event.*

masculine male	masculino	Esas botas se ven **masculinas**. *Those boots look **masculine**.*
mental	mental	La salud **mental** es sumamente importante. ***Mental** health is extremely important.*
nervous	nervioso	Estoy **nervioso** por el examen. *I'm **nervous** about the exam.*
physical	físico	Debo hacerme un examen **físico**. *I have to get a **physical** exam done.*
political	político	No recomiendo hablar de temas **políticos**. *I don't recommend talking about **political** matters.*
popular	popular	Mi hermana es **popular** en la escuela. *My sister is **popular** at school.*
precious	precioso	El diamante es una piedra **preciosa**. *A diamond is a **precious** stone.*
recent	reciente	La noticia es muy **reciente**. *The news is very **recent**.*
representative	representativo	La estatua es **representativa** de la persona real. *The statue is **representative** of the real person.*
resident	residente	Por fin, obtendré el estatus de **residente**. *Finally, I will obtain **resident** status.*
responsible	responsable	Intento ser muy **responsable** en el trabajo. *I try to be very **responsible** at work.*
serious	serio	Mi abuelo es una persona muy **seria**. *My grandfather is a very **serious** person.*
significant	significativo	El tiempo es muy **significativo** para mí. *Time is very **significant** to me.*
strict	estricto	Mi vecino es **estricto** con sus hijos. *My neighbor is **strict** with his children.*
terrible	terrible	Tengo un resfriado **terrible**. *I have a **terrible** cold.*
typical	típico	Me gusta la comida **típica** de mi pueblo. *I like my town's **typical** food.*
violent	violento	Este huracán es muy **violento**. *This hurricane is very **violent**.*
visual	visual	La pintura tiene buenos efectos **visuales**. *The painting has good **visual** effects.*

3. TRANSPORTATION I

Transportation in Spanish is "**el transporte**." Below are some means of transportation and vocabulary related to transportation and traffic:

airplane	**avión**[m]	*penalty*	**pena**[f]
airport	**aeropuerto**[m]	*pick-up truck*	**camioneta**[f]

bicycle	**bicicleta**[f] **bici**[f]	*police officer*	**agente**[m] **de policía** **oficial**[m] **de policía**
boat	**barco**[m]	*ship*	**navío**[m]
brakes	**frenos**[m]	*sign*	**señal**[f]
bus	**autobús**[m]	*speed*	**velocidad**[f]
car[1]	**auto**[m] **coche**[m] **carro**[m]	*subway*	**metro**[m] **subterráneo**[m]
driver	**conductor**[m] **conductora**[f]	*ticket (air, train)*	**boleto**[m] **billete**[m]
driver's license[2]	**permiso**[m] **de conducir** **licencia**[f] **de conducir**	*ticket (fine)*	**multa**[f]
engine	**motor**[m]	*tire*	**neumático**[m] **llanta**[f]
envelope	**sobre**[m]	*traffic*	**tráfico**[m]
flight	**vuelo**[m]	*train*	**tren**[m]
gasoline	**gasolina**[f]	*train station*	**estación**[f] **de tren**
package	**paquete**[m]	*truck*	**camión**[m]

[1] There is also the word "**automóvil**[m]" which is often considered too formal for typical conversation. Instead, "**coche**" is widely used in Spain, "**carro**" is mainly used in Mexico and some other Latin American countries, and "**auto**" is used the most in South America.

[2] Also called, in Spain, sometimes "**carnet**[m] **de conducir**" and "**carné**[m] **de conducir**."

4. NATURE I

Some vocabulary related to *nature*, or "**la naturaleza**," are:

air	**aire**[m]	*ocean*	**océano**[m]
beach	**playa**[f]	*park*	**parque**[m]
camp	**campamento**[m]	*planet*	**planeta**[m]
canteen	**cantina**[f]	*plant*	**planta**[f]
cloud	**nube**[f]	*river*	**río**[m]
coast	**costa**[f]	*root*	**raíz**[f]
countryside	**campo**[m]	*sand*	**arena**[f]
desert	**desierto**[m]	*sea*	**mar**[m] [3]

[3] Although in real life the word "**mar**" is used as a *masculine* noun among most Spanish speakers, the Real Academia Española (RAE) considers it an ambiguous noun that accepts both genders. Using "**mar**" as a *feminine* noun is common among sailors and people who are linked to the sea. It is also common to use it as a feminine noun when describing the state of the sea, e.g., "**la mar gruesa**" *(the rough sea)*.

earth	**tierra**[f]	*sky*	**cielo**[m]
fire	**fuego**[m]	*snow*	**nieve**[f]
flower	**flor**[m]	*space*	**espacio**[m]
grass	**césped**[m] **pasto**[m]	*star*	**estrella**[f]
ground	**tierra**[f]	*sun*	**sol**[m]
ice	**hielo**[m]	*tree*	**árbol**[m]
island	**isla**[f]	*universe*	**universo**[m]
lake	**lago**[m]	*weather*	**tiempo**[m]
moon	**luna**[f]	*wind*	**viento**[m]
mountain	**montaña**[f]	*world*	**mundo**[m]

5. PLACES

A *place* in Spanish is "**un lugar.**" This is a list of the most common places we encounter in our daily life:

apartment	**apartamento**[m] **departamento**[m]	*hospital*	**hospital**[m]
area	**área**[f]	*hotel*	**hotel**[m]
bakery	**panadería**[f]	*location*	**ubicación**[f]
bank	**banco**[m]	*market*	**mercado**[m]
bar	**bar**[m]	*office*	**oficina**[f]
bookstore	**librería**[f]	*parking*	**estacionamiento**[m]
bridge	**puente**[m]	*port* *harbor*	**puerto**[m]
building	**edificio**[m]	*restaurant*	**restaurante**[m]
center	**centro**[m]	*school*	**escuela**[f]
city	**ciudad**[f]	*shop*	**tienda**[f]
club	**club**[m]	*suburb*	**suburbio**[m]
court	**corte**[f]	*theater*	**teatro**[m]
district	**distrito**[m]	*university*	**universidad**[f]
factory	**fábrica**[f]	*village*	**pueblo**[m]
farm [1]	**finca**[f] **granja**[f] **hacienda**[f]	*work*	**trabajo**[m]

---

[1] The word "**granja**" is often used to refer to a farm for raising animals, whereas "**hacienda**" is used to refer to a crops farm. An alternative word to "**hacienda**" is some Latin American countries is "**estancia**[f]". In general, the word "**finca**" can be used to either type of farms.

6. FOOD I

An important subject in Spanish is *food*, or "**la comida**." Here is some useful food vocabulary:

apple	**manzana**[f]	lemon	**limón**[m]
apricot	**albaricoque**[m]	lettuce	**lechuga**[f]
banana	**banana**[f 1]	mango	**mango**[m]
beef	**carne de vaca**	meat	**carne**[f]
beer	**cerveza**[f]	milk	**leche**[f]
bread	**pan**[m]	oil	**aceite**[m]
broccoli	**brócoli**[m]	olive	**aceituna**[f] **oliva**[f]
carrot	**zanahoria**[f]	orange	**naranja**[f]
cheese	**queso**[m]	pork	**carne de cerdo**
chicken	**pollo**[m]	refreshment	**refresco**[m]
coffee	**café**[m]	rice	**arroz**[m]
egg	**huevo**[m]	salad	**ensalada**[f]
eggplant	**berenjena**[f]	salt	**sal**[f]
fruit	**fruta**[f]	sugar	**azúcar**[m]
grape	**uva**[f]	tea	**té**[m]
grapefruit	**pomelo**[m] **toronja**[f]	tomato	**tomate**[m]
ice cream	**helado**[m]	vegetable	**verdura**[f] **vegetal**[m]
juice	**jugo**[m]	water	**agua**[f]
lamb	**cordero**[m]	wine	**vino**[m]

[1] In Spain, Mexico, and some other Latin American countries, the word "**plátano**[m]" is used instead of *"banana."* This can be confusing as some other Spanish speakers use the word "**plátano**" to refer to a *"plantain."*

7. CLOTHES I

The word *clothes* in Spanish is "**la ropa**," and it is singular. Here you can learn some vocabulary related to clothing:

appearance	**apariencia**[f]	pants	**pantalón**[m]
band	**cinta**[f]	pocket	**bolsillo**[m]
belt	**cinturón**[m]	purse	**bolso**[m]
bra	**sostén**[m] **corpiño**[m]	ring	**anillo**[m]

coat	**abrigo**[m]	*shirt*	**camisa**[f]
glasses	**gafas**[f] **lentes**[m] **anteojos**[m]	*sunglasses*	**gafas**[f] **de sol** **lentes**[m] **de sol** **anteojos**[m] **de sol**
glove	**guante**[m]	*skirt*	**falda**[f]
hat	**sombrero**[m]	*t-shirt*	**camiseta**[f][1]
jacket	**chaqueta**[f]	*underwear*	**ropa**[f] **interior**
makeup	**maquillaje**[m]	*wallet*	**cartera**[f] **billetera**[f]

---

[1] In some countries, you may hear "**playera**[f]" or "**remera**[f]" instead of "**camiseta**."

8. EDUCATION

The following are vocabulary related to *education* or "**la educación**":

absence	**ausencia**[f]	*graduate*	**graduado**[m]
academy	**academia**[f]	*history* *story*[2]	**historia**[f]
arithmetic	**aritmética**[f]	*homework*	**deberes**[m] **tarea**[f]
astronomy	**astronomía**[f]	*list*	**lista**[f]
bachelor's degree	**licenciatura**[f] **bachillerato**[m]	*master's degree*	**maestría**[f]
backpack	**mochila**[f]	*meaning*	**significado**[m]
biology	**biología**[f]	*method*	**método**[m]
board	**tablero**[m]	*microscope*	**microscopio**[m]
break (pause)	**pausa**[f] **descanso**[m]	*notebook*	**cuaderno**[m] **libreta**[f]
career	**carrera**[f]	*physics*	**física**[f]
chalkboard	**pizarra**[f]	*requirement*	**requisito**[m]
chemistry	**química**[f]	*response* *answer*	**respuesta**[f]
clarification	**aclaración**[f]	*ruler*	**regla**[f]
class	**clase**[f]	*schedule*	**horario**[m]
course	**curso**[m]	*scholarship*	**beca**[f]
course material	**material**[m] **del curso**	*sheet (paper)*	**hoja**[f]

---

[2] A factual account is often referred to as "**historia**[f]," whereas a fictional tale is referred to as "**cuento**[m]" or "**relato**[m]."

degree	**título**^m	*summary*	**resumen**^m
doctorate	**doctorado**^m	*system*	**sistema**^m
eraser	**borrador**^m	*technique*	**técnica**^m
faculty	**facultad**^f	*theory*	**teoría**^f
good grades	**buenas notas**^f	*way*	**manera**^f

9. SHOPPING

To go shopping in Spanish is "**ir de compras**," and *the market* is "**el mercado**." Here you learn some vocabulary related to shopping:

bill	**cuenta**^f	*on-sale*	**en venta**
brand	**marca**^f	*opening time*	**horarios**^m **de apertura**
card	**tarjeta**^f	*order*	**pedido**^m
cash	**efectivo**^m	*payment*	**pago**^m
chain	**cadena**^f	*penny*	**centavo**^m
complaint	**queja**^f	*price*	**precio**^m
cost	**costo**^m	*purchase*	**compra**^f
delivery	**entrega**^f	*receipt*	**recibo**^m
discount	**descuento**^m **rebaja**^f	*register*	**caja registradora**^f
fee [1]	**pago**^m **cargo**^m	*row (line)*	**fila**^f
invoice	**factura**^f	*sale*	**venta**^f
kiosk	**quiosco**^m	*shopping mall*	**centro**^m **comercial**
label *tag*	**etiqueta**^f	*spree* *binge*	**juerga**^f
line *queue*	**fila**^f **cola**^f	*surprise*	**sorpresa**^f
merchant	**comerciante**^m	*type*	**tipo**^m
money	**dinero**^m	*value*	**valor**^m [2]

---

[1] Depending on the context, the word *"fee"* in English can be translated as:

1. "**pago**^m" or "**cargo**^m" (service)
2. "**precio**^m" (ticket)
3. "**cuota**^f" (membership)
4. "**matrícula**^f" (tuition or course)

[2] The word "**valor**^m" can also mean *"courage"* or *"bravery."*

10. MATERIALS

Vocabulary related to *materials*, or "**los materiales**," can be useful to be familiar with. Here is a list of some common vocabulary:

cement	**cemento**[m]	*metal*	**metal**[m]
copper	**cobre**[m]	*petroleum*	**petróleo**[m]
cotton	**algodón**[m]	*plastic*	**plástico**[m]
diamond	**diamante**	*silk*	**seda**[f]
dust *powder*	**polvo**[m]	*silver*	**plata**[f][1]
fiber	**fibra**[f]	*steel*	**acero**[m]
glass	**vidrio**[m]	*substance*	**sustancia**[f]
gold	**oro**[m]	*synthesis*	**síntesis**[f]
iron	**hierro**[m]	*texture*	**textura**[f]
lead	**plomo**[m]	*thread*	**hilo**[m]
leather	**cuero**[m]	*wood*	**madera**[f]
magnet	**imán**[m]	*wool*	**lana**[f]

---

[1] The word "**plata**" is one of the most common ways to informally refer to *"money"* in most of Latin America.

LEVEL III: ELEMENTARY

I. Introductory Topics & Grammar

Start by reading the introductory topics of this level. You will notice that some concepts are unique to the Spanish language. Use the Anki cards to practice with reviews and exercises.

1. VERBS LIKE "GUSTAR"

Some expressions use a different sentence structure in Spanish compared to that used in English to express the same meaning. The most common example is the use of verbs like **"gustar"** (*to please*). Let us examine this sentence in Spanish:

Me gusta el auto.

This is often translated as: "*I like the car.*"

A more accurate and literal translation would be:

"*The car is pleasing to me.*"

Note that the verb conjugation is in the third-person singular form because **"el auto"** is the subject that does the act of pleasing, and **"me"** is the object. Thus, the conjugation of the verb **"gustar"** must agree with the subject **"el auto."**

Let us take another example. If you want to say that someone is interested in ancient cultures, the best way to say that is:

Le interesan las culturas antiguas.

Here, we use the verb **"interesar"** (*to interest*), and the sentence is translated as:

"Ancient cultures interest him (or her)."

Note that the verb is conjugated as **"interesan"** because **"las culturas antiguas"** is the subject, and **"le"** is the object. Thus, the conjugation of the verb **"interesar"** must agree with the subject **"las culturas antiguas."**

As you can see, we use the indirect object **"le"** to express the meaning *"to him"* or *"to her,"* that is, that the ancient cultures interest him or her. However, remember that **"le"** can also mean *"to him,"* *"to her,"* or even *"to you"* (formal). To remove ambiguity, one might optionally say:

"<u>A María</u> le interesan las culturas antiguas," or **"<u>A ella</u> le interesan las culturas antiguas."**

This is translated as:

"Ancient cultures interest María," or *"Ancient cultures interest her."*

Below are more examples of expressions with the verb **"gustar."**

English Example	Prep. Object Pronoun	Indirect Object Pronoun	Spanish Equivalent
I like reading.	mí	me	A **mí me** gusta leer.
You like reading. (singular informal)	ti	te	A **ti te** gusta leer.
He likes reading.	él	le	A **él le** gusta leer.
She likes reading.	ella	le	A **ella le** gusta leer.
You like reading. (singular formal)	usted	le	A **usted le** gusta leer.
We like reading.	nosotros/-as	nos	A **nosotros nos** gusta leer.
You like reading. (plural informal)	vosotros/-as	os	A **vosotros os** gusta leer.
They like reading.	ellos/ellas	les	A **ellos les** gusta leer.
You like reading. (plural formal)	ustedes	les	A **ustedes les** gusta leer.

❖ Note again how the verb "**gustar**" does not change conjugation in the examples above because "**leer**" *(to read)* is singular; thus, it takes the second-person conjugation "**gusta.**"

❖ In cases where ambiguity is not an issue, the introductory "**a + prepositional object pronoun**" can be omitted., e.g., "**A mí me gusta leer**" is just an emphasis of "**Me gusta leer,**" and both mean "*I like reading.*"

❖ The verb "**gustar**" is used to express the liking of things rather than of persons. If said about a person, it usually has a physical or sexual meaning to the act of liking, e.g., "**Me gustan las mujeres altas**" (*I like tall women*). If you want to express the liking of a person for his traits, use the verb "**caer bien**" (*to like, to suit, or to get along*), e.g., "**Me cae bien Julio. Él es una buena persona**" (*I like Julio. He is a good person*).

Here is a list of verbs like "**gustar**" that are common in Spanish:

Verb	Meaning	Example	
aburrir	*to bore*	Me **aburren** los videojuegos.	*Video games are boring to me.*
agradar	*to please*	Nos **agrada** el lugar.	*We like the place.*
alegrar	*to gladden*	¿Te **alegra** estudiar?	*Do you like studying?*
bastar	*to be enough*	A él eso le **basta**.	*That's enough for him.*
caer bien	*to like or to get along*	Me **cae bien** tu amigo.	*I like your friend.*
caer mal	*to not like or to not get along*	Nos **caen mal** estos políticos.	*We don't like these politicians.*
convenir	*to suit or to be convenient*	Llámame si te **conviene**.	*Call me if it is convenient for you.*
costar	*to cost or to be difficult*	Me **cuesta** aprender inglés.	*I find it difficult to learn English.*
interesar	*to interest*	No me **interesa** el tema.	*I am not interested in the topic.*
dar asco	*to be disgusted*	Me **da asco** tu comportamiento.	*Your behavior disgusts me.*
disgustar	*to disgust*	Me **disgustan** esos problemas.	*Those problems disgust me.*
doler	*to be painful*	A ella le **duele** la espalda.	*She has back pain.*

encantar	*to love something*	Me **encanta** este restaurante.	*I love this restaurant.*
faltar	*to be lacking*	Me **falta** un libro más.	*I am missing one more book.*
fascinar	*to fascinate*	A ella le **fascina** el hockey.	*Hockey fascinates her.*
hacer falta	*to be missing*	¿Te **hace falta** algo?	*Do you need something?*
importar	*to be important*	No me **importa**.	*I don't care.*
molestar	*to bother*	Te llamo si no te **molesta**.	*I'll call you if it doesn't bother you.*
parecer	*to seem*	Me **parece** interesante.	*It seems interesting to me.*
resultar[1]	*to find*	Me **resulta** muy interesante el tema.	*I find the topic very interesting.*
tocar[2]	*to be one's turn or responsibility*	Me **toca** traer la comida.	*It's my turn to bring food.*
volver loco	*to be crazy about*	Me **vuelven loco** los gatos.	*I am crazy about cats.*

[1] The verb "**resultar**" also means *"to result in"* or *"to turn out to be,"* e.g., "**La cirugía puede resultar en efectos secundarios**" (*The surgery can result in side effects*).

[2] The verb "**tocar**" has several other meanings, such as *"to touch," "to play (music)," "to ring (bell)," "to knock (on door),"* and *"to honk (horn)."*

2. "Por" vs. "Para"

The difference between the prepositions "**por**" and "**para**" is challenging for most Spanish learners. There are a few rules that you need to follow and some expressions that you need to memorize. However, with practice, you can get this right. In general, both "**por**" and "**para**" can mean *"for."* Nevertheless, in many contexts, they can also mean *"by," "per," "in order to," "because of,"* and some other meanings. Let us take a look at some of these contexts.

Uses of "Por"

1. To denote *reason* or *motive*, for example:

Llegaremos tarde **por** el tráfico.	*We'll be late **because of** the traffic.*
Él murió **por** falta de agua.	*He died **due to** a lack of water.*

2. To denote *duration*, for example:

| Te esperé **por** dos horas. | *I waited for you **for** two hours.* |
| Estaré en España **por** tres días. | *I will be in Spain **for** three days.* |

3. To denote *agency*, usually meaning *"by,"* for example:

| El libro fue escrito **por** un autor anónimo. | *The book was written **by** an anonymous author.* |
| Son amados **por** sus padres. | *They are loved **by** their parents.* |

4. To denote *equivalency* or *exchange*, for example:

| Cambié mi auto **por** otro nuevo. | *I changed my car **for** a new one.* |
| La harina cuesta dos dólares **por** kilo. | *The flour costs two dollars **per** kilo.* |

5. To denote *travel itinerary*, usually meaning *"through,"* for example:

| Quiero ir a Suiza **por** Italia. | *I want to go to Switzerland **through** Italy.* |
| Podemos pasar **por** el parque. | *We can go **through** the park.* |

6. To denote *means of travel or communication*, usually meaning *"by"* or *"via,"* for example:

| Ellos viajaron **por** avión. | *They traveled **by** plane.* |
| Te voy a contactar **por** teléfono. | *I am going to contact you **by** phone.* |

Uses of "Para"

1. To denote a *goal* or *objective*, usually meaning *"in order to,"* for example:

| Trabajo **para** ganar dinero. | *I work **in order to** earn money.* |
| Voy a la universidad **para** estudiar. | *I go to the university **to** study.* |

2. To denote *destination* or *direction*, for example:

| El tren sale **para** Nueva York. | *The train leaves **for** New York.* |
| Viajaremos **para** Colombia. | *We will travel **to** Colombia.* |

3. To denote the *recipient of an object*, for example:

| Es **para** ti. | *This is **for** you.* |
| Este regalo es **para** mi amigo. | *This gift is **for** my friend.* |

4. To denote a *deadline*, for example:

Tengo que hacerlo **para** mañana.	*I have to do it **by** tomorrow.*
Necesito terminar **para** las nueve.	*I need to finish **by** 9 o'clock.*

5. To denote an *opinion*, for example:

Para mí, es ridículo.	***For** me, it's ridiculous.*
Para ella, el fútbol no es divertido.	***In her opinion**, soccer is not fun.*

6. To denote the *contrast of an idea*, for example:

Para un niño, habla muy bien.	***For** a child, he speaks very well.*
Tiene buena salud **para** su edad.	*He's in good health **for** his age.*

Common Expressions with "Por" and "Para"

There are certain expressions that use "**por**," such as:

por Dios	*Oh my God!*	**por las dudas** / **por si acaso**	*just in case*
por favor	*please*	**por ejemplo**	*for example*
por suerte	*luckily*	**por supuesto**	*of course*
por ciento	*percent*	**por tu culpa**	*because of you*

and others that use "**para**," such as:

para siempre	*forever*	**para variar**	*just for a change*
para colmo	*to top it all*	**para empezar**	*for starters*
para nada	*not at all*	**para entonces**	*by then*
para otra ocasión / **para otro momento**	*for another time*	**para que**	*so that*

3. THE VERB "TO KNOW": "SABER" VS. "CONOCER"

There are two verbs in Spanish that mean *"to know"* in English. The two verbs are "**saber**" and "**conocer**." Knowing when to use "**saber**" and when to use "**conocer**" should not be difficult if you understand the subtle difference between the two concepts of *"knowing."*

In short, the verb "**saber**" is used to describe knowledge of facts, concepts, languages, skills, abilities, etc. On the other hand, the verb "**conocer**" is used to describe recognition or familiarity with a person, a place, or an object, including a movie, a site, a brand, etc.

Below is a reminder of the present tense conjugation of both verbs.

	saber	conocer
yo	sé	conozco
tú	sabes	conoces
él/ella/usted	sabe	conoce
nosotros/-as	sabemos	conocemos
vosotros/-as	sabéis	conocéis
ellos/ellas/ustedes	saben	conocen

Here are some examples that use the verbs "**saber**" and "**conocer**" and highlight the difference:

"saber" and "conocer" Examples	Explanation
¿**Sabes** si hay alguien dentro? *Do you **know** if there is someone inside?*	Referring to a fact (whether someone is inside or not), use "**saber**."
¿**Sabes** inglés? *Do you **know** English?*	Referring to a language, use "**saber**."
Ella no **sabe** nadar. *She doesn't **know** how to swim.*	Referring to a skill, use "**saber**."
No **sé** dónde hay una escuela. *I don't **know** where there is a school.*	Referring to a fact (whether a school exists nearby), use "**saber**."
No **conozco** la ciudad muy bien. *I don't **know** the city very well.*	Referring to recognizing a place, use "**conocer**."
No **conocen** a mis padres. *They don't **know** my parents.*	Referring to recognizing a person, use "**conocer**."
¿**Conoces** esa película? *Do you **know** that movie?*	Referring to recognizing a movie, use "**conocer**."

To know each other using "Conocer"

The verb "**conocer**" is used to refer to the reciprocal act of knowing each other, for example:

Nos conocemos muy bien.	*We **know each other** very well.*
No **se conocen**[1].	*They don't **know each other**.*

---

[1] More on the use of reflexive verbs will be covered in detail in **Level IV, Lesson 4**.

Expressions that use "Saber"

The verb "**saber**" is used in many expressions in Spanish, for example:

lo sé	*I know*	**que yo sepa** [1]	*as far as I know*
para que lo sepas [1]	*just so you know*	**¡qué sé yo!**	*how should I know?*
sin saberlo yo	*without my knowledge*	**vete a saber**	*your guess is as good as mine*
a saber	*who knows?*	**de haberlo sabido** [2]	*if I'd only known*

---

[1] Both "**sepa**" and "**sepas**" are subjunctive forms of "**saber**" which we will study in **Level IV Lesson 7**.

[2] The pluperfect tense will be covered in more detail in **Level VI, Lesson 3**.

Use of "Saber" and "Conocer" in the Preterite Tense

The preterite is one of the tenses used in Spanish to describe past events. We will cover the preterite in more detail in **Level IV, Lesson 2**, and **Level V, Lesson 1**. For now, keep in mind that "**saber**" in the preterite form can also mean *"to find out"* in the past, while "**conocer**" in the preterite form can also mean *"to meet"* in the past, for example:

Mi hermano **supo** que estaba enfermo.	*My brother **found out** that I was sick.*
Conocí a mi esposa en la universidad.	*I **met** my wife at university.*

4. INDEFINITE ADJECTIVES & PRONOUNS

Indefinite adjectives describe a noun in a vague or non-specific way, e.g., "**otra** gente" (*other people*), "**cada** persona" (*each person*), "**varias** cosas" (*several things*), "**todas** las escuelas" (*all schools*). On the other hand, an indefinite pronoun replaces the noun in a vague and non-specific way, e.g., "**Te digo algo**" (*I tell you something*), "**Hablé con alguien**" (*I spoke to someone*), "**Todo está bien**" (*All is well*). Many indefinite pronouns are identical to their indefinite adjective counterpart, e.g., "**todo**" (*all*), "**otro**" (*other*), "**mucho**" (*much or many*).

Unlike most adjectives in Spanish, indefinite adjectives precede the noun they describe. Some also change form to agree with the noun in gender and number. Indefinite adjectives and pronouns are used abundantly in Spanish. Thus, it is very useful to learn the most common ones.

Here is a list of the most common indefinite adjectives and pronouns:

	Meaning		Examples	
bastante **suficiente**	*enough*	indef. adj. & pron.	Tengo **bastante** dinero.	*I have **enough** money.*
demasiado, -a, -os, -as	*too much, too many*	indef. adj. & pron.	Este auto es **demasiado** caro.	*This car is **too** expensive.*
uno a otro **una a otra**	*each other*	indef. adj. & pron.	Deben ayudarse **unos a otros**.	*They must help **each other**.*
uno u otro **una u otra**	*one or the other*	indef. adj. & pron.	Debes elegir **una u otra** de estas casas.	*You must choose **one or the other** of these houses.*
ambos, -as	*both*	indef. adj. & pron.	**Ambas** opciones están disponibles.	***Both** options are available.*
ni uno, -a	*not a single one*	indef. adj. & pron.	**Ni una** sola persona apareció.	***Not a single** person showed up.*
ni uno ni otro **ni una ni otra**	*neither the one nor the other*	indef. adj. & pron.	No puedo elegir **ni uno ni otro**.	*I can choose **neither one nor the other**.*
los otros **las otras**	*the others*	indef. adj. & pron.	**Los otros** no están disponibles.	***The others** are not available.*
los demás	*the rest of*	indef. adj. & pron.	Me gustan los gatos y **los demás** animales.	*I like cats and **the rest of** the animals.*
mismo, -a, -os, -as	*same, self*	indef. adj. & pron.	Es la **misma** persona que vimos anoche.	*It is the **same** person we saw last night.*
cierto, -a, -os, -as	*certain*	indef. adj. & pron.	Solo **ciertas** personas pueden hacer eso.	*Only **certain** people can do that.*
otro, -a, -os, -as	*other, another*	indef. adj. & pron.	Quisiera **otra** copa de agua por favor.	*I'd like **another** glass of water, please.*
todo, -a	*all, every*	indef. adj. & pron.	**Todo** el año llueve en el país.	***All** year round, it rains in the country.*
todos, -as	*all, everybody*	indef. adj. & pron.	**Todos** nosotros somos de Australia.	***All** of us are from Australia.*

poco, -a	*little, not much*	indef. adj. & pron.	Necesitamos **poco** tiempo para llegar.	*We need **little** time to arrive.*
pocos, -as	*few*	indef. adj. & pron.	Tiene **pocos** amigos en la escuela.	*He has **few** friends at school.*
mucho, -a, -os, -as	*much, many*	indef. adj. & pron.	Hay **muchas** opciones para los jóvenes.	*There are **many** options for young people.*
varios, -as	*several*	indef. adj. & pron.	**Varios** campos están abiertos para todos.	***Several** fields are open to everyone.*
cualquier(a)	*any, whichever*	indef. adj. & pron.	Dame **cualquier** periódico.	*Give me **any** newspaper.*
propio, -a, -os, -as	*own, self, same*	indef. adj. & pron.	Lo hizo con sus **propias** manos.	He did it with his **own** hands.
tal(es)	*such a, such*	indef. adj. & pron.	Nunca he visto **tal** celebración.	I have never seen **such a** celebration.
ninguno, -a	*no one, not any*	indef. adj. & pron.	**Ninguna** casa era grande.	**Not any** of the houses were big.
algún alguna, -os, -as	*some, any, a/an*	indef. adj.	Solo tengo una casa y **algunos** libros.	*I only have a house and **some** books.*
alguno, -a, -os, -as	*one, someone, any, anyone*	indef. pron.	**Alguno** de ustedes me puede ayudar.	***One** of you can help me.*
cada	*each, every*	indef. adj.	Jugamos al fútbol **cada** sábado.	We play soccer **every** Saturday.
algo	*something*	indef. pron.	Quiero decir **algo** muy importante.	I want to say **something** very important.
alguien	*somebody*	indef. pron.	Hablé con **alguien** muy interesante.	I talked with **someone** very interesting.
nada	*nothing*	indef. pron.	Hoy no voy a hacer **nada** en todo el día.	I am going to do **nothing** all day today.
nadie	*nobody*	indef. pron.	Hoy no hay **nadie** en la oficina.	**Nobody** is in the office today.
quienquiera	*whoever*	indef. pron.	**Quienquiera** que sea, voy a cumplir.	**Whoever** it is, I will comply.

❖ Note that "**cada**" *(each)* can only be used as an indefinite adjective because it is always followed by a noun, e.g., "**cada libro**" *(each book)*, "**cada persona**" *(each person)*, etc. On the other hand, "**algo**" (*something*), "**alguien**" (*somebody*), "**nada**" (*nothing*), "**nadie**" (*nobody*), and "**quienquiera**" (*whoever*) can only be used as indefinite pronouns because they cannot be followed by a noun, e.g., "**No pasó nada**" (*Nothing happened*).

❖ Although both "**bastante**" and "**suficiente**" are often translated as *"enough"* in English, "**suficiente**" indicates that something is just barely enough, whereas "**bastante**" often has a more positive connotation that indicates an abundance and is not typically used in negative contexts.

For example, both "**Tengo suficiente dinero**" and "**Tengo bastante dinero**" indicate that you have enough money. Nevertheless, the former indicates that you have *just* enough to get by or to buy something, for example, whereas the latter indicates that you have quite a lot of it.

On the other hand, you would say "**No tengo suficiente dinero**" to indicate that you do not have enough money to buy something, for example, but you would not say "**No tengo bastante dinero**" unless you want to emphasize that you do not have quite a lot of it.

5. PRESENT PROGRESSIVE TENSE

The present progressive tense, similar to its use in English, describes an event that continues to take place in the present, e.g., "**Yo estoy hablando**" (*I am speaking*). It is formed by adding the auxiliary verb "**estar**" to the present participle, also known as the gerund. The gerund is formed by attaching "**-ando**" to the stem of "**-ar**" ending verbs and "**-iendo**" to the stem of "**-er**" and "**-ir**" ending verbs.

"**-ar**" verbs	subject pronoun + "**estar**" in present tense + (verb stem+ **ando**)
"**-er**" verbs	subject pronoun + "**estar**" in present tense + (verb stem+ **iendo**)
"**-ir**" verbs	subject pronoun + "**estar**" in present tense + (verb stem+ **iendo**)

Let us look at some examples:

		-ar ending e.g., hablar	-er ending e.g., comer	-ir ending e.g., vivir
yo	estoy			
tú	estás			
él/ella/usted	está	hablando	comiendo	viviendo
nosotros/-as	estamos			
vosotros/-as	estáis			
ellos/ellas/ustedes	están			

Unlike in English, it is possible to use the present simple tense to describe something happening continuously at the moment to convey the same meaning as the present progressive tense. For example, "**¿Qué haces ahora?**" and "**¿Qué estás haciendo ahora?**" can both mean *"What are you doing now?"* Similarly, "**Hablo con mi amigo**" and "**Estoy hablando con mi amigo**" both mean *"I am talking to my friend."*

Irregular Gerunds

We have mentioned that a gerund can be easily constructed by attaching "**-ando**" to an "**-ar**" ending verb and "**-iendo**" to an "**-er**" or "**-ir**" ending verb. Nevertheless, there are a few irregular verbs that require some practice:

❖ The gerund of the verb "**ir**" (*to go*), which is a very common verb in Spanish, is "**yendo**," e.g., "**Yo estoy yendo al aeropuerto**" (*I am going to the airport*). To say *"I'm coming"* in Spanish, you could use "**Estoy yendo**" or "**Ya voy**" because in Spanish we use the verb "**ir**" based on the point of reference of the speaker rather than that of the destination.

❖ In verbs ending in "**-er**" or "**-ir**," if the stem (the remaining part of the verb after removing the "**-er**" or "**-ir**" ending) ends in a vowel, "**-iendo**" becomes "**-yendo**," e.g., the gerund of "**leer**" *(to read)* is "**leyendo**," the gerund of "**atraer**" *(to attract)* is "**atrayendo**," the gerund of "**destruir**" *(to destroy)* is "**destruyendo**," and that of "**huir**" *(to run away)* is "**huyendo**."

❖ Many verbs ending in "**-ir**" that change stem in third-person forms of the present tense conjugation from "**e**" to "**i**" or from "**o**" to "**u**" maintain the same stem change in the gerund form, e.g., "**decir**" *(to say)* becomes "**diciendo**," "**pedir**" *(to ask for)* becomes "**pidiendo**," "**dormir**" becomes "**durmiendo**," and "**morir**" *(to die)* becomes "**muriendo**."

❖ In the verbs ending in "**-er**" or "**-ir**," if the stem ends in "**-ll**" or "**-ñ**," "**-iendo**" becomes "**-endo**." There are few verbs in this group, most of which are not very common, e.g., "**bullir**" *(to boil)* becomes "**bullendo**," "**mullir**" *(to fluff)* becomes "**mullendo**," and "**teñir**" *(to dye)* becomes "**tiñendo**," where the latter changes the first "**e**" to "**i**" as an exception to the rule.

6. PRESENT PERFECT TENSE

The present perfect tense in Spanish, like in English, is used to describe events that happened recently or started in the past and continue in the present. It is a compound tense, meaning it requires an auxiliary verb, in this case, the *irregular* verb "**haber**" in the present tense, followed by the past participle. The auxiliary "**haber**" serves a similar function to the auxiliary *"have"* in English, e.g., *"I have done my homework."*

"**-ar**" verbs	subject pronoun + "**haber**" in present tense + (verb stem+ **ado**)
"**-er**" verbs	subject pronoun + "**haber**" in present tense + (verb stem+ **ido**)
"**-ir**" verbs	subject pronoun + "**haber**" in present tense + (verb stem+ **ido**)

Let us look at some verb examples and the conjugation of "**haber**."

		-ar ending e.g., hablar	-er ending e.g., comer	-ir ending e.g., vivir
yo	he			
tú	has			
él/ella/usted	ha			
nosotros/-as	hemos	habl**ado**	com**ido**	viv**ido**
vosotros/-as	habéis			
ellos/ellas/ustedes	han			

Here are some more examples:

		Examples	
yo	he	Yo **he visitado** Egipto.	*I **have visited** Egypt.*
tú	has	Tú **has bebido** el café.	*You **have drunk** the coffee.*
él/ella/usted	ha	Ella **ha hablado** con su madre.	*She **has spoken** to her mother.*
nosotros/-as	hemos	Nosotros **hemos comido**.	*We **have eaten**.*
vosotros/-as	habéis	Vosotros **habéis llegado**.	*You **have arrived**.*
ellos/ellas/ustedes	han	Ellos **han vivido** aquí.	*They **have lived** here.*

Irregular Past Participles

There are a few verbs with irregular past participles that need to be memorized.

Verb	Past Participle	Meaning	Examples	
abrir	abierto	*to open*	He **abierto** la puerta.	*I have **opened** the door.*
absolver	absuelto	*to absolve*	Lo han **absuelto**.	*They have **absolved** him.*
cubrir	cubierto	*to cover*	Hemos **cubierto** el suelo.	*We have **covered** the floor.*
decir	dicho	*to say*	Te lo he **dicho**.	*I have **told** you so.*
escribir	escrito	*to write*	Ella ha **escrito** una carta.	*She has **written** a letter.*
freír	frito	*to fry*	¿Has **frito** la papa?	*Have you **fried** the potato?*
hacer	hecho	*to do*	He **hecho** la tarea.	*I have **done** the task.*
imprimir	impreso	*to print*	He **impreso** la foto.	*I have **printed** the photo.*
morir	muerto	*to die*	Él ha **muerto**.	*He has **died**.*
poner	puesto	*to put*	Él nos ha **puesto** en peligro.	*He has **put** us in danger.*
proveer	provisto	*to provide*	Hemos **provisto** el agua.	*We have **provided** water.*

resolver	resuelto	*to resolve*	Ella ha **resuelto** el problema.	*She has **resolved** the problem.*
romper	roto	*to break*	Ella ha **roto** la ventana.	*She has **broken** the window.*
satisfacer	satisfecho	*to satisfy*	Mi trabajo me ha **satisfecho**.	*My work has **satisfied** me.*
ver	visto	*to see*	No lo he **visto**.	*I haven't **seen** him.*
volver	vuelto	*to return*	Ella no ha **vuelto**.	*She hasn't **returned**.*

❖ Among the above exceptions, it is acceptable for the verbs "**freír**," "**imprimir**," and "**proveer**" to use the past participle in the regular form as "**freído**," "**imprimido**," and "**proveído**." However, only irregular forms are acceptable if used as adjectives.

❖ The verbs above can be used with prefixes that change the meaning, but the irregular form remains the same. For example, the past participles of "**revolver**" (*to scramble*), "**devolver**" (*to return*), and "**envolver**" (*to wrap*) are "**revuelto**," "**devuelto**," and "**envuelto**," respectively, which are all similar to the past participle of the original verb "**volver**" without the prefix, i.e., "**vuelto**."

❖ Another minor orthographic irregularity is in the case of "-**er**" and "-**ir**" verbs if the stem ends in a vowel, e.g., the stem of "**leer**" *(to read)* is "**le-**." In this case, the "**i**" in the past participle ending is accented, i.e., "-**ído**." Thus, the past participle of "**leer**" is "**leído**." Other examples include "**caer**" *(to fall)*, "**creer**" *(to believe)*, "**oír**" *(to hear)*, "**poseer**" *(to possess)*, "**reír**" *(to laugh)*, and "**traer**" *(to bring)*. An exception to the accented "**i**" rule is verbs with a "-**uir**" ending. In this case, the "**i**" is not accented, e.g., "**destruir**" *(to destroy)* becomes "**destruido**."

Past Participle as Adjective

Many adjectives in Spanish are the same as the past participle, especially when active meaning is conveyed.

		Examples	
agradecido	*grateful*	Estoy **agradecido** por tu ayuda.	*I'm **grateful** for your help.*
atrevido	*daring*	Él es una persona muy **atrevida**.	*He is a very **daring** person.*
divertido	*amusing*	Su comportamiento era muy **divertido**.	*His behavior was very **amusing**.*
experimentado	*experienced expert*	Él es un médico muy **experimentado**.	*He is a very **experienced** doctor.*

In some cases, the past participle and the adjective are different. It is useful to remember that the following words use different adjective and past participle forms:

Infinitive	Meaning	Adjective	Past Participle
atender	*to look after*	atento	atendido
bendecir	*to bless*	bendito	bendecido
confundir	*to confuse*	confuso, confundido	confundido
corromper	*to corrupt*	corrupto, corrompido	corrompido
despertar	*to wake up*	despierto	despertado
maldecir	*to curse*	maldito	maldecido
poseer	*to possess*	poseso, poseído	poseído
presumir	*to presume*	presunto	presumido
suspender	*to suspend*	suspenso, suspendido	suspendido

For example:

Yo he **despertado**.	*I have **woken up**.*	**"despertado"** is the past participle
Yo estoy **despierto**.	*I am **awake**.*	**"despierto"** is an adjective

Me han **confundido**.	*They have **confused** me.*	**"confundido"** is the past participle
Ella estaba **confusa**.	*She was **confused**.*	**"confusa"** is an adjective

Finally, despite not being grammatically correct or recognized by the Real Academia Española (RAE), the present perfect progressive tense is sometimes heard by native speakers to describe an action that was initiated in the past and continues to happen.

A sentence in the present perfect progressive tense is formed as follows:

subject pronoun + "**haber**" in present tense + "**estado**"+ *gerund*

			-ar ending hablar	-er ending comer	-ir ending vivir
yo	he	estado	hablando	comiendo	viviendo
tú	has				
él/ella/usted	ha				
nosotros/-as	hemos				
vosotros/-as	habéis				
ellos/ellas/ustedes	han				

For example:

He estado hablando con él por dos horas.	*I **have been talking** with him for two hours.*
Ha estado viviendo aquí por mucho tiempo.	*He **has been living** here for a long time.*

In formal speech, one must not use this grammatically incorrect tense. The alternative is to use the present perfect tense, which we studied previously. The present perfect tense is the grammatically correct alternative to the present perfect progressive tense.

Thus, the above two examples should be rewritten as follows:

He hablado con él.	*I **have talked** with him.*
Ha vivido aquí por mucho tiempo.	*He **has lived** here for a long time.*

7. SPECIAL USES OF "HABER" & "TENER"

The verbs "**haber**" and "**tener**" are widely used in Spanish. Here, we discuss some special uses other than the ones encountered elsewhere in the book.

The Verb "Haber"

We have encountered the auxiliary verb "**haber**" in the present perfect tense, e.g., "**Yo he comido**" (*I have eaten*), and we will encounter it again in the future perfect tense, e.g., **"Yo habré comido"** (*I will have eaten*), and in other tenses.

	Present Tense	**Future Tense**
yo	he	habré
tú	has	habrás
él/ella/usted	ha	habrá
nosotros/-as	hemos	habremos
vosotros/-as	habéis	habréis
ellos/ellas/ustedes	han	habrán

Another common and special use of the verb **"haber"** is the expression **"Hay …,"** which is translated as *"There is/are …,"* and is the same for singular and plural. The form **"hay"** is considered in the present tense and does not take a personal pronoun as a subject.

Hay …	*There is/are …*
Ha habido …	*There has/have been …*
Había/Hubo …	*There was/were …*
Habrá …	*There will be …*

Both **"había"** and **"hubo"** mean *"there was/were."* The first is more often used. There is a subtle difference that we will come to understand as we study the difference between the two past tense forms in Spanish, namely the preterite and the imperfect.

Another use of the verb **"haber"** in the form **"hay que…(*infinitive*)"** is to express obligation, meaning *"One must …"* or *"It must be that you …."* For example:

Hay que tener cuidado en la ciudad.	***One must*** *be careful in the city.*
Hay que hacer ejercicio frecuentemente.	***One must*** *exercise frequently.*

The expression **"Hay cupo"** means *"There is room,"* whereas **"No hay cupo"** means *"There is no space or vacancy."*

The Verb "Tener"

We have also encountered the verb **"tener"** (*to have*) as an irregular verb in the present tense.

yo	tengo
tú	tienes
él/ella/usted	tiene
nosotros/-as	tenemos
vosotros/-as	tenéis
ellos/ellas/ustedes	tienen

In addition to the obvious use of "**tener**" to indicate possession, e.g., "**Yo tengo dos gatos**" (*I have two cats*), there are some less obvious uses of the verb "**tener**" in Spanish:

1. Age

In English, we use the verb *"to be"* to describe age, as in *"how old <u>are</u> you?"* and *"I <u>am</u> 30 years old."* In Spanish, the verb "**tener**" is used instead. In Spanish, we literally say, *"I have 30 years old"* rather than, *"I am 30 years old."* Here are a few more examples:

¿Cuántos años **tienes**?	*How old **are** you?*
Tengo 40 años.	*I **am** 40 years old.*
Ella **tiene** 20 años.	*She **is** 20 years old.*

2. Expressions with "**Tener**" that describe a feeling, pain, illness, or desire.

Some expressions in Spanish describe a feeling or desire using the verb "**tener**," while their equivalent in English uses the verb *"to be,"* e.g., "**<u>Tengo</u> miedo**" (*I <u>am</u> afraid*). The word "**miedo**" means *"fear."* Thus, we literally say, *"I have fear."* Some other examples are:

tener hambre	*to be hungry*	**tener sed**	*to be thirsty*
tener frío	*to be cold*	**tener calor**	*to be hot*
tener sueño	*to be sleepy*	**tener cuidado**	*to be careful*
tener alergia	*to be allergic*	**tener razón**	*to be right*
tener suerte	*to be lucky*	**tener prisa**	*to be in a hurry*
tener celos	*to be jealous*	**tener éxito**	*to be successful*
tener ganas de	*to want or desire*	**tener vergüenza**	*to be ashamed*

3. Tener que ...

One way to express the obligation *"have to ..."* is by using "**tener que**" followed by the *infinitive*, for example:

Yo **tengo que** hacerlo.	*I **have to** do it.*
Ellos **tienen que** pagar.	*They **have to** pay.*
Nosotros **tenemos que** ir.	*We **have to** go.*

4. Other Expressions

There are many other idioms and expressions that use the verb "**tener**." One common expression is "**Tiene sentido**," which means *"It makes sense."* Some other expressions are:

tener lugar	*to take place*	**tener la palabra**	*to have the floor*
tener mala cara	*to look bad*	**tener la culpa**	*to take the blame*
tener que ver con	*to have to do with*	**tener mucho que hacer**	*to have a lot to do*

8. Telling Time & Describing the Weather

Telling time and describing the weather are fundamental language skills for any language learner.

Expressing Time in Hours

In Spanish, the verb "**ser**" (*to be*) is used in the third-person forms to describe time.

The singular form "**es**" is used for *"one o'clock,"* while other hours (from two to twelve o'clock) use the plural form "**son**."

Es la una.	*It's one o'clock.*
Son las tres.	*It's three o'clock.*
Son las once.	*It's eleven o'clock.*

Expressing Minutes

To express time in hours and minutes, we use the conjunction "**y**" *(and)* or "**con**" *(with).*

Es la una **y** treinta. Es la una **con** treinta.	*It's one-thirty.*
Son las cinco **y** veinticuatro. Son las cinco **con** veinticuatro.	*It's five twenty-four.*

If you want to say it is minutes to a certain hour, e.g., "*It's five to ten,*" use "**menos**" *(minus).*

Es la una **menos** diez.	*It's ten to one.*
Son las diez **menos** cinco.	*It's five to ten.*

An alternative way is to use "**para**." Either "**es**" or "**son**" can be used.

Es un cuarto **para** las seis. **Son** un cuarto **para** las seis.	*It's quarter to six.*

The "*15 minutes*" and "*30 minutes*" can sometimes be replaced with "**cuarto**" *(quarter)* and "**media**" *(half),* respectively.

Es la una menos **cuarto**.	*It's a quarter to one.*
Son las cuatro y **media**.	*It's four-thirty.*

The expressions "**a.m.**" and "**p.m.**" are commonly used in Spanish as in English.

Other Time Expressions

Here are some expressions that are used to express time with examples:

de la mañana	*in the morning*	*It's 9 a.m.*	Son las nueve **de la mañana**.
de la tarde	*in the afternoon*	*It's 1 p.m.*	Es la una **de la tarde**.
de la noche	*in the evening at night*	*It's 7 p.m.*	Son las siete **de la noche**.
de la madrugada	*in the wee hours*	*It's 4 a.m.*	Son las cuatro **de la madrugada**.

mediodía	noon	It's noon.	Es **mediodía**.
medianoche	midnight	It's midnight.	Es **medianoche**.
en punto	sharp	It's two o'clock sharp.	Son las dos **en punto**.
más o menos	around	It's around three o'clock.	Son las tres **más o menos**.

Weather Expressions

Describing the weather in Spanish often involves the use of some idiomatic expressions that make little sense if translated into English literally. For example, the expression **"Hace mucho calor"** translates literally to *"It makes much heat."* However, it just means that it is too hot. Similarly, the expression **"Hay sol,"** which means that the sun is shining, makes little sense when translated literally as *"There is sun."*

Here we list a few common ways of describing the weather using some of these idiomatic expressions as well as other simple expressions.

Weather Expressions using the verb "hacer"

¿Qué tiempo hace?	*What's the weather like?*
Hace buen tiempo.	*The weather is good.*
Hace mal tiempo.	*The weather is bad.*
Hace (mucho) frío.	*It's (too) cold.*
Hace calor.	*It's hot.*
Hace sol.	*It's sunny.*
Hace viento.	*It's windy.*
Hace fresco.	*It's brisk.*

Weather Expressions using the verb "hay"

The verb **"hay"** means *"there is/are"* and is used in many weather expressions.

Hay sol.	*The sun is shining.*
Hay luna.	*The moon is out.*
Hay nubes.	*It's cloudy.*
Hay niebla.	*It's foggy.*
Hay neblina.	*It's misty.*

Hay humedad.	*It's humid.*
Hay relámpagos.	*There is lightning.*
Hay granizo.	*It's hailing.*
Hay lloviznas.	*It's sprinkling.*
Hay un vendaval.	*There is a windstorm.*

Weather Expressions using the verb "estar"

We can also use the verb "**estar**" in the third-person singular form followed by an adjective to describe the weather.

Está soleado.	*It's sunny.*
Está nublado.	*It's cloudy.*
Está lluvioso.	*It's rainy.*
Está oscuro.	*It's dark.*

Weather Expressions using a simple verb

One can also use a simple verb expression in the third-person singular form, such as "**llueve**," the third-person singular form of the present tense of the verb "**llover**" (*to rain*). Other examples include:

Llueve.	*It's raining.*
Nieva.	*It's snowing.*
Llovizna.	*It's sprinkling.*
Truena.	*It's thundering.*

9. ADVERBS

An adverb is a word that modifies a verb, an adjective, or another adverb. They usually answer questions such as how? how often? how long? when? where? etc.

A lot of Spanish adverbs have the ending "**-mente**," e.g., "**rápidamente**" (*quickly*), "**fuertemente**" (*strongly*), etc. This is, more or less, similar to the ending "*-ly*" in English. Nevertheless, there are many other adverbs and adverbial phrases that do not follow this simple rule. We will attempt to classify the most common adverbs into some categories for easier memorization.

Forming an Adverb

Many adverbs in Spanish can be formed by simply adding "-**mente**" to the *feminine* singular adjective. Here are some examples:

Adverb in English	Masculine singular adjective	Feminine singular adjective	Adverb in Spanish
slowly	lento	lenta	lentamente
quickly	rápido	rápida	rápidamente
easily	fácil	fácil	fácilmente
quietly	tranquilo	tranquila	tranquilamente
exactly	exacto	exacta	exactamente
normally	normal	normal	normalmente
relatively	relativo	relativa	relativamente
automatically	automático	automática	automáticamente
lightly	ligero	ligera	ligeramente
generally	general	general	generalmente
originally	original	original	originalmente
partially	parcial	parcial	parcialmente
substantially	sustancial	sustancial	sustancialmente
literally	literal	literal	literalmente

A commonly used adverb formed this way is "**recientemente**," which means "**recently**," and is often abbreviated as "**recién**."

Yo **recién** llegué.	*I recently arrived.*
el **recién** nacido	*the newly born*

Not all adverbs in Spanish are formed by adding the "-**mente**" ending, similar to the fact that not all English adverbs are formed by adding *"-ly"* to the corresponding adjective. Some other ways of forming adverbs, especially adverbs of manner, are summarized with this example:

"**de manera**" + feminine adjective	Él me habló **de manera** respetuosa.
"**de modo**" + masculine adjective	Él me habló **de modo** respetuoso.
"**con**" or "**sin**" + noun	Él me habló **con** respeto.

All three sentences above can be translated as *"He spoke to me respectfully."* The first two form the adverb from the corresponding adjective, while the third forms the adverb from the corresponding noun. The word "**con**" means *"with,"* while "**sin**" means *"without."* Thus, "**Él me habló sin respeto**" is translated as *"He spoke to me disrespectfully."*

The Adverb "Tan"

Another common adverb in Spanish is "**tan**," which is often translated as *"such"* or *"so,"* for example:

¡Es un gato **tan** lindo!	*He is **such** a pretty cat.*
¡Este gato es **tan** lindo!	*This cat is **so** pretty.*

The Adverb "Solo"

The word "**solo**" can be used as an adjective or adverb. When used as an adverb, "**solo**" means *"only"* or *"just,"* and is synonymous with "**solamente**." When used as an adjective, on the other hand, it means *"alone."*

The adverb used to be written with an accent as "**sólo**" until 2010, when the Real Academia Española (RAE) changed that rule, leaving it up to the context of a given sentence to determine the meaning. This leaves room for confusion in certain situations. For instance, the sentence "**Trabajo <u>solo</u> los fines de semana**" could mean *"I work <u>alone</u> on weekends"* or *"I work <u>only</u> on weekends."*

The Adverbs "También" and "Tampoco"

The adverb "**también**" is used to express agreement with an *affirmative* statement, whereas the adverb "**tampoco**" is used to express agreement with a *negative* statement. For example:

A: Yo hablo español.	*A: I speak Spanish.*
B: Yo **también**.	*B: Me **too**.*
A: Yo no hablo español.	*A: I don't speak Spanish.*
B: Yo **tampoco**.	*B: Me **neither**.*

To show disagreement with affirmative and negative statements, we simply use "**no**" *(no)* and "**sí**" *(yes)*, respectively, for example:

A: Yo hablo español.	A: I speak Spanish.
B: Yo **no**.	B: I **don't**.
A: Yo no hablo español.	A: I don't speak Spanish.
B: Yo **sí**.	B: I **do**.

If a verb like "**gustar**" is used, the subject pronoun is replaced with a prepositional "**a**" followed by the prepositional object pronoun. For example:

A: Me gusta el té.	A: I like tea.
B: <u>A mí</u> **también**.	B: Me **too**.
A: No me gusta el té.	A: I don't like tea.
B: <u>A mí</u> **tampoco**.	B: Me **neither**.

We apply the same concept in the case of disagreement, for example:

A: Me gusta el té.	A: I like tea.
B: <u>A mí</u> **no**.	B: I **don't**.
A: No me gusta el té.	A: I don't like tea.
B: <u>A mí</u> **sí**.	B: I **do**.

Adverbial Phrases with "Vez" and "Veces"

The feminine noun "**vez**" and its plural "**veces**" are used to describe the frequency of occurrence. The English equivalents are often *"time,"* and its plural *"times,"* e.g., *"how many times did you win?"* Here is a list of some adverbial phrases that use "**vez**":

esta vez	*this time*	rara vez [1]	*rarely* *seldom*
la próxima vez	*next time*	**la última vez**	*last time*
cada vez	*each time* *every time*	**tal vez**	*perhaps* *maybe*
por primera vez	*for the first time*	**por última vez**	*for the last time*

---

[1] An alternative expression is "**raramente**."

a la vez [1]	at the same time	alguna vez [2]	sometime once
en vez de	instead of	de vez en cuando	from time to time
una vez	one time once	a mi vez	for my part in my turn
otra vez [3]	again	cada vez menos	less and less

[1] An alternative expression is "**al mismo tiempo**."

[2] If used in a question, it can also mean *"ever,"* e.g., "**¿Alguna vez has ido a Paraguay?** " *(Have you ever been to Paraguay?)*.

[3] An alternative expression is "**de nuevo**."

Examples of adverbial verbs that use the plural noun **"veces"** include:

a veces	sometimes	tres veces	three times
muchas veces	many times often	varias veces	several times
algunas veces	at times sometimes	¿Cuántas veces?	How many times?

Other Adverbs

Given that an adverb can be created easily from a corresponding adjective, it is difficult to cover a vast number of adverbs in the limited space of this book.

Moreover, there are often multiple adverbs that convey a similar meaning. Here are some examples:

1. To say *"certainly"* or *"surely,"* you could use one of the following options: **"ciertamente," "seguramente," "claro," "por supuesto,"** or even **"sin duda"** *(undoubtedly)*.

2. To say *"perhaps"* or *"maybe,"* you could use: **"tal vez," "quizás," "quizá,"** or **"a lo mejor."**

3. To say *"really," "truly,"* or *"actually,"* you could use: **"realmente," "verdaderamente," "de verdad,"** or **"en realidad."** Remember that **"actualmente,"** in Spanish, means *"currently,"* not *"actually."*

4. To say *"finally,"* you could use: **"finalmente," "al final," "por fin," "al fin,"** or **"por último."** [1]

In this section, we list some of the most common adverbs and adverbial phrases. You will learn more adverbs as you practice Spanish by reading, listening, and understanding the general rules explained in this lesson.

Adverbs of Place

cerca	*near*	lejos	*far*
delante	*in front*	detrás atrás	*behind*
dentro adentro	*inside*	fuera afuera	*outside*
adelante	*ahead*	alrededor	*around*
en ninguna parte	*nowhere*	a bordo	*on board*
en todas partes	*everywhere*	en casa	*at home*

Adverbs of Time

pronto	*soon*	luego más tarde	*later*
temprano	*early*	tarde	*late*
antes	*before*	después	*after*
siempre	*always*	nunca jamás	*never*
a menudo muchas veces	*often*	de repente	*suddenly*
usualmente	*usually*	entonces	*then*
brevemente	*briefly*	frecuentemente con frecuencia	*frequently*
al principio	*in the beginning*	al final	*in the end*
todos los días cada día	*every day*	día por medio cada otro día	*every other day*

---

[1] There are some differences between these expressions, all meaning *"finally"*:

- **"por último"** means *"lastly"* (in a list or order).
- **"por fin"** and **"al fin"** mean *"at last"* (often regarding something that is hoped for).
- **"finalmente"** and **"al final"** (the former is more formal) can mean *"lastly"* (in a list or order) or *"in the end"* (not necessarily regarding something that is hoped for).

a corto plazo	*in the short term*	**a largo plazo**	*in the long term*
a tiempo	*on time*	**mientras tanto** **entretanto**	*meanwhile*
inmediatamente **de inmediato**	*immediately*	**enseguida**	*right away* *immediately*
anteanoche	*the night before last*	**diariamente** **a diario**	*daily*
semanalmente	*weekly*	**mensualmente**	*monthly*

Adverbs of Quantity

muy	*very*	**mucho**	*a lot*
demasiado	*too much*	**poco**	*a little*
más	*more*	**menos**	*less*
tanto	*so much*	**bastante**	*enough*
casi	*almost*	**para nada**	*not at all*

Adverbs of Manner

como	*as* *like*	**así**	*like this*
juntos	*together*	**separadamente** **por separado**	*separately*
poco a poco	*little by little*	**paso a paso**	*step by step*
deprisa	*quickly* *in a hurry*	**apenas**	*barely* *hardly*
seriamente **en serio**	*seriously*	**alto** **en voz alta**	*loudly*
además	*moreover*	**cara a cara**	*face to face*
afortunadamente	*fortunately*	**desafortunadamente**	*unfortunately*
por suerte	*luckily*	**por desgracia** **desgraciadamente**	*unfortunately*

Adverbial Expressions

de buena gana	*willingly*	**de mala gana**	*unwillingly*
a sabiendas	*knowingly*	**a la moda**	*fashionably*
de memoria	*by heart*	**a pie**	*on foot*
en camino	*on the way*	**en el exterior** [1]	*overseas*

---

[1] The expression "**en el exterior**" can also mean *"outside"* or *"outdoors."*

II. Vocabulary Building

Go over the vocabulary in this section and use the provided Anki cards to study and memorize the new vocabulary efficiently.

1. VERBS III

Below is a list of some important verbs needed for this level. Use the Anki cards created for this section to help you memorize the meaning of each verb in proper contexts.

English	Spanish	Examples
access	acceder	Por esa escalera **accedes** al sótano. *Down those stairs you **access** the basement.*
advance	avanzar	Para **avanzar** en la universidad, hay que estudiar. *To **advance** in university, you have to study.*
arrange (order)	ordenar arreglar	**Ordenaré** mis archivos alfabéticamente. *I **will arrange** my files alphabetically.*
arrange (organize)	organizar	**Organizaré** una reunión a las 2. *I **will arrange** a meeting at 2 o'clock.*
break (object)	romper	Debes **romper** tres huevos para la receta. *You have to **break** three eggs for the recipe.*
breathe	respirar	Tienes que **respirar** profundo antes de zambullirte. *You have to **breathe** deeply before diving in.*
bring	traer	¿Me puedes **traer** ese vaso? *Can you **bring** me that glass?*
carry	llevar[1]	**Llevaré** estas bolsas a la casa. *I will **carry** these bags to the house.*
continue	continuar seguir	**Continúo** viendo esa serie. *I **continue** to watch that series.*
correct	corregir	**Estoy corrigiendo** los exámenes de ayer. *I **am correcting** yesterday's exams.*
cross	cruzar	Debes **cruzar** el puente para llegar. *You must **cross** the bridge to arrive.*
direct	dirigir	**Dirige** muy bien a la orquesta. *He **directs** the orchestra very well.*
discuss	discutir	No **discutiré** eso contigo. *I **will** not **discuss** that with you.*

---

[1] Depending on the context, the verb "**llevar**" can have other meanings such as *"to give a ride," "to bring," "to be ahead by,"* and *"to be older by."* It can also sometimes mean *"to be or to spend time on,"* e.g., "**Llevo horas estudiando**" *(I have been studying for hours).*

do again	volver [1]	Debo **volver** a hacer esta receta. *I have to* ***do*** *this recipe* ***again***.
dream	soñar	Siempre **sueño** con ir a Australia. *I always* ***dream*** *of going to Australia*.
employ	emplear	Mi empresa **emplea** muchos obreros. *My company* ***employs*** *many workers*.
fail	fallar fracasar	No es fácil **fracasar**. *It isn't easy to* ***fail***.
fill	llenar	**Lleno** siempre la cubitera. *I always* ***fill*** *the ice tray*.
finish	terminar acabar	Si **termino** con esto, vamos. *If I* ***finish*** *this, we'll go*.
fix (attach)	fijar	Dame el destornillador para **fijar** el marco a la pared. *Give me the screwdriver to* ***fix*** *the frame to the wall*.
fix (repair)	arreglar reparar	**Estoy arreglando** el grifo. *I* ***am fixing*** *the faucet*.
fly	volar	**Volaré** hasta San Francisco. *I* ***will fly*** *to San Francisco*.
follow	seguir	Me puedes **seguir** en redes sociales. *You can* ***follow*** *me on social media*.
guess	adivinar	Siempre **adivino** mi regalo de cumpleaños. *I always* ***guess*** *my birthday gift*.
hate	odiar detestar	**Odio** cuando me pican los mosquitos. *I* ***hate*** *it when mosquitoes bite me*.
have lunch	almorzar	No puedo; **estoy almorzando**. *I can't; I* ***am having lunch***.
keep **save** **guard**	guardar	Siempre **guardo** las sobras. *I always* ***save*** *the leftovers*.
kill	matar	Ese veneno **mata** las pulgas. *That poison* ***kills*** *fleas*.
lack	faltar carecer de	Le **falta** sabor a este guisado. *This stew* ***lacks*** *flavor*.
last	durar	Esos víveres deberían **durar** toda la semana. *Those groceries should* ***last*** *the entire week*.
mix **blend**	mezclar	Debes **mezclar** los ingredientes secos primero. *You must* ***mix*** *the dry ingredients first*.
must	deber [2]	**Debes** visitar a tu abuela. *You* ***must*** *visit your grandmother*.

---

[1] The verb "**volver**" also means *"to return"* or *"to come back."*

[2] The verb "**deber**" can also mean *"to owe,"* e.g., "**Te debo 100 euros**" *(I owe you 100 euros)*.

name	nombrar	No sabemos a quién **nombrar** como asistente. *We don't know who to **name** as an assistant.*
notify	avisar notificar	¿Puedes **avisar**me cuando llegue? *Can you **notify** me when it arrives?*
offer	ofrecer	El mercado **ofrece** muchos productos. *The market **offers** a lot of products.*
perform **fulfill**	realizar	Los científicos **realizarán** un experimento. *The scientists **will perform** an experiment.*
possess	poseer	**Posee** una habilidad sorprendente. *He **possesses** a surprising skill.*
pull	tirar jalar	Debes **tirar** de esa cuerda para que caiga. *You have to **pull** on that rope for it to fall.*
push	empujar	Te **estoy empujando** hacia adelante. *I **am pushing** you forward.*
remind	recordar [1]	¿Me puedes **recordar** la fecha, por favor? *Can you **remind** me of the date, please?*
rent	alquilar	**Estoy alquilando** un apartamento. *I **am renting** an apartment.*
ride	montar	Me gusta **montar** a caballo. *I like **riding** horses.*
seem	parecer	**Parece** que es por allí. *It **seems** it's that way.*
sign	firmar	El actor **está firmando** autógrafos. *The actor **is signing** autographs.*
smell	oler	Debes **oler** esta canela. *You must **smell** this cinnamon.*
sound	sonar	El timbre **suena** demasiado fuerte. *The doorbell **sounds** too loud.*
spell	deletrear	¿Me puedes **deletrear** esa palabra? *Can you **spell** that word for me?*
split **break**	partir	Esta calle **parte** la ciudad en dos. *This street **splits** the city in two.*
switch on **turn on**	encender	Debo **encender** la luz para ver. *I have to **turn on** the light to see.*
test **taste**	probar [2]	Me gusta **probar** toda la comida que hay. *I like to **taste** all the food there is.*
thank	agradecer	Les **agradezco** a mis amigos por ayudarme. *I **thank** my friends for helping me.*
train	entrenar	Debo **entrenar** para la carrera. *I have to **train** for the race.*

---

[1] The verb "**recordar**" can also mean *"to remember."*
[2] The verb "**probar**" can also mean *"to prove."*

trust	confiar	**Confío** en tu juicio. *I **trust** your judgment.*
warn	advertir	Te **advierto** que no te gustará. *I **warn** you that you won't like it.*
wish	desear	Los jóvenes **desean** ser más independientes. *Young people **wish** to be more independent.*

In addition to the above new verbs, we add a few more English cognates that are easy to memorize.

English	Spanish	Examples
abuse	abusar	No es bueno **abusar** de la confianza. *It's not good to **abuse** trust.*
accelerate	acelerar	Trato de no **acelerar** mucho cuando conduzco. *I try to not **accelerate** too much when I drive.*
accompany	acompañar	¿Me puedes **acompañar** a la puerta? *Can you **accompany** me to the door?*
adjust	ajustar	Quiere **ajustar** la luz de la habitación. *He wants to **adjust** the light in the room.*
affect	afectar	Tener sueño **afecta** a mis reacciones. *Being sleepy **affects** my reactions.*
assist	asistir [1]	Debes **asistir** a la gente cuando puedas. *You must **assist** people when you can.*
cease	cesar	Esa marca va a **cesar** de existir. *That brand is going to **cease** to exist.*
celebrate	celebrar	**Celebraré** mi cumpleaños en un crucero. *I **will celebrate** my birthday on a cruise.*
combat	combatir	Es difícil **combatir** los mosquitos. *It's hard to **combat** the mosquitoes.*
compete	competir	Le encanta **competir** con su hermano. *She loves to **compete** with her brother.*
condemn **convict**	condenar	No debes **condenar** sin pruebas. *You shouldn't **condemn** without proof.*
confine	confinar	El ejército **ha confinado** a los rebeldes. *The army **has confined** the rebels.*
consent	consentir	Leo los términos antes de **consentir**los. *I read the terms before I **consent** to them.*

---

[1] The verb **"asistir"** also means *"to attend,"* e.g., **"asistir a una clase"** *(to attend a class)*, which is the more common use of the verb **"asistir."** The verb **"ayudar"** is often used to describe the act of giving help or assistance. The verb **"atender,"** on the other hand, means *"to attend to, to serve, or care for."*

contemplate	contemplar	Me gusta **contemplar** el arte callejero. *I like to **contemplate** street art.*
contrast	contrastar	Ese color de puerta **contrasta** con la pared. *That door color **contrasts** with the wall.*
contribute	contribuir	Creo que puedo **contribuir** a este proyecto. *I think I can **contribute** to this project.*
convert	convertir	**Convertiré** la imagen a otro formato. *I **will convert** the image to another format.*
convince	convencer	No soy fácil de **convencer**. *I'm not easy to **convince**.*
criticize	criticar	Mi abuela siempre **critica** todo. *My grandmother always **criticizes** everything.*
demonstrate	demostrar	**Demostraré** cómo se hace. *I **will demonstrate** how it's done.*
destroy	destruir	La guerra puede **destruir** una gran ciudad. *War can **destroy** a large city.*
detect	detectar	Puede **detectar** si aumentas la velocidad. *It can **detect** if you increase your speed.*
devastate	devastar	La casa está **devastada**. *The house is **devastated**.*
evade	evadir	El sospechoso trata de **evadir** a la policía. *The suspect is trying to **evade** the police.*
examine	examinar	¿Puedes **examinar** este lunar? *Can you **examine** this mole?*
foment	fomentar	Intento **fomentar** la lectura en la clase. *I try to **foment** reading in the class.*
implement	implementar	Estoy **implementando** hábitos saludables. *I **am implementing** healthy habits.*
indicate	indicar	¿Me puedes **indicar** dónde está el baño? *Can you **indicate** to me where the bathroom is?*
intensify	intensificar	La sal **intensifica** los sabores. *Salt **intensifies** flavors.*
multiply	multiplicar	No me gusta **multiplicar** números. *I don't like to **multiply** numbers.*
object	objetar	Lamento tener que **objetar** lo que dices. *I am sorry to have to **object** to what you're saying.*
obtain	obtener	El año que viene **obtendré** la certificación. *Next year I **will obtain** the certification.*
occur	ocurrir	El choque seguramente **ocurrirá**. *The crash **will** surely **occur**.*
optimize	optimizar	Debes **optimizar** la velocidad de tu Internet. *You have to **optimize** your internet speed.*
produce	producir	Las abejas **producen** miel. *Bees **produce** honey.*

require	requerir	**Requiere** un certificado. *It **requires** a certificate.*
serve	servir	Es generoso **servir** a los demás cuando es posible. *It is generous to **serve** others when possible.*
supervise oversee	supervisar	Mi jefe **supervisa** a 30 personas. *My boss **supervises** 30 people.*
torture	torturar	No es humano **torturar** a los prisioneros. *It's not humane to **torture** prisoners.*
vandalize	vandalizar	**Han vandalizado** la pared. *They **have vandalized** the wall.*
vibrate	vibrar	Mi celular **está vibrando**. *My cell phone **is vibrating**.*

2. ADJECTIVES III

Below is a list of some common adjectives in Spanish that we need at this level. Use the Anki cards created for this section to help you memorize the meaning of each word in proper contexts. Notice that an adjective must agree with the noun in number and gender.

English	Spanish	Examples
accurate	exacto preciso	La hora de mi reloj no es **exacta**. *The time on my watch isn't **accurate**.*
alone	solo [1]	Me gusta descansar **solo**. *I like to rest **alone**.*
ancient	antiguo	Las pirámides de Egipto son **antiguas**. *Egypt's pyramids are **ancient**.*
attracted	atraído	Las polillas son **atraídas** por la luz. *Moths are **attracted** to light.*
aware conscious	consciente	¿Eres **consciente** de la hora que es? *Are you **aware** of what time it is?*
bitter	amargo	Me gusta mi café **amargo**. *I like my coffee **bitter**.*
blind	ciego	Tengo una víbora **ciega**. *I have a **blind** snake.*
brave	valiente	Eres muy **valiente** al dar ese discurso. *You're very **brave** giving that speech.*

---

[1] When used as an adverb, "**solo**" means *"only"* or *"just,"* and it is synonymous with "**solamente**."

bright (light)	brillante luminoso	Júpiter se ve muy **brillante** en el cielo. *Jupiter looks very **bright** in the sky.*
cloudy	nublado	El día está un poco **nublado**. *The day is a bit **cloudy**.*
covered	cubierto	El suelo está **cubierto** de lodo. *The floor is **covered** in mud.*
cowardly	cobarde	Mi perro es muy **cobarde**. *My dog is very **cowardly**.*
dark	oscuro	Este bosque es muy **oscuro**. *This forest is very **dark**.*
deep profound	profundo	Es la parte **profunda** de la piscina. *This is the **deep** part of the pool.*
depressed	deprimido	Escucho música cuando me siento **deprimido**. *I listen to music when I feel **depressed**.*
depressing	deprimente	Los funerales son **deprimentes**. *Funerals are **depressing**.*
desirable	deseable	Vivir en la ciudad es muy **deseable**. *Living in the city is very **desirable**.*
drunk	borracho	No debes conducir si estás **borracho**. *You must not drive if you are **drunk**.*
exhausted	agotado exhausto	Cortar leña me deja **agotado**. *Cutting firewood leaves me **exhausted**.*
fat	gordo	No es educado decirle a alguien que se ve **gordo**. *It's not polite to tell someone they look **fat**.*
main principal	principal	El punto **principal** es mantener la calma. *The **main** point is to remain calm.*
naked bare	desnudo	Quiero saber la verdad **desnuda**. *I want to know the **naked** truth.*
narrow	estrecho	Cuidado con esas escaleras **estrechas**. *Be careful with those **narrow** stairs.*
own	propio	Me compraré mi **propio** auto. *I'm going to buy my **own** car.*
powerful	poderoso	Esta máquina es muy **poderosa**. *This machine is very **powerful**.*
proud	orgulloso	Estoy **orgulloso** de cómo me quedó la pintura. *I'm **proud** of how my painting came out.*
rainy	lluvioso	Estará **lluvioso** todo el fin de semana. *It will be **rainy** all weekend.*
raw	crudo	Ese pollo está **crudo**. *That chicken is **raw**.*
relaxed	relajado	Dormir me deja **relajado**. *Sleep leaves me **relaxed**.*
relaxing	relajante	Dormir temprano es **relajante**. *Sleeping early is **relaxing**.*

retired	jubilado retirado	Mis abuelos están **retirados**. *My grandparents are **retired**.*
rude	grosero	No debes ser **grosero** con la gente. *You shouldn't be **rude** to people.*
sensitive	sensible	Tengo una piel muy **sensible**. *I have very **sensitive** skin.*
spicy	picante	¡Me encanta la comida **picante**! *I love **spicy** food!*
successful	exitoso	Espero ser **exitoso** en mi nuevo empleo. *I hope I'm **successful** in my new job.*
tender **gentle**	tierno [1]	La carne está bien **tierna**. *The meat is very **tender**.*
thick	grueso	No quiero un trozo **grueso** de pastel. *I don't want a **thick** slice of cake.*
thin	fino [2] delgado [2]	Cortaré las patatas bien **finas**. *I'll cut the potatoes very **thin**.*
tiring	agotador fatigoso cansador	Quedarse despierto toda la noche es **agotador**. *Staying up all night is **tiring**.*
united	unido	Están **unidos** contra el enemigo. *They are **united** against the enemy.*
valuable	valioso	La vasija de mi abuela es muy **valiosa**. *My grandma's vase is very **valuable**.*
wide	ancho	El sofá es muy **ancho**. *The couch is very **wide**.*
winning	ganador	Tiene la receta **ganadora**. *He has the **winning** recipe.*
wise	sabio	Mi profesor es muy **sabio**. *My professor is very **wise**.*

In addition to the above new adjectives, we add a few more English cognates that are easy to memorize.

English	**Spanish**	**Examples**
approximate	aproximado	¿Puedes calcular la demora **aproximada**? *Can you calculate the **approximate** delay?*
arrogant	arrogante	La gente **arrogante** no me agrada. *I don't like **arrogant** people.*

---

[1] The adjective "**tierno**" *(tender)* can also refer to human behavior, e.g., "**Ellos son tiernos con sus hijos**" *(They are tender with their children)*.

[2] Although "**fino**" and "**delgado**" can be synonyms, we use "**delgado**" more often with persons and animals, whereas "**fino**" is used more often with objects.

attractive	atractivo	Esta es una oferta **atractiva**. *This is an **attractive** offer.*
calm	calmado	Me siento **calmado** cuando paseo por la playa. *I feel **calm** when I go for a walk on the beach.*
defined	definido	Tus rizos son muy **definidos**. *Your curls are very **defined**.*
double	doble	Si trabajo el sábado, me pagan el **doble**. *If I work on Saturday, I get paid **double**.*
emotional	emocional	Los dramas me ponen **emocional**. *Dramas make me **emotional**.*
equivalent	equivalente	Un par es **equivalente** a dos. *A pair is **equivalent** to two.*
financial	financiero	Mi situación **financiera** es privada. *My **financial** situation is private.*
independent	independiente	Los jóvenes desean ser más **independientes**. *Young people wish to be more **independent**.*
intense	intenso	Ese perfume es muy **intenso** para mí. *That perfume is very **intense** to me.*
limited	limitado	El espacio del patio es **limitado**. *The patio's space is **limited**.*
logical	lógico	Esta explicación no es **lógica**. *This explanation is not **logical**.*
major	mayor	Mi **mayor** logro han sido mis calificaciones. *My **major** accomplishment has been my grades.*
maximum	máximo	Lleno la botella a su capacidad **máxima**. *I fill the bottle to its **maximum** capacity.*
medical	médico	Tengo un problema **médico**. *I have a **medical** issue.*
minimum	mínimo	No se recomienda solo hacer lo **mínimo**. *It's not recommended to just do the **minimum**.*
modest	modesto	Ese millonario es muy **modesto**. *That millionaire is very **modest**.*
multiple	múltiples	He pedido de ese lugar **múltiples** veces. *I've ordered from that place **multiple** times.*
oppressive	opresivo	Es difícil vivir bajo un régimen **opresivo**. *It is difficult to live under an **oppressive** regime.*
ridiculous	ridículo	¡Mi respuesta será **ridícula**! *My answer will be **ridiculous**!*
separate	separado	Sus padres están **separados**. *His parents are **separated**.*
sexual	sexual	El acoso **sexual** es totalmente inaceptable. ***Sexual** harassment is totally unacceptable.*
similar	similar parecido	Mis hermanos y yo somos muy **similares**. *My siblings and I are very **similar**.*

solid	sólido	La superficie no se ve **sólida**. *The surface doesn't look **solid**.*
technical	técnico	No entiendo los aspectos **técnicos** del auto. *I don't understand the **technical** aspects of the car.*
traditional	tradicional	Me gusta la decoración más **tradicional**. *I like the more **traditional** decor.*
unlimited	ilimitado	Lo que se puede aprender es **ilimitado**. *What can be learned is **unlimited**.*
valid	válido	Yo creo que tiene una razón **válida**. *I believe that he has a **valid** reason.*

3. RELIGION I

Below is some vocabulary related to *religion*, or "**la religión**," that you may need:

God	**Dios**	*angel*	**ángel**[m]
Koran	**Corán**[m]	*belief*	**creencia**[f]
Islam	**islam**[m]	*church*	**iglesia**[f]
Muslim	**musulmán**[m]	*faith*	**fe**[f]
Bible	**Biblia**[f]	*devil*	**diablo**[m]
Christianity	**cristianismo**[m]	*demon*	**demonio**[m]
Christian	**cristiano**[m]	*heaven*	**paraíso**[m]
Christmas	**Navidad**[f]	*hell*	**infierno**[m]
Catholic	**católico**[m]	*miracle*	**milagro**[m]
Catholicism	**catolicismo**[m]	*mosque*	**mezquita**[f]
Protestantism	**protestantismo**[m]	*pope*	**papa**[m]
Protestant	**protestante**[m]	*prayer*	**oración**[f]
Judaism	**judaísmo**[m]	*prophet*	**profeta**[m]
Jewish	**judío**[m]	*sin*	**pecado**[m]
Buddhism	**budismo**[m]	*soul*	**alma**[f]
Buddhist	**budista**[m]	*atheism*	**ateísmo**[m]
Hinduism	**hinduismo**[m]	*atheist*	**ateo**[m]
Hindu	**hindú**[m]	*Satan*	**Satán**[m]

4. MEDIA I

The *media*, a singular word in English, is a plural word in Spanish, that is, "**los medios**." Here is some related vocabulary:

advertising	**publicidad**[f]	*press*	**prensa**[f]
antenna	**antena**[f]	*public TV*	**televisión pública**

cable TV	**televisión por cable**	*radio station*	**estación**[f] **de radio**
cinema	**cine**[m]	*rumor*	**rumor**[m]
documentary	**documental**[m]	*scandal*	**escándalo**[m]
fact check	**revisión**[f] **de hechos**	*soap opera*	**telenovela**[f]
magazine	**revista**[f]	*television*	**televisión**[f] **tele**[f]
movie	**película**[f]	*TV channel*	**canal**[m] **(de tele)**
news	**noticias**[f]	*TV series*	**serie**[f] **(de tele)**
news report	**informe**[m] **de noticias**	*TV show*	**programa**[m] **(de tele)**
newspaper	**periódico**[m] **diario**[m]	*voice*	**voz**[f]

5. HOUSE I

Here we learn a set of vocabulary related to the *house*, or "**la casa**," in Spanish:

address	**dirección**[f]	*glass (of water)*	**vaso**[m]
alarm clock	**despertador**[m]	*glue*	**pegamento**[m] **cola**[f]
armchair	**sillón**[m]	*ground floor*	**planta baja**[f]
bag	**bolsa**[f]	*headboard*	**cabecera**[f]
balcony	**balcón**[m]	*kettle*	**hervidor**[m 1] **tetera**[f 1]
basement	**sótano**[m]	*key*	**llave**[f]
basin	**lavabo**[m]	*kitchen*	**cocina**[f]
basket	**cesta**[f] **canasta**[f]	*knife*	**cuchillo**[m]
bathroom	**baño**[m]	*ladle*	**cucharón**[m]
bathtub	**bañera**[f]	*lamp*	**lámpara**[f]
bed	**cama**[f]	*living room*	**sala**[f] **de estar**
bedroom	**dormitorio**[m] **recámara**[f]	*mail*	**correo**[m]
blanket	**manta**[f] **cobija**[f]	*mirror*	**espejo**[m]
book	**libro**[m]	*outlet (electricity)*	**toma**[f] **de corriente**
bottle	**botella**[f]	*oven*	**horno**[m]

---

[1] In some South American countries, "**pava**[f]" and "**caldera**[f]" are also used.

bowl	**cuenco**^m **tazón**^m **bol**^m	*painting*	**pintura**^f **cuadro**^m
box	**caja**^f	*photo*	**foto**^f **fotografía**^f
carpet	**alfombra**^f	*pillow*	**almohada**^f
ceiling	**techo**^m	*refrigerator*	**refrigerador**^m **heladera**^f
cellar	**bodega**^f	*roof*	**tejado**^m
chair	**silla**^f	*room*	**habitación**^f **cuarto**^m
chimney	**chimenea**^f	*saucepan*	**cacerola**^f
cigar	**cigarro**^m	*scale (kitchen)*	**balanza**^f
cigarette	**cigarrillo**^m	*sink*	**fregadero**^m
clock	**reloj**^m	*sofa*	**sofá**^m **diván**^m
cup	**taza**^f **copa**^f	*spoon*	**cuchara**^f
desk	**escritorio**^m	*stairs*	**escalera**^f
dishes *plates*	**platos**^m	*stove*	**estufa**^f **fogón**^m **cocina**^f
door	**puerta**^f	*study (room)*	**despacho**^m
extractor	**extractor**^m	*table*	**mesa**^f
fan	**ventilador**^m	*telephone*	**teléfono**^m
faucet	**grifo**^m **llave**^f	*thing*	**cosa**^f
floor	**piso**^m	*towel*	**toalla**^f
fork	**tenedor**^m	*trash* *garbage*	**basura**^f
freezer	**congelador**^m	*wall*	**pared**^f
frying pan	**sartén**^f [1]	*wardrobe*	**armario**^m **guardarropa**^m
garage	**garaje**^m	*window*	**ventana**^f

[1] Although the Real Academia Española (RAE) classifies it as a feminine noun, it is considered masculine in many parts of Latin America, whereas in Spain it is considered feminine.

6. SPORTS I

Sport, or "**el deporte**," contains a lot of vocabulary that we encounter in our daily life. Here we have some commonly used ones. If you are interested in *soccer*, or "**el fútbol**," you can refer to **Appendix D** for a more extensive set of vocabulary. In addition, an extra set of flashcards dedicated to soccer vocabulary is available for readers who purchased this book, for free for a limited time, at https://www.adrosverse.com/books-and-flashcards/ using the same coupon code provided in **Appendix A**.

ball	**balón**[m] **pelota**[f] **bola**[f]	*national team*	**selección**[f]
baseball	**béisbol**[m]	*offside*	**fuera de juego**
basketball	**baloncesto**[m]	*period*	**período**[m]
boxing	**boxeo**[m]	*punch*	**puñetazo**[m] **trompada**[f]
championship	**campeonato**[m]	*race*	**carrera**[f]
chess	**ajedrez**[m]	*referee*	**árbitro**[m]
court *field*	**cancha**[f]	*round*	**ronda**[f]
draw (tie)	**empate**[m]	*scorer*	**goleador**[m]
entry *admission*	**entrada**[f]	*shot (soccer)*	**tiro**[m] **disparo**[m]
exercise	**ejercicio**[m]	*stadium*	**estadio**[m]
game	**juego**[m]	*swimming*	**natación**[f]
goal [1]	**gol**[m]	*team*	**equipo**[m]
in top shape	**en plena forma**	*tennis*	**tenis**[m]
injury	**lesión**[f]	*trainer* *coach*	**entrenador**[m]
locker room	**vestuario**[m]	*training*	**entrenamiento**[m]
match	**partido**[m]	*wound*	**herida**[f]

---

[1] Another common term for *"goal"* is "**tanto**[m]," e.g., "**marcar un tanto**" *(to score a goal)*. An impressive goal is a "**golazo**[m]." Referring to the structured net, also called *"goal"* in English, we use "**portería**[f]" or "**arco**[m]."

7. COLORS II

Some more colors and color-related words to add to your Spanish vocabulary are:

burgundy	**borgoña**[m,f] **burdeos**[m,f]	*shade*	**sombra**[f]
magenta	**magenta**[m,f]	*tone*	**tono**[m]
pink	**rosa**[m,f] **rosado**[m]	*violet*	**violeta**[m,f]

8. TECHNOLOGY

Let us go over some vocabulary related to *technology* or "**la tecnología**":

alert	**alerta**[f]	*key (code)*	**clave**[m]
appliance	**aparato**[m]	*keyboard*	**teclado**[m]
atom	**átomo**[m]	*integrated circuit*	**circuito integrado**
attachment	**archivo adjunto**	*laboratory*	**laboratorio**[m]
backup file	**archivo de respaldo**	*laptop*	**portátil**[m]
battery	**batería**[f]	*network*	**red**[f]
binary	**binario**[m]	*password*	**contraseña**[f] **clave**[m]
button	**botón**[m]	*patent*	**patente**[f]
cable	**cable**[m]	*permission*	**permiso**[m]
calculator	**calculadora**[f]	*printer*	**impresora**[f]
camera	**cámara**[f]	*program*	**programa**[m]
CD player	**reproductor de CD**	*reminder*	**recordatorio**[m]
cell phone	**celular**[m]	*remote control*	**control remoto**[m]
charger	**cargador**[m]	*satellite*	**satélite**[m]
circuit	**circuito**[m]	*search*	**búsqueda**[f]
code	**código**[m]	*screen*	**pantalla**[f]
computer	**computadora**[f][1]	*short circuit*	**cortocircuito**[m]
database	**base**[f] **de datos**	*speaker*	**altavoz**[m]
domain	**dominio**[m]	*symbol*	**símbolo**[m]
downloading	**descarga**[f]	*telescope*	**telescopio**[m]
email	**correo electrónico**[m] **email**[m]	*testing*	**prueba**[f]
energy	**energía**[f]	*transmitter*	**transmisor**[m]

[1] The word "**computadora**[f]" is commonly used in Latin America, although "**computador**[m]" is also used is some countries like Chile and Colombia. In Spain, the word "**ordenador**[m]" is used instead.

file	**archivo**[m]	*uploading*	**carga**[f]
fuse	**fusible**[m]	*volume*	**volumen**[m]
headphones	**auriculares**[m]	*weblink*	**enlace**[m]
home appliances	**electrodomésticos**[m]	*wire*	**alambre**[m]
input (device)	**entrada**[f]	*wireless*	**inalámbrico**[m]

9. TRAVEL

Travel, or "**el viaje,**" is another important topic with commonly used vocabulary, such as:

adventure	**aventura**[f]	*outskirts*	**afueras**[f]
accommodation	**alojamiento**[m]	*passenger*	**pasajero**[m]
arrival	**llegada**[f]	*passport*	**pasaporte**[m]
carry-on luggage	**equipaje**[m] **de mano**	*pharaoh*	**faraón**[m]
customs	**aduana**[f]	*public transportation*	**transporte público**[m]
delay	**demora**[f] **retraso**[m] **tardanza**[f]	*remote zone*	**zona alejada**[f]
departure	**salida**[f]	*resort (vacation)*	**complejo turístico**[m]
duty (tariff)	**aranceles**[m]	*security safety*	**seguridad**[f]
duty-free	**libre de impuestos**	*souvenir*	**recuerdo**[m] **souvenir**[m]
guide	**guía**[m,f]	*suitcase*	**maleta**[f] **valija**[f]
holidays vacation	**vacaciones**[f]	*tour*	**gira**[f] **excursión**[f]
itinerary	**itinerario**[m]	*tourist*	**turista**[m,f]
journey	**viaje**[m] **recorrido**[m]	*traveler*	**viajero**[m]
luggage	**equipaje**[m]	*trip*	**viaje**[m]

10. LANGUAGE

There is a subtle difference between "**el idioma**" and "**el lenguaje,**" both meaning *language.* Whereas "**idioma**" is used to describe the real spoken language, e.g., "**el idioma español**" *(the*

Spanish language), "**lenguaje**" is used to describe the way and the ability of humans and other beings to communicate, e.g., "**el lenguaje oral**" *(oral language).* To describe computer languages, we also use "**lenguaje,**" e.g., "**el lenguaje Java**" *(the Java language).* Here is some vocabulary related to language:

acronym	**acrónimo**ᵐ	*native*	**nativo**ᵐ
adjective	**adjetivo**ᵐ	*noun*	**sustantivo**ᵐ
alphabet	**alfabeto**ᵐ	*paragraph*	**párrafo**ᵐ
Arabic	**árabe**ᵐ	*passage*	**pasaje**ᵐ
auxiliary	**auxiliar**ᵐ	*passive*	**pasivo**ᵐ
clause	**cláusula**ᶠ	*phrase*	**frase**ᶠ
conjunction	**conjunción**ᶠ	*Portuguese*	**portugués**
conjugation	**conjugación**ᶠ	*preposition*	**preposición**ᶠ
dialect	**dialecto**ᵐ	*pronoun*	**pronombre**ᵐ
dictionary	**diccionario**ᵐ	*proverb*	**refrán**ᵐ **proverbio**ᵐ
discourse	**discurso**ᵐ	*semantics*	**semántica**ᶠ
emphasis	**énfasis**ᵐ	*sentence*	**oración**ᶠ
figurative	**figurativo**ᵐ	*slang*	**jerga**ᶠ
fluency	**fluidez**ᶠ	*subjunctive*	**subjuntivo**ᵐ
fluent	**fluido**ᵐ	*suffix*	**sufijo**ᵐ
grammar	**gramática**ᶠ	*superlative*	**superlativo**ᵐ
Hindi	**hindi**ᵐ	*syllable*	**sílaba**ᶠ
idiom	**modismo**ᵐ	*tale*	**cuento**ᵐ
indicative	**indicativo**ᵐ	*translation*	**traducción**ᶠ
infinitive	**infinitivo**ᵐ	*Urdu*	**urdu**ᵐ
interjection	**interjección**ᶠ	*verb*	**verbo**ᵐ
letter	**letra**ᶠ	*verb tense*	**tiempo verbal**ᵐ
level	**nivel**ᵐ	*vocabulary*	**vocabulario**ᵐ
Mandarin	**mandarín**ᵐ	*vowel*	**vocal**ᵐ
mood	**modo**ᵐ	*word*	**palabra**ᶠ

LEVEL IV: INTERMEDIATE

I. Introductory Topics & Grammar

At this intermediate level, we encounter new topics, some familiar thanks to our knowledge of English and some new and unique to the Spanish language. Use the Anki cards to reinforce these topics in your memory with reviews and exercises.

1. DEGREES OF COMPARISON

In this lesson, we will examine different ways of comparing nouns, indicating their equality, inequality, or the extreme degree of an adjective. We will study the comparison of equality, comparison of inequality, and superlatives.

Comparison of Equality

The two most common expressions in this category are:

1. **tan** + (adjective/adverb) + **como** …   *as (adjective/adverb) as …*

Este auto es **tan** caro **como** una casa.	*This car is **as** expensive **as** a house.*
Ella es **tan** alta **como** su hermana.	*She is **as** tall **as** her sister.*
Él habla **tan** claro **como** un profesor.	*He speaks **as** clearly **as** a teacher.*

2. **tanto/-a** + (noun) + **como** …   *as much/many (noun) as …*

Él tiene **tanto** dinero **como** un millonario.	*He has **as much** money **as** a millionaire.*
Hay **tanta** gente acá **como** en Londres.	*There are **as many** people here **as** in London.*

Comparison of Inequality

The following formula is used to express inequality when comparing two adjectives, adverbs, or nouns:

más/menos … **que** …   *more/less … than …*

For example:

Ella es **más** alta **que** su hermana.	*She is taller than her sister.*
Él habla **más** claro **que** un profesor.	*He speaks more clearly than a teacher.*
Él tiene **más** dinero **que** el presidente.	*He has more money than the president.*
Somos **menos** ricos **que** nuestros padres.	*We are less rich than our parents.*
Él habla **menos** claro **que** un profesor.	*He speaks less clearly than a teacher.*
Él tiene **menos** paciencia **que** mi hermano.	*He has less patience than my brother.*

There are a few exceptions to the above formula:

bueno	*good*	**mejor**	*better*
malo	*bad*	**peor**	*worse*
viejo	*old*	**mayor**	*older*
joven	*young*	**menor**	*younger*
grande	*large*	**mayor**	*larger*
pequeño	*small*	**menor**	*smaller*

It is also common to hear "**más grande**" and "**más pequeño**" in a less formal speech, which mean *"larger/older"* and *"smaller/younger,"* respectively.

Superlatives

There are two ways to express the large or extreme degrees of an adjective.

1. Relative Superlatives

el/la/los/las + **más/menos** + (adjective)	*the* + *most/least* + (adjective)

Inserting a noun between the definite article "**el/la/los/las**" and "**más/menos**" is optional.

Ella es **la más** inteligente de su clase.	*She is **the most** intelligent in her class.*
Somos **los menos** afectados por la crisis.	*We are **the least** affected by the crisis.*
Es **el** tema **más** importante en el país.	*This is **the most** important topic in the country.*
Es **el** político **menos** corrupto del parlamento.	*He is **the least** corrupt politician in the parliament.*

The same exceptions used in the comparison of inequality still apply here.

bueno	*good*	mejor	*best*
mal	*bad*	peor	*worst*
viejo	*old*	mayor	*oldest*
joven	*young*	menor	*youngest*
grande	*large*	mayor	*largest*
pequeño	*small*	menor	*smallest*

2. Absolute Superlatives

One can express an absolute superlative by simply preceding the adjective with an adverb such as **"muy"** (*very*) or **"extremamente/sumamente"** (*extremely*). For example:

Este estadio está **muy** frío.	*This stadium is **very** cold.*
El café está **sumamente** caliente.	*The coffee is **extremely** hot.*

Another way is to use a prefix like **"super-"** or **"re-,"** for example:

Este estadio está **super**frío.	*This stadium is **super** cold.*
El café está **re**caliente.	*The coffee is **super**-hot.*

Another common way to express absolute superlatives is by using adjectives ending in **"-ísimo"** for masculine or **"-ísima"** for masculine, translated as *"very," "quite,"* or *"extremely."* It is usually constructed by removing the vowel at the end of the adjective (if it exists) and attaching the suffix **"-ísimo."**

grande	*large*	grandísimo	*extremely large*
mucho	*much/many*	muchísimo	*too much/many*
bueno	*good*	buenísimo	*really good*
pequeño	*small*	pequeñísimo	*tiny*
caliente	*hot*	calientísimo [1]	*extremely hot*

---

[1] Both the regular form **"calientísimo"** and the irregular form **"calentísimo"** are acceptable.

Adjectives ending with **"g,"** which sounds like *"get,"* or **"c,"** which sounds like *"cold,"* undergo orthographic change to maintain the same pronunciation.

| amargo | *bitter* | **amarg<u>u</u>ísimo** | *extremely bitter* |
| **fresco** | *fresh* | **fres<u>qu</u>ísimo** | *extremely fresh* |

Adjectives ending with "**z**" undergo an orthographic change that replaces "**z**" with "**c**."

| **feliz** | *happy* | **feli<u>c</u>ísimo** | *extremely happy* |

Adjectives ending with "**-ble**" must change the suffix to "**-bil**" before adding "**-ísimo**."

| **amable** | *kind* | **ama<u>bil</u>ísimo** | *extremely kind* |
| **miserable** | *miserable* | **misera<u>bil</u>ísimo** | *extremely miserable* |

Some adjectives ending with "**-n**" take the suffix "**-císimo**" instead of "**-ísimo**."

| **joven** | *young* | **joven<u>c</u>ísimo** | *extremely young* |

Many qualitative adjectives ending with "**-ro**," "**-ra**," or "**-re**" take the suffix "**-érrimo**" instead of "**-ísimo**."

íntegro	*full* *whole*	**integ<u>érrimo</u>**	*extremely full*
áspero	*harsh*	**asp<u>érrimo</u>**	*extremely harsh*
mísero	*meager*	**mis<u>érrimo</u>**	*extremely meager*
libre	*free*	**lib<u>érrimo</u>**	*extremely free*
salubre	*healthy*	**salub<u>érrimo</u>**	*extremely healthy*

Other adjectives are completely irregular.

amigo	*friend*	**amicísimo** [1]	*extremely friendly*
antiguo	*ancient*	**antiquísimo**	*extremely ancient*
fiel	*faithful*	**fidelísimo**	*extremely faithful*
sabio	*wise*	**sapientísimo**	*extremely wise*
sagrado	*sacred*	**sacratísimo**	*extremely sacred*
simple	*simple*	**simplicísimo**	*extremely simple*

---

[1] A more common alternative form is "**amiguísimo**."

2. PAST TENSE: PRETERITE & IMPERFECT

There are two past tenses in Spanish that are translated as the simple past tense in English. In this lesson, we will have a short introduction about the difference between the two tenses, and we will learn their conjugation. The two tenses are called the *preterite tense* and the *imperfect tense*. Knowing which one to use is usually a challenge for Spanish learners.

Uses

The *preterite tense* is used to describe:

1. Completed actions that have definite beginning and end points, usually identified by expressions such as: **"ayer"** *(yesterday)*, **"anoche"** *(last night)*, **"la semana pasada"** *(last week)*, **"en 1852"** *(in 1852)*, etc.
2. Actions that lasted a defined duration of time, usually identified by expressions such as: **"por dos horas"** *(for two hours)*, **"toda la noche"** *(all night)*, **"tres veces"** *(three times)*, **"de la una hasta las tres"** *(from one to three o'clock)*, **"el otro día"** *(the other day)*, etc.

On the other hand, we use the *imperfect tense* to describe:

1. Habits in the past.
2. Description of people, places, and objects in the past.
3. Time and age in the past.
4. Actions that were continuously happening when another action interrupted in the past.

Conjugation

Before diving into examples, let us look at the conjugation of the imperfect and the preterite.

1. Preterite Tense

Regular verbs in the preterite are conjugated as follows:

	-ar ending hablar	-er ending comer	-ir ending vivir
yo	habl**é**	com**í**	viv**í**
tú	habl**aste**	com**iste**	viv**iste**

él/ella/usted	habl**ó**	com**ió**	viv**ió**
nosotros/-as	habl**amos**	com**imos**	viv**imos**
vosotros/-as	habl**asteis**	com**isteis**	viv**isteis**
ellos/ellas/ustedes	habl**aron**	com**ieron**	viv**ieron**

Notice that the "**nosotros/-as**" conjugation is the same as that of the present tense, e.g., "**nosotros hablamos**" can mean *"we speak"* or *"we spoke,"* depending on the context.

There are quite a few verbs that are irregular in the preterite tense. We will focus here on six important verbs and cover the rest in **Level V, Lesson 1**.

	ser	ir	dar	tener	estar	hacer
yo	fui	fui	di	tuve	estuve	hice
tú	fuiste	fuiste	diste	tuviste	estuviste	hiciste
él/ella/usted	fue	fue	dio	tuvo	estuvo	hizo
nosotros/-as	fuimos	fuimos	dimos	tuvimos	estuvimos	hicimos
vosotros/-as	fuisteis	fuisteis	disteis	tuvisteis	estuvisteis	hicisteis
ellos/ellas/ustedes	fueron	fueron	dieron	tuvieron	estuvieron	hicieron

Notice that the verbs "**ser**" and "**ir**" have the same conjugation in the preterite. The verbs "**ser**," "**ir**," and "**dar**" have unique patterns of conjugation in the preterite and thus must be memorized. On the other hand, there are a few other irregular verbs that are conjugated in the preterite in a manner similar to "**tener**," "**estar**," and "**hacer**." We will cover many of these irregular verbs in **Level V, Lesson 1**.

2. Imperfect Tense

Regular verbs in the imperfect are conjugated as follows:

	-ar ending hablar	-er ending comer	-ir ending vivir
yo	habl**aba**	com**ía**	viv**ía**
tú	habl**abas**	com**ías**	viv**ías**
él/ella/usted	habl**aba**	com**ía**	viv**ía**
nosotros/-as	habl**ábamos**	com**íamos**	viv**íamos**
vosotros/-as	habl**abais**	com**íais**	viv**íais**
ellos/ellas/ustedes	habl**aban**	com**ían**	viv**ían**

There are only three verbs that are irregular in the imperfect. These verbs are:

	ser	ir	ver
yo	era	iba	veía
tú	eras	ibas	veías
él/ella/usted	era	iba	veía
nosotros/-as	éramos	íbamos	veíamos
vosotros/-as	erais	ibais	veíais
ellos/ellas/ustedes	eran	iban	veían

Examples

Let us now look at some examples and determine when to use the imperfect and when to use the preterite. It takes practice, but hopefully, these examples are a good start to illustrate the difference.

*I **visited** my mother last night.* Yo **visité** a mi madre anoche.	Preterite	Action with defined time in the past (last night)
*I **was** at the gym for two hours.* **Estuve** en el gimnasio durante dos horas.	Preterite	Action with defined time in the past (for two hours)
*I **talked** to her the other day.* **Hablé** con ella el otro día.	Preterite	Action with defined time in the past (the other day [1])
*When I was a child, I **used to live** in a village.* De niña **vivía** en un pueblo.	Imperfect	Habit in the past, indicated by *"used to"*
*My school professor **was** tall.* Mi profesor de la escuela **era** alto.	Imperfect	Description in the past
*When I **was** 15 years old, I used to play tennis.* Cuando **tenía** 15 años, jugaba al tenis.	Imperfect	Time and age in the past
*I **was** at work when you called me.* **Estaba** en el trabajo cuando me llamaste.	Imperfect	Actions continuously happening in the past when another action interrupted

---

[1] Although *"the other day"* may seem vague and undefined, it is considered a defined time from a grammatical viewpoint.

In general, use the preterite if you are talking about actions with a defined time or period in the past. Look for expressions such as: *yesterday, last night, last week, ago, in 1994, from … to …, two times, for three hours, the other day,* etc. These expressions may not be explicitly used, but the meaning can implicitly refer to a defined time or period in the past, which necessitates the use of the preterite.

On the other hand, use the imperfect when you see phrases such as: *"when I was a child," "when I was younger," "when I was 15 years old,"* etc.

Cuando era joven, podía correr mucho.	*When I was young, I could run a lot.*
De niño me gustaba la fruta.	*When I was a child, I used to like fruits.*
Cuando era un adolescente, tomaba café.	*When I was a teenager, I used to drink coffee.*

Also, use the imperfect when comparing the present to the past, for example:

Hoy en día es fácil viajar, **pero antes** era muy difícil.	*Today it is easy to travel,* **but before,** *it used to be difficult.*

Another important use of the imperfect tense is to express a past intention of doing something that does not end up being done in the present. These are expressions such as *"I was going to …," "I was thinking of …,"* and *"I wanted to …."*

The general formula of such expressions is as follows:

> *Imperfect tense* of (**"ir a," "pensar,"** or **"querer"**) + *infinitive*

For example:

Iba a llamarte, pero me dormí.	***I was going to*** *call you, but I fell asleep.*
Pensaba en salir, pero ya es muy tarde.	***I was thinking of*** *going out, but it's already too late.*
Quería venir, pero tuve un accidente.	***I wanted to*** *come, but I had an accident.*

3. CONJUNCTIONS

Conjunctions are important components of any language as they allow the speaker to join sentences and convey useful meanings.

The most common conjunctions in Spanish are:

Conjunction	Meaning	Example
y	*and*	Me gusta la primavera **y** el verano. *I like spring **and** summer.*
o	*or*	Voy a tomar café **o** té. *I am going to drink tea **or** coffee.*
si	*if*	**Si** estoy cansado, no voy a salir. ***If** I am tired, I won't go out.*
pero mas sino	*but*	Quiero dormir **pero** no puedo. *I want to sleep, **but** I can't.* Yo trabajo, **mas** no tengo dinero. *I work, **but** I have no money.* No voy el sábado **sino** el domingo. *I won't go on Saturday, **but rather** on Sunday.*
según	*according to*	**Según** los médicos, el café no es malo. ***According to** the doctors, coffee is not bad.*
excepto salvo	*except*	Voy al gimnasio todos los días **excepto** los viernes. *I go to the gym every day **except** Friday.*
entonces	*then*	Bueno, **entonces** te voy a esperar. *Okay, **then** I will wait for you.*
sin embargo	*however*	Estoy cansado. **Sin embargo**, puedo salir contigo. *I am tired. **However**, I can go out with you.*
no obstante	*nevertheless*	El clima es seco; **no obstante**, a veces llueve. *The climate is dry. **Nevertheless**, sometimes it rains.*
para que a fin de que	*so that* *in order to*	Resumiré el libro **para que** puedas entenderlo. Resumiré el libro **a fin de que** puedas entenderlo. *I will summarize the book **so that** you can understand it.*
porque	*because*	Estudio español **porque** quiero vivir en México. *I study Spanish **because** I want to live in Mexico.*
a causa de	*because of*	No podemos salir **a causa de** la nieve. *We can't go out **because of** the snow.*
en vez de en lugar de	*instead*	**En vez de** salir hoy, vamos a ver una película. ***Instead of** going out tonight, we'll watch a movie.*
pues puesto que ya que	*since* *because* *for*	Voy al café, **pues** tengo bastante tiempo libre. Voy al café, **puesto que** tengo bastante tiempo libre. Voy al café, **ya que** tengo bastante tiempo libre. *I'll go to the coffee shop **since** I have enough free time.*
dado que	*given that*	Es un momento importante, **dado que** el ganador se lo lleva todo. *This is an important moment, **given that** winner takes all.*

por lo tanto	*therefore*	Era tarde; **por lo tanto,** no salimos anoche. *It was late; **therefore**, we didn't go out last night.*
de lo contrario	*otherwise*	Espero que no llueva; **de lo contrario,** no salimos. *I hope it doesn't rain; **otherwise**, we don't go out.*
aunque	*although* *even if*	Entiendo lo que dijo, **aunque** no puedo explicarlo. *I understand what he said, **although** I can't explain it.*
a pesar de	*in spite of* *despite*	**A pesar de** ser bajo, es un muy buen jugador. ***Despite** being short, he is a very good player.*
como	*as* *since*	**Como** hace frío, voy a llevar mi abrigo. ***As** it is cold, I will wear my coat.*
así que	*so*	Es difícil decidir, **así que** hay que pensarlo. *It is difficult to decide, **so** one must think about it.*
es decir	*in other words* *that is*	Hablo inglés y español, **es decir**, soy bilingüe. *I speak English and Spanish, **in other words**, I'm bilingual.*
siempre que con tal (de) que	*provided that* *as long as*	Te ayudaré **siempre que** lo necesites. Te ayudaré **con tal de que** lo necesites. *I will help you **as long as** you need it.*
mientras (que)	*while* *as long as*	Compremos algo **mientras** estamos aquí. *Let's buy something **while** we are here.*
o ... o ... ya sea ... o ...	*either... or...*	Bueno, **o** nos vamos ahora **o** más tarde. Bueno, nos vamos **ya sea** ahora **o** más tarde. *Okay, we **either** leave now **or** later.*
ni ... ni ...	*neither ...* *nor ...*	Mi italiano no es **ni** bueno **ni** malo. *My Italian is **neither** good **nor** bad.*
además de	*besides*	**Además de** la comida, pediré bebidas también. ***Besides** food, I will order drinks too.*
aparte de	*apart from*	**Aparte de**l clima, no me gusta este lugar. ***Apart from** the weather, I don't like this place.*
a diferencia de	*unlike*	**A diferencia de** usted, no sé alemán. ***Unlike** you, I don't know German.*

❖ If the word following "**y**" *(and)* starts with an "**i**" or has the *"ee"* sound, e.g., "**hijo**" *(son)* at the beginning of the word, the "**y**" is replaced with "**e**," e.g., "**español e inglés**" *(Spanish <u>and</u> English)*, "**hijos e hijas**" *(sons <u>and</u> daughters)*, etc. An exception to this rule is if the word starts with a diphthong, such as "**ie**" or "**io**" sounds, e.g., "**agua y hielo**" *(water and ice)*.

❖ If the word following "**o**" *(or)* starts with an "**o**" or has the "**o**" sound (e.g., "**hogar**") at the beginning of the word, the "**o**" is replaced with "**u**," e.g., "**siete u ocho**" *(seven <u>or</u> eight)*, "**ayer u hoy**" *(yesterday <u>or</u> today)*.

❖ The words **"pero,"** **"mas,"** and **"sino"** can all mean *"but."* However, **"pero"** is the one you will encounter the most in daily life. The word **"mas"** is considered formal and is used more in written Spanish. Finally, the word **"sino"** is used to mean *"but"* or *"but rather"* when the first part of the sentence is negative, e.g., **"No es invierno sino verano"** (*It is not winter but summer*).

❖ Both **"para que"** and **"a fin de que"** mean *"so that"* or *"in order to."* However, **"para que"** is more commonly used, while **"a fin de que"** is considered more formal.

❖ The conjunctions **"para que,"** **"a fin de que,"** **"siempre que,"** **"con tal (de) que,"** and **"mientras que"** are usually followed by the subjunctive mood as will be explained in **Level IV, Lesson 7** and **Level V, Lesson 5**.

❖ The conjunction **"aunque"** means *"although"* or *"even though"* if followed by indicative mood, and means *"even if"* if followed by subjunctive mood. More on this is covered in **Level VI, Lesson 5**.

4. REFLEXIVE PRONOUNS & VERBS

A verb is considered reflexive if the subject and the object are the same. This means that the subject is doing the action to itself, not to something or someone else. For instance, *"I wash myself"* is reflexive, while *"I wash my car"* is not reflexive.

Some verbs in Spanish are commonly used in the reflexive form. Let us take one example that we are familiar with. The verb **"llamar"** means *"to call,"* e.g., **"Mi mamá me llama todos los viernes"** (*My mom calls me every Friday*). However, the reflexive form of the verb **"llamarse,"** which literally means *"to call oneself,"* is used to express one's name. For instance, **"Me llamo Carlos"** means *"My name is Carlos,"* which is literally *"I call myself Carlos."*

There are many verbs in Spanish that have reflexive forms. We will discuss some examples; however, let us first learn how to conjugate reflexive verbs.

	Object Personal Pron.	e.g., llamar
yo	me	llamo
tú	te	llamas
él/ella/usted	se	llama
nosotros/-as	nos	llamamos
vosotros/-as	os	llamáis
ellos/ellas/ustedes	se	llaman

As shown in the table, we add the object personal pronoun before the verb. Note that the subject and object personal pronouns are of the same gender and number because the subject and the object are essentially the same.

When the verb is used in reflexive form, the infinitive ends in **"se,"** e.g., **"llamarse."** Here are more examples of reflexive verbs.

abrigarse	*to bundle up*	**aburrirse**	*to get bored*
afeitarse	*to shave*	**alegrarse (de)**	*to be glad (about)*
bañarse	*to take a bath*	**cansarse**	*to get tired*
cuidarse	*to take care of oneself*	**disgustarse (de)**	*to become upset (about)*
despertarse	*to wake up*	**divertirse**	*to have fun*
distraerse	*to distract oneself*	**enamorarse**	*to fall in love*
emborracharse	*to get drunk*	**fijarse en**	*to take notice of*
enojarse (con)	*to get mad (at)*	**levantarse**	*to get up*
lavarse	*to wash oneself*	**olvidarse**	*to forget*
maquillarse	*to put on makeup*	**quedarse**	*to stay*
peinarse	*to comb one's hair*	**reponerse**	*to get well or to recover*
sentarse	*to sit down*	**sentirse**	*to feel*
subirse	*to get up*	**torcerse**	*to twist or sprain*
vestirse	*to get dressed*	**volverse**	*to become*

Let us look at some examples:

Bañarse en la tina es relajante.	***Bathing*** *in the tub is relaxing.*
Me aburro rápido en casa.	*I **get bored** fast at home.*
Ella siempre **se despierta** temprano.	*She always **wakes up** early.*
Ayer **nos divertimos** mucho.	*We **had** a lot of **fun** yesterday.*

One can add the reflexive pronoun to verbs that are not regularly reflexive to make them reflexive, for example:

hablarse	*to speak to oneself*	**verse**	*to see oneself*
escribirse	*to write to oneself*	**comprarse**	*to buy for oneself*
compararse	*to compare oneself*	**escucharse**	*to listen to oneself*

Some verbs are used *only* in reflexive form, for example:

arrepentirse	*to repent*	**atreverse a**	*to dare*
darse cuenta de	*to realize*	**jactarse de**	*to boast*
quejarse de	*to complain about*	**suicidarse**	*to commit suicide*

Some verbs change their meaning when they are used in reflexive form, for example:

aburrir	*to bore*	**aburrirse**	*to get bored*
acordar	*to agree*	**acordarse**	*to remember*
acostar	*to lay down or put to bed*	**acostarse**	*to lie down or go to bed*
casar	*to join in marriage*	**casarse con**	*to get married to*
despedir	*to fire or dismiss*	**despedirse**	*to say goodbye*
dormir	*to sleep*	**dormirse**	*to fall asleep*
ir	*to go*	**irse**	*to leave or go away*
morir	*to die from a sudden event, such as war or accident*	**morirse**	*to die from natural causes or die figuratively (e.g., of love)*
negar	*to deny*	**negarse**	*to refuse*
parecer	*to seem*	**parecerse**	*to resemble*
poner	*to put*	**ponerse**	*to put on*
probar	*to try or to taste*	**probarse**	*to try on*
quitar	*to take away*	**quitarse**	*to take off (shoes, clothes, etc.)*

Some verbs do not change their meaning but imply emphasis when used in the reflexive form. These cases are hard to translate into English.

comer	*to eat*	Quiero **comer** esta torta.	*I want to **eat** this cake.*
comerse	*to eat up or devour*	Quiero **comerme** esta torta.	*I want to **eat up** this cake.*

The verb "Quedar" and its reflexive form "Quedarse"

The verb "**quedar**" and its reflexive form, "**quedarse**," are very common verbs in Spanish and can have different meanings depending on the context. We will cover some of the possible meanings of both verbs.

The following are some of the most common meanings of the verb "**quedar**" with examples:

Meaning	Examples	
to remain or to be left	¿**Queda** comida para mañana? *Is there any food **left** for tomorrow?*	Solo **quedan** dos asientos. *Only two seats **are left**.*
to be located	¿Dónde **queda** tu oficina? *Where **is** your office?*	Perú **queda** en América del Sur. *Peru **is located** in South America.*
to meet or to plan to meet	¿Dónde **quedamos** hoy? *Where shall we **meet** today?*	**Quedaré** con un cliente mañana. *I will **meet** with a client tomorrow.*
to suit or to fit	Te **quedan** bien estos zapatos. *These shoes **fit** you well.*	Ya no me **queda** esta camisa. *This shirt doesn't **fit** me anymore.*
to finish (competition)	**Quedarán** últimos en el grupo. *They **will finish** last in the group.*	**Quedó** segundo en la carrera. *He **finished** second in the race.*
to become [1] or to end up	**Quedó** huérfano hace 5 años. *He **became** an orphan 5 years ago.*	**Quedé** cansado después del viaje. *I **ended up** tired after the trip.*
to appear or look	No quiero **quedar** como un idiota. *I don't want to **look** like an idiot.*	Lo ayudó y **quedó** como un héroe. *He helped him and **looked** like a hero.*

---

[1] There are many verbs in Spanish that are translated as *"to become."* We will cover these verbs in more detail in **Level VI, Lesson 6**.

On the other hand, here are two common meanings of the reflexive verb "**quedarse**" in different contexts:

Meaning	Examples	
to stay	Me **quedé** con mi mamá ayer. *I **stayed** with my mom yesterday.*	Nos **quedaremos** en el hotel. *We **will stay** in the hotel.*
to keep	Puede **quedarse** con el cambio. *You can **keep** the change.*	**Me** lo **quedaré** como recuerdo. *I **will keep** it as a souvenir.*

In addition, **"quedar"** and **"quedarse"** can have different meanings when used in some common idioms in Spanish. For more on the use of idioms in Spanish, you can refer to **Appendix E**.

5. The Verb "Soler"

The verb **"soler"** has no exact equivalent in English but can mean *"usually"* or *"used to."* It indicates that an action is frequent in the present or was frequent in the past. Because it is used to describe a repeated action, when used in the past, only the imperfect tense is used.

	Present	**Imperfect**
yo	sue**lo**	sol**ía**
tú	sue**les**	sol**ías**
él/ella/usted	sue**le**	sol**ía**
nosotros/-as	sol**emos**	sol**íamos**
vosotros/-as	sol**éis**	sol**íais**
ellos/ellas/ustedes	sue**len**	sol**ían**

The conjugated **"soler"** is followed by a verb in the infinitive form, for example:

Yo **suelo** ir al gimnasio tres veces por semana.	I **usually** go to the gym three times a week.
Mi hermano **solía** tomar café todas las mañanas.	My brother **used to** drink coffee every morning.
Suele llover mucho en esta región.	It **usually** rains a lot in this region.
Suelo llegar temprano a la clase.	I **usually** arrive early to the class.
Solíamos ir a la playa con más frecuencia en verano.	We **used to** go to the beach more often in the summer.
Solían juntarse más en el pasado.	They **used to** get together more in the past.

6. Time Expressions: Todavía, Aún, Ya, Hace, Acabar, and Desde

In this section, we will learn more advanced time expressions that are common in Spanish.

1.   "Todavía," "Aún," and "Ya"

When followed by a verb in the present tense, both "**todavía**" and "**aún**[1]" generally mean *"still"* in affirmative and negative expressions. Both "**todavía**" and "**aún**" can also mean *"yet"* in a negative expression when followed by a verb in the present perfect tense, for example:

Todavía vivo en España.	I *still live in Spain.*
Todavía no hablo bien inglés.	I *still don't speak English well.*
Todavía no he vuelto a casa.	I *haven't returned home* **yet**.

One can think of "**ya**" as the opposite response to "**todavía no**" and of "**ya no**" as the opposite response to "**todavía**." Below are some examples in both the present tense and the present perfect tense:

a) Present Tense ("**ya no**" as the opposite of "**todavía**")

Todavía vivo en España.	I *still live in Spain.*
Ya no vivo en España.	I *don't live in Spain* **anymore**.

b) Present Tense ("**ya**" as the opposite of "**todavía no**")

Todavía no hablo bien inglés.	I *still don't speak English well.*
Ya hablo bien inglés.	I **already** *speak English well.*

c) Present Perfect Tense ("**ya**" as the opposite of "**todavía no**")

Todavía no he vuelto a casa.	I *haven't returned home* **yet**.
Ya he vuelto a casa.[2]	I *have* **already** *returned home.*

In addition, "**ya**" can mean *"now"* or *"shortly"* if it is followed by a verb in the present tense that implies a future action. A common

---

[1] Notice the accent on the "**u**" in "**aún**." The word "**aun**" without an accent on the "**u**" can have other meanings depending on the context, for example:

- "Ayudó mucho, **aun** como amigo" *(He helped a lot, **even** as a friend).*
- "No vino nadie, **ni aun** mi hermano" *(No one came, **not even** my brother).*
- "**Aun cuando** estoy enfermo, voy al trabajo" *(**Even if** I am sick, I go to work).*
- "**Aun así**, no es possible" *(**Even so**, it is not possible).*

[2] In Latin American Spanish, it is common to use the preterite with "**ya**" to describe finished actions, e.g., "**Ya volví a casa**" *(I have already returned home).* The English equivalent, however, still uses the present perfect to express the same meaning.

expression representing this case is "**ya voy**," which means *"I'm coming."* Similarly, "**ya vuelvo**" means *"I will return shortly."*

Keep in mind that the above cases are not the only uses of "**ya**." There are many other cases in which it is used to express emphasis, frustration, or other sentiments where literal translation is often difficult, e.g., "**Ya lo creo**" *(I think so)*, "**¡Basta ya!**" *(Enough is enough!)*.

The expression "**ya que**" is often translated as *"considering that"* or *"since,"* e.g., "**Ya que estás aquí, podemos hablar**" *(Since you are here, we can talk)*.

2. "Hace"

The verb "**hacer**" can be used to describe something that happened in the past. Depending on the context, it can mean the equivalent of *"ago"* or *"for,"* as shown in the following examples:

❖ Actions that happened and ended in the past:

Hace tres meses **que** hablé con mi hermana.	*It was three months **ago** that I talked with my sister.*
Me desperté **hace** 15 minutos.	*I woke up 15 minutes **ago**.*

❖ Actions that started in the past and continue into the present:

Hace 10 meses **que** hablamos.	*It's **been** 10 months since we have been talking.*
Trabajo aquí **desde hace** dos años.	*I've **been** working here for two years.*

❖ Actions that happened in the past and were interrupted in the past:

Hacía 5 años **que** trabajaba allí cuando cerraron la empresa.	*It's **been** 5 years that I used to work there when they closed the company.*
Trabajaba allí desde **hacía** 5 años cuando cerraron la empresa.	*I used to work there **for** 5 years when they closed the company.*

3. "Acabar"

The verb "**acabar**" is an important verb that expresses the timing of an action.

❖ If used on its own, the verb **"acabar"** often means *"to finish or complete"* or *"to use up or exhaust the supplies of,"* for example:

Yo **acabé** mis estudios el último año.	I **finished** my studies last year.
Debemos **acabar** las sobras antes de cocinar.	We must **finish** the leftovers before cooking.

❖ The verb can also be in the reflexive form **"acabarse,"** which means *"to reach an end"* or *"to run out or run its course before dying off,"* for example:

El partido **se acabó**.	The match **ended**.
Se acabó la leche de la nevera.	The milk in the fridge **ran out**.
Si **se acaba** todo eso, me iré de vacaciones.	If all this **ends**, I'll go on vacation.

❖ The verbal expression **"acabar de"** followed by the infinitive is used to describe an event that has just finished in the present, for example:

Acabo de llegar a casa.	I **have just arrived** home.
Ella **acaba de** comer.	She **has just finished** eating.

If the expression **"acabar de"** is used to describe something in the distant past that had just finished when another event took place, the imperfect tense of the verb **"acabar"** is used, for example:

Acababa de llegar a la casa cuando él me llamó.	I **had just arrived** home when he called me.
Ellos **acababan de comer** cuando llegamos.	They **had just finished eating** when we arrived.

❖ The verbal expression **"acabar por"** in the *preterite* followed by the infinitive is used to describe the meaning of finally doing something or ending up doing something unexpectedly, for example:

Yo **acabé por** ir a Italia.	I **ended up** going to Italy.
Tú **acabaste por** hacer la tarea.	You **finally** did the task.
Acabamos por viajar solos.	We **ended up** traveling alone.

❖ The verbal expression **"acabar con"** in the preterite tense followed by the infinitive means *"to finish off," "to put an end to,"* or *"to ruin."*

Tú **acabaste con** nuestra amistad.	*You **ruined** our friendship.*
La guerra **acabó con** nuestros planes.	*The war **ruined** our plans.*
La lluvia **acabó con** el partido.	*The rain **finished off** the match.*

4. **"Desde"**

Depending on the context, **"desde"** can mean *"since"* or *"from."*

❖ If used to indicate the location or place from which the action originates, it is translated as *"from,"* for example:

Trabajo **desde** la oficina.	*I work **from** the office.*
Hacemos compras **desde** casa.	*We do the shopping **from** home.*
Me gusta ver la ciudad **desde** arriba.	*I like seeing the city **from** above.*

❖ If used to indicate time, it is usually translated as *"since,"* for example:

Desde que era niño, he jugado al fútbol.	***Since** I was a child, I have played football.*
Desde entonces, no fuimos allá.	***Since** then, we didn't go there.*

There are some exceptions where **"desde"** can be translated as *"from,"* even though it indicates time, for example:

Desde hoy en adelante, voy a ir al gimnasio.	***From** now on, I'll go to the gym.*
Te dije eso **desde** el principio.	*I told you that **from** the beginning.*

7. PRESENT SUBJUNCTIVE I

All the tenses we have encountered so far were in the indicative mood. The indicative mood is what we use to express facts. This is the mood we encounter often. There are five moods in total in Spanish: infinitive, indicative, subjunctive, imperative, and conditional. The subjunctive mood is used to express opinion, possibility, and feelings such as fear, doubt, hope, desire, etc.

Remember that the present indicative is formed as follows:

	-ar ending **hablar**	-er ending **comer**	-ir ending **vivir**
yo	habl**o**	com**o**	viv**o**
tú	habl**as**	com**es**	viv**es**
él/ella/usted	habl**a**	com**e**	viv**e**
nosotros/-as	habl**amos**	com**emos**	viv**imos**
vosotros/-as	habl**áis**	com**éis**	viv**ís**
ellos/ellas/ustedes	habl**an**	com**en**	viv**en**

On the other hand, the present subjunctive is formed as follows:

We begin from the *first-person singular in the present indicative*, i.e., **"hablo," "como," "vivo,"** etc., and we extract the stem **"habl-," "com-," "viv-,"** etc. Then, we add the endings shown in the table below. Note that verbs ending in **"er"** or **"ir"** are conjugated in the same way in the present subjunctive.

	-ar ending **hablar**	-er ending **comer**	-ir ending **vivir**
yo	habl**e**	com**a**	viv**a**
tú	habl**es**	com**as**	viv**as**
él/ella/usted	habl**e**	com**a**	viv**a**
nosotros/-as	habl**emos**	com**amos**	viv**amos**
vosotros/-as	habl**éis**	com**áis**	viv**áis**
ellos/ellas/ustedes	habl**en**	com**an**	viv**an**

You must remember to use the stem from the first-person **"yo"** form in the present indicative, not the stem from the infinitive. This is especially important with verbs that are irregular in the first-person **"yo"** form in the present indicative. For example, use the stem from **"yo tengo"** to use the verb **"tener"** in the present subjunctive. Below are some examples:

	tener **teng-**	**querer** **quier-**	**jugar** **jueg-**	**dormir** **duerm-**	**conocer** **conozc-**
yo	tenga	quiera	juegue	duerma	conozca
tú	tengas	quieras	juegues	duermas	conozcas
él/ella/usted	tenga	quiera	juegue	duerma	conozca
nosotros/-as	tengamos	queramos	juguemos	durmamos	conozcamos
vosotros/-as	tengáis	queráis	juguéis	durmáis	conozcáis
ellos/ellas/ustedes	tengan	quieran	jueguen	duerman	conozcan

Notice that, in these examples, the verbs "**querer**," "**jugar**," and "**dormir**" change the conjugation stem in the "**nosotros/-as**" and "**vosotros/-as**" forms.

Because we start the conjugation from the stem of the "**yo**" form of the present indicative, the present subjunctive carries over the same stem change: "**e**" to "**i**," "**e**" to "**ie**," "**o**" to "**ue**," "**u**" to "**ue**," and "**i**" to "**ie**." To form the present subjunctive, the "**nosotros/-as**" and "**vosotros/-as**" forms use the stem after removing these changes. Sometimes a slight change is applied, such as using the stem "**durm-**" instead of "**dorm-**" with the verb "**dormir**."

The following verbs are irregular in the subjunctive:

	ir	ser	estar	saber	dar	haber
yo	vaya	sea	esté	sepa	dé	haya
tú	vayas	seas	estés	sepas	des	hayas
él/ella/usted	vaya	sea	esté	sepa	dé	haya
nosotros/-as	vayamos	seamos	estemos	sepamos	demos	hayamos
vosotros/-as	vayáis	seáis	estéis	sepáis	deis	hayáis
ellos/ellas/ustedes	vayan	sean	estén	sepan	den	hayan

The subjunctive is usually used in subordinate clauses that use the conjunction *"that,"* where the main clause expresses opinions and feelings such as fear, doubt, hope, desire, etc.

	Examples
Impersonal opinion	**Es importante que** comas bien. *It is important that you eat well.*
Happiness	**Me alegro de que** estés bien. *I'm glad you are well.*
Doubt	**Tengo dudas de que** vaya a llover hoy. *I doubt that it will rain today.*
Hope	**Espero que** estés feliz. *I hope that you are happy.*
Desire	**Quiero que** estudies bien. *I want you to study well.*

Expressing Opinions

Knowing when to use the indicative mood and when to use the subjunctive mood when expressing an opinion in Spanish can be a little tricky. Nevertheless, these are the main guidelines:

1. Impersonal Opinions

For impersonal opinions, such as *"it is important that …,"* *"it is good that …,"* and *"it is bad that …,"* we generally use the subjunctive mood, for example:

Es importante que visites a tu familia.	***It is important that*** *you visit your family.*
Es bueno que estés aquí hoy.	***It is good that*** *you are here today.*

However, if the impersonal opinion expresses some sense of certainty, such as *"it is true that …"* and *"it is obvious that …,"* the indicative mood is used, for example:

Está claro que vamos a ganar este partido.	***It is clear that*** *we are going to win this match.*
Es obvio que no estoy interesado.	***It is obvious that*** *I am not interested.*
Es verdad que quiero salir hoy.	***It is true that*** *I want to go out today.*

If the above expressions are in the negative, the subjunctive mood must be used, for example:

No es verdad que quiera salir hoy.	***It is not true that*** *I want to go out today.*

2. Personal Opinions

If the main clause expresses an opinion in the negative, the subordinate clause is in the subjunctive mood, for example:

No pienso que esta casa sea muy grande.	***I don't think that*** *this house is too big.*
No creo que haya gente viviendo allí.	***I don't believe that*** *there are people living there.*
No me parece que ella hable español.	***It doesn't seem to me that*** *she speaks Spanish.*

If the main clause is in the affirmative, the subordinate clause must be in the indicative, not in the subjunctive mood, for example:

Pienso que esta casa es muy grande.	***I think that*** *this house is too big.*
Creo que hay gente viviendo allí.	***I believe that*** *there are people living there.*
Me parece que ella habla español.	***It seems to me that*** *she speaks Spanish.*

Note also that it is the main clause that determines the use of the indicative or the subjunctive. For instance, in the sentence "**Creo que ella no habla español**," we use the indicative because the main clause "**Creo que**" is in the affirmative.

Expressing Possibilities

Most expressions that express the possibility of something being one way or the other can use indicative or subjunctive mood without any preference, for example:

Tal vez **salgo/salga** hoy.	*Perhaps I* **will go out** *today.*
Quizás **hablamos/hablemos** mañana.	*Maybe we* **talk** *tomorrow.*
Probablemente **voy/vaya** al parque solo.	*I* **will** *probably* **go** *to the park alone.*
Posiblemente **vienes/vengas** tarde.	*Possibly you* **will come** *late.*

A notable exception that only uses the indicative is "**a lo mejor**" (*maybe*), for example:

No hay nadie aquí. A lo mejor **están** en el parque.	*There is no one here. Maybe they* **are** *at the park.*

Expressing Desires, Wishes, Feelings, Requests, and Recommendations

In general, desires, wishes, feelings, and requests are expressed in the subjunctive mood, for example:

Quiero que coman con nosotros.	*I* ***want you to*** *eat with us.*
Espero que nos veamos pronto.	*I* ***hope that*** *we see each other soon.*
Me alegro de que **estés bien.**	*I'm* ***glad*** *you are well.*
Te pido que me ayudes a preparar la cena.	*I* ***ask you to*** *help me prepare dinner.*
Te ruego que no fumes en casa.	*I* ***beg you*** *not* ***to*** *smoke at home.*
Te recomiendo que vayas a la playa.	*I* ***recommend that*** *you go to the beach.*

Note that when a verb is used to express desire, the subjunctive mood is only used if the subject and the performer of the action are not the same, for example:

Quiero que **estudies** bien.	*I* *want you to* **study** *well.*

If the subject and the performer of the action are the same, we use the infinitive following the verb, for example:

| Quiero **estudiar** bien. | *I want to* **study** *well.* |

8. PERSONAL "A"

Another example of Spanish grammar that has no equivalent in English is the use of the personal "**a**." The preposition "**a**" is used frequently in Spanish, e.g., "**Voy a la escuela**" *(I go to school).*

A special use of the preposition "**a**" is to precede the direct object when it is a defined person or a group of defined persons. In this case, the preposition "**a**" is known as personal "**a**," for example:

Yo vi **a** mi mamá ayer.	*I saw my mom yesterday.*
Él llama **a** su amigo frecuentemente.	*He calls his friend frequently.*
Ella visitó **a** sus padres anoche.	*She visited her parents last night.*
Comprendo **a** mi profesor fácilmente.	*I understand my professor easily.*

Notice that the English translation of the above sentences has no direct equivalent of the personal "**a**" in Spanish.

If we refer generally, and not specifically to a person, we do not use the personal "**a**," for example:

| Yo vi dos mujeres charlando ayer. | *I saw two women chatting yesterday.* |
| Él necesita un médico inmediatamente. | *He needs a doctor immediately.* |

Generally, a pet is treated as a person in Spanish. The personal "**a**" is used when referring to a pet, but not with ordinary animals, for example:

| Le doy un baño **a** mi gato todos los meses. | *I give my cat a bath every month.* |
| Vi un conejo en el zoológico. | *I saw a rabbit in the zoo.* |

In the first sentence above, the *"cat"* is a pet. Thus, the personal "**a**" is used. On the other hand, the *"rabbit"* in the second sentence is an ordinary animal that does not require the use of the personal "**a**."

Pronouns referring to a person or persons are also treated in the same way as a specific person or persons. Thus, the personal "**a**" is used. This includes each of the following pronouns when used as a direct object referring to people: **"alguien"** (*somebody*), **"nadie"** (*nobody*), **"quien"** (*whom*), **"alguno"** (*some*), and **"ninguno"** (*none*), for example:

| No vi **a** nadie ayer. | *I didn't see anybody yesterday.* |
| Tengo que llamar **a** alguien. | *I have to call someone.* |

If a direct object is personified to express emotion or attachment, the personal **"a"** can be used to imply such emotion, for example:

| Extraño mucho **a** mi país. | *I miss my country a lot.* |
| Abrazaría **a** la almohada como si fuera mi amiga. | *I'd hug my pillow as if it were my friend.* |

The only verbs that generally do not use the personal **"a,"** even when referring to a specific person or persons, are **"haber"** and **"tener,"** for example:

| Hay 15 estudiantes en la clase. | *There are 15 students in the class.* |
| Tengo cinco primos. | *I have five cousins.* |

The only exception to the verb **"tener"** is when it is used to mean holding someone physically or emotionally close to you. In this case, the personal **"a"** is used, for example:

| Cuando hay un problema, tengo **a** mi familia. | *When there is a problem, I have my family.* |
| Tendré **a** mi hermano en los brazos. | *I will have my brother in my arms.* |

9. FUTURE PERFECT TENSE

The future perfect tense in Spanish, similar to its use in English, describes events that will happen and be completed in the future by a certain time or happen after another event is completed in the future. It also uses the auxiliary verb **"haber,"** but in the future tense followed by a past participle. The auxiliary **"haber"** in future tense serves a similar function to the auxiliary *"will have"* in English, e.g., *"I will have done my homework by the time they come."*

The verb **"haber"** in the future form is conjugated as follows:

		-ar ending **hablar**	-er ending **comer**	-ir ending **vivir**
yo	habré			
tú	habrás			
él/ella/usted	habrá			
nosotros/-as	habremos	habl**ado**	com**ido**	viv**ido**
vosotros/-as	habréis			
ellos/ellas/ustedes	habrán			

As we studied in **Level III, Lesson 6**, some verbs have irregular past participle forms.

Let us look at some examples:

		Examples	
yo	habré	Yo **habré visitado** Egipto en enero.	*I **will have visited** Egypt in January.*
tú	habrás	Tú **habrás bebido** el café.	*You **will have drunk** the coffee.*
él/ella/usted	habrá	Ella **habrá hablado** con su madre.	*She **will have spoken** to her mother.*
nosotros/-as	habremos	Nosotros **habremos comido**.	*We **will have eaten**.*
vosotros/-as	habréis	Vosotros **habréis llegado**.	*You **will have arrived**.*
ellos/ellas/ustedes	habrán	Ellos **habrán vivido** aquí.	*They **will have lived** here.*

II. Vocabulary Building

Go over the vocabulary in this section and use the provided Anki cards to study and memorize the new vocabulary efficiently.

1. VERBS IV

Below is a list of verbs that we need at this level:

English	Spanish	Examples
achieve	lograr	**Logró** sus metas para ese mes. *He **achieved** his goals for that month.*
add	añadir agregar	**Añadí** una taza de agua a la mezcla que preparé. *I **added** a cup of water to the mixture that I prepared.*
advise	aconsejar asesorar	Mi amigo me **aconsejó** sobre las universidades el año pasado. *My friend **advised** me about the universities last year.*

apologize	disculparse	**Me disculpo**, lo hice sin querer. *I **apologize**, I did it unintentionally.*
assemble	ensamblar	Vamos a **ensamblar** la mesa más tarde. *We are going to **assemble** the table later.*
avenge	vengar	El héroe quería **vengar** la muerte de su padre. *The hero wanted to **avenge** his father's death.*
avoid	evitar [1]	Yo quería **evitar** verlo en el café. *I wanted to **avoid** seeing him in the café.*
bake	hornear cocer	Acabo de **hornear** esta tarta. *I just **baked** this pie.*
bathe	bañarse	**Bañarse** en la tina es relajante. ***Bathing** in the tub is relaxing.*
bet **gamble**	apostar	Siempre **apostaba** mucho dinero. *He **used to** always **bet** a lot of money.*
bounce	rebotar	Las pelotas de básquetbol **rebotan** mucho. *Basketballs **bounce** a lot.*
brush	cepillar(se)	Iré a **cepillarme** los dientes. *I'm going to **brush** my teeth.*
burn	quemar	No estaba ahí cuando **quemó** la comida. *I wasn't there when he **burned** the food.*
catch up **reach**	alcanzar	Lo **alcanzaré** en la siguiente ronda. *I **will catch up** with him in the next round.*
challenge	retar desafiar	Te **reto** a un duelo. *I **challenge** you to a duel.*
charm	encantar	Me **encantó** desde el comienzo. *It **charmed** me from the beginning.*
chase **pursue**	perseguir	Me **persiguió** un perro de la calle anoche. *A dog from the streets **chased** me last night.*
cheat **(in exam)**	hacer trampa copiar	**Hizo trampa** con las preguntas del último examen. *He **cheated** on the last exam's questions.*
cheat **(deceive)**	engañar	Los magos **engañan** a sus espectadores. *Magicians **cheat** their spectators.*
check [2] **(information)**	verificar comprobar	¿Puedes **verificar** tus respuestas primero? *Can you **check** your answers first?*
claim	reclamar	**Reclamaré** un reembolso. *I **will claim** a reimbursement.*
comb	peinar(se)	¿Puedes **peinarte** los rizos? *Can you **comb** your curls?*

---

[1] The verb "**evitar**" can also mean *"to prevent"* depending on the context.

[2] The verb "**chequear**" which comes from the English verb *"to check"* is also widely used in Latin America.

congratulate	felicitar	No me **felicitó** el día de mi graduación. *She didn't **congratulate** me on my graduation day.*
cut	cortar(se)	**Me cortaré** el cabello bien corto. *I **will cut** my hair really short.*
decrease	disminuir decrecer	Si gastas en eso, tus fondos **disminuirán**. *If you spend on that, your funds **will decrease**.*
delay	retrasar tardar	Los envíos están **retrasados**. *The shipments are **delayed**.*
demand **require**	exigir	Mi trabajo anterior **exigía** que usara uniforme. *My previous job **demanded** that I wear a uniform.*
deserve	merecer	**Mereces** ese premio. *You **deserve** that award.*
develop	desarrollar	Recientemente **desarrollé** un gusto por el café amargo. *I recently **developed** a taste for bitter coffee.*
dial	marcar	**Marcó** el número equivocado. *He **dialed** the wrong number.*
digest	digerir	Me resulta difícil **digerir** la lactosa. *It's hard for me to **digest** lactose.*
doubt	dudar	**Dudo** que puedas terminarte una pizza entera. *I **doubt** you can finish a whole pizza.*
download	descargar	Antes **descargaba** música de manera ilegal. *In the past, I used to **download** music illegally.*
dress	vestir(se)	Es bueno que **se vista** sobriamente. *It's good that he **dresses** soberly.*
embarrass	avergonzar	Mi niño siempre me **avergüenza** en público. *My kid always **embarrasses** me in public.*
enjoy	disfrutar (de) gozar de	**Disfrutaré de** mis vacaciones. *I **will enjoy** my vacation.*
entertain	entretener	Esa obra de anoche me **entretuvo** mucho. *That play last night **entertained** me a lot.*
erase	borrar	**Borré** mis mensajes sin querer. *I **erased** my messages by accident.*
escape	escaparse huirse	Mi ratón **se escapa** de la jaula todo el tiempo. *My mouse **escapes** from its cage all the time.*
fall	caerse	**Me caí** por las escaleras la semana pasada. *I **fell down** the stairs last week.*
fast (food)	ayunar	Hay gente que **ayuna** días enteros. *There are people who **fast** for whole days.*
feel	sentir(se)	**Me siento** feliz y contento de escuchar eso. *I **feel** happy and content to hear that.*
fight **struggle** **wrestle**	luchar	El guerrero **está luchando** por su libertad. *The warrior **is fighting** for his freedom.*

fight **quarrel**	pelear	Los hermanos siempre **pelean**. *Siblings always **quarrel**.*
focus **concentrate**	centrarse concentrarse enfocarse	**Me concentro** mejor si no tengo hambre. *I **focus** better if I'm not hungry.*
freeze	congelar helar	No olvides **congelar** la verdura. *Don't forget to **freeze** the vegetables.*
fry	freír	Voy a **freír** esas patatas. *I'm going to **fry** those potatoes.*
get up	levantarse	¿Puedes **levantarte**? *Can you **get up**?*
grill **roast**	asar	**Asaremos** vegetales en la parrilla. *We **will grill** vegetables on the barbecue.*
guide	guiar	**Me guiaré** con el mapa. *I **will guide myself** with the map.*
have fun	divertirse	La gente va al parque a **divertirse**. *People go to the park to **have fun**.*
heal	curar(se) sanar(se)	Espero que la quemadura **se cure** pronto. *I hope the burn **heals** soon.*
heat up	calentar	La estufa a leña **calentaba** mejor en el pasado. *The wood stove **heated up** better in the past.*
hide	esconder(se) ocultar(se)	**Escondo** mi dinero en el armario. *I **hide** my money in the closet.*
hit **strike**	golpear	Lo **golpeó** un auto mientras cruzaba la calle. *A car **hit** him while he was crossing the street.*
hug **embrace**	abrazar	Lo **abrazó** en el momento en que lo vio. *He **hugged** him the moment he saw him.*
improve	mejorar	**Mejoré** mucho mi estilo en este último año. *I **improved** my style a lot during this last year.*
increase	aumentar incrementar	En verano la temperatura **aumenta** mucho. *In the summer, the temperature **increases** a lot.*
introduce **present**	presentar(se)	¿Puedes **presentarte**? *Can you **introduce yourself**?*
involve	involucrar	No quiero **involucrar** a otra gente en esto. *I don't want to **involve** other people in this.*
launch **throw**	lanzar	El 16 de julio de 1969, EEUU **lanzó** el Apolo 11. *On July 16, 1969, the US **launched** Apollo 11.*
lift **raise**	levantar	**Levantaré** el sofá para revisar. *I **will lift** the couch to check.*
look **appear**	verse lucir	**Se ve** muy bien hoy. *He **looks** very good today.*

look after	cuidar de atender	¿Puedes **cuidar de** tu sobrino hoy? *Can you look after your nephew today?*
lower **descend**	bajar	¿Puedes **bajar** el volumen? *Can you lower the volume?*
manage to	lograr conseguir	**He conseguido** terminar mi trabajo a tiempo. *I have managed to finish my work on time.*
maintain	mantener	La nevera ayuda a **mantener** los alimentos. *The fridge helps in maintaining food.*
marry	casar(se)	Mi prima **se casó** en primavera. *My cousin got married in the spring.*
measure	medir[1]	**Mediré** el largo de tu pie. *I will measure your foot's length.*
melt	derretir fundir	Debes **derretir** el chocolate para utilizarlo. *You have to melt the chocolate to use it.*
miss **(emotionally)**	extrañar	Te **extrañaba**, así que vino a verte. *He missed you, so he came to see you.*
paint	pintar	Le gusta **pintar** paisajes hermosos. *He likes to paint beautiful landscapes.*
park (car)	estacionar[2]	¿Está prohibido **estacionar** aquí? *Is it prohibited to park here?*
place an **order**	pedir encargar	Buenas noches, quiero **encargar** comida. *Good evening, I want to order food.*
protect	proteger	Las mamás oso **protegen** a sus crías. *Mother bears protect their offspring.*
prove	probar[3]	Debes **probar** que puedes hacerlo. *You must prove you can do it.*
punish	castigar	Lo **castigué** por su mal comportamiento anoche. *I punished him due to his bad behavior last night.*
put up with **endure**	aguantar soportar	Odio tener que **soportar** el frío. *I hate having to put up with the cold.*
recognize **acknowledge**	reconocer	No te **reconocí** con ese peinado. *I didn't recognize you with that hairstyle.*
reduce	reducir disminuir	Debes **reducir** la velocidad en calles vecinales. *You must reduce your speed on neighborhood streets.*
register	registrar(se)	Puedes **registrarte** aquí. *You can register here.*

---

[1] The verb "**medir**" is also used to ask about the height, e.g., "**¿Cuánto mides?**" is translated as *"How tall are you?"* although it literally asks about measurement.

[2] The verb "**parquear**" is also used in some parts of Latin America, and the verb "**aparcar**" is used in Spain.

[3] The verb "**probar**" can also mean *"to test"* or *"to taste."*

remember	recordar acordarse	**Recuerdo** el lago que visitamos. *I **remember** the lake we visited.*
replace	reemplazar	**Reemplacé** mi cafetera vieja con una nueva. *I **replaced** my old coffee machine with a new one.*
retire	jubilarse retirarse	**Me jubilaré** en dos años. *I **will retire** in two years.*
return	regresar volver	Mi primo **regresó** de su viaje ayer. *My cousin **returned** from his trip yesterday.*
review **go over**	repasar	**Repasaremos** ese capítulo juntos. *We **will go over** that chapter together.*
ruin	arruinar	El tabaco **arruina** tu salud. *Tobacco **ruins** your health.*
run away	huir escapar	A los niños les gusta **huir** en las tiendas. *Children like to **run away** in stores.*
save **rescue**	salvar rescatar	No pude **salvar** la tarta luego de que se quemó. *I couldn't **save** the pie after it burned.*
save **spare**	ahorrar	**Ahorraré** más dinero para este viaje. *I **will save** more money for this trip.*
scratch **(oneself)**	rascarse	**Me rasqué** la picadura de mosquito casi al instante. *I **scratched** the mosquito bite almost instantly.*
scratch **(surface)**	arañar	Mi gato **araña** los sillones. *My cat **scratches** the armchairs.*
scream **yell**	gritar	No está bien que le **grites** a tu hijo. *It's not right for you to **yell** at your son.*
shave	afeitar(se)	**Me afeitaré** mañana. *I will **shave** tomorrow.*
shine	brillar	¡Ese diamante **brilla** mucho! *That diamond **shines** a lot!*
shoot **fire**	disparar tirar	**Dispara** muy bien. *He **shoots** very well.*
sink	hundir(se)	Creo que ese juguete no **se hundirá**. *I think that toy **will not sink**.*
sit	sentar(se)	Puedes **sentarte** a mi lado. *You can **sit** next to me.*
skate	patinar	Amo **patinar** en invierno. *I love to **skate** in winter.*
ski	esquiar	Es divertido **esquiar** en las montañas. *It's fun to **ski** in the mountains.*
spend **(money)**	gastar	Es genial que no **gastes** tanto en ropa. *It's great that you don't **spend** so much on clothes.*
spend **(time)**	pasar	Amo **pasar** el rato en la playa. *I love to **spend** time on the beach.*

spy	espiar	No es agradable que **espíes** a tus hermanos. *It's not nice of you to **spy** on your siblings.*
stand	estar de pie [1]	No me gusta **estar de pie** en el autobús. *I don't like to **stand** while on the bus.*
stay **remain**	quedarse	¿Quieres **quedarte** a dormir? *Do you want to **stay** over?*
stop [2]	parar(se) detener(se)	Debes **parar** en la esquina. *You have to **stop** at the corner.*
succeed	tener éxito	**Tuve éxito** luego de muchos intentos. *I **succeeded** after many tries.*
suck	chupar	Debes **chupar** por el popote. *You have to **suck** through the straw.*
suffer	sufrir padecer	Mi abuela **sufre** de artritis. *My grandmother **suffers** from arthritis.*
suggest	sugerir	Me **sugirió** que comiera cuatro frutas al día. *He **suggested** that I eat four fruits a day.*
suppose	suponer	**Supongo** que no tienes planes para hoy. *I **suppose** you don't have any plans for today.*
survive	sobrevivir	Mis plantas **sobrevivieron** al invierno pasado. *My plants **survived** last winter.*
suspect	sospechar	Yo **sospechaba** que el viejo era el asesino. *I **suspected** the old man was the killer.*
sustain	sostener	Una vida saludable es fácil de **sostener**. *A healthy life is easy to **sustain**.*
swear	jurar	El testigo **ha jurado** decir la verdad. *The witness **has sworn** to tell the truth.*
sweat	sudar	**Sudo** mucho en el gimnasio. *I **sweat** a lot at the gym.*
switch off	apagar	¿Puedes **apagar** la luz? *Can you **switch off** the light?*
tackle **address**	abordar	**Abordaré** este tema en la próxima clase. *I **will address** this subject in the next class.*
take a **shower**	ducharse	¿**Te habrás duchado** para cuando yo llegue? *Will you **have showered** by the time I arrive?*
take apart	desmontar desarmar	**Desarmaré** el armario para la mudanza. *I **will take apart** the closet for the move.*

[1] The verb **"estar de pie"** in this context means *"to be standing in upright position."* To refer to the act of getting up to stand, one must use the verb **"ponerse de pie."**

[2] To use the verb *"stop"* to refer to ceasing an activity, **"dejar de"** is used instead, e.g., **"Debes dejar de fumar"** (*You must stop smoking*).

take out	sacar	¿Puedes **sacar** la basura? *Can you **take out** the trash?*
take (photo)	sacar	¿Me puedes **sacar** una foto? *Can you **take** a photo of me?*
throw	arrojar echar	¡Deja de **arrojar** piedras! *Stop **throwing** rocks!*
tire **exhaust**	cansar fatigar agotar	Cuidar a los niños me **cansa**. *Taking care of children **tires** me.*
tour **roam**	recorrer	Me gustaría **recorrer** la ciudad. *I'd like to **tour** the city.*
treat	tratar	Siempre **trato** a los demás con respeto. *I always **treat** others with respect.*
trip **stumble**	tropezar	Debes tener cuidado de no **tropezar**. *You have to be careful not to **trip**.*
twist	torcer(se)	**Me torcí** el tobillo mientras jugaba al tenis. *I **twisted** my ankle while playing tennis.*
upload	subir cargar	**Subiré** los videos en una hora. *I **will upload** the videos in an hour.*
wake up	despertarse	Me cuesta **despertarme** temprano. *It's hard for me to **wake up** early.*
wear **put on**	llevar vestir ponerse	No olvides **llevar** puesta una bufanda. *Don't forget to **wear** a scarf.*
weigh	pesar	Me **pesaré** el lunes. *I **will weigh** myself on Monday.*
wet	mojar	De niño **mojaba** la cama. *When I was a child, I used to **wet** the bed.*
whistle	silbar pitar	Siempre **silbo** mientras me baño. *I always **whistle** while I bathe.*
worry	preocupar(se)	Siempre **me preocupo** por los exámenes. *I always **worry** about exams.*
worsen	empeorar	La enfermedad de mi abuelo **empeoró** el año pasado. *My grandfather's disease **worsened** last year.*

In addition to the above new verbs, we add a few more English cognates that are easy to memorize.

English	Spanish	Examples
act	actuar	**Actúo** de manera educada siempre. *I always **act** in a polite manner.*

adapt	adaptar(se)	Los niños **se adaptan** rápido en la escuela. *Children **adapt** quickly in school.*
affirm	afirmar	**Afirmó** que está allí. *He **affirmed** he is there.*
alter	alterar	**Alteraré** el vestido un poco. *I **will alter** the dress a bit.*
arrest	arrestar	Lo **arrestaron** por robar. *They **arrested** him for stealing.*
assign **allocate**	asignar	Me **asignaron** la misma tarea tres veces. *They **assigned** me the same task three times.*
capture	capturar	**Capturaron** al ladrón rápidamente anoche. *They **captured** the thief quickly last night.*
cause	causar	No quería **causar** un alboroto. *I didn't want to **cause** a fuss.*
communicate	comunicar(se)	Es más fácil **comunicarse** con un celular. *It's easier to **communicate** with a cell phone.*
connect	conectar(se)	Debes **conectarte** al servidor. *You have to **connect** to the server.*
console	consolar	La tuvo que **consolar** cuando lloraba. *He had to **console** her when she was crying.*
debate	debatir	Van a **debatir** sobre el presupuesto. *They're going to **debate** about the budget.*
declare	declarar	**Declararon** su independencia hace 50 años. *They **declared** their independence 50 years ago.*
dedicate **devote**	dedicar(se)	**Dedico** mi tiempo libre a la escritura. *I **dedicate** my free time to writing.*
deteriorate	deteriorar(se)	Si no cuidas la pintura, **se** puede **deteriorar**. *If you don't take care of the paint, it can **deteriorate**.*
determine	determinar	El gobierno **determina** el presupuesto anual. *The government **determines** the annual budget.*
differ	diferir	El precio **difiere** con el del cartel. *The price **differs** from that on the sign.*
dismantle	desmantelar	Intenté **desmantelar** mi reloj. *I tried to **dismantle** my clock.*
dispense	dispensar	Esta farmacia **dispensa** recetas todo el día. *This pharmacy **dispenses** prescriptions all day long.*
dispute	disputar(se)	**Se están disputando** la herencia. *They **are disputing** the inheritance.*
dissolve	disolver(se)	La sal **se disuelve** bien en agua. *The salt **dissolves** well in water.*
exhibit	exhibir	**Exhibieron** sus obras en la galería el año pasado. *They **exhibited** her works in a gallery last year.*
generate	generar	La represa **genera** electricidad para la ciudad. *The dam **generates** electricity for the city.*

imagine	imaginar(se)	No **me imagino** cómo debe ser. *I can't **imagine** how it must be.*
incorporate	incorporar	Intento **incorporar** más ejercicios a mi rutina. *I try to **incorporate** more exercises into my routine.*
insist	insistir	**Insistió** tanto que lo dejaron entrar. *He **insisted** so much, they let him in.*
invade	invadir	El ejército temía **invadir** la ciudad. *The army feared **invading** the city.*
invent	inventar	¿Quién **inventó** esta tecnología? *Who **invented** this technology?*
mark	marcar	**Marcaron** su pasaporte en el aeropuerto al entrar. *They **marked** his passport at the airport upon entering.*
negotiate	negociar	Los países **negocian** un tratado de comercio. *The countries **negotiate** a trade agreement.*
occupy	ocupar	**Ocuparon** dos asientos en la mesa la última vez. *They **occupied** two seats at the table last time.*
offend	ofender	No quise **ofender**te. *I didn't mean to **offend** you.*
operate	operar	El cirujano **opera** a los pacientes los jueves. *The surgeon **operates** on patients on Thursdays.*
prepare	preparar	Me tengo que **preparar** para el examen mañana. *I have to **prepare** for the exam tomorrow.*
provoke	provocar	No es bueno **provocar** a los animales salvajes. *It's not good to **provoke** wild animals.*
publish	publicar	Voy a **publicar** este poema. *I'm going to **publish** this poem.*
qualify	calificar	No **calificas** para este programa. *You do not **qualify** for this program.*
refrigerate	refrigerar	Debes **refrigerar** el refresco. *You have to **refrigerate** the soda.*
resist	resistirse	No puedo **resistirme** al pastel. *I can't **resist** cake.*
reveal disclose	revelar	Él **revela** cómo es realmente. *He **reveals** how he truly is.*
simulate	simular	La realidad virtual intenta **simular** la vida real. *Virtual reality tries to **simulate** real life.*
subscribe	suscribir(se) [1]	**Se suscribieron** al gimnasio por un año. *They **subscribed** to the gym for a year.*

---

[1] This verb has another acceptable but less common alternative, i.e., "**subscribir(se)**."

2. ADJECTIVES IV

Below is a list of adjectives that we need at this level. Adding them to your vocabulary will improve your comprehension of Spanish speech and writing.

English	Spanish	Examples
accustomed	acostumbrado	Estoy **acostumbrado** al clima frío. *I'm **accustomed** to the cold weather.*
advantageous	ventajoso	Es **ventajoso** ser organizado. *It's **advantageous** to be organized.*
alive	vivo	¡Ese calamar sigue **vivo**! *That squid is still **alive**!*
angry	enojado enfadado	Estaba muy **enojado**. *I was very **angry**.*
asleep	dormido	Me quedé **dormido** en el sillón. *I fell **asleep** on the couch.*
capable of	capaz de	Soy **capaz de** aprobar el examen. *I'm **capable of** passing the exam.*
confused	confundido	Esa pregunta me dejó **confundido**. *That question left me **confused**.*
confusing	confuso	El orden que siguen es muy **confuso**. *The order they follow is very **confusing**.*
conservative	conservador	Hoy, ganó el partido **conservador**. *Today, the **conservative** party won.*
costly	costoso	Ese restaurante es muy **costoso**. *That restaurant is very **costly**.*
credible	creíble	Me pareció una historia **creíble**. *It seemed like a **credible** story to me.*
crushed **smashed**	aplastado	Se utiliza ajo **aplastado** para esta receta. *You use **crushed** garlic for this recipe.*
daily	diario	Comienzo mi rutina **diaria** con el desayuno. *I start my **daily** routine with breakfast.*
dangerous	peligroso	Es **peligroso** salir de noche. *It's **dangerous** to go out at night.*
dead	muerto fallecido	Mi bisabuelo lleva muchos años **muerto**. *My great-grandfather has been **dead** for many years.*
defeated	derrotado	Fui **derrotado** en el juego. *I was **defeated** in the game.*
destroyed	destruido	Los imperios antiguos fueron **destruidos**. *The ancient empires were **destroyed**.*
developed	desarrollado	La trama del libro está bien **desarrollada**. *The book's plot is nicely **developed**.*
disadvantageous	desventajoso	Es **desventajoso** no tener ahorros. *It's **disadvantageous** to not have savings.*

disappointed	decepcionado	Quedé **decepcionado** al ver que no viniste. *I was **disappointed** to see you didn't come.*
disgusting	repugnante asqueroso	Esta mochila huele **asqueroso**. *This backpack smell is **disgusting**.*
distinctive	distintivo	Las vacas tienen un olor **distintivo**. *Cows have a **distinctive** smell.*
doubtful	dudoso	Respondí de manera **dudosa**. *I answered in a **doubtful** manner.*
enormous	enorme	¡Ese elefante es **enorme**! *That elephant is **enormous**!*
entertaining	entretenido	El espectáculo estuvo **entretenido**. *The show was **entertaining**.*
enthusiastic	entusiasta	Este profesor es muy **entusiasta**. *This teacher is very **enthusiastic**.*
entire	entero	Quiero ver el mundo **entero**. *I want to see the **entire** world.*
environmental	ambiental	La polución tiene un impacto **ambiental**. *Pollution has an **environmental** impact.*
excited	emocionado	Estoy **emocionado** por la nueva película. *I'm **excited** for the new movie.*
exciting	emocionante	Las montañas rusas son **emocionantes**. *Roller coasters are **exciting**.*
exhausting	agotador	El senderismo es **agotador**. *Hiking is **exhausting**.*
few	pocos	Tengo **pocos** amigos. *I have **few** friends.*
flat	plano llano	El piso está bien **plano** allí. *The floor is very **flat** there.*
foreign	extranjero	Me gustan los condimentos **extranjeros**. *I like **foreign** condiments.*
free (liberty)	libre	Eres **libre** de hacer lo que quieras. *You are **free** to do whatever you want.*
free (money)	gratis	¡Compra uno, lleva otro **gratis**! *Buy one, get one **free**!*
furnished	amoblado amueblado	El apartamento viene totalmente **amoblado**. *The apartment comes completely **furnished**.*
grateful	agradecido	Estoy **agradecido** a mis padres por todo. *I am **grateful** to my parents for everything.*
guilty	culpable	Me sentí **culpable** después de comer la galleta. *I felt **guilty** after eating the cookie.*
handmade	hecho a mano	Esta manta fue **hecha a mano**. *This blanket was **handmade**.*
handsome	guapo	Mi marido es muy **guapo**. *My husband is very **handsome**.*

hated	odiado	Ese personaje es muy **odiado**. *That character is very **hated**.*
heavy	pesado	Esta mochila está demasiado **pesada**. *This backpack is too **heavy**.*
hidden	escondido oculto	Estaba **escondido** entre las rocas. *It was **hidden** between the rocks.*
humble	humilde	El actor era muy **humilde**. *The actor was very **humble**.*
incredible	increíble	El espectáculo fue **increíble**. *The show was **incredible**.*
jealous	celoso	La hermana mayor estaba **celosa** de la menor. *The older sister was **jealous** of the younger one.*
known	conocido	Es un autor muy **conocido**. *He is a very well-**known** author.*
lazy	perezoso	Mi perro es muy **perezoso**. *My dog is very **lazy**.*
loved	amado	Este es mi **amado** peluche. *This is my **beloved** teddy.*
opposite	opuesto	Se encuentra en el lado **opuesto**. *He's on the **opposite** side.*
picky	exigente	Mi hermana es muy **exigente**. *My sister is very **picky**.*
portable	portátil	Es una consola **portátil**. *It's a **portable** console.*
pregnant	embarazada	Mi prima anunció que está **embarazada**. *My cousin announced that she's **pregnant**.*
quiet **silent** **(persons)**	callado en silencio	Suelo mantenerme **callado** en público. *I tend to remain **quiet** in public.*
satisfied	satisfecho	Comí hasta quedar **satisfecho**. *I ate until I was **satisfied**.*
sour	agrio ácido	Me encantan las gomitas **ácidas**. *I love **sour** gummies.*
sunny	soleado	Ayer estuvo muy **soleado**. *It was very **sunny** yesterday.*
tasty	sabroso	Este pastel está muy **sabroso**. *This cake is very **tasty**.*
unknown	desconocido	Es un restaurante **desconocido**. *It's an **unknown** restaurant.*
used	usado	A veces compro ropa **usada**. *I sometimes buy **used** clothes.*
warm **tepid**	tibio	Me gustaría tomar un café **tibio**. *I would like to have a **warm** coffee.*

| weekly | semanal | Tendremos reuniones **semanales**.
*We'll have **weekly** meetings.* |

In addition to the above new adjectives, we add a few English cognates that are easy to memorize.

English	Spanish	Examples
acceptable	aceptable	La comida estuvo **aceptable**. *The food was **acceptable**.*
ample **broad**	amplio	Tiene **amplio** conocimiento sobre la materia. *He has **broad** knowledge on the matter.*
cellular	celular	El cambio es a nivel **celular**. *The change is at a **cellular** level.*
concise	conciso	El artículo es **conciso**. *The article is **concise**.*
consistent	consistente	Tu argumento debe ser **consistente**. *Your argument must be **consistent**.*
content **pleased** **glad**	contento	Quedó muy **contento** al verte bien. *He was very **pleased** to see you well.*
contrary	contrario	**Contrario** a lo que parece, me gusta el invierno. ***Contrary** to what it seems, I like winter.*
cruel	cruel	Es difícil tratar con personas **crueles**. *It is difficult to deal with **cruel** people.*
effective	efectivo	Es un medicamento muy **efectivo**. *It's a very **effective** medication.*
efficient	eficiente eficaz	Trabaja de manera muy **eficiente**. *He works in a very **efficient** way.*
electrical	eléctrico	Debes tener cuidado con la conexión **eléctrica**. *You must be careful with the **electrical** connection.*
exaggerated	exagerado	Creo que sus estimaciones de costos son **exageradas**. *I believe that their cost estimates are **exaggerated**.*
existent **existing**	existente	Este es el único termo **existente** aquí. *This is the only **existing** thermos here.*
genuine	genuino	Nuestra amistad es **genuina**. *Our friendship is **genuine**.*
impacted	impactado [1]	El planeta fue **impactado** por un cometa. *The planet was **impacted** by a comet.*
impressed	impresionado	Quedé **impresionado** con su voz. *I was **impressed** with his voice.*

---

[1] The adjective "**impactado**" can also mean *"shocked"* or *"impressed."*

impressive	impresionante	El tamaño del edificio es **impresionante**. *The size of the building is **impressive**.*
influenced	influenciado	Su estilo de arte fue **influenciado** por otros. *His art style was **influenced** by others.*
legal	legal	Necesito asesoramiento **legal**. *I need **legal** advice.*
lethal	letal	Fumar mucho puede ser **letal**. *Smoking a lot can be **lethal**.*
modern	moderno	Siempre me asombra la tecnología **moderna**. ***Modern** technology always amazes me.*
nuclear	nuclear	El pueblo cuenta con una planta **nuclear**. *The town relies on a **nuclear** plant.*
obese	obeso	El veterinario me dijo que mi gato es **obeso**. *The vet told me that my cat is **obese**.*
obligatory **mandatory**	obligatorio	Tienen un uniforme **obligatorio**. *They have an **obligatory** uniform.*
offended	ofendido	Resultó muy **ofendido** por lo que ocurrió. *He ended up very **offended** by what happened.*
offensive	ofensivo	Nunca utilizo lenguaje **ofensivo**. *I never use **offensive** language.*
pathetic	patético	Me sentí **patético** con esta vestimenta. *I felt **pathetic** in this outfit.*
preventive	preventivo	Es mejor tomar medidas **preventivas**. *It's better to take **preventive** measures.*
prosperous	próspero	Creo que esta cosecha será muy **próspera**. *I believe this harvest will be very **prosperous**.*
psychological	psicológico	Sus temores son todos **psicológicos**. *His fears are all **psychological**.*
punctual	puntual	Es importante ser **puntual** en el trabajo. *It's important to be **punctual** at work.*
pure	puro	Esta es miel **pura** de las colmenas. *This is **pure** honey from the hives.*
realistic	realista	Siempre me pongo metas **realistas**. *I always set **realistic** goals for myself.*
severe	severo	Los castigos son **severos** en este caso. *The punishments are **severe** in this case.*
specific	específico	Me gustó en ese color **específico**. *I liked it in that **specific** color.*
stupendous **terrific**	estupendo	Pasamos un rato **estupendo** en el parque. *We had a **stupendous** time at the park.*
supreme	supremo	Ha hecho un esfuerzo **supremo** para tener éxito. *He has made a **supreme** effort to succeed.*
temporary	temporario temporal	Debo solicitar una visa de residencia **temporaria**. *I must apply for a **temporary** residence visa.*

trivial	trivial	No te preocupes por cosas **triviales**. *Don't worry over **trivial** things.*
unacceptable	inaceptable	El comportamiento de su gato era **inaceptable**. *His cat's behavior was **unacceptable**.*
unique	único	Su talento es verdaderamente **único**. *His talent is truly **unique**.*
vacant	vacante [1]	Ese cargo lleva años **vacante**. *That position has been **vacant** for years.*
various **several**	varios	Tengo **varias** ollas de ese estilo. *I have **several** pots of that style.*

[1] The word "**vacante**" often refers to a seat or position. To refer to a vacant room or apartment, we use "**desocupado**" *(unoccupied)* or "**disponible**" *(available)*.

3. PEOPLE II

We go over more vocabulary to describe people in our daily life.

accountant	**contador**ᵐ **contable**ᵐ	*leader*	**líder**ᵐ
actor	**actor**ᵐ	*owner*	**dueño**ᵐ **propietario**ᵐ
actress	**actriz**ᶠ	*pharmacist*	**farmacéutico**ᵐ
architect	**arquitecto**ᵐ	*philosopher*	**filósofo**ᵐ
artist	**artista**ᵐ,ᶠ	*poet*	**poeta**ᵐ **poetisa**ᶠ
author	**autor**ᵐ	*police station*	**comisaría**ᶠ
business partner	**socio**ᵐ **de negocios**	*policeman*	**policía**ᵐ
butcher	**carnicero**ᵐ	*programmer*	**programador**ᵐ
cashier	**cajero**ᵐ	*reporter*	**reportero**ᵐ
chauffeur	**chofer**ᵐ	*researcher*	**investigador**ᵐ
chef	**cocinero**ᵐ	*retirement*	**jubilación**ᶠ **retiro**ᵐ
chief	**jefe**ᵐ	*scientist*	**científico**ᵐ
colleague	**colega**ᵐ,ᶠ	*secretary*	**secretario**ᵐ
crowd	**multitud**ᶠ	*singer*	**cantante**ᵐ,ᶠ
dancer	**bailador**ᵐ **bailarina**ᶠ	*society*	**sociedad**ᶠ
designer	**diseñador**ᵐ	*soldier*	**soldado**ᵐ
director	**director**ᵐ	*speaker*	**orador**ᵐ
doctor	**médico**ᵐ	*spy*	**espía**ᵐ,ᶠ
employee	**empleado**ᵐ	*statue*	**estatua**ᶠ

employer	**empleador**[m]	*teacher*	**profesor**[m] **maestro**[m]
engineer	**ingeniero**[m]	*union*	**sindicato**[m]
interview	**entrevista**[f]	*veterinarian*	**veterinario**[m]
journalist	**periodista**[m,f]	*victim*	**víctima**[f]
lawyer	**abogado**[m]	*waiter*	**camarero**[m] **mozo**[m]

4. HEALTH I

Health, or "**la salud**," is always an important topic in any language. Here is some related vocabulary in Spanish:

burn	**quemadura**[f]	*mind*	**mente**[f]
disorder (medical)	**trastorno**[m]	*narcotic*	**narcótico**[m]
drug (narcotic)	**droga**[f] **narcótico**[m]	*needle*	**aguja**[f]
drug (medicine)	**medicina**[f] **fármaco**[m]	*pain*	**dolor**[m]
fever	**fiebre**[f]	*painkiller*	**analgésico**[m]
floss	**hilo dental**[m]	*pill* *lozenge*	**pastilla**[f]
flu	**gripe**[f]	*public health*	**salud pública**[f]
illness	**enfermedad**[f]	*surgery*	**cirugía**[f]
insurance	**seguro**[m]	*symptom*	**síntoma**[m]
medical coverage	**cobertura médica**[f]	*vaccine*	**vacuna**[f]
medication	**medicamento**[m]	*well-being*	**bienestar**[m]

5. LAW

The law, or "**la ley**," usually has its specific set of vocabulary. We go over some important vocabulary here:

acceptance	**aceptación**[f]	*lie*	**mentira**[f]
accomplice	**cómplice**[m,f]	*murder*	**asesinato**[m]
background check	**verificación**[f] **de antecedentes**[m]	*murderer*	**asesino**[m]
bail *bond*	**fianza**[f]	*offense*	**ofensa**[f]
case	**caso**[m]	*pickpocket*	**carterista**[m,f]
clue	**pista**[f]	*prosecutor*	**fiscal**[m]

court	**tribunal**^m **juzgado**^m	*lieutenant*	**teniente**^m
crime	**crimen**^m **delito**^m	*meeting*	**reunión**^f
delinquency	**delincuencia**^f	*mistake*	**error**^m **equivocación**^f
evidence	**evidencia**^f	*patrol*	**patrulla**^f
fault *guilt* *blame*	**culpa**^f	*punishment*	**castigo**^m
fingerprint	**huella dactilar**^f	*quarrel*	**pelea**^f
footprint	**huella**^f	*raid (police)*	**redada**^f
fraud	**fraude**^m **estafa**^f	*records*	**registros**^m **récords**^m
gang	**pandilla**^f **banda**^f **cuadrilla**^f	*report*	**reporte**^m **informe**^m
harassment	**acoso**^m	*request*	**solicitud**^f
hearing	**audiencia**^f	*right*	**derecho**^m
hit *blow*	**golpe**^m	*scammer* *swindler*	**estafador**^m
judge	**juez**^m	*sentence*	**sentencia**^f
jury	**jurado**^m	*suicide*	**suicidio**^m
justice	**justicia**^f	*trial*	**juicio**^m
lawsuit	**demanda judicial**^f **pelito**^m	*witness*	**testigo**^m

6. MEASUREMENTS

The verb *"to measure"* in Spanish is **"medir,"** and *measurement* is **"medición."** Below is some useful vocabulary related to measurements:

angle	**ángulo**^m	*line*	**línea**^f
average	**promedio**^m	*meter*	**metro**^m
barrel	**barril**^m	*mile*	**milla**^f

bundle	**bulto**[m] **lío**[m]	*piece* [1]	**pedazo**[m] **trozo**[m] **pieza**[f]
centimeter	**centímetro**[m]	*pound*	**libra**[f]
circle	**círculo**[m]	*quantity* *amount*	**cantidad**[f]
contents	**contenidos**[m]	*rectangle*	**rectángulo**[m]
degree	**grado**[m]	*sphere*	**esfera**[f]
diameter	**diámetro**[m]	*square*	**cuadrado**[m]
edge	**borde**[m]	*step*	**paso**[m]
form *shape*	**forma**[f]	*temperature*	**temperatura**[f]
fragment	**fragmento**[m]	*ton*	**tonelada**[f]
height	**altura**[f]	*unit*	**unidad**[f]
hole	**agujero**[m]	*weight*	**peso**[m]
inch	**pulgada**[f]	*width*	**ancho**[m] **anchura**[f]
kilometer	**kilómetro**[m]	*yard*	**yarda**[f]

[1] Whereas "**pedazo**" and "**trozo**" are used to refer to a piece of paper, meat, cake, etc., "**pieza**" is used to refer to a piece of music, art, cloth or to a component of a larger construction such as a machine or an engine.

7. HOUSE II

Here, we add more vocabulary related to *the house*, or "**la casa**."

air conditioner	**aire acondicionado**[m]	*light*	**luz**[f]
ashtray	**cenicero**[m]	*lighter*	**encendedor**[m] [2]
ax	**hacha**[f] [3]	*lock*	**cerradura**[f]
bench	**banco**[m]	*mattress*	**colchón**[m]
blender	**licuadora**[f]	*microwave*	**microondas**[m]
bucket	**cubo**[m] **balde**[m]	*napkin*	**servilleta**[f]
calendar	**calendario**[m]	*nail (hardware)*	**clavo**[m]
candle	**vela**[f] **candela**[f]	*pantry*	**despensa**[f]

[2] The word "**mechero**[m]" is also used in Spain.

[3] Even though this is a feminine noun, it takes the definite article "**el**" in the singular form. You can revisit **Level I, Lesson 6** for further review.

chest (container)	**baúl**^m **cofre**^m **acra**^f	*paper tissue*	**pañuelo**^m **de papel**
chores	**quehaceres**^m	*paper towel*	**toalla**^f **de papel**
clay	**arcilla**^f	*plug*	**enchufe**^m
cleaning *cleanliness*	**limpieza**^f	*plumbing* [1]	**plomería**^f **fontanería**^f
cloth	**paño**^m **trapo**^m	*plunger*	**desatascador**^m
coal	**carbón**^m	*pool*	**piscina**^f
column	**columna**^f	*porcelain*	**porcelana**^f
cottage	**cabaña**^f **casita**^f **de campo**	*portrait*	**retrato**^m
crease	**pliegue**^m	*pot (cookware)*	**olla**^f
curtain *drape*	**cortina**^f	*project*	**proyecto**^m
dining room	**comedor**^m	*property*	**propiedad**^f
drain	**desagüe**^m	*rice cooker*	**olla arrocera**^f
driveway	**entrada**^f **de coches**	*saw*	**sierra**^f
dryer	**secadora**^f	*screw*	**tornillo**^m
elevator	**ascensor**^m **elevador**^m	*shelf*	**estante**^m **repisa**^f
fence	**valla**^f **cerca**^f	*shower*	**ducha**^f
fire (incident)	**incendio**^m	*soap*	**jabón**^m
flashlight	**linterna**^f	*strap*	**correa**^f
frame	**cuadro**^m	*tangle*	**maraña**^f
furniture	**muebles**^m	*teaspoon*	**cucharilla**^f
garden	**jardín**^m	*tenant*	**inquilino**^m
gift	**regalo**^m	*tent*	**carpa**^f **tienda**^f
grill	**parrilla**^f	*tray*	**bandeja**^f
hallway	**pasillo**^m **corredor**^m	*toaster*	**tostadora**^f
heating	**calefacción**^f	*toilet paper*	**papel**^m **higiénico**

---

[1] The word "**fontanería**" is used more often in Spain and Central America to refer to the *"plumbing"* profession whereas "**plomería**" is used often in Latin America in general. In addition, some countries in South America use the alternative word "**gasfitería**^f."

hut	**cabaña**[f] **choza**[f]	*toilet*	**inodoro**[m]
instrument	**instrumento**[m]	*tool*	**herramienta**[f]
ironing board	**tabla**[f] **de planchar**	*toothbrush*	**cepillo**[m] **de dientes**
iron	**plancha**[f]	*toothpaste*	**dentífrico**[m]
item	**artículo**[m]	*trashcan*	**bote**[m] **de basura**
jewelry	**joyas**[f]	*tube*	**tubo**[m]
kit	**kit**[m]	*utensil*	**utensilio**[m]
ladder	**escalera**[f]	*utilities*	**servicios públicos**[m]
landlord *owner*	**propietario**[m] **dueño**[m]	*vacuum cleaner*	**aspiradora**[f]
laundry *dirty clothes*	**ropa sucia**[f]	*view*	**vista**[f]
lawn	**césped**[m] **pasto**[m]	*wall (external)*	**muro**[m]
lawn mower	**cortacésped**[m]	*wall (internal)*	**pared**[f]
leak[1] *(gas)*	**escape**[m] **fuga**[f]	*washing machine*	**lavadora**[f]
letter	**carta**[f]	*wax*	**cera**[f]
light bulb	**bombilla**[f]	*yard* *patio*	**patio**[m]

[1] Referring to a *leak in a container* we use "**agujero**[m]," to a *leak in a roof* we use "**gotera**[f]," and to a *leak in a boat* we use "**rotura**[f]." For a *leak of information*, we use "**filtración**[f]."

8. FOOD II

Here is more vocabulary related to *food*, or "**la comida**":

almond	**almendra**[f]	*melon*	**melón**[m]
appetizer	**aperitivo**[m]	*nuts*	**nuez**[f]
avocado	**aguacate**[m] **palta**[f][2]	*onion*	**cebolla**[f]
bacon	**tocino**[m]	*peanut*[3]	**maní**[m] **cacahuete**[m]

[2] The word "**palta**" is often used to refer to *"avocado"* in Argentina, Chile, and Bolivia.
[3] The word "**maní**[m]" is more common in Latin America, whereas "**cacahuete**[m]" is used in Spanish, Mexico, and a few other countries.

beans	**habas**[f] **frijoles**[m]	*pear*	**pera**[f]
blueberry	**arándano**[m]	*pepper*[1] *(fruit)*	**pimiento**[m]
breakfast	**desayuno**[m]	*pistachio*	**pistacho**[m]
burger	**hamburguesa**[f]	*pomegranate*	**granada**[f]
butter	**mantequilla**[f]	*potato*	**papa**[f] **patata**[f]
cabbage	**repollo**[m] **col**[f]	*raspberry*	**frambuesa**[f]
cake	**torta**[f]	*recipe*	**receta**[f]
can	**lata**[f]	*sandwich*	**sándwich**[m]
coconut	**coco**[m]	*seafood*	**mariscos**[m]
corn	**maíz**[m]	*shrimp*	**camarón**[m]
cranberry	**arándano**[m] **agrio**	*soup*	**sopa**[f]
cucumber	**pepino**[m]	*spice*	**especia**[f]
currant	**grosella**[f]	*straw*[2]	**pajita**[f]
dessert	**postre**[m]	*strawberry*	**fresa**[f]
fries	**papas fritas**[f 3]	*sweet potato*	**batata**[f]
lentils	**lentejas**[f]	*takeaway*	**para llevar**
meal	**comida**[f]	*watermelon*	**sandía**[f]

[1] Whereas "**pimiento**[m]" refers to *"pepper"* as a fruit, *"pepper"* as a spice is referred to as "**pimienta**[f]."

[2] The word *"straw"* has other alternatives in many Spanish-speaking countries, e.g. "**popote**[m]" in Mexico, "**pitillo**[m]" in Colombia and Venezuela, "**sorbeto**[m]" in Cuba, "**sorbete**[m]" in Argentina, and "**carrizo**[m]" in Panama.

[3] In Spain, "**patatas fritas**[f]" is often used instead.

9. CLOTHES II

Here we add more vocabulary related to *clothes*, or "**la ropa**."

accessories	**accesorios**[m]	*perfume*	**perfume**[m]
attire	**atuendo**[m]	*raincoat*	**impermeable**[m]
blouse	**blusa**[f]	*sandals*	**sandalias**[f]
bow (knot) *ribbon*	**lazo**[m]	*scarf*	**bufanda**[f] **pañuelo**[m]
bracelet	**pulsera**[f] **brazalete**[m]	*shoes*	**zapatos**[m]
checkered shirt	**camisa a cuadros**	*sideburn*	**patilla**[f]
cleavage	**escote**[m]	*size (clothes)*	**tamaño**[m]
diaper	**pañal**[m]	*size (shoes)*	**talla**[f]
disguise	**disfraz**[f]	*sleeve*	**manga**[f]

dress	**vestido**^m	*socks*	**medias**^f **calcetines**^m
fabric	**tela**^f	*stain*	**mancha**^f
fitting room	**probador**^m	*stockings*	**calcetas**^f **medias**^f
garment	**prenda**^f	*striped shirt*	**camisa rayada**
haircut	**corte**^m **de pelo**	*suit*	**traje**^m
mask	**mascarilla**^f **barbijo**^m	*sweater*	**suéter**^m
necklace	**collar**^m	*swimsuit*	**traje**^m **de baño** [1]
pajamas	**pijama**^f [2]	*tie*	**corbata**^f
pattern	**patrón**^m	*watch*	**reloj**^m **de pulsera**

[1] The word "**malla**^f" is used in some South American countries, and "**bañador**^m" is used in Spain.

[2] The word "**pijama**" is masculine in Spain and the southern part of South America, but feminine in most other Spanish-speaking countries.

10. DIRECTIONS II

Below is some useful vocabulary to describe directions:

alley	**callejón**^m	*destination*	**destino**^m
around the corner	**a la vuelta de la esquina**	*downstairs*	**abajo** **al piso inferior**
arrow	**flecha**^f	*highway*	**autopista**^f **carretera**^f
at the beginning of	**al comienzo de**	*in the middle of*	**en el medio de**
at the corner	**en la esquina**	*neighborhood*	**barrio**^m
at the end of	**al final de**	*next block*	**siguiente cuadra**^f
avenue	**avenida**^f	*side*	**lado**^m
bottom	**fondo**^m	*somewhere*	**en alguna parte**^f **en algún lugar**^m
corner [3]	**esquina**^f **rincón**^m	*upstairs*	**arriba** **al piso superior**

[3] In Spanish, there are two words for *"corner."* If you refer to an *inner* corner, e.g., of a room or an object, use "**rincón**." If you refer to an *outer* corner, such as that of a street, page, table, or in sports like soccer, use "**esquina**."

I. Introductory Topics & Grammar

As you plow through the language to reach this advanced level, take your time to go over the new topics, which will become a little more challenging but much more interesting. Use the Anki cards to reinforce these topics in your memory with reviews and exercises.

1. IRREGULAR VERBS IN THE PRETERITE TENSE

We have previously covered the following irregular verbs in the preterite tense:

	ser	ir	dar	tener	estar	hacer
yo	fui	fui	di	tuve	estuve	hice
tú	fuiste	fuiste	diste	tuviste	estuviste	hiciste
él/ella/usted	fue	fue	dio	tuvo	estuvo	hizo
nosotros/-as	fuimos	fuimos	dimos	tuvimos	estuvimos	hicimos
vosotros/-as	fuisteis	fuisteis	disteis	tuvisteis	estuvisteis	hicisteis
ellos/ellas/ustedes	fueron	fueron	dieron	tuvieron	estuvieron	hicieron

In addition to the above irregular verbs in the preterite, there are a few more verbs and patterns that are useful to memorize. Use your Anki cards to practice more examples until you master this lesson. You can also use the summary in the cheat sheets in **Appendix B** as a quick reference.

Verbs ending in "-ducir" as well as "decir" and "traer"

Verbs ending in "-**ducir**" replace the "**c**" with "**j**" in their stem to form the preterite stem ending in "**duj**-." The verbs "**decir**" and "**traer**" are treated similarly, and their stems are "**dij**-" and "**traj**-," respectively. Notice also that the third-person plural form of these verbs ends in "-**eron**" instead of "-**ieron**."

Examples of verbs in this category include: **"traducir"** (*to translate*), **"producir"** (*to produce*), **"reducir"** (*to reduce*), **"conducir"** (*to drive*), **"introducir"** (*to introduce*), **"deducir"** (*to deduce*), and **"seducir"** (*to seduce*).

	traducir	**producir**	**reducir**	**decir**	**traer**
yo	traduje	produje	reduje	dije	traje
tú	tradujiste	produjiste	redujiste	dijiste	trajiste
él/ella/usted	tradujo	produjo	redujo	dijo	trajo
nosotros/-as	tradujimos	produjimos	redujimos	dijimos	trajimos
vosotros/-as	tradujisteis	produjisteis	redujisteis	dijisteis	trajisteis
ellos/ellas/ustedes	tradujeron	produjeron	redujeron	dijeron	trajeron

Verbs "estar," "tener," and "andar"

The verbs **"estar," "tener,"** and **"andar"** (*to walk* or *to go*) take the stems **"estuv-," "tuv-,"** and **"anduv-,"** respectively.

	estar	**tener**	**andar**
yo	estuve	tuve	anduve
tú	estuviste	tuviste	anduviste
él/ella/usted	estuvo	tuvo	anduvo
nosotros/-as	estuvimos	tuvimos	anduvimos
vosotros/-as	estuvisteis	tuvisteis	anduvisteis
ellos/ellas/ustedes	estuvieron	tuvieron	anduvieron

Verbs that change the first vowel from "a" or "o" to "u"

The two verbs **"haber"** and **"poder"** take the stems **"hub-"** and **"pud-,"** respectively, whereas the verbs **"poner," "saber,"** and **"caber"** (*to fit*) undergo an extra-letter change and take the stems **"pus-," "sup-,"** and **"cup-,"** respectively.

	haber	**poder**	**poner**	**saber**	**caber**
yo	hube	pude	puse	supe	cupe
tú	hubiste	pudiste	pusiste	supiste	cupiste
él/ella/usted	hubo	pudo	puso	supo	cupo
nosotros/-as	hubimos	pudimos	pusimos	supimos	cupimos
vosotros/-as	hubisteis	pudisteis	pusisteis	supisteis	cupisteis
ellos/ellas/ustedes	hubieron	pudieron	pusieron	supieron	cupieron

Verbs that change stem in the third-person forms

There are three groups in this category:

1. Verbs that change "**e**" to "**i**" in the third-person singular and plural forms.
   Examples of these verbs: "**pedir**" *(to ask or request)*, "**mentir**" *(to lie)*, "**sentir**" *(to feel)*, "**seguir**" *(to follow)*, "**servir**" *(to serve)*, "**hervir**" *(to boil)*, "**preferir**" *(to prefer)*, "**convertir**" *(to convert)*, "**despedir**" *(to dismiss)*, "**impedir**" *(to prevent)*, "**divertirse**" *(to have fun)*, "**sugerir**" *(to suggest)*, "**vestirse**" *(to dress)*, "**repetir**" *(to repeat)*, "**reír**" *(to laugh)*, and "**sonreír**" *(to smile)*. Notice that these verbs are all "**-ir**" verbs.

	pedir	**mentir**	**seguir**	**preferir**	**reír**
yo	pedí	mentí	seguí	preferí	reí
tú	pediste	mentiste	seguiste	preferiste	reíste
él/ella/usted	pidió	mintió	siguió	prefirió	rió
nosotros/-as	pedimos	mentimos	seguimos	preferimos	reímos
vosotros/-as	pedisteis	mentisteis	seguisteis	preferisteis	reísteis
ellos/ellas/ustedes	pidieron	mintieron	siguieron	prefirieron	rieron

2. Verbs that change "**o**" to "**u**" in the third-person singular and plural forms.
   Examples of these verbs: "**dormir**" *(to sleep)* and "**morir**" *(to die)*, which are also "**-ir**" verbs.

	dormir	**morir**
yo	dormí	morí
tú	dormiste	moriste
él/ella/usted	durmió	murió
nosotros/-as	dormimos	morimos
vosotros/-as	dormisteis	moristeis
ellos/ellas/ustedes	durmieron	murieron

3. Verbs that change "**e**" or "**i**" to "**y**" in the third-person singular and plural forms.

   Examples of these verbs: "**caer**" *(to fall)*, "**leer**" *(to read)*, "**roer**" *(to nibble)*, "**oír**" *(to hear)*, "**influir**" *(to influence)*, and "**concluir**" *(to* *conclude)*. Notice that if the final vowel of the stem is silent, this rule does not apply, e.g., "**seguir**" *(to follow)*, "**perseguir**" *(to chase or pursue)*, "**conseguir**" *(to get)*.

	caer	leer	roer	oír	influir
yo	caí	leí	roí	oí	influí
tú	caíste	leíste	roíste	oíste	influiste
él/ella/usted	cayó	leyó	royó	oyó	influyó
nosotros/-as	caímos	leímos	roímos	oímos	influimos
vosotros/-as	caísteis	leísteis	roísteis	oísteis	influisteis
ellos/ellas/ustedes	cayeron	leyeron	royeron	oyeron	influyeron

The changes in the table above prevent the presence of three consecutive vowels, e.g., "**cayó**" (the "**y**" replaces "**e**," preventing the presence of the three consecutive vowels "-**aeo**-").

Verbs "venir," "querer," and "ver"

Finally, the verbs "**venir**" and "**querer**" take the stems "**vin-**" and "**quis-**," respectively, whereas the verb "**ver**" does not follow a specific rule.

	ver	venir	querer
yo	vi	vine	quise
tú	viste	viniste	quisiste
él/ella/usted	vio	vino	quiso
nosotros/-as	vimos	vinimos	quisimos
vosotros/-as	visteis	vinisteis	quisisteis
ellos/ellas/ustedes	vieron	vinieron	quisieron

2. IMPERATIVE MOOD & GIVING COMMANDS

The imperative mood is generally used to give commands or instructions in the affirmative or the negative. We have so far encountered the indicative and the subjunctive moods. The imperative is considered a separate mood in Spanish.

The imperative mood can be used in the singular or plural form and can be formal or informal. When using the imperative mood with the plural, there is only one format for both formal and informal. Thus, we have three cases:

1. Singular informal (i.e., **tú**)
2. Singular formal (i.e., **usted**)
3. Plural (i.e., **ustedes**)

Each of the above can be used in the affirmative or the negative. In addition to these three cases of imperative commands, we will study commands using "**nosotros**," indirect commands, and commands using the infinitive.

In Spain, the plural informal form "**vosotros**" can be used. However, we will skip that as it is not used outside of Spain.

Singular Informal Imperative

To give commands to a single person in an informal way, we use the *present indicative* in the third-person singular form, i.e., "**usted**," in the affirmative and the *present subjunctive* in the second-person singular form, i.e., "**tú**," in the negative, for example:

Cómprame un café.	***Buy** me a coffee.*
Camina despacio.	***Walk** slowly.*
No me **mientas**.	***Don't lie** to me.*
No hables rápido.	***Don't speak** fast.*

There are eight common irregular verbs in the affirmative singular informal command form.

Infinitive	Command	Example	
ser	sé	**Sé** cortés.	***Be** polite.*
ir	ve	**Ve** a la escuela.	***Go** to school.*
venir	ven	**Ven** aquí.	***Come** here.*
tener	ten	**Ten** cuidado.	***Take** caution.*
decir	di	**Di** la verdad.	***Tell** the truth.*
hacer	haz	**Haz** la tarea.	***Do** the homework.*
poner	pon	**Pon** el lápiz aquí.	***Put** the pencil here.*
salir	sal	**Sal** con tus amigos.	***Go out** with your friends.*

Singular Formal Imperative

To give commands to a single person in a formal way, we use the *present subjunctive* in the third-person singular form in both the affirmative and in the negative; that is, the form used with "**usted**," for example:

Señora, **entre** desde aquí, por favor.	*Ma'am, **enter** from here, please.*
Señor, **no fume** aquí, por favor.	*Sir, **don't smoke** here, please.*

Plural Imperative

To give commands to a group of people, we use the *present subjunctive* in the third-person plural form in both the affirmative and in the negative; that is, the form used with "**ustedes**," for example:

Chicos, **hagan** la tarea.	*Boys, **do** the homework.*
Señores, **no fumen** aquí, por favor.	*Gentlemen, **don't smoke**, please.*

Commands using "Nosotros"

Similar to the expression *"let's do something"* in English, commands using "**nosotros**" in Spanish express the same idea and can be affirmative or negative. Both use the *present subjunctive*, for example:

Hagamos nuestra tarea.	***Let's do** our homework.*
No fumemos.	***Let's not smoke.***

The only exception is "**vamos**," which is often used to mean *"let's go"* instead of "**vayamos**" in the affirmative. In the negative, however, "**no vayamos**" is how you say *"let's not go"* in Spanish.

Indirect Commands

Another way to express commands mostly in the affirmative is by using "**que**" followed by the *present subjunctive*, for example:

Que **entren.**	*Let them **enter.***
Que **tengas** un buen día.	***Have** a nice day.*

Infinitive Commands

A less polite and less often used form to express commands is using
the *infinitive*, for example:

Caminar despacio.	*Walk slowly.*
No **llorar**.	*No crying.*

3. EXPRESSIONS OF PAIN & ILLNESS

There are some commonly used expressions in Spanish to describe
pain, symptoms, and illness. We will discuss three categories of
these expressions:

1. Using the verb **"doler"** *(to hurt)* to express pain in a particular
   body part, for example:

Me **duele** la cabeza.	*My head hurts.*
A mi mamá le **duele** la mano.	*My mom's hand hurts.*
Nos **duelen** las piernas.	*Our legs hurt.*
¿Te **duelen** los dientes?	*Do your teeth hurt?*

The expression **"me duele"** literally means *"it hurts me."* Thus, **"me
duele la cabeza"** literally means *"the head hurts me,"* which we
translate as *"my head hurts."*

2. Using the verb **"tener"** *(to have)* to describe symptoms, including
   pain, for example:

Tengo fiebre.	*I have a fever.*
Tenemos resaca.	*We have a hangover.*
Tuvimos estrés.	*We had stress.*
Ella **tiene** dolor de estómago.	*She has a stomachache.*

3. Using the verb **"estar"** *(to be)* to describe symptoms, for
   example:

Estoy mareado.	*I am dizzy.*
Él **está** cansado.	*He is tired.*
¿**Estás** resfriado?[1]	*Do you have a cold?*

---

[1] The verb **"tener"** can also be used to say: **"¿Tienes un resfriado?"** *(Do you have a cold?)*.

4. SIMPLE CONDITIONAL TENSE

The simple conditional tense is used to describe a hypothetical situation, express wishes, give advice, or make a polite request. It is similar in its use to the simple conditional tense in English, e.g., "*I would do the laundry if I had time.*" The regular verb conjugation is the same for all verb endings and is formed by adding the conjugation ending to the *infinitive* rather than to the stem.

	-ar ending hablar	-er ending comer	-ir ending vivir
yo	hablaría	comería	viviría
tú	hablarías	comerías	vivirías
él/ella/usted	hablaría	comería	viviría
nosotros/-as	hablaríamos	comeríamos	viviríamos
vosotros/-as	hablaríais	comeríais	viviríais
ellos/ellas/ustedes	hablarían	comerían	vivirían

Irregular Verbs

There are a few irregular verbs in the simple future tense; twelve are commonly used and will be discussed here.

Some verbs ending in "**-er**" and "**-ir**" drop the "**e**" or "**i**" from the infinitive ending and replace it with a "**d**." There are five common verbs in this category: "**tener**" *(to have)*, "**poner**" *(to put)*, "**valer**" *(to value* or *to be worth)*, "**venir**" *(to come)*, and "**salir**" *(to go out* or *to exit)*.

	tener tendr-	poner pondr-	venir vendr-	salir sladr-
yo	tendría	pondría	vendría	saldría
tú	tendrías	pondrías	vendrías	saldrías
él/ella/usted	tendría	pondría	vendría	saldría
nosotros/-as	tendríamos	pondríamos	vendríamos	saldríamos
vosotros/-as	tendríais	pondríais	vendríais	saldríais
ellos/ellas/ustedes	tendrían	pondrían	vendrían	saldrían

Some verbs ending in "**-er**" simply drop the "**e**" from the infinitive ending. There are also five common verbs in this category: "**saber**" (*to know*), "**poder**" (*can*), "**caber**" *(to fit)*, "**querer**" *(to want)*, and "**haber**," which is an auxiliary verb equivalent to the English auxiliary verb *"have."*

	saber sabr-	poder podr-	querer querr-	haber habr-
yo	sabría	podría	querría	habría
tú	sabrías	podrías	querrías	habrías
él/ella/usted	sabría	podría	querría	habría
nosotros/-as	sabríamos	podríamos	querríamos	habríamos
vosotros/-as	sabríais	podríais	querríais	habríais
ellos/ellas/ustedes	sabrían	podrían	querrían	habrían

The verbs "**decir**" (*to say*) and "**hacer**" (*to do*) change their stem to "**dir-**" and "**har-**" to form the simple conditional tense conjugation. These two verbs are irregular and must be memorized.

	decir dir-	hacer har-
yo	diría	haría
tú	dirías	harías
él/ella/usted	diría	haría
nosotros/-as	diríamos	haríamos
vosotros/-as	diríais	haríais
ellos/ellas/ustedes	dirían	harían

Below are some examples that use the simple conditional tense.

Viajaría cada año si tuviera dinero.	I **would travel** *every year if I had money.*
Si yo fuera tú, **no iría** al gimnasio hoy.	*If I were you, I* **wouldn't go** *to the gym today.*
Si tuviera mucho dinero, **compraría** un palacio.	*If I had a lot of money, I* **would buy** *a palace.*
Podrías estudiar más horas para el examen.	**You could** *study more hours for the exam.*
¿**Podrías** pasarme la pimienta?	**Could you** *pass me the pepper?*
¿**Viviríamos** en una ciudad pequeña?	**Would we live** *in a small city?*
Dormirían todo el día si no tuvieran trabajo.	**They would sleep** *all day if they didn't have work.*
Diría la verdad si me preguntaran.	I **would tell** *the truth if they asked me.*

5. PRESENT SUBJUNCTIVE II

We discussed some of the uses of the subjunctive mood in **Level IV, Lesson 7**, mainly expressing opinions, possibilities, desires, wishes, feelings, requests, and recommendations. We will cover other cases here in which the subjunctive mood ought to be used.

Time Expressions in the Future

Let us examine the following time expressions:

cuando	*when*
apenas, en cuanto, tan pronto como, ni bien	*as soon as*
hasta que	*until*
antes de que	*before*
después de que	*after*

When one of the above expressions is used in the present or the past, we use the indicative, for example:

Vi a mi hermano cuando **llegué** a casa.	*I saw my brother when I **arrived** home.*
Leo el correo tan pronto como lo **recibo**.	*I read the mail as soon as I **receive** it.*
Envié el paquete después de que me **pagaron**.	*I sent the parcel after they **paid** me.*

However, if used to describe an action in the future, the sentence after the above time expressions shall be in the subjunctive, for example:

Veré a mi hermano cuando **llegue** a casa.	*I will see my brother when I **arrive** home.*
Leeré el correo tan pronto como lo **reciba**.	*I will read the mail as soon as I **receive** it.*
Voy a enviar el paquete después de que me **paguen**.	*I will send the parcel after they **pay** me.*

The Expression "Ojalá"

The expression **"ojalá"** is derived from the Arabic influence on the Spanish language and is used to express hope that something would happen or would have happened. We will cover the use of **"ojalá"** in the present subjunctive, which can be translated roughly as *"hopefully"* to express hope for something to happen in the present or the future, for example:

Ojalá que **no llueva** esta noche.	*Hopefully, it **won't rain** tonight.*
Ojalá que mi hermano **venga** hoy.	*Hopefully, my brother **will come** today.*

"Ojalá" can also be used to express hope that something has happened or would have happened in the past. We will cover that in the lessons to come with the imperfect and perfect subjunctive.

The Use of "Para que"

The preposition **"para,"** meaning *"for," "to,"* or *"in order to,"* is used to indicate the purpose or the objective.

When used alone without **"que"** afterward, it is followed by the verb in the infinitive, for example:

Compré un auto **para** viajar.	*I bought a car **to** travel.*
Uso este libro **para** aprender español.	*I use this book **to** learn Spanish.*

Notice in the sentences above that the subject is the same before and after **"para."** Thus, we used the infinitive.

If the subject before and after **"para"** is different, we use **"para que"** followed by the subjunctive, for example:

Compré un auto **para que** podamos viajar.	*I bought a car **so that** we can travel.*
Uso este libro **para que** aprendamos español.	*I use this book **so that** we learn Spanish.*

Another alternative to "**para que**," which is more formal but has the same meaning, is "**a fin de que**," and it is similarly followed by the subjunctive, for example:

Compré un auto **a fin de que** viajemos.	*I bought a car **so that** we travel.*
Uso este libro **a fin de que** aprendamos español.	*I use this book **so that** we learn Spanish.*

The Use of "Mientras"

The word "**mientras**" has many different uses, most of which use the indicative mood. However, the following two cases use the present subjunctive:

1. "**Mientras**" (=*as long as*)

Mientras (que) estés cansado, no tienes que trabajar.	***As long as*** *you're tired, you don't have to work.*
Mientras (que) el café sea bueno, lo tomaré.	***As long as*** *the coffee is good, I'll drink it.*

Notice that the verb after "**mientras**" and "**mientras que**" in the above examples is in the present *subjunctive*. The use of "**que**" in this case is optional.

If "**mientras**" is followed by the *indicative* and not the subjunctive, it means *"while"* and describes two events that happen simultaneously, for example:

Voy a cenar **mientras** tú ves la tele.	*I'm going to have dinner **while** you watch TV.*
Mientras escucho música, hago la tarea.	***While*** *I listen to music, I do the homework.*
Mientras estaba caminando por la calle, pensaba en el trabajo.	***While*** *I was walking down the street, I was thinking about work.*

2. "**Mientras más/menos**" (= *the more, the less*)

To form expressions that start with *"the more"* or *"the less"* in Spanish, we can use "**mientras**" followed by "**más**" or "**menos**," respectively. If the sentence refers to something that happens in the *present*, the *indicative* mood is used. However, if the sentence refers to something that will happen in the *future*, the *subjunctive* mood is used instead, for example:

Mientras más <u>sé</u>, más quiero aprender.	***The more*** *I know, the more I want to learn.*
Mientras menos <u>agregues</u>, menos desorden crearás.	***The less*** *you add, the less mess you will create.*

Notice that the first example uses the indicative mood, whereas the second uses the subjunctive mood.

An alternative to "**mientras más/menos**" that is more common, is "**cuanto más/menos**," which has the same meaning, for example:

Cuanto más <u>sé</u>, más quiero aprender.	***The more*** *I know, the more I want to learn.*
Cuanto menos <u>agregues</u>, menos desorden crearás.	***The less*** *you add, the less mess you will create.*

The expression "**cuanto/mientras más/menos**" can also be followed by a noun or adjective instead of a verb, for example:

Mientras/cuanto más ejercicio, más saludable.	***The more*** *exercise, the healthier.*
Mientras/cuanto más salado, más sabroso.	*The saltier, the tastier.*

One thing to notice is that one must use the correct number and gender if "**cuanto**" is used instead of "**mientras**," for example:

Mientras/cuan<u>tas</u> más personas me llamen hoy, más feliz estaré.	***The more*** *people call me today, the happier I will be.*
Mientras/cuan<u>ta</u> menos ventilación en la casa, menos saludable.	***The less*** *ventilation in the house, the less healthy.*

If "**mejor/peor**" (*better/worse*) is used, the second "**más/menos**" is not needed, for example:

Mientras/cuanta menos ventilación en la casa, **peor** la calidad del aire.	*The less ventilation in the house, the* ***worse*** *the air quality.*

More Expressions that use the Subjunctive

It is really hard to include all expressions that use the subjunctive in this limited space. However, a few expressions are still worth mentioning as we are likely to encounter them more frequently.

First, the expressions **"siempre que"** and **"con tal de que"** mean *"as long as"* or *"provided that."* They are both similar in meaning and context to **"mientras que"** followed by the subjunctive, for example:

Mientras que el café sea bueno, lo tomaré.	*As long as the coffee is good, I'll drink it.*
Siempre que el café sea bueno, lo tomaré.	*As long as the coffee is good, I'll drink it.*
Con tal de que el café sea bueno, lo tomaré.	*As long as the coffee is good, I'll drink it.*

Second, the expressions **"por mucho que"** and **"por más que"** both mean **"no matter how much"** or **"however much."** Both expressions are usually followed by the subjunctive, for example:

Iré al gimnasio **por más que** me sienta cansado.	*I will go to the gym **no matter how much** I feel tired.*
Por mucho que lo quiera, no cenaré hoy.	*As much as I want it, I won't have dinner today.*
Por mucho que insistas, no lo haré.	***No matter how much** you insist, I won't do it.*

Another common expression that is usually followed by the subjunctive is **"a menos que,"** which means *"unless,"* for example:

A menos que tengas bastante dinero, será difícil vivir aquí.	***Unless** you have enough money, it will be difficult to live here.*
No vamos a avanzar **a menos que** seamos pacientes.	*We won't advance **unless** we are patient.*

Finally, the expression **"sin que,"** which means *"without,"* is often followed by the subjunctive and used in a similar context to **"a menos que,"** for example:

Dejaré la llave **sin que** él la vea.	*I will leave the key **without** him seeing.*

| No vamos a avanzar **sin que** seamos pacientes. | *We won't advance **without** being patient.* |

6. PERFECT SUBJUNCTIVE

We have previously studied the subjunctive mood and the present subjunctive tense. The subjunctive mood is used to express opinion, possibility, and feelings such as fear, doubt, hope, desire, etc.

We have also studied the present perfect tense in the indicative mood. The present perfect tense is used to describe events that happened recently or started in the past and continue in the present.

Now, we will study the case when we want to express opinions, possibilities, and feelings, such as fear, doubt, hope, desire, etc., about something that happened recently or started in the past and continues in the present. In other words, we want to describe the present perfect but in the subjunctive mood, i.e., the perfect subjunctive.

The perfect subjunctive, similar to the present perfect in the subjunctive, uses the past participle. However, the only difference is that the auxiliary verb **"haber"** is conjugated in the subjunctive.

		-ar ending **hablar**	-er ending **comer**	-ir ending **vivir**
yo	haya			
tú	hayas			
él/ella/usted	haya			
nosotros/-as	hayamos	habl**ado**	com**ido**	viv**ido**
vosotros/-as	hayáis			
ellos/ellas/ustedes	hayan			

Let us look at some examples:

		Examples	
yo	haya	Es bueno que **haya descansado** después del partido.	*It is good that I **have relaxed** after the match.*
tú	hayas	Espero que **hayas disfrutado** tu viaje.	*I hope that you **have enjoyed** your trip.*

él/ella/usted	haya	Me pone triste que no me **haya llamado**.	*It makes me sad that he **hasn't called** me.*
nosotros/-as	hayamos	Dudo que **hayamos visto** tu casa antes de hoy.	*I doubt that we **have seen** your house before today.*
vosotros/-as	hayáis	Estoy feliz de que **hayáis llegado**.	*I am happy that you **have arrived**.*
ellos/ellas/ustedes	hayan	No creo que **hayan vivido** aquí.	*I don't believe they **have lived** here.*

Another less common use is to describe things that will have been completed in the future. It is, in effect, expressing the future perfect in the subjunctive mood, for example:

Espero que **hayas terminado** de escribir el libro para el próximo año.	*I hope that you **will have finished** writing the book <u>by next year</u>.*

Note that "**para el próximo año**" (*by next year*) is what clarified the meaning to be in the future. Otherwise, without reference to some future time, it is more likely to assume the following meaning:

Espero que **hayas terminado** de escribir el libro.	*I hope that you **have finished** writing the book.*

7. IMPERFECT SUBJUNCTIVE

The imperfect subjunctive, similar to the present perfect in the subjunctive, is used to express desires and wishes. However, these desires and wishes are often in the past or refer to unlikely events or possibilities, for example:

Si yo **fuera** tú, no iría.	*If I **were** you, I wouldn't go.*

Conjugation

The stem used to form the imperfect subjunctive conjugation comes from the *third-person plural form* of the *preterite* rather than the infinitive, that is, the preterite that follows "**ellos**" or "**ellas**" minus "**-ron**," for example:

Infinitive	Third-person plural preterite	Imperfect subjunctive stem
tener	ellos/ellas tuvieron	tuvie-
ir	ellos/ellas fueron	fue-
comer	ellos/ellas comieron	comie-

Next, one of the following two endings is attached to the stem. Both endings are equally acceptable, although the first group is more widely used. All verbs follow these conjugation rules, and there are no irregular verbs.

yo	-ra	-se	hablara/hablase
tú	-ras	-ses	hablaras/hablases
él/ella/usted	-ra	-se	hablara/hablase
nosotros/-as	-ramos	-semos	habláramos/hablásemos
vosotros/-as	-rais	-seis	hablarais/hablaseis
ellos/ellas/ustedes	-ran	-sen	hablaran/hablasen

Uses of the Imperfect Subjunctive

Let us discuss the common uses of the imperfect subjunctive and check some examples.

1. Expressing Past Desires, Wishes, Feelings, Requests, and Recommendations.

Whereas the present subjunctive is used to express opinion, possibility, and feelings such as fear, doubt, hope, desire, etc., about something in the present or the future, the imperfect subjunctive can be used similarly, but when the hope, desire, feeling, etc. itself is in the past.

For example, using the present subjunctive, we can say:

Quiero que **vengas** a mi casa.	*I want you to* **come** *to my house.*
Me pone triste que no me **llamen**.	*It makes me sad that they don't* **call** *me.*

If that hope or desire occurred in the past, the imperfect subjunctive should be used:

Quería que **vinieras** a mi casa.	*I wanted you to* **come** *to my house.*
Me ponía triste que no me **llamaran**.	*It made me sad that they didn't* **call** *me.*

2. Unlikely or Hypothetical Conditional Statements.

As discussed previously, conditional statements that contain hypothetical or unlikely assumptions, such as *"if I were you," "if I were the president,"* and *"if I had a lot of money,"* use the imperfect subjunctive, for example:

Si yo **fuera** tú, no iría al gimnasio hoy.	*If I **were** you, I wouldn't go to the gym today.*
Si **tuviera** mucho dinero, compraría un palacio.	*If I **had** a lot of money, I would buy a palace.*

3. Expressions with **"ojalá"** that contain *unlikely* or *hypothetical* events in the *present* or the *future*.

We have previously discussed the use of **"ojalá"** in the present subjunctive to express hope for something to happen in the present or the future, for example:

Ojalá que **no llueva** esta noche.	*Hopefully, it **won't rain** tonight.*
Ojalá que **venga** mi hermano hoy.	*Hopefully, my brother **will come** today.*

"Ojalá" can also be used along with the imperfect subjunctive to express hope that something, which is *unlikely* or *improbable*, would happen in the present or the future, for example:

Ojalá que **pudiéramos** ganar mucho dinero en un año.	*I wish we **could** make a lot of money in one year.*
Ojalá que **viniera** mi hermano hoy, pero siempre está ocupado.	*I wish my brother **would come** today, but he is always busy.*

You can refer to **Appendix H** for a summary of the uses of **"ojalá"** in Spanish.

4. Polite Requests

It is also very common to use the imperfect subjunctive to make polite requests, for example:

| **Quisiera** un café, por favor. | *I would like a coffee, please.* |
| **Quisiera** que vinieras mañana. | *I would like you to come tomorrow.* |

8. PAST & CONDITIONAL PROGRESSIVE TENSE

The past progressive tense, similar to its use in English, describes an event that continued to take place in the past, e.g., "**Yo estaba hablando**" (*I was speaking*). It is formed by adding the imperfect tense of the auxiliary verb "**estar**" to the present participle, also known as the gerund.

> subject pronoun + imperfect tense of the verb "**estar**" + *gerund*

		-ar ending **hablar**	-er ending **comer**	-ir ending **vivir**
yo	estaba			
tú	estabas			
él/ella/usted	estaba			
nosotros/-as	estábamos	habl**ando**	com**iendo**	viv**iendo**
vosotros/-as	estabais			
ellos/ellas/ustedes	estaban			

For example:

| Mi mamá **estaba cocinando** cuando mi papá entró a la casa. | *My mom **was cooking** when my dad entered the house.* |
| **Estábamos nadando** mientras estabas estudiando. | *We **were swimming** while you were studying.* |

On the other hand, the conditional progressive tense is used to describe an event that would be happening now had another event happened earlier, e.g., "**Yo estaría jugando si no estuviera lesionado**" (*I would be playing if I weren't injured*). It is formed by adding the conditional form of the auxiliary verb "**estar**" to the gerund.

> subject pronoun + conditional form of the verb "**estar**" + *gerund*

		-ar ending hablar	-er ending comer	-ir ending vivir
yo	estaría			
tú	estarías			
él/ella/usted	estaría	hablando	comiendo	viviendo
nosotros/-as	estaríamos			
vosotros/-as	estaríais			
ellos/ellas/ustedes	estarían			

For example:

Estaría hablando con mi hermano si hubiera ido a su casa ayer.	*I **would be talking** to my brother had I gone to his house yesterday.*
No estaría comiendo mucho si estuviera a dieta.	*I **wouldn't be eating** much if I were on a diet.*

9. INTERJECTIONS

Interjections are mere exclamation words or expressions that usually represent feelings like surprise or anger. Interjections are often followed by an exclamation mark.

		Examples
¡Qué …!	*What…!*	**¡Qué** hermoso gato! ***What** a beautiful cat!*
¡Cómo …!	*How…!*	**¡Cómo** canta él! ***How** he sings!*
¡Cuánto…!	*How much…!*	**¡Cuánto** la quiero! ***How** much I love her!*
¡Ay!	*Oh!* *Ouch!*	**¡Ay!** No lo sabía. ***Oh**! I didn't know.*
¡Ajá!	*Aha!*	**¡Ajá!** Ahora entiendo. ***Aha**! I understand now.*
¡Bravo!	*Well done!*	**¡Bravo!** Jugaron bien. ***Well done**! They played well.*
¡Dale!	*Alright!*	-¿Vamos hoy? -**¡Dale!** *-Do we go today? -**Alright**!*
¡Dios mío!	*Oh my God!*	**¡Dios mío!** ¿Qué pasó? ***Oh my God**! What happened?*

¡Gracias a Dios!	*Thank God!*	**¡Gracias a Dios** no vino! ***Thank God*** *he didn't come!*
¡Por Dios!	*For God's sake!*	¿Qué pasó, **por Dios**? *What happened,* ***for God's sake?***
¡Claro!	*Of course!*	-¿Tienes hambre? -**¡Claro!** *-Are you hungry? -**Of course.***
¡Menos mal!	*(Relief)*	**¡Menos mal** que no me vio! ***Good thing*** *he didn't see me!*
¡Buen provecho!	*Bon appétit!*	Aquí tiene. **¡Buen provecho!** *Here you go.* ***Bon appétit!***
¡Buena suerte!	*Good luck!*	Nos vemos. **¡Buena suerte!** *See you soon.* ***Good luck!***
¡Qué horror!	*How awful!*	Fue malo. **¡Qué horror!** *It was bad.* ***How awful!***
¡Qué lástima!	*What a pity!*	Perdimos. **¡Qué lástima!** *We lost.* ***What a pity!***
¡Cuidado!	*Careful!*	**¡Cuidado!** Está oscuro. ***Careful!*** *It's dark.*
¡Ojo!	*Look out!*	**¡Ojo!** Es peligroso. ***Look out!*** *It's dangerous.*
¡Ojalá!	*I hope so!*	-¿Todo bien? -**¡Ojalá!** *-Everything's okay? -**I hope so!***
¡Obvio!	*Obviously!*	-¿Te gusta? -**¡Obvio!** *-Do you like it? -**Obviously!***
¡Oye!	*Hey! Listen!*	**¡Oye!** Lo siento. ***Hey!*** *I'm sorry.*
¡Vale!	*Alright!*	-¿Vamos hoy? -**¡Vale!** *-Do we go today? -**Alright!***
¡Vamos!	*Come on!*	**¡Vamos!** Podemos ganar. ***Come on!*** *We can win.*

Many interjections and exclamations tend to vary a lot from one Spanish-speaking country to another and from one region to another. For instance, **"vale"** and **"dale"** are identical in meaning and use. In Spain, you are likely to hear the former, whereas, in Argentina, you are more likely to hear the latter. Therefore, it is important to keep that in mind when you learn expressions in this category.

II. Vocabulary Building

Go over the vocabulary in this section and use the provided Anki cards to study and memorize the new vocabulary efficiently.

1. VERBS V

Below is a list of some important verbs that we need at this level. Use the Anki cards created for this section to help you memorize the meaning of each verb in proper contexts.

English	Spanish	Examples
accomplish	cumplir [1] lograr	**He cumplido** mi meta de volverme saludable. *I **have accomplished** my goal of becoming healthy.*
admonish	amonestar	Tuve que **amonestar** a mis alumnos hoy. *I had to **admonish** my students today.*
afford	permitirse	Es rico y puede **permitirse** cualquier gasto. *He is rich and can **afford** any expense.*
age	envejecer	Esta carne **ha envejecido** muy bien. *This meat **has aged** very well.*
agree	estar de acuerdo	**Estuve de acuerdo** con su discurso al escucharlo. *I **agreed** with his speech upon listening to him.*
amaze	asombrar	Siempre me **asombra** la tecnología moderna. *Modern technology always **amazes** me.*
anger	enojar enfadar	Su trato a los clientes me **enoja**. *His treatment of customers **angers** me.*
announce **advertise**	anunciar [2]	Mi tía **anunciará** su embarazo el sábado. *My aunt **will announce** her pregnancy on Saturday.*
approach **(motion)**	acercarse	Vi como **se acercaba** la ardilla a mis plantas. *I saw how the squirrel **approached** my plants.*
assure **ensure**	asegurar	Te **aseguro** que te gustará. *I **assure** you that you will like it.*
attract	atraer(se)	Los polos opuestos **se atraen**. *Opposite poles **attract** one another.*

---

[1] The verb "**cumplir**" can also mean *"to turn a certain age,"* e.g., "**Mañana cumplo 30 años**" *(I'll turn 30 tomorrow).*

[2] The verb "**anunciar**" can also mean *"to advertise,"* e.g., "**Anunciaron el festival en el periódico**" *(They advertised the festival in the newspaper).*

babysit	cuidar al niño	**Cuido a los niños** de mi vecina de vez en cuando. *I **babysit** my neighbor's kids from time to time.*
bark	ladrar	Mi perro **ladra** mucho. *My dog **barks** a lot.*
be born	nacer	Mi sobrino **nacerá** por cesárea. *My nephew **will be born** through a C-section.*
be worth	valer	Esa versión del libro **vale** una fortuna. *That version of the book **is worth** a fortune.*
become dark	anochecer	Debemos volver antes de que **anochezca**. *We have to come back before it **becomes dark**.*
beg	rogar mendigar	No quisiera tener que **mendigar**. *I wouldn't like to have **to beg**.*
bend	doblar curvar	**Dobló** el tenedor con la mano sin querer. *He inadvertently **bent** the fork with his hand.*
benefit	beneficiar(se)	Te puedes **beneficiar** de ese arreglo. *You can **benefit** from that arrangement.*
bite	morder	Él **mordió** el queso porque tenía hambre. *He **bit off** the cheese because he was hungry.*
blackmail	chantajear	**Chantajeó** a sus amigos cuando lo confrontaron. *He **blackmailed** his friends when they confronted him.*
blame	culpar	No lo **culpo** por querer irse. *I don't **blame** him for wanting to leave.*
bleed	sangrar	No me gusta ver gente **sangrar**. *I don't like to see people **bleed**.*
blink	parpadear	Debes **parpadear** para hidratar los ojos. *You have to **blink** to hydrate your eyes.*
bloom **blossom**	florecer	Las rosas **florecen** en la primavera. *Roses **bloom** in the spring.*
boil	hervir	El agua **hierve** a 100 grados Celsius. *The water **boils** at 100 degrees Celsius.*
borrow	tomar prestado	¿Puedo **tomar prestado** tu cepillo? *Can I **borrow** your brush?*
bow	inclinarse	En Japón es costumbre **inclinarse** al saludar. *In Japan it's customary to **bow** when saluting.*
brag **boast** **show off**	jactarse alardear presumir [1]	Me agradaría si no **se jactara** de todo. *I'd like him if he **would** not **brag** about everything.*
break down	averiarse descomponerse	**Se descompuso** mi auto ayer. *My car **broke down** yesterday.*
breastfeed	amamantar	La gata **está amamantando** a sus crías. *The cat **is breastfeeding** its babies.*

---

[1] The verb "**presumir**" can also mean *"to presume."*

bribe	sobornar	Nunca debes **sobornar** a la policía. *You should never **bribe** the police.*
burst	reventar	La botella **reventó** por la presión. *The bottle **burst** because of the pressure.*
cage	enjaular	En el circo **enjaulan** a los animales. *In the circus they **cage** the animals.*
carry out	llevar a cabo	El viernes **llevarán a cabo** un espectáculo. *On Friday, they **will carry out** a show.*
carve	tallar	**Talló** sus nombres en un árbol el año pasado. *He **carved** their names on a tree last year.*
catch **trap**	atrapar	La policía logró **atrapar** al ladrón. *The police managed to **catch** the thief.*
chew	masticar mascar	Es de mala educación **mascar** chicle en clase. *It's bad manners to **chew** gum in class.*
clap **applaud**	aplaudir	Todos **aplaudieron** cuando terminó de cantar. *Everyone **applauded** when he finished singing.*
clarify	aclarar clarificar	¿Puedes **aclarar** esta respuesta? *Can you **clarify** this answer?*
classify **sort**	clasificar	¿Puedes **clasificar** estas carpetas? *Can you **classify** these folders?*
climb	subir trepar(se)	¡No **te trepes** al árbol! *Don't **climb** the tree!*
complain	quejarse	No **te quejes** tanto. *Don't **complain** so much.*
collide	chocar	Lograron evitar que **chocara**. *They managed to avoid him **colliding**.*
conceal	ocultar encubrir	Su amigo intentó **ocultar** lo que había robado. *His friend tried to **conceal** what he had stolen.*
cool down	enfriar	Debes dejar que el pan **se enfríe**. *You have to let the bread **cool down**.*
cough	toser	**Tosí** mucho con la gripe el mes pasado. *I **coughed** a lot with the flu last month.*
crack	agrietar(se) rajar(se)	**Se agrietará** si le echas agua caliente. *It **will crack** if you pour hot water into it.*
crawl	gatear(se)	Aprendió a **gatear** siendo muy pequeño. *He learned how to **crawl** when he was very little.*
curl	rizar enrular	Voy a **rizar** mi cabello para salir. *I'm going to **curl** my hair to go out.*
dare	atreverse osar	**Me atreveré** a hablar ante un público. *I **will dare** to talk in front of an audience.*
deal with	tartar con	Es difícil **tratar con** personas crueles. *It is difficult to **deal with** cruel people.*

dent	abollar mellar	El choque **abolló** mi auto. *The crash **dented** my car.*
deprive	privar	No es bueno **privarse** todo el tiempo. *It's not good to **deprive** yourself all the time.*
discourage	desalentar	No quiero **desalentar**te a que sigas. *I don't want to **discourage** you from continuing.*
disturb	perturbar	No debes **perturbar** a los perros del vecino. *You shouldn't **disturb** the neighbor's dogs.*
drag	arrastrar	**Arrastré** una caja con el auto por accidente. *I accidentally **dragged** a box with my car.*
drag & drop	arrastrar y soltar	**Arrastra y suelta** los elementos en la página. ***Drag and drop** the elements on the page.*
drop	caer	La lluvia repentinamente **cayó** del cielo. *The rain suddenly **dropped** from the sky.*
empty	vaciar	¿Puedes **vaciar** tus bolsillos? *Can you **empty** your pockets?*
encourage	alentar animar	Mi mamá me **alienta** mucho en mi vida. *My mom **encourages** me a lot in my life.*
enrich	enriquecer(se)	No creo que me vaya a **enriquecer**, pero intentaré. *I don't believe I'm going to **enrich** myself, but I'll try.*
envy	envidiar	**Envidio** su estilo. *I **envy** her style.*
erupt	estallar reventar	El edificio **estalló** en llamas. *The building **erupted** in flames.*
execute	ejecutar	El soldado **ejecutó** la orden enseguida. *The soldier **executed** the order right away.*
exhaust **deplete**	agotar	Debo **agotar** todas las oportunidades. *I have to **exhaust** all the chances.*
explode	explotar [1]	Escuché cómo **explotaban** las palomitas. *I heard how the popcorn kernels **were exploding**.*
exploit	explotar [1]	En esa empresa **explotan** a sus empleados. *In that company, they **exploit** their employees.*
extract	extraer	Me **extrajeron** las muelas del juicio. *They **extracted** my wisdom teeth.*
familiarize **acquaint**	familiarizar(se)	Debes **familiarizarte** con los pasos. *You have to **familiarize yourself** with the steps.*
flirt	coquetear ligar	No es bueno **coquetear** con colegas. *It's not good to **flirt** with colleagues.*
flow	fluir	El agua **fluye** en el conducto para generar energía. *The water **flows** in the duct to generate power.*

---

[1] Depending on the context, the verb "**explotar**" can mean *"to exploit"* or *"to explode."*

fulfill **comply**	cumplir	Nunca **ha cumplido** con las reglas. *He **has** never **complied** with the rules.*
graduate	graduarse	**Me graduaré** este año. *I **will graduate** this year.*
grant **concede**	conceder	Me **concederán** una beca completa. *They **will grant** me a full scholarship.*
greet	saludar	Debes **saludar** a tus invitados cuando llegan. *You have to **greet** your guests when they arrive.*
haggle **bargain**	regatear	**Regateé** el precio de mi auto cuando lo compré. *I **haggled** over the price of my car when I bought it.*
happen	suceder pasar	Él fue franco sobre lo que podría **pasar**. *He was frank about what could **happen**.*
hinder	dificultar	La altura de la colina **dificulta** el aterrizaje. *The height of the hill **hinders** landing.*
hold	sujetar sostener	¿Puedes **sostener** a mi bebé un segundo? *Can you **hold** my baby for a second?*
hook	enganchar	**Enganchó** un pescado en el primer intento ayer. *He **hooked** a fish on the first try yesterday.*
hunt	cazar	No me gusta **cazar**. *I don't like to **hunt**.*
inhabit	habitar	Muchos osos **habitan** esta zona. *Many bears **inhabit** this zone.*
inherit	heredar	**Heredó** la casa de su abuela. *He **inherited** his grandmother's house.*
insert	insertar introducir	Esa era una ranura para **insertar** discos. *That was a slot to **insert** disks.*
inspect	inspeccionar	**Inspeccionó** mi auto en detalle. *He **inspected** my car in detail.*
interrupt	interrumpir	No me **interrumpas** cuando hablo. *Do not **interrupt** me when I'm talking.*
interview	entrevistar	**Entrevistaré** a la celebridad. *I **will interview** the celebrity.*
invest	invertir	No **inviertas** dinero del presupuesto del hogar. *Don't **invest** money from the household's budget.*
judge	juzgar	No me gusta que me **juzguen** sin conocerme. *I don't like that they **judge** me without knowing me.*
keep away **ward off**	alejar	Uso repelente para **alejar** a los mosquitos. *I use repellant to **ward off** mosquitoes.*
kidnap	secuestrar	Escuché que **secuestraron** a otra persona. *I heard they **kidnapped** another person.*
kill off **top off**	rematar	**Remataron** a los zombis en la película. *They **killed off** the zombies in the movie.*

knock (door)	tocar	**Toca** la puerta antes de entrar. *Knock on the door before you enter.*
knot	anudar	**Anudó** la bolsa correctamente esta vez. *He tied the bag correctly this time.*
land	aterrizar	El avión **aterrizó** temprano. *The airplane landed early.*
lend	prestar	¿Me puedes **prestar** dinero? *Can you lend me money?*
lie down	acostarse	Debo **acostarme** a descansar. *I have to lie down to rest.*
locate	ubicar	¿Pudiste **ubicar** a tu mamá? *Were you able to locate your mom?*
make a mistake **go wrong**	equivocarse	**Me equivoqué** comprando esta marca de té. *I made a mistake buying this brand of tea.*
make sense	tener sentido	Todo **tiene sentido** para mí ahora. *It all makes sense to me now.*
mature	madurar	Ese aguacate tiene que **madurar** más. *That avocado needs to mature more.*
misinterpret	malinterpretar	**Malinterpretó** lo que dije la última vez. *He misinterpreted what I said last time.*
moan	gemir	Me asusta mi gato cuando **gime**. *My cat scares me when she moans.*
move (emotionally)	conmover conmocionar	Esa película siempre me **conmueve**. *That movie always touches me.*
move (direction)	mover(se)	¿Puedes **moverte** un lugar? *Can you move a spot?*
move (residence)	mudarse trasladarse	Desearía que mi vecino **se mudara**. *I wish my neighbor would move.*
obey	obedecer	Mi perro siempre me **obedece**. *My dog always obeys me.*
obstruct	obstruir	Ese poste **obstruye** el camino. *That post obstructs the way.*
oppose to	oponerse a	Siempre **se opone a** mis propuestas. *He always opposes my proposals.*
overcome exceed	superar	Quiero **superar** mi mejor puntaje. *I want to surpass my best mark.*
pardon	perdonar	Debes **perdonar** sus modales. *You'll have to pardon his manners.*
participate	participar tomar parte	Quisiera **participar** en el desfile. *I'd like to participate in the parade.*
paste	pegar	**Pega** esa punta con la otra. *Paste that edge with the other one.*
pedal	pedalear	Siempre **pedaleo** mucho cuando uso la bici. *I always pedal a lot when I use the bicycle.*

play (instrument)	tocar	De chico **tocaba** la flauta. *As a child, I **played** the flute.*
polish	pulir	**Pulió** todos los cubiertos el año pasado. *She **polished** all the cutlery last year.*
pour	verter	**Vertió** el jugo en su vaso y se fue. *She **poured** the juice in her cup and left.*
preach	predicar	Debemos **predicar** la paz entre las personas. *We must **preach** peace among people.*
prevent	prevenir impedir evitar[1]	Ser precavido **evita** muchos accidentes. *Being cautious **prevents** lots of accidents.*
proceed	proceder	**Procede** con precaución. ***Proceed** with caution.*
promise	prometer	Me **prometió** que se portaría bien esta vez. *He **promised** me he'd behave well this time.*
propose	proponer	**Propondré** que coloquen un semáforo. *I **will propose** they put a stoplight.*
quit	dejar (de) abandonar	Dijo que quiere **abandonar** la banda. *She said she wants to **quit** the band.*
recover **retrieve**	recuperar	Debo **recuperarme** luego de correr. *I have to **recover** after running.*
recruit	reclutar	Uno esperaría que **reclutaran** más personas. *One would expect them to **recruit** more people.*
reflect	reflejar	Está tan limpio que **refleja** todo. *It's so clean it **reflects** everything.*
refresh	refrescar	Tuve que **refrescar** la página varias veces. *I had to **refresh** the page several times.*
refuse **reject**	rechazar rehusar(se) negar(se)	**Me rehúso** a pagar esa cantidad. *I **refuse** to pay that amount.*
reimburse	reembolsar	Esta empresa no **reembolsa** los gastos de envío. *This company doesn't **reimburse** the shipping costs.*
reinforce	reforzarse	Su libro ayudó a **reforzar** el nuevo concepto. *His book helped **reinforce** the new concept.*
release	soltar liberar	**Liberó** a su mariposa mascota anoche. *He **released** his pet butterfly last night.*
repent	arrepentirse	Es importante **arrepentirse** para aprender. *It's important to **repent** in order to learn.*
reprimand	reprender	No me gusta tener que **reprender**lo. *I don't like having to **reprimand** him.*

---

[1] The verb **"evitar"** can also mean *"to avoid"* depending on the context.

resign	renunciar dimitir	**Renunció** a su cargo en la empresa. *He **resigned** from his position in the company.*
restrict	restringir	El acceso a esa zona es **restringido**. *Access to that zone is **restricted**.*
result in turn out to be	resultar [1]	El tema **resultó** muy difícil. *The topic **turned out to be** very difficult.*
rhyme	rimar	Intento que mis poemas **rimen**. *I try to make my poems **rhyme**.*
risk	arriesgar	No quisiera que **arriesgara** todo su sueldo. *I wouldn't want him to **risk** all his salary.*
roll	rodar	**Rodó** por la colina sin querer. *He **rolled** down the hill by accident.*
rub	frotar	Debes **frotar** la crema para que funcione. *You have to **rub** the cream on for it to work.*
scare	asustar espantar dar miedo	Me **asustan** los fantasmas. *Ghosts **scare** me.*
scatter	esparcir	El viento **esparció** todos mis papeles. *The wind **scattered** all of my papers.*
schedule	agendar programar	Te **agendaré** para la semana próxima. *I **will schedule** you for next week.*
scold	regañar	**Regañan** a su hijo todo el tiempo. *They **scold** their son all the time.*
sculpt	esculpir	Aprendió a **esculpir** figuras de su padre. *He learned to **sculpt** figures from his father.*
sew	coser	**Coseré** mis medias. *I **will sew** my socks.*
slim down	adelgazar	**Adelgazó** mucho este año. *He **slimmed down** a lot this year.*
sneeze	estornudar	En la primavera **estornudo** mucho. *In the spring I **sneeze** a lot.*
spin	girar	Las ruedas empezaron a **girar** enseguida. *The wheels started to **spin** right away.*
startle	sobresaltar	Me **sobresaltó** el ruido mientras leía. *The noise **startled** me as I was reading.*
store	almacenar guardar	**Almacenaré** los víveres. *I **will store** the groceries.*
stroll go for a walk	pasear	Me siento calmado cuando **paseo** por la playa. *I feel calm when I **go for a walk** on the beach.*

---

[1] The verb "**resultar**" also means *"to find,"* e.g., "**Me resulta muy interesante el tema**" (*I find the topic very interesting*).

substitute	sustituir	**Sustituiré** el azúcar por el edulcorante. *I **will substitute** the sugar for sweetener.*
subtract	sustraer restar	Debes **restar** $100 de la deuda. *You have to **subtract** $100 from the debt.*
sue	demandar a	Dijeron que iban a **demandar a** la tienda. *They said they were going to **sue** the store.*
surf sail navigate	navegar	Amaba **navegar** por el mar. *He loved to **sail** across the sea.*
swing	oscilar	El péndulo del reloj **oscila** correctamente. *The clock's pendulum **swings** correctly.*
take advantage of	aprovechar	**Aprovecharé** la oferta y compraré tres. *I **will take advantage of** the offer and I'll buy three.*
take off	despegar	**Despegaremos** en media hora. *We **will take off** in half an hour.*
tempt	tentar	Esos pasteles siempre me **tientan**. *Those cakes always **tempt** me.*
threaten	amenazar	No estaría bien que **amenazara** a sus hijos. *It wouldn't be okay if he **threatened** his children.*
tie	atar(se)	Debes saber **atarte** las agujetas tú solo. *You have to know how to **tie** your shoelaces by yourself.*
trim	recortar	Quiero **recortar** solo las puntas. *I want to **trim** only the tips.*
turn	girar	**Gira** a la derecha y luego sigue derecho. ***Turn** right and then keep going straight ahead.*
undergo	someterse a	**Se someterá a** una cirugía el mes que viene. *He **will undergo** surgery next month.*
update	actualizar	Debo **actualizar** el sistema operativo. *I have to **update** the operating system.*
wander roam	vagar	Me gusta **vagar** por el centro comercial. *I like to **wander** through the mall.*
welcome	dar la bienvenida	Los consejeros nos **dieron la bienvenida** ayer. *The advisors **welcomed** us yesterday.*
whisper	susurrar	Por favor **susurra** para no despertar al bebé. *Please **whisper** to not wake up the baby.*
witness	atestiguar presenciar	**Presencié** el accidente en persona. *I **witnessed** the accident in person.*
wrap	envolver	Soy malo para **envolver** regalos. *I'm bad at **wrapping** gifts.*
yield	ceder	Debes **ceder** el lugar en esa esquina. *You have to **yield** your spot in that corner.*

In addition to the above new verbs, we add a few more English cognates that are easy to memorize.

English	Spanish	Examples
absorb	absorber	La tierra **absorbió** el agua inmediatamente. *The soil **absorbed** all the water immediately.*
adhere	adherir(se)	El imán se **adhirió** al refrigerador. *The magnet **adhered** to the fridge.*
administer	administrar	Debo **administrar** un grupo de 10. *I have **to administer** a group of 10.*
audit	auditar	Debo **auditar** los documentos. *I have to **audit** the documents.*
authorize	autorizar	**Autorizó** el uso de su imagen. *She **authorized** the use of her image.*
automate	automatizar	Busco **automatizar** los procesos. *I am seeking **to automate** the processes.*
coincide	coincidir	Nuestros horarios **coinciden** todos los días. *Our schedules **coincide** every day.*
collaborate	colaborar	**Colaboraron** para comprar este auto. *They **collaborated** to buy this car.*
compile	compilar	**Compilé** fotos de mi niñez el otro día. *I **compiled** photos of my childhood the other day.*
cooperate	cooperar	**Cooperaron** para construir esa casa. *They **cooperated** to build that house.*
coordinate	coordinar	Debemos **coordinar** la salida. *We have to **coordinate** the outing.*
denote	denotar	Este resultado **denota** una falla general. *This result **denotes** a general failure.*
derive	derivar	Esta palabra **deriva** del latín. *This word **derives** from Latin.*
deviate	desviarse	Es peligroso **desviarse** del sendero. *It's dangerous to **deviate** from the trail.*
disperse	dispersar(se)	El grupo **se dispersó** enseguida. *The group **dispersed** immediately.*
distinguish	distinguir	No logra **distinguir** entre el verde y el rojo. *He can't **distinguish** between green and red.*
diverge	divergir	La película **divergió** de la historia real. *The movie **diverged** from the real story.*
emerge	emerger	**Emergió** luego de meses aislado. *He **emerged** after months isolated.*
emit	emitir	**Emitieron** una alerta por el mal clima anoche. *They **emitted** an alert about the bad weather last night.*
err	errar	Prefiere **errar** por cauteloso. *He prefers to **err** for being cautious.*
evaluate **assess**	evaluar	Debo **evaluar** los daños. *I have to **assess** the damages.*
forge	forjar	Mi abuelo **forja** espadas. *My grandfather **forges** swords.*

improvise	improvisar	No me gusta **improvisar** sobre la marcha. *I don't like to **improvise** on the fly.*
induce	inducir	Los médicos decidieron **inducir** el parto. *The doctors decided to **induce** the labor.*
inhale	inhalar	Amo **inhalar** aire fresco. *I love to **inhale** fresh air.*
inhibit	inhibir(se)	**Se inhiben** cuando están en público. *They **get inhibited** when in public.*
insinuate	insinuar	**Estás insinuando** algo que no dije. *You **are insinuating** something I didn't say.*
inspire	inspirar	Estaba **inspirado** en los grandes autores. *He was **inspired** by the great writers.*
legislate	legislar	Intentan **legislar** sobre este tema. *They are trying to **legislate** on this issue.*
mobilize	movilizar(se)	La resistencia **se movilizó** contra la ocupación inmediatamente. *The resistance **mobilized** against the occupation immediately.*
narrate	narrar	Me gusta **narrar** historias. *I like to **narrate** stories.*
oblige compel	obligar	Las leyes nos **obligan** a comportarnos. *Laws **oblige** us to behave.*
originate	originarse	Esa fruta **se origina** en otro continente. *That fruit **originates** from another continent.*
persist	persistir	Estas hierbas **persisten** aunque las corte. *These weeds **persist** even if I cut them.*
personalize	personalizar	Siempre **personalizo** mis cuadernos. *I always **personalize** my notebooks.*
persuade	persuadir	Debes **persuadir** a mamá para que me deje. *You have to **persuade** mom so she'll let me.*
prolong	prolongar	Intenté **prolongar** mi rutina. *I tried to **prolong** my routine.*
recite	recitar	Deberá **recitar** un poema completo. *She will have to **recite** a complete poem.*
refute	refutar	En el debate, él **refutaba** todo lo que yo decía. *In the debate, he **refuted** everything I said.*
reproduce	reproducir	Intento **reproducir** la receta de mi mamá. *I'm trying to **reproduce** my mom's recipe.*
scan (computer)	escanear	¿Puedes **escanear** estas páginas, por favor? *Can you **scan** these pages, please?*
stimulate	estimular	El café me **estimula** a trabajar más. *Coffee **stimulates** me to work more.*
subsist	subsistir	He logrado **subsistir** en la naturaleza. *I've managed to **subsist** in nature.*

theorize	teorizar	Los expertos **teorizaron** la solución posible el año pasado. *The experts **theorized** the possible solution last year.*
transform	transformar(se)	**Se transformó** casi en otra persona recientemente. *He **transformed** almost into another person recently.*
transplant	trasplantar	**Trasplantaron** un riñón en su cuerpo. *They **transplanted** a kidney into his body.*

2. ADJECTIVES V

Below is a list of some common adjectives that we need at this level. Use the Anki cards created for this section to help you memorize the meaning of each word in proper contexts. Notice that an adjective must agree with the noun in number and gender.

English	Spanish	Examples
acute **sharp**	agudo	Odio los ruidos **agudos**. *I hate **sharp** noises.*
agitated	agitado	¿Te sientes **agitado**? *Are you feeling **agitated**?*
alleged	presunto	Es un **presunto** ladrón. *He's an **alleged** thief.*
astonished	asombrado	Quedé **asombrado** por mi calificación. *I was **astounded** by my grade.*
astonishing	asombroso	¡Eso fue **asombroso**! *That was **astonishing**!*
bald	calvo	Mi profesor de la universidad era **calvo**. *My university teacher was **bald**.*
based on	basado en	El libro estaba **basado en** hechos reales. *The book was **based on** real events.*
beaten **(defeated)**	vencido	Me sentí **vencido** luego de la pelea. *I felt **beaten** after the fight.*
beaten **(whipped)**	batido	Pones crema **batida** encima del pastel. *You put **whipped** cream on top of the pie.*
blurry	borroso	Veo todo **borroso** sin mis gafas. *I see everything **blurry** without my glasses.*
brief	breve	Me excusaré por un **breve** momento. *I'll excuse myself for a **brief** moment.*
brunette	morena	Esa mujer es **morena**. *That woman is a **brunette**.*

cautious	precavido cauteloso prudente	Siempre soy **cauteloso** en la calle. *I'm always **cautious** on the street.*
challenging	retador desafiante	La carrera es muy **desafiante**. *The race is very **challenging**.*
charitable	caritativo	Es un trabajo **caritativo**. *It's a **charitable** job.*
clumsy **awkward**	torpe	De niña era muy **torpe**. *As a child I was very **clumsy**.*
committed	comprometido	Están **comprometidos** con la causa ahora. *They're **committed** to the cause now.*
deaf	sordo	Mi primo nació siendo **sordo**. *My cousin was born **deaf**.*
dear	querido estimado	Era una persona muy **querida** para mí. *He was a very **dear** person to me.*
dented	abollado	El auto quedó **abollado** después del accidente. *The car was **dented** after the accident.*
dizzy	mareado	Las montañas rusas me dejan **mareado**. *Roller coasters leave me **dizzy**.*
edible	comestible	Lo creas o no, esas flores son **comestibles**. *Believe it or not, those flowers are **edible**.*
embarrassed	avergonzado	Me sentí muy **avergonzado** con lo que dijo. *I was very **embarrassed** by what he said.*
embarrassing	vergonzoso	Fue un momento un tanto **vergonzoso**. *It was a moment that was a bit **embarrassing**.*
envious	envidioso	Es muy feo ser **envidioso**. *It's very ugly to be **envious**.*
fidgety **restless**	inquieto azogado	Estás **inquieto** hoy. *You're **fidgety** today.*
flattered	halagado	Me siento **halagado** por tu interés. *I am **flattered** by your interest.*
flawed	defectuoso	Tuve que devolverlo porque estaba **defectuoso**. *I had to return it because it was **flawed**.*
floating	flotante	Me encantó ese pato **flotante**. *I loved that **floating** duck.*
following	siguiente	No puedo esperar para el **siguiente** capítulo. *I can't wait for the **following** episode.*
former	anterior	El dueño **anterior** de la casa la pintó. *The **former** owner of the house painted it.*
grated	rallado	Uso mucho queso **rallado**. *I use a lot of **grated** cheese.*
hospitable	hospitalario	Mi primo siempre es muy **hospitalario**. *My cousin is always very **hospitable**.*

immigrant	inmigrante	Soy hijo de padres **inmigrantes**. *I'm the child of **immigrant** parents.*
injured	lesionado	Fue **lesionado** durante la carrera. *He was **injured** during the race.*
in order	en orden ordenado	Me gusta mantener la casa **en orden**. *I like to keep my house **in order**.*
linked	vinculado	Él está **vinculado** a muchos rumores. *He is **linked** to many rumors.*
long-lasting	duradero	Tienen una relación muy **duradera**. *They have a very **long-lasting** relationship.*
loose	holgado suelto	Esa camisa te queda muy **holgada**. *That shirt is very **loose** on you.*
luxurious	lujoso	El restaurante era muy **lujoso**. *The restaurant was very **luxurious**.*
pale	pálido	Te ves muy **pálido**. *You look very **pale**.*
picturesque	pintoresco	Es un paisaje **pintoresco**. *It's a **picturesque** landscape.*
populated **populous**	poblado	Este pueblo no está muy **poblado**. *This town isn't very **populated**.*
reliable	confiable	Sabes que es una persona **confiable**. *You know he's a **reliable** person.*
round	redondo	La burbuja se ve **redonda**. *The bubble looks **round**.*
sacred	sagrado	Esta tierra es **sagrada** para mucha gente. *This ground is **sacred** to many people.*
safe	seguro a salvo	Se siente **seguro** contigo. *He feels **safe** with you.*
scared	asustado espantado	Mi cachorro estaba **asustado** cuando lo vi. *My puppy was **scared** when I saw him.*
scary	aterrador asustadizo de miedo	Los zombis son **aterradores**. *Zombies are **scary**.*
shredded	triturado	Vi papeles **triturados** en la cesta. *I saw **shredded** papers in the basket.*
square	cuadrado	Intenté que el invernáculo fuera **cuadrado**. *I tried to make the greenhouse **squared**.*
steep	escarpado empinado	La montaña es muy **empinada**. *The mountain is very **steep**.*
stingy	tacaño	Una persona muy **tacaña** no es un buen amigo. *A very **stingy** person is not a good friend.*
subtle	sutil	Me gusta usar maquillaje **sutil**. *I like to wear **subtle** makeup.*

sudden	repentino	El cambio fue muy **repentino**. *The change was very **sudden**.*
suitable	adecuado apropiado idóneo	Es un maestro **idóneo** para esos niños. *He's a **suitable** teacher for those children.*
surprised	sorprendido	Puso cara de **sorprendido**. *He put on a **surprised** face.*
surprising	sorprendente	Fue un hecho **sorprendente**. *It was a **surprising** event.*
suspicious	sospechoso	Su comportamiento es muy **sospechoso**. *His behavior is very **suspicious**.*
tight	apretado ajustado	Está muy **apretado** dentro de este coche. *It is very **tight** inside this car.*
unbearable	insoportable inaguantable	El dolor era **inaguantable**. *The pain was **unbearable**.*
unbeatable	invencible imbatible	Fue **invencible** durante mucho tiempo. *He was **unbeatable** for a long time.*
unprecedented	sin precedentes	Fue un resultado **sin precedentes**. *It was an **unprecedented** result.*
unworthy	indigno	Es **indigno** de mi confianza. *He's **unworthy** of my trust.*
veiled	velado	La novia caminó al altar **velada**. *The bride walked to the altar **veiled**.*
wavy	ondulado	Mi cabello es **ondulado**. *My hair is **wavy**.*
wicked **evil**	malvado	El villano era muy **malvado**. *The villain was very **wicked**.*
wild **savage**	salvaje silvestre	Esta planta es una flor **silvestre**. *This plant is a **wild** flower.*
willing to	dispuesto a	Estoy **dispuesto a** ayudarte en todo. *I'm **willing to** help you with everything.*
wooden	de madera	Tenía muchos juguetes **de madera**. *He had a lot of **wooden** toys.*
worthy of	digno de	Es **digno del** título que se ganó. *He's **worthy of** the title he earned.*
woven	tejido	Es un lindo cárdigan **tejido**. *It's a nice **woven** cardigan.*
wrinkled	arrugado	Esa camisa está muy **arrugada**. *That shirt is very **wrinkled**.*
zealous	celoso	Era muy **celoso** en su ideología. *He was very **zealous** in his ideology.*

In addition to the above new adjectives, we add a few English cognates that are easy to memorize.

English	Spanish	Examples
absurd	absurdo	La trama me pareció **absurda**. *The plot seemed **absurd** to me.*
adequate	adecuado	Tiene un precio **adecuado**. *It has an **adequate** price.*
aggregate	agregado	Dice que no tiene azúcar **agregado**. *It says it doesn't have **aggregated** sugar.*
ambitious	ambicioso	Mi hermano siempre ha sido **ambicioso**. *My brother has always been **ambitious**.*
anonymous	anónimo	Esa pintura fue hecha por un artista **anónimo**. *That painting was made by an **anonymous** artist.*
appropriate	apropiado	¿Este atuendo te parece **apropiado**? *Does this outfit seem **appropriate** to you?*
archeological	arqueológico	Esta reliquia **arqueológica** es de otra época. *This **archeological** relic is from another era.*
balanced	balanceado	Llevo una dieta **balanceada**. *I have a **balanced** diet.*
conscientious	concienzudo	Mi padre es muy **concienzudo**. *My father is very **conscientious**.*
consecutive	consecutivo	Están en orden **consecutivo**. *They are in **consecutive** order.*
cosmopolitan	cosmopolita	No me considero una persona **cosmopolita**. *I don't consider myself a **cosmopolitan** person.*
curved	curvo curvado	Mi casa tiene una pared **curvada**. *My house has a **curved** wall.*
definite	definitivo	Este será su puesto **definitivo**. *This will be his **definitive** spot.*
deliberate	deliberado	Lo hizo de manera **deliberada**. *He did it in a **deliberate** manner.*
delicate	delicado	Lavo la ropa **delicada** a mano. *I wash **delicate** clothes by hand.*
desperate	desesperado	Estaba **desesperado** por obtener el empleo. *I was **desperate** to obtain the job.*
erroneous	erróneo	La primera vez tuvo un resultado **erróneo**. *The first time, he had an **erroneous** result.*
essential	esencial	El agua es **esencial** para la vida. *Water is **essential** for life.*
explicit	explícito	La película tiene violencia **explícita**. *The movie has **explicit** violence.*
federal	federal	La infracción de los derechos de autor es un delito **federal**. *Copyright infraction is a **federal** offense.*

frantic	frenético	Se puso **frenético** porque no estaba allí. *He was **frantic** because it wasn't there.*
homogenous	homogéneo	Mezcla hasta que la masa sea **homogénea**. *Stir until the dough is **homogeneous**.*
humanitarian	humanitario	Participo en varias obras **humanitarias**. *I participate in various **humanitarian** works.*
immersed	inmerso	Estaba completamente **inmerso** en la trama. *I was completely **immersed** in the plot.*
individual[1]	individual	Aquí tienes un postre **individual**. *Here you have an **individual** dessert.*
insufferable	insufrible	A veces las lecciones son **insufribles**. *Sometimes the lessons are **insufferable**.*
intimate	íntimo	Solo tuvieron una boda **íntima**. *They just had an **intimate** wedding.*
involuntary **inadvertent**	involuntario	El hipo es un reflejo **involuntario**. *A hiccup is an **involuntary** reflex.*
junior	júnior	Entrará en un nivel **júnior**. *He'll enter at a **junior** level.*
legitimate	legítimo	Al final, tuvo un heredero **legítimo**. *In the end, he had a **legitimate** heir.*
mere	mero	Era una **mera** espectadora del suceso. *She was a **mere** spectator of the event.*
meticulous	meticuloso	Soy muy **meticuloso** cuando cocino. *I am very **meticulous** when I cook.*
metropolitan	metropolitano	Queda en la zona **metropolitana** del país. *It's in the **metropolitan** area of the country.*
pertinent **relevant**	pertinente	Necesito información **pertinente**. *I need **pertinent** information.*
pioneer	pionero	Fue un **pionero** en su campo. *He was a **pioneer** in his field.*
privileged	privilegiado	No es una persona **privilegiada**. *He's not a **privileged** person.*
reciprocal	recíproco	El amor que tenían era **recíproco**. *The love they had was **reciprocal**.*
sinister	siniestro	Me asustó su risa **siniestra**. *His **sinister** laugh scared me.*
spontaneous	espontáneo	Me gusta sacar fotos **espontáneas**. *I like to take **spontaneous** photos.*

---

[1] The adjective *"individual"* in English is referred to using the adjective **"individual"** in Spanish spelled the same way, whereas the noun *"individual"* referring to a person uses the Spanish word **"individuo[m]."**

sterile	estéril	Debes limpiarlo con una gasa **estéril**. *You have to clean it with a sterile gauze.*
synthetic	sintético	Prefiero usar telas **sintéticas**. *I prefer to use synthetic fabrics.*
theoretical	teórico	No soy bueno para las ciencias **teóricas**. *I'm not good at theoretical sciences.*
tremendous	tremendo	La crianza tiene un impacto **tremendo** en nuestras vidas. *Upbringing has a tremendous impact on our lives.*
urban	urbano	Esta zona tiene varias leyendas **urbanas**. *This zone has various urban legends.*
vague	vago [1]	La descripción del libro es muy **vaga**. *The book's description is too vague.*
vigorous	vigoroso	Hice un entrenamiento **vigoroso**. *I did vigorous training.*
visionary	visionario	Da Vinci es considerado un pensador **visionario**. *Da Vinci is considered a visionary thinker.*

---

[1] The adjective "**vago**" also means *"lazy"* referring to a person, or can be used as a noun meaning a *"slacker"* or an *"idle person."*

3. ANIMALS II

Here we add more animal vocabulary to our list.

alligator	**caimán**[m]	*howl (of a wolf)*	**aullido**[m]
ant	**hormiga**[f]	*hunting*	**caza**[f]
bark (of a dog)	**ladrido**[m]	*ivory*	**marfil**[m]
bat (animal)	**murciélago**[m]	*kangaroo*	**canguro**[m]
bear	**oso**[m]	*lion*	**león**[m]
beaver	**castor**[m]	*monkey*	**mono**[m]
bee	**abeja**[f]	*octopus*	**pulpo**[m]
beehive	**colmena**[f]	*ostrich*	**avestruz**[m]
breed	**raza**[f]	*owl*	**búho**[m]
cage	**jaula**[f]	*oyster*	**ostra**[f]
camel	**camello**[m]	*parrot*	**loro**[m]
caterpillar	**oruga**[f]	*paw*	**pata**[f]
cattle	**ganado**[m]	*peacock*	**pavo real**[m]
cheetah	**guepardo**[m]	*penguin*	**pingüino**[m]
chick	**polluelo**[m] **pollito**[m]	*petting*	**caricia**[f]
cockroach	**cucaracha**[f]	*poaching*	**caza**[f] **furtiva**
creature	**criatura**[f]	*predator*	**depredador**[m]

crocodile	**cocodrilo**[m]	*prey*	**presa**[f]
deer	**ciervo**[m]	*seagull*	**gaviota**[f]
dinosaur	**dinosaurio**[m]	*seal*	**foca**[f]
dove *pigeon*	**paloma**[f]	*shark*	**tiburón**[m]
eagle	**águila**[f]	*slaughterhouse*	**matadero**[m]
elephant	**elefante**[m]	*snake*	**serpiente**[f] **culebra**[f]
extinction	**extinción**[f]	*spider*	**araña**[f]
falcon	**halcón**[m]	*spiderweb*	**telaraña**[f]
feather	**pluma**[f]	*squirrel*	**ardilla**[f]
fishing rod	**caña**[f] **de pescar**	*tail*	**cola**[f]
fox	**zorro**[m]	*tiger*	**tigre**[m]
frog	**rana**[f]	*turtle* *tortoise*	**tortuga**[f]
gill	**branquia**[f]	*vulture*	**buitre**[m]
giraffe	**jirafa**[f]	*wasp*	**avispa**[f]
goat	**cabra**[f]	*whale*	**ballena**[f]
goose	**ganso**[m]	*wing*	**ala**[f]
herd	**manada**[f] **rebaño**[m]	*wolf*	**lobo**[m]
hippopotamus	**hipopótamo**[m]	*worm*	**gusano**[m]

4. POLITICS

Politics, in Spanish, is "**la política**," and it is singular. Below is some related vocabulary:

agenda	**agenda**[f]	*governor*	**gobernador**[m]
ambassador	**embajador**[m]	*grant* *subsidy*	**subvención**[f]
anthem	**himno**[m]	*heritage*	**patrimonio**[m]
awareness	**conciencia**[f]	*mayor*	**alcalde**[m]
ballot box	**urna electoral**[f]	*mayoress*	**alcaldesa**[f]
bill (law)	**proyecto**[m] **de ley**	*measures*	**medidas**[f]
candidate	**candidato**[m]	*minister*	**ministro**[m]
citizen	**ciudadano**[m]	*ministry*	**ministerio**[m]
citizenship	**ciudadanía**[f]	*monarchy*	**monarquía**[f]
congress	**congreso**[m]	*nomination*	**nominación**[f]

constitution	**constitución**[f]	*official (government employee)*	**funcionario**[m]
controversy	**polémica**[f] **controversia**[f]	*parliament*	**parlamento**[m]
council (committee)	**consejo**[m]	*podium*	**podio**[m]
coup d'état	**golpe**[m] **de estado**	*policy*	**póliza**[f] **política**[f]
county	**condado**[m]	*political party*	**partido político**[m]
crown	**corona**[f]	*political post*	**puesto político**[m]
democracy	**democracia**[f]	*power*	**poder**[m]
demonstration	**manifestación**[f]	*prince*	**príncipe**[m]
dictatorship	**dictadura**[f]	*princess*	**princesa**[f]
donor	**donante**[m,f]	*protocol*	**protocolo**[m]
dual-citizenship	**doble nacionalidad**	*rebel*	**rebelde**[m]
dynasty	**dinastía**[f]	*referendum*	**referéndum**[m]
election	**elección**[f]	*republic*	**república**[f]
electoral campaign	**campaña electoral**[f]	*senate*	**senado**[m]
embassy	**embajada**[f]	*senator*	**senador**[m]
emperor	**emperador**[m]	*skeptic*	**escéptico**[m]
empire	**imperio**[m]	*slip of the tongue*	**lapsus**[m] **desliz**[m]
ethics	**ética**[f]	*trick*	**truco**[m]
exit polls	**encuestas de salida** **encuestas a boca de urna**	*unrest*	**agitación**[f] **disturbios**[m]
flag	**bandera**[f]	*vice president*	**vicepresidente**[m]
government	**gobierno**[m]	*vote*	**voto**[m]

5. COUNTRIES & NATIONALITIES II

More vocabulary to expand our knowledge about countries and nationalities is in the table below:

Algeria	**Argelia**[f]	*Algerian*	**argelino/-a**
Austria	**Austria**[f]	*Austrian*	**austríaco/-a** **austriaco/-a**
Belarus	**Bielorrusia**[f]	*Belarusian*	**bielorruso/-a**
Belgium	**Bélgica**[f]	*Belgian*	**belga**
Belize	**Belice**[f]	*Belizean*	**beliceño/-a**
Central America	**América**[f] **Central**	*Central American*	**centroamericano/-a**
Chile	**Chile**[m]	*Chilean*	**chileno/-a**

Costa Rica	**Costa Rica**[f]	*Costa Rican*	**costarricense**
Denmark	**Dinamarca**[f]	*Danish*	**danés/-esa**
Ecuador	**Ecuador**[m]	*Ecuadorian*	**ecuatoriano/-a**
Finland	**Finlandia**[f]	*Finnish*	**finlandés/-esa**
Greece	**Grecia**[f]	*Greek*	**griego/-a**
Guatemala	**Guatemala**[f]	*Guatemalan*	**guatemalteco/-a**
Haiti	**Haití**[m]	*Haitian*	**haitiano/-a**
Honduras	**Honduras**[f]	*Honduran*	**hondureño/-a**
Hungary	**Hungría**[f]	*Hungarian*	**húngaro/-a**
India	**India**[f]	*Indian*	**indio/-a**
Ireland	**Irlanda**[f]	*Irish*	**irlandés/-esa**
Lebanon	**Líbano**[m]	*Lebanese*	**libanés/-esa**
Middle East	**Medio**[m] **Oriente**	*Middle Eastern*	**del Medio Oriente**
Netherlands	**Países Bajos**[m]	*Dutch*	**holandés/-esa**
Nicaragua	**Nicaragua**[f]	*Nicaraguan*	**nicaragüense**
North America	**América**[f] **del Norte**	*North American*	**norteamericano/-a**
Norway	**Noruega**[f]	*Norwegian*	**noruego/-a**
Peru	**Perú**[m]	*Peruvian*	**peruano/-a**
Philippines	**Filipinas**[f]	*Filipino*	**filipino/-a**
Romania	**Rumania**[f] **Rumanía**[f]	*Romanian*	**rumano/-a**
South Korea	**Corea**[f] **del Sur**	*South Korean*	**surcoreano/-a**
Sweden	**Suecia**[f]	*Swedish*	**sueco/-a**
Switzerland	**Suiza**[f]	*Swiss*	**suizo/-a**
Syria	**Siria**[f]	*Syrian*	**sirio/-a**
Thailand	**Tailandia**[f]	*Thai*	**tailandés/-esa**
Ukraine	**Ucrania**[f]	*Ukrainian*	**ucraniano/-a**
United Kingdom	**Reino Unido**[m]	*British*	**británico/-a** [1]
United States	**Estados Unidos**[m]	*American*	**estadounidense** [2]
Venezuela	**Venezuela**[f]	*Venezuelan*	**venezolano/-a**
Wales	**Gales**[f]	*Welsh*	**galés/-esa**

[1] The term "**británico**" is also used to refer to the citizens of *Great Britain* or "**Gran Bretaña**."
[2] Although "**estadounidense**" is the correct term to refer to someone from the US and "**americano**" refers to a male person from the American continent, the term "**americano**" is widely accepted referring to a male person from the US.

6. TRANSPORTATION II

We continue to add more vocabulary related to transportation.

anchor	**ancla**[f]	*ride (bike)*	**paseo**[m]
bus stop	**parada**[f] **de autobús**	*ride (car)*	**vuelta**[f]

chassis	**chasis**[m] **armazón**[m]	*rush hour*	**hora pico** **hora punta**
cobblestone	**adoquines**[m]	*sailing boat*	**velero**[m]
convertible (car)	**descapotable**[m]	*scratch*	**arañazo**[m] **rasguño**[m]
curb [1]	**borde**[m] **bordillo**[m]	*seat*	**asiento**[m]
dashboard	**tablero**[m]	*seat belt*	**cinturón**[m] **de seguridad**
dent	**abolladura**[f]	*ship*	**navío**[m]
flat tire	**pinchazo**[m]	*shipwreck*	**naufragio**[m]
fuel	**combustible**[m]	*speed bump* [2]	**badén**[m]
glove compartment	**guantera**[f]	*speed limit*	**límite**[m] **de velocidad**
gravel	**grava**[f]	*steering wheel*	**volante**[m]
hood (car)	**capó**[m]	*toll*	**peaje**[m]
landing	**aterrizaje**[m]	*traffic jam*	**embotellamiento**[m]
lane	**carril**[m]	*traffic light*	**semáforo**[m]
notice (warning)	**aviso**[m]	*truck*	**maletero**[m]
pedestrian	**peatón**[m]	*tunnel*	**túnel**[m]
postage stamp	**estampilla**[f] **sello**[m]	*undocumented*	**indocumentado**[m]
pothole	**bache**[m]	*van*	**furgoneta**[f]
railway	**ferrocarril**[m]	*warning*	**advertencia**[f]
rearview mirror	**retrovisor**[m]	*wheel*	**rueda**[f]

[1] This word varies between Spanish-speaking countries. The word "**bordillo**[m]" is used in Spain, "**sardinel**[m]" in the Northern part of South America, "**cordón**[m]" in the Southern part of South America, and "**cuenta**[f]" in some Caribbean countries.

[2] This is another word that varies a lot between Spanish-speaking countries. In addition to "**badén**[m]," you may hear "**policía acostada**[f]" across Latin America, "**tope**[m]" in Mexico, "**resalto**[m]" in Spain and Chile, and "**lomo**[m] **de burro**" in Argentina.

7. NATURE II

Let us go over more vocabulary related to nature.

ash	**ceniza**[f]	*mud*	**lodo**[m] **barro**[m]
bank (river)	**orilla**[f]	*organ*	**órgano**[m]
bay	**bahía**[f]	*passage*	**pasaje**[m]
beauty	**belleza**[f]	*path*	**camino**[m]

branch	**rama**^f	*peak*	**pico**^m **cumbre**^f **cima**^f
brook	**arroyo**^m	*pearl*	**perla**^f
bush	**arbusto**^m	*pollutant*	**contaminante**^m
carbon dioxide	**dióxido**^m **de carbono**	*pollution*	**contaminación**^f
cliff	**acantilado**^m	*pond*	**estanque**^m **charca**^f
darkness *gloom*	**oscuridad**^f	*puddle*	**charco**^m
dawn	**amanecer**^m **alba**^f **madrugada**^f	*rainbow*	**arcoíris**^m
dew	**rocío**^m	*ranch*	**hacienda**^f **estancia**^f
dusk *nightfall*	**anochecer**^m	*ravine*	**barranco**^m
earthquake	**terremoto**^m **sismo**^m	*ray* *beam*	**rayo**^m
eclipse	**eclipse**^m	*reef*	**arrecife**^m
environment	**ambiente**^m **medioambiente**^m	*rock*	**roca**^f
flood	**inundación**^f **diluvio**^m	*seashell*	**concha**^f
fog	**niebla**^f	*slope*	**cuesta**^f
forecast	**pronóstico**^m	*soil*	**suelo**^m
forest	**bosque**^m	*sound*	**sonido**^m
frost	**escarcha**^f	*species*	**especie**^f
fumes *smoke*	**humo**^m	*spectrum*	**espectro**^m
galaxy	**galaxia**^f	*stick*	**palo**^m
gap	**brecha**^f	*stone*	**piedra**^f
geology	**geología**^f	*storm*	**tormenta**^f
grove	**arboleda**^f	*strength* *force*	**fuerza**^f
heat	**calor**^m	*sunrise*	**salida**^f **del sol**
heatwave	**ola**^f **de calor**	*sunset*	**puesta**^f **del sol**
hemisphere	**hemisferio**^m	*surface*	**superficie**^f
hill	**colina**^f **cerro**^m	*swamp*	**pantano**^m

horizon	**horizonte**^{m}	*thorn*	**espina**^{f}
humidity	**humedad**^{f}	*thunder*	**truenos**$^{m\ 1}$
hurricane	**huracán**^{m}	*trail*	**sendero**^{m}
hydrogen	**hidrógeno**^{m}	*trench*	**zanja**^{f} **trinchera**^{f}
instinct	**instinto**^{m}	*trunk (tree)* *log (tree)*	**tronco**^{m}
jungle	**selva**^{f}	*twilight*	**crepúsculo**^{m}
leaf (tree)	**hoja**^{f}	*vacuum*	**vacío**^{m}
lightning	**relámpago**^{m}	*valley*	**valle**^{m}
marvel	**maravilla**^{f}	*vine*	**vid**^{f} **parra**^{f}
mist	**neblina**^{f}	*volcano*	**volcán**^{m}
molecule	**molécula**^{f}	*waterfall*	**cascada**^{f}
mountain range	**cordillera**^{f} **sierra**^{f}	*wave*	**ola**^{f}

[1] Use the plural form "**truenos**" to refer to the uncountable sense of thunder.

8. HEALTH II

We add more vocabulary related to health.

allergy	**alergia**^{f}	*injection*	**inyección**^{f}
ambulance	**ambulancia**^{f}	*microbe*	**microbio**^{m}
anti-allergy drug	**antialérgico**^{m}	*migraine*	**migraña**^{f}
antibiotic	**antibiótico**^{m}	*operating room*	**quirófano**^{m}
arthritis	**artritis**^{f}	*outbreak*	**brote**^{m}
bandage	**vendaje**^{m} **venda**^{f}	*pandemic*	**pandemia**^{f}
bee sting	**picadura**^{f} **de abeja**	*paralysis*	**parálisis**^{f}
cholesterol	**colesterol**^{m}	*pest*	**peste**^{f}
cough	**tos**^{f}	*plague*	**plaga**^{f}
cramp	**calambre**^{m}	*pneumonia*	**neumonía**^{f}
cream	**crema**^{f}	*prescription*	**receta**^{f}
diabetes	**diabetes**^{f}	*psychology*	**psicología**^{f}
diagnosis	**diagnóstico**^{m}	*pulse (health)*	**pulso**^{m}
dizziness	**mareo**^{m}	*remedy*	**remedio**^{m}
dose	**dosis**^{f}	*rupture*	**ruptura**^{f}
drop	**gota**^{f}	*scar*	**cicatriz**^{f}
emergency room	**sala**^{f} **de emergencias**	*seizure*	**convulsiones**^{f}

epidemic	**epidemia**f	*shiver* / *chill*	**escalofrío**m
epilepsy	**epilepsia**f	*side effect*	**efecto secundario**m
first aid	**primeros auxilios**m	*smallpox*	**viruela**f
food poisoning	**intoxicación alimentaria**f	*sneeze*	**estornudo**m
fracture	**fractura**f	*stroke*	**derrame cerebral**m
germ	**germen**m	*stitches*	**puntos**m / **suturas**f
heart attack	**infarto**m / **ataque**m **al corazón**	*stuffy nose*	**nariz tapada**f
heart burn	**acidez**f	*sunstroke*	**insolación**f
high pressure	**alta presión**f	*syringe*	**jeringuilla**f
hygiene	**higiene**f	*treatment*	**tratamiento**m
immunity	**inmunidad**f	*vomit*	**vómito**m

9. FOOD III

We continue to add to our set of vocabulary related to food.

all-you-can-eat buffet	**bufé libre**m / **tenedor libre**m	*ginger*	**jengibre**m
asparagus	**espárrago**m	*jam*	**mermelada**f
baking	**cocción**f / **hornada**f	*layer*	**capa**f
beet	**remolacha**f	*leftovers*	**las sobras**
bite	**bocado**m	*mushroom*	**hongo**m
blackberry	**mora**f	*noodles*	**fideos**m
carbohydrate	**carbohidrato**m	*oat*	**avena**f
cashew	**anacardo**m	*peach*	**durazno**m / **melocotón**m
cauliflower	**coliflor**f	*peas*	**guisantes**m
chewing gum	**chicle**m / **goma**f **de mascar**	*pine nut*	**piñón**m
chickpea	**garbanzo**m	*plum*	**ciruela**f
cookie	**galleta**f	*potion*	**poción**f / **pócima**f
crust	**corteza**f	*pumpkin*	**calabaza**f
dairy	**lácteos**m	*quince*	**membrillo**m
date	**dátil**m	*radish*	**rábano**m
fat	**grasa**f	*sausage*	**salchicha**f
fig	**higo**m	*seed*	**semilla**f

flour	**harina**[f]	*soy*	**soja**[f]
garlic	**ajo**[m]	*slice*[1]	**rebanada**[f] **rodaja**[f]
glucose	**glucosa**[f]	*spinach*	**espinaca**[f]
grain	**grano**[m]	*starch*	**almidón**[m]
green beans	**judías verdes**[f]	*turnip*	**nabo**[m]
harvest *crop*	**cosecha**[f]	*wheat*	**trigo**[m]
hazelnut	**avellana**[f]	*zucchini*	**calabacín**[m]

[1] There are multiple words in Spanish that can be translated as *"slice"* in English depending on the context:

1. *slice (of bread)*: **rebanada**[f]
2. *slice (of fruit or vegetable)*: **rodaja**[f]
3. *slice (of cake or pie)*: **trozo**[m], **pedazo**[m], **rebanada**[f]
4. *slice (of sausage or cheese)*: **loncha**[f]
5. *slice (of meat)*: **tajada**[f]

10. ANATOMY II

Below is some more advanced vocabulary related to anatomy:

armpit	**axila**[f]	*lung*	**pulmón**[m]
blood vessel	**vaso sanguíneo**[m]	*nail*	**uña**[f]
bone	**hueso**[m]	*neck*	**cuello**[m]
cell	**célula**[f]	*nerve*	**nervio**[m]
chest	**pecho**[m]	*reflex*	**reflejo**[m]
chin	**mentón**[m] **barbilla**[f]	*skeleton*	**esqueleto**[m]
elbow	**codo**[m]	*skull*	**cráneo**[m] **calavera**[f]
dimple	**hoyuelo**[m]	*spine*	**columna vertebral**[f]
forehead	**frente**[f]	*spleen*	**bazo**[m]
hip	**cadera**[f]	*tear*	**lágrima**[f]
intestine	**intestino**[m]	*throat*	**garganta**[f]
joint	**articulación**[f]	*tongue*	**lengua**[f]
kidney	**riñón**[m]	*vein*	**vena**[f]
liver	**hígado**[m]	*waist*	**cintura**[f]

LEVEL VI: FLUENT

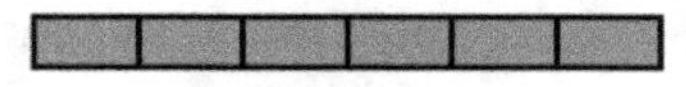

I. Introductory Topics & Grammar

Congratulations on reaching the fluent level. It must feel great to have achieved this accomplishment. At this level, all you need is to perfect a few concepts that are preventing you from achieving fluency. Use the Anki cards to reinforce these topics in your memory with reviews and exercises.

1. ORDINAL NUMBERS II

Ordinal numbers between 11 and 19 are as follows:

once	11	undécimo, undécima	11.º / 11.ª
doce	12	duodécimo, duodécima	12.º / 12.ª
trece	13	decimotercero, decimotercera	13.º / 13.ª
catorce	14	decimocuarto, decimocuarta	14.º / 14.ª
quince	15	decimoquinto, decimoquinta	15.º / 15.ª
dieciséis	16	decimosexto, decimosexta	16.º / 16.ª
diecisiete	17	decimoséptimo, decimoséptima	17.º / 17.ª
dieciocho	18	decimoctavo, decimoctava	18.º / 18.ª
diecinueve	19	decimonoveno, decimonovena	19.º / 19.ª

Ordinal numbers beyond 10 are not commonly used. However, it can be useful to know them. Ordinal numbers are adjectives and must agree in gender and number with the noun.

veinte	20	vigésimo, vigésima	20.º / 20.ª
treinta	30	trigésimo, trigésima	30.º / 30.ª
cuarenta	40	cuadragésimo, cuadragésima	40.º / 40.ª
cincuenta	50	quincuagésimo, quincuagésima	50.º / 50.ª
sesenta	60	sexagésimo, sexagésima	60.º / 60.ª
setenta	70	septuagésimo, septuagésima	70.º / 70.ª
ochenta	80	octogésimo, octogésima	80.º / 80.ª
noventa	90	nonagésimo, nonagésima	90.º / 90.ª
cien	100	centésimo, centésima	100.º / 100.ª

doscientos	200	ducentésimo, ducentésima	200.º / 200.ª
trescientos	300	tricentésimo, tricentésima	300.º / 300.ª
cuatrocientos	400	cuadrigentésimo, cuadrigentésima	400.º / 400.ª
quinientos	500	quingentésimo, quingentésima	500.º / 500.ª
seiscientos	600	sexcentésimo, sexcentésima	600.º / 600.ª
setecientos	700	septingentésimo, septingentésima	700.º / 700.ª
ochocientos	800	octingentésimo, octingentésima	800.º / 800.ª
novecientos	900	noningentésimo, noningentésima	900.º / 900.ª
mil	1.000	milésimo, milésima	1000.º / 1000.ª
millón	1.000.000	millonésimo, millonésima	1000000.º / 1000000.ª

❖ Numbers following the names of kings and queens are ordinal from first to tenth, and cardinal above that, e.g., **Isabel segunda (2.ª)**, **Eduardo tercero (3.º)**, **Luis catorce (14)**, **Alfonso trece (13)**, etc.

❖ Fractional numbers from 11th and above are formed from cardinal numbers by adding "**-avo**" to the end of the cardinal number, e.g., 1/16 = **un dieciseisavo**.

Collective Numbers

A collective number refers to a set or group of items. Examples include:

un par	*a pair, a couple*
una decena	*a set of ten*
una docena	*a dozen*
una treintena	*a set of 30*
un centenar/ una centena	*a set of 100, around 100*
un millar	*around a thousand*

2. "Should/Could/Would Have …"

To convey the meaning of *"would/could/should have …"* in Spanish, we resort to the conditional tense.

❖ *"Would have"* + past participle = "**Haber**" in conditional tense + past participle, for example:

Yo lo **habría hecho**.	*I **would have done** it.*
Ellos **habrían pagado**.	*They **would have paid**.*
Nosotros **habríamos venido**.	*We **would have come**.*

❖ *"Could have"* + past participle = "**Poder**" in conditional tense + "**haber**" + past participle, for example:

Yo lo **podría haber hecho**.	*I **could have done** it.*
Ellos **podrían haber pagado**.	*They **could have paid**.*
Nosotros **podríamos haber venido**.	*We **could have come**.*

❖ *"Should have"* + past participle = "**Deber**" in conditional tense + "**haber**" + past participle, for example:

Yo lo **debería haber hecho**.	*I **should have done** it.*
Ellos **deberían haber pagado**.	*They **should have paid**.*
Nosotros **deberíamos haber venido**.	*We **should have come**.*

Another way to express *"should have …"* is by using "**tener**" in the conditional tense:

"Should have" … + past participle = "**Tener**" in conditional tense + "**que haber**" + past participle, for example:

Yo **tendría que haberlo hecho**.	*I **should have done** it.*
Ellos **tendrían que haber pagado**.	*They **should have paid**.*
Nosotros **tendríamos que haber venido**.	*We **should have come**.*

3. PLUPERFECT INDICATIVE TENSE

The pluperfect tense, literally *the more than perfect*, describes the past before the simple past. If two actions took place in the past, the one that occurred before is often described in the pluperfect. In case you encounter it in Spanish, the name of this tense is "**el pretérito pluscuamperfecto**."

The pluperfect indicative is formed as follows:

"**Haber**" in the imperfect + past participle

The pluperfect indicative uses the verb "**haber**" in the imperfect and is conjugated as follows:

		-ar ending hablar	-er ending comer	-ir ending vivir
yo	había			
tú	habías			
él/ella/usted	había	hab**lado**	com**ido**	viv**ido**
nosotros/-as	habíamos			
vosotros/-as	habíais			
ellos/ellas/ustedes	habían			

For example:

Antes de conocernos, nunca **había ido** a España.	*Before we met, I **had** never **been** to Spain.*
Cuando visité a mi mamá, mi hermana ya **había llegado**.	*When I visited my mom, my sister **had** already **arrived**.*
Después de que el partido **había sido** cancelado, los espectadores se fueron a casa.	*After the game **had been** canceled, the spectators went home.*

4. PLUPERFECT SUBJUNCTIVE TENSE

The pluperfect subjunctive is formed as follows:

"**Haber**" in the imperfect subjunctive + past participle

The verb "**haber**" in the imperfect subjunctive is conjugated as follows:

		-ar ending hablar	-er ending comer	-ir ending vivir
yo	hubiera			
tú	hubieras			
él/ella/usted	hubiera	hab**lado**	com**ido**	viv**ido**
nosotros/-as	hubiéramos			
vosotros/-as	hubierais			
ellos/ellas/ustedes	hubieran			

The pluperfect in the subjunctive mood has different uses than the pluperfect in the indicative mood studied earlier. It is mostly used to describe an event that already happened in the past, but we wish it did not happen or happened differently, or we want to discuss what would happen if we hypothetically changed that past event.

We will discuss three examples in which the pluperfect subjunctive is used:

1. One common use is with the word "**ojalá**," which is roughly translated as *"I wish"* or *"we wish,"* for example:

Ojalá **hubiera estudiado** medicina.	*I wish I* **had studied** *medicine.*
Ojalá mi abuelo **no hubiera muerto**.	*I wish my grandfather* **hadn't died**.

In all the events described in the above sentences, it is clear that it is *impossible* to change the *past*. Therefore, any wish to even hypothetically talk about such a change must be expressed in the pluperfect subjunctive.

The interested reader may refer to **Appendix H** for a summary of the uses of "**ojalá**" in Spanish.

2. The pluperfect subjunctive is also used in conditional statements to convey the above meaning of the impossible past, for example:

Si **hubiera estudiado** medicina, …	*If I* **had studied** *medicine, …*
Si mi abuelo no **hubiera muerto**, …	*If my grandfather* **hadn't died**, …

The conditional statements above are usually followed by

❖ a verb in simple conditional, or

❖ *"would have"* + past participle

Si **hubiera estudiado** medicina, **sería** rico hoy.	*If I* **had studied** *medicine, I* **would be** *rich today.*
Si mi abuelo no **hubiera muerto**, **habría pasado** tiempo con él.[1]	*If my grandfather* **hadn't died**, *I* **would have spent** *time with him.*

---

[1] It is not uncommon to hear "**habría**" replaced with "**hubiera**" in informal conversation, e.g., "**Si mi abuelo no hubiera muerto, <u>hubiera</u> pasado tiempo con él**." According to the RAE, this sentence is considered grammatically acceptable.

Another way to describe a hypothetical or impossible past is using the expression "**como si**," translated as *"as if,"* for example:

| Habla como si **hubiera estudiado** medicina. | He *talks as if he **had studied** medicine.* |
| Lloró como si su abuelo **hubiera muerto**. | He *cried as if his grandfather **had died**.* |

3. One use of the pluperfect in the subjunctive is similar to that in the indicative mood. As studied earlier, the pluperfect in the indicative mood is used to describe the past before the simple past. If doubt or hope is added to the action described in the pluperfect, the subjunctive mood should be used. Let us look at the following examples for comparison:

a) Pluperfect in the indicative mood:

| Antes de conocernos, **habías ido** a España. | *Before we met, you **had been** to Spain.* |
| Cuando visité a mi mamá, mi hermana ya **había llegado**. | *When I visited my mom, my sister **had** already **arrived**.* |

b) Pluperfect in the subjunctive mood:

| Antes de conocernos, me gustó que ya **hubieras ido** a España. | *Before we met, I was delighted that you **had** already **been** to Spain.* |
| Cuando visité a mi mamá, dudé que mi hermana **hubiera llegado**. | *When I visited my mom, I doubted that my sister **had** already **arrived**.* |

Finally, remember that there is another accepted but less common conjugation of "**haber**" in the pluperfect subjunctive. For example, we could replace "**hubiera**" in the above examples with "**hubiese**," which does not change the meaning.

5. USE OF "AUNQUE," "SI BIEN," AND "A PESAR DE"

"**Aunque**" and "**si bien**" convey the same meaning of *"although"* or *"even though"* if followed by the *indicative*, for example:

Aunque/Si bien no quiero comer, iré al café contigo.	***Although*** *I don't want to eat, I will go to the café with you.*
Aunque/Si bien hice mucho ejercicio, no bajé de peso.	***Even though*** *I exercised a lot, I didn't lose weight.*

On the other hand, **"aunque"** conveys the meaning of *"even if"* when followed by the *subjunctive*, for example:

Aunque no quiera comer, iré al café contigo.	***Even if*** *I don't want to eat, I will go to the café with you.*
Aunque haga mucho ejercicio, no bajo de peso.	***Even if*** *I exercise a lot, I don't lose weight.*

Notice that only **"aunque,"** and not **"si bien,"** can be used in these examples, followed by the subjunctive.

"A pesar de" means *"despite"* or *"in spite of."* It can be used in one of three formulas:

1. A pesar de + Infinitive, for example:

A pesar de estar cansado, quiero salir con mis amigos.	***In spite of*** *being tired, I want to go out with my friends.*

2. A pesar de + Noun, for example:

A pesar de las advertencias, Ana sigue fumando.	***Despite*** *the warnings, Ana continues to smoke.*

3. A pesar de que + Indicative Tense, for example:

A pesar de que estoy triste, voy a celebrar mi cumpleaños.	***Despite the fact that*** *I am sad, I will celebrate my birthday.*

6. VERBS OF CHANGE

In Spanish, selecting the proper verb to describe a change can be tricky. This depends on the nature of change in a state or emotion:

❖ whether the change is temporary or permanent

❖ whether the change is voluntary or involuntary

❖ whether the change is sudden or the result of a process

Below are the most common verbs to describe a change in Spanish:

1. "Ponerse"

This verb describes temporary, involuntary, and sudden changes, especially in emotions, for example:

Se puso triste después de la muerte de su esposa.	*He **became** sad after the death of his wife.*
Me pongo feliz cada vez que te veo.	*I **become** happy every time I see you.*

2. "Volverse"

This verb describes permanent, involuntary, and sudden changes. It usually describes changes into a negative state of mind, for example:

Se volvió loca cuando escuchó la noticia.	*She **went** crazy when she heard the news.*
Se va a **volver** obsesivo a causa de eso.	*He'll **become** obsessive because of this.*

3. "Hacerse"

This verb describes permanent and voluntary changes, regardless of whether the change is sudden or the result of a process. It is usually used to refer to change in religion, belief, or ideology, for example:

Esa famosa cantante **se hizo** musulmana.	*That famous singer **became** Muslim.*
Se hizo socialista.	*He **became** a socialist.*

4. "Quedar"

This verb describes a change that is the result of a process or an accident, regardless of whether it is permanent or temporary and regardless of whether it is voluntary or involuntary, for example:

Quedó muy cansado después del partido.	*He **got** tired after the match.*
Ella **quedó** embarazada.	*She **got** pregnant.*
Él **quedó** paralítico a causa del accidente.	*He **got** paralyzed because of the accident.*

5. "**Convertirse en**"

This verb describes a change that is the result of a process that leads to an important change, regardless of whether it is permanent or temporary and regardless of whether it is voluntary or involuntary, for example:

Nueva York **se convirtió** en la capital financiera global.	*New York* **became** *the global financial capital.*
Su proyecto **se convertirá** en un gran negocio.	*His project* **will become** *a large business.*

6. "**Llegar a**"

This verb describes a change that is the result of a process that involved an effort to achieve the goal, regardless of whether it is permanent or temporary and regardless of whether it is voluntary or involuntary, for example:

Messi **llegó a ser** el mejor jugador de fútbol.	*Messi* **became** *the best football player.*
Este senador **llegará a ser** el presidente del país.	*This senator* **will become** *the president of the country.*

The table below presents a summary of the verbs of change:

ponerse	temporary	involuntary	sudden	emotions
volverse	permanent	involuntary	sudden	negative state of mind
hacerse	permanent	voluntary	-	belief or ideology
quedar	-	-	-	process or accident
convertirse en	-	-	process	important change
llegar a	-	-	process	involves effort

7. REFLEXIVE PASSIVE, IMPERSONAL, & ACCIDENTAL "SE"

One way to describe something in the passive voice in Spanish is by moving the noun acted upon to the beginning of the sentence to emphasize it and using a *"to be"* verb followed by the adjective or the past participle. For example:

| El tejido fue **hecho** de material reciclado (por la fábrica). | *The textile was **made** from recycled material (by the factory).* |
| El contrato será **firmado** (por la empresa). | *The contract will be **signed** (by the company).* |

The performer of the action in the above two examples, denoted by **"por …"** (*by* …), can be omitted as it is deemed not to be of great significance.

Reflexive Passive "Se"

Another way to construct the passive voice in Spanish is by using the reflexive passive **"se"** with *transitive* verbs. The basic formula consists of **"se"** followed by the third-person verb in singular or plural, depending on the noun which follows the verb.

> **"Se"** + third-person *transitive* verb (sing. or plural) + noun (sing. or plural)

This is the passive construction you are likely to encounter in ads, commercials, cookbook instructions, or when the performer of the action is unknown or not as important. For example:

Se buscan personas con experiencia.	***Wanted** people with experience.*
Se venden celulares aquí.	*Cell phones **are sold** here.*
Se alquila un apartamento.	*An apartment **for rent**.*
Se cortan las manzanas, y **se mezclan** los ingredientes.	*The apples **are cut**, and the ingredients **are mixed**.*

Notice that only transitive verbs can be used to construct sentences using the reflexive passive **"se,"** and the noun that follows the third-person verb can represent thing(s) or person(s).

Impersonal "Se"

In English, we sometimes make general statements or observations such as:

We *work better as a team.*

They *sleep early in the village.*

It *feels better without social pressure.*

It *is better alone than in bad company.*

Notice that in the above sentences, we used the subject pronouns *(we, they,* and *it)* to convey a general meaning. For instance, the subject *"we"* in the sentence *"We work better as a team"* does not necessarily refer to the speaker(s) but rather refers to the general fact that humans work better as a team rather than individually. In other words, work is better as a team.

Notice also that the verbs *"to work"* and *"to sleep"* are *intransitive,* meaning that they do not need an object for the meaning to be complete. On the other hand, *"to feel"* and *"to be"* are *copular* verbs, meaning they connect a subject to an adjective, adverb, noun, or phrase. Examples of copular verbs include: *seem, feel, appear, look, become, taste, get, sound, turn, grow,* and *find.*

In Spanish, there is a special way to express such observations or statements using **"se"** followed by the *singular* third-person conjugation of the verb. Because the subject is undefined, we call this construction *impersonal.*

The previous examples in English can be translated as follows:

We work better as a team.	**Se trabaja** mejor en equipo.
They sleep early in the village.	**Se duerme** temprano en el pueblo.
It feels better without social pressure.	**Se siente** mejor sin presión social.
It is better alone than in bad company.	**Se está** mejor solo que mal acompañado.

As you can see, the verb is always singular regardless of any implicit assumptions about the subject, which is grammatically absent.

> **"Se"** + third-person *intransitive* or *copular* verb (always singular)

Although often used with *intransitive* and *copular* verbs, the impersonal "**se**" can also be used with *transitive* verbs in one case, that is, if the direct complement is a person(s) preceded by the personal "**a**," e.g., "**Se busca a personas con experiencia**" *(Wanted people with experience)*. In this case, as is the practice with impersonal "**se**" sentences, the third-person verb is in singular form regardless of the number of the noun following the personal "**a**."

"**Se**" + third-person *transitive* verb (always sing.) + Personal "**a**" + Person(s)

If you find it sometimes difficult to distinguish between the reflexive passive "**se**" and the impersonal "**se**," consider the following rules:

1. If the third-person verb is *intransitive* or *copular*, the impersonal "**se**" must be used.
2. If the third-person verb is *transitive* and the noun that follows the verb is a thing or things, not a person or persons, the reflexive passive "**se**" must be used.

Confusion arises only when the third-person verb is *transitive* and the noun that follows the verb is a person or persons, not a thing or things. In this case, either the reflexive passive "**se**" or the impersonal "**se**" can be used. Consider the following two examples:

Se buscan personas con experiencia.	***Wanted*** *people with experience.*
Se busca a personas con experiencia.	***Wanted*** *people with experience.*

The two examples above have identical English translations and use the same transitive verb, "**buscar**" *(to search or look for)*. The second example, however, differs in two ways:

1. The direct complement is person(s) preceded by the personal "**a**," which makes the subject lacking from a grammatical point of view.
2. The third-person verb is in the singular form.

Thus, the second example uses the impersonal "**se**," whereas the first example uses the reflexive passive "**se**."

Accidental "Se"

Another interesting use of "**se**" in Spanish is the "**accidental se**" or the blameless form, in which the speaker does not claim responsibility for the action. It indicates that the action is due to an accident rather than a deliberate act. Examples of this are:

Se me cayó el Internet.	*My internet dropped off.*
Se me olvidaron las llaves.	*I forgot the keys.*
No se nos quedó [1] la dirección.	*We can't remember the address.*

---

[1] The reflexive verb "**quedarse**" here means *"to remember."*

It is more like saying that the internet dropped off on me or the keys were forgotten on me, rather than taking the blame or responsibility for the accidental action of dropping or forgetting something.

You can distinguish the accidental "**se**" from the reflexive passive "**se**" and the impersonal "**se**" by the reflexive pronoun, which precedes the accidental "**se**" and reveals the *real* performer of the act.

The table below summarizes the differences between the reflexive passive, the impersonal, and the accidental "**se**":

	Pronoun(s)	Verb		Noun		Example
Reflexive Passive	Se	Transitive Only	Sing. or Plural	Thing or Person	Sing. or Plural	Aquí se habla español.
Impersonal	Se	Intransitive or Copular	Always Sing.	Absent		Se trabaja mejor en equipo.
		Transitive		Personal "a" + Person(s)		Se busca a gente joven.
Accidental	Se + Refl. Pron.	Transitive Only	Sing. or Plural	Thing or Person	Sing. or Plural	Se me cayó la llave.

8. DIMINUTIVES & AUGMENTATIVES

In Spanish, and especially in Latin America, the use of diminutives and augmentatives is ubiquitous. Understanding some rules and familiarity with some vocabulary in this category will help you perfect your Spanish and bring it closer to native speakers.

Diminutives

In the English language, we sometimes form the diminutive by suffixing *"-y"* or *"-ie,"* as in *"doggie"* for *"dog"* and *"kitty"* for *"kitten,"* indicating small size and sometimes the state or quality of being familiarly known, lovable, pitiable, or contemptible. Sometimes other suffixes are used, such as *"-ette"* in *"kitchenette"* and *"novelette,"* *"-let"* in *"booklet"* and *"droplet,"* and *"-ling"* in *"ducking"* and *"gosling"* (a *young goose).*

In Spanish, the purpose of using the diminutive is often similar to that in English, although in a few cases, the diminutive may be used to express sarcasm or negativity. It is also important to remember that the diminutive can be used for nouns, adjectives, and sometimes adverbs.

There are two general rules to form the diminutive in Spanish. However, there are a few exceptions that we will cover as well as some orthographic changes and regional variations. Let us start with the two general rules:

Rule # 1: Diminutives with the "-**ito**/-**ita**" Suffix

For words that end in "**o**," "**a**," or a consonant other than "**n**" or "**r**," add the ending "-**ito**" for masculine and "-**ita**" for feminine at the end of the word.

In the case of words ending with "**o**" or "**a**," remove the "**o**" or "**a**" to avoid the double vowel. For example:

pollo[m] *(chicken)*	poll~~o~~	+	-ito	=	pollito *(chick)*
pato[m] *(duck)*	pat~~o~~	+	-ito	=	patito *(duckling)*
casa[f] *(house)*	cas~~a~~	+	-ita	=	casita *(small house)*

mesa[f] (table)	mesa	+	-ita	=	mesita (small table)
mano[f] (hand)	mano	+	-ita	=	manita[1] (little hand)
pastel[m] (cake)	pastel	+	-ito	=	pastelito (small cake)
reloj[m] (clock)	reloj	+	-ito	=	relojito (small clock)

---

[1] Notice that "**mano**" takes the suffix "**-ita**" because it is a feminine noun, even though it ends with an "**o**."

<u>Rule # 2</u>: Diminutives with the "**-cito/-cita**" Suffix

For words that end in "**e**," "**n**," or "**r**," add the ending "**-cito**" for masculine and "**-cita**" for feminine at the end of the word. For example:

café[m] (coffee)	café	+	-cito	=	cafecito (little coffee)
calle[f] (street)	calle	+	-cita	=	callecita (little street)
suave[m,f] (soft)	suave	+	-cito -cita	=	suavecito (very soft) suavecita (very soft)
favor[m] (favor)	favor	+	-cito	=	favorcito (little favor)
amor[m] (love)	amor	+	-cito	=	amorcito (sweetie)
camión (truck)	camión	+	-cito	=	camioncito (little truck)
rincón (corner)	rincón	+	-cito	=	rinconcito (little corner)

In some words, especially the ones ending in "**c**" or "**z**," an extra "**e**" is added before the suffix "**-cito**" or "**-cita**." For example:

flor[f] (flower)	flor	+	-ecita	=	florecita[2] (small flower)

---

[2] The diminutive "**florcita**" is also used in some parts of Latin America.

In addition to the aforementioned suffixes, there are three less common suffixes used to form the diminutive: "**-illo/-illa**," "**-ico/-ica**," "**-zuelo/-zuela**." There are very few words that use these three suffixes, the most common of which are: "**bolsillo**" *(pouch or pocket)*, which is diminutive of "**bolso**" *(bag)*, "**barbilla**" *(chin)*, which is diminutive of "**barba**" *(beard)*, "**mantequilla**" *(butter)*, which is diminutive of "**manteca**" *(lard)*, and "**Venezuela**" *(Little Venice)*, which is diminutive of "**Venecia**" *(Venice)*. The "**-ico**" suffix is used in some regions of Spain and the Caribbean to form some uncommon diminutives, such as "**perrico**," which is a diminutive of "**perro**" *(dog)* instead of the more common "**perrito**."

The variation of diminutives across regions is not uncommon. For example, while the standard diminutive of the word "**sol**" *(sun)* is "**solecito**" *(little sun)*, "**solcito**" is the diminutive used in Argentina.

To highlight the regional aspect of the use of diminutives, consider the term "**ticos**," the name the Costa Ricans are called and proudly call themselves due to their ubiquitous use of the "**-tico**" ending to form diminutives, e.g., "**momentico**," "**pizzatica**," "**perritico**," "**chiquitico**," etc.

While the aforementioned rules cover most diminutives, some words remain difficult to categorize, such as "**nuevo**" *(new)*, the diminutive of which is "**nuevecito**" *(brand-new)*, and "**pez**" *(fish)*, the diminutive of which is "**pececito**" *(small fish)*. Note also that the meaning sometimes changes when the word is in the diminutive form.

Finally, when necessary, orthographic changes are applied to maintain the correct pronunciation sounds and spelling rules. These are similar to the rules we encountered in verb conjugation rules throughout the book. For example:

"c" to "qu"	poco[m] *(little)*	po**c**o	+	-ito	=	po**qu**ito *(very little)*
	chico[m] *(small, boy)*	chi**c**o	+	-ito	=	chi**qu**ito *(tiny, little boy)*
	chica[f] *(girl)*	chi**c**a	+	-ita	=	chi**qu**ita *(little girl)*
"g" to "gu"	amigo[m] *(friend)*	ami**g**o	+	-ito	=	ami**gu**ito *(little friend)*
	trago[m] *(sip)*	tra**g**o	+	-ito	=	tra**gu**ito *(little sip)*
"z" to "c"	lápiz[m] *(pencil)*	lápi**z**	+	-ito	=	lapicito *(small pencil)*
	luz[f] *(light)*	lu**z**	+	-ecita	=	lucecita[1] *(little light)*

---

[1] The diminutive "**lucita**" is also used in some regions.

For a more extensive list of diminutives, refer to **Appendix F**.

Augmentatives

Augmentatives are the opposite of diminutives. They indicate that something is large or intense, sometimes in an undesirable way. Augmentatives can apply to nouns and adjectives. In the English language, although not as versatile and common, augmentatives are formed by using prefixes rather than suffixes. You can think of the prefix *"super-"* in *"superpower"* and *"supernatural,"* the prefix *"mega-"* in *"megaphone"* and *"megastore,"* the prefix *"grand-"* in *"grandmaster"* and *"grandfather,"* the prefix *"over-"* in *"overgrown"* and *"overqualified,"* and the prefix *"arch-"* in *"archrival"* and *"archenemy."*

In Spanish, we use suffixes, such as: **"-ón/-ona," "-azo/-aza," "-ote/-ota," "-udo/-uda,"** and **"-achón/-achona,"** to form augmentatives. Unfortunately, there are no rules to guess which suffix to use. Practice is the only way. Thus, we will classify the augmentatives based on the meaning they convey rather than the suffix they use.

1. Augmentatives that indicate a large size

Some examples in this category include:

perro[m] *(dog)*	perro	+	-ote	=	perrote[m] *(big or mean dog)*
			-azo	=	perrazo[m] *(big or mean dog)*
hombre[m] *(man)*	hombre	+	-ón	=	hombrón[m] *(big strong man)*
casa[f] *(house)*	casa	+	-ona	=	casona[f] *(big house)*
animal[m] *(animal)*	animal	+	-ote	=	animalote[m] *(big or nasty animal)*

2. Augmentatives that indicate intensity

Some examples in this category include:

bueno[m] *(good)*	bueno	+	-azo	=	buenazo[m] *(good-natured)*
éxito[m] *(success)*	éxito	+	-azo	=	exitazo[m] *(great success)*
coche[m] *(car)*	coche	+	-azo	=	cochazo[m] *(amazing car)*
película[f] *(movie)*	película	+	-ón	=	peliculón[m] *(blockbuster)*

3. Augmentatives that indicate a strike or blow

The suffix "**-azo**" is often used to form masculine words that refer to a specific type of strike, hit, or blow. Examples in this category include:

codo[m] *(elbow)*	cod~~o~~	+ -azo	=	codazo[m] *(elbow jab)*
cabeza[f] *(head)*	cabez~~a~~	+ -azo	=	cabezazo[m] *(headbutt)*
martillo[m] *(hammer)*	martill~~o~~	+ -azo	=	martillazo[m] *(hammer blow)*
misil[m] *(missile)*	misil	+ -azo	=	misilazo[m] *(missile strike)*

4. Augmentatives that form new words

In some cases, new words with their own meanings can be formed using augmentatives. Examples in this category include:

silla[f] *(chair)*	sill~~a~~	+ -ón	=	sillón[m] *(armchair)*
cintura[f] *(waist)*	cintur~~a~~	+ -ón	=	cinturón[m] *(belt)*
rata[f] *(rat)*	rat~~a~~	+ -ón	=	ratón[m] *(mouse)*
caja[f] *(box)*	caj~~a~~	+ -ón	=	cajón[m] *(drawer)*
papel[m] *(paper)*	papel	+ -ote	=	papelote[m] *(worthless[1] paper)*

---

[1] This can be literal or figurative.

Notice that in some cases, the augmentative word changes gender, often from feminine to masculine, as in the feminine words "**película**," "**silla**," and "**rata**," the augmentatives of which are masculine: "**peliculón**," "**sillón**," and "**ratón**," respectively.

Some words have multiple augmentative forms. These forms may convey the same meaning or a different meaning. For example, the augmentatives "**cabezón**," "**cabezote**," and "**cabezudo**" all mean *stubborn* or *big-headed*, literally or figuratively, formed from the word "**cabeza**" *(head)*. On the other hand, the augmentative "**cabezazo**," also formed from the word "**cabeza**," has a different meaning, that is, a *headbutt* or a *header* (in sports).

In addition to the dropping of "**o**" or "**a**" to avoid the double vowel, some words undergo some minor changes, such as the "**ue**" change to "**o**" in "**cordón**" *(shoelace)*, "**portazo**" *(door slam)*, and "**fortachón**" *(beefy)*, augmentatives of "**cuerda**" *(rope or string)*, "**puerta**" *(door)*, and "**fuerte**" *(strong)*, respectively.

Finally, some words remain hard to guess and must be learned by practice, such as "**grandullón**" *(overgrown)* and "**favorzote**" *(huge favor)*, augmentatives of "**grande**" *(big)* and "**favor**" *(favor)*, respectively.

For a more extensive list of augmentatives, refer to **Appendix F**.

9. USE OF "VOS" IN SOME SPANISH-SPEAKING COUNTRIES

In some Spanish-speaking countries, such as Argentina, Uruguay, Paraguay, Nicaragua, Costa Rica, and El Salvador, the second-person pronoun "**tú**" is not used. Instead, the pronoun "**vos**" is used.

Keep in mind that the pronoun "**vos**" is conjugated differently. For example, instead of saying "**Tú hablas inglés**," we say "**<u>Vos hablás</u> inglés**." The pronoun "**vos**" is used instead of "**tú**." The "**r**" in the infinitive ending of "**hablar**" is replaced with "**s**," and an accent is added to the vowel before the last "**s**" to stress the last syllable.

The use of "**vos**" as a second-person pronoun is referred to as *voseo*, as opposed to the use of "**tú**," which is referred to as *tuteo*.

In general, using "**vos**" instead of "**tú**" does not change the conjugation of verbs in Spanish sentences except for the present indicative and the affirmative imperative mood. We will study these two cases separately.

Voseo in the Present Indicative

Forming the present indicative using "**vos**" is straightforward and has fewer irregular cases than using "**tú**." Regular verbs in the present indicative tense follow the conjugation rules shown below:

	-ar ending hablar	-er ending comer	-ir ending vivir
yo	hablo	como	vivo
vos	hablás	comés	vivís
él/ella/usted	habla	come	vive
nosotros/-as	hablamos	comemos	vivimos
vosotros/-as	habláis	coméis	vivís
ellos/ellas/ustedes	hablan	comen	viven

As seen above, to form the second-person present indicative using "**vos**," the "**r**" in the infinitive ending is replaced with "**s**," and an accent is added to the vowel before the last "**s**" to stress the last syllable, for example:

¿Qué **querés** comer esta noche?	*What do you **want** to eat tonight?*
¿Dónde **vivís**?	*Where do you **live**?*
Vos **tenés** una casa grande.	*You **have** a big house.*

The only irregular verbs in *voseo* are:

Infinitive	Second person in the present indicative
ser	sos
ir	vas
haber	has

For example:

¿De dónde **sos**?	*Where **are** you from?*
Vos **vas** a la escuela todos los días.	*You **go** to school every day.*
Vos **has** comido el postre.	*You **have** eaten the dessert.*

Voseo in the Affirmative Imperative Mood

Forming the singular imperative mood in the affirmative using "**vos**" is straightforward and has only one irregular case. Regular verbs follow the conjugation rule shown below:

	-ar ending hablar	-er ending comer	-ir ending vivir
vos	hablá	comé	viví

To conjugate the verb, the "**r**" in the infinitive ending is removed, and an accent is added to the last vowel to stress the last syllable, for example:

¡Vení acá!	**Come** *here!*
¡Tené cuidado!	*Be careful!*
Comé algo saludable.	**Eat** *something healthy.*

The only irregular case using "**vos**" in the imperative is the verb "**ir**," which has the imperative form "**andá**," for example:

Andá al gimnasio temprano.	**Go** *to the gym early.*

Conjugation of the imperative mood in the negative using "**vos**" is identical to that using "**tú**," for example:

No **vayas** a la escuela mañana.	*Don't **go** to school tomorrow.*
No **comas** mucho postre.	*Don't **eat** a lot of dessert.*

Voseo in all Other Cases

Finally, it is important to note that conjugation of all other moods and tenses using "**vos**" is identical to that of using "**tú**," for example:

Vos **viniste** muy temprano hoy.	*You **came** early today.*
Vos **estabas** dormido cuando llegué.	*You **were** sleeping when I arrived.*

II. Vocabulary Building

Go over the vocabulary in this section and use the provided Anki cards to study and memorize the new vocabulary efficiently.

1. VERBS VI

Below is a list of some important verbs that we need at this level:

English	Spanish	Examples
acquire	adquirir	**Adquirió** el apartamento sin problemas el año pasado. *He **acquired** the apartment with no problems last year.*
adore **worship**	adorar	Mi hija **adoraba** a su abuela cuando era joven. *My daughter **adored** her grandma when she was young.*

advocate	abogar	Ella **aboga** siempre por los más débiles. *She always **advocates** for the weakest.*
align	alinear(se)	Me gusta **alinear** los frascos correctamente. *I like to **align** the jars correctly.*
ally	aliar(se)	Los gobiernos **se aliaron** entre sí durante muchos años. *The governments **allied** with one another for many years.*
approve **pass (exam)**	aprobar	**Aprobé** todas las materias el semestre pasado. *I **passed** all the subjects last semester.*
attack	atacar agredir	El perro de la vecina siempre **ataca** al cartero. *My neighbor's dog always **attacks** the mailman.*
attend	asistir a	**Habría asistido a** la reunión de haberlo sabido. *I **would've attended** the meeting if I had known.*
be noticeable **be able to tell**	notarse	**Se nota** que no está feliz. *You **can tell** he is not happy.*
behave	comportarse portarse	Espero que **te comportes** como un caballero. *I hope you will **behave** like a gentleman.*
betray	traicionar	No **traiciones** la confianza de tu amigo. *Don't **betray** your friend's trust.*
bill **check in**	facturar	La empresa **facturó** a sus clientes hoy. *The company **billed** their clients today.*
bless	bendecir	El cura **bendijo** a la pareja. *The priest **blessed** the couple.*
blush	sonrojarse	**Se sonrojó** al escuchar la historia. *He **blushed** upon hearing the story.*
brake **(vehicle)**	frenar	Si no **hubiera frenado**, habría chocado. *If I **had** not **braked**, I would have crashed.*
broadcast **transmit**	transmitir	**Están transmitiendo** en vivo. *They **are broadcasting** live.*
bury	enterrar sepultar	Tuvimos que **sepultar** al pez mascota. *We had to **bury** the pet fish.*
charge **lunge into**	embestir	El cordero **embistió** al carro. *The lamb **lunged into** the cart.*
charge (fee)	cobrar	**Cobran** muy caras las entradas. *They **charge** a lot for tickets.*
chop down	talar	**Están talando** los árboles del parque. *They **are chopping down** the trees in the park.*
clear	despejar	**Despeja** el camino, por favor. *Clear the way, please.*
collapse	derrumbarse	Ese edificio está por **derrumbarse**. *That building is about to **collapse**.*
collect or raise **(money)**	recaudar	**Están recaudando** fondos para la organización benéfica. *They **are raising** money for the charity.*

commit	cometer	No quiso **cometer** un crimen. *He didn't want to **commit** a crime.*
compose	componer	**Compuso** esa hermosa canción. *She **composed** that beautiful song.*
compress	comprimir	Tuve que **comprimir** los archivos. *I had to **compress** the files.*
compromise	comprometer	Decidieron **comprometer** algunas ideas. *They decided to **compromise** some ideas.*
confuse	confundir(se)	Su explicación nos **ha confundido**. *His explanation **has confused** us.*
conquer	conquistar	Intentaron **conquistar** esa isla. *They tried to **conquer** that island.*
contain	contener	Este tubo puede **contener** un líquido peligroso. *This tube may **contain** a dangerous liquid.*
contradict	contradecir	No quiero tener que **contradecir**te. *I don't want to **contradict** you.*
correspond	corresponderse	Las medias no **corresponden** al mismo par. *The socks don't **correspond** to the same pair.*
cram	atestar	Estaba **atestado** de gente. *It was **crammed** with people.*
crease	plegar	**Pliega** los bordes de la hoja. ***Crease** the edges of the paper.*
cross out	tachar rayar	**Estaban tachando** tu nombre. *They **were crossing out** your name.*
curse	maldecir	Sabes que no debes **maldecir**. *You know you shouldn't **curse**.*
damage **harm**	dañar	Tuvo mucho cuidado de no **dañar** la pintura. *He was very careful not to **damage** the paint.*
dazzle	deslumbrar	El espectáculo los **deslumbrará**. *The show **will dazzle** you.*
defeat	derrotar vencer	Me **venció** en esta ronda. *He **defeated** me in this round.*
deliver **turn in**	entregar	**Están entregándo**lo ahora mismo. *They **are delivering** it right now.*
deny	negar	No se le debe **negar** el agua a nadie. *No one should **deny** water to others.*
deplete	agotar mermar	Escalar la montaña ayer lo **agotó**. *Climbing the mountain yesterday **depleted** him.*
detain	detener	Lo **habría detenido** la policía de todos modos. *The police **would have stopped** him anyway.*
diagnose	diagnosticar	El médico será quien me **diagnosticará**. *The doctor will be the one who will **diagnose** me.*
dig	cavar excavar	**Están excavando** en la cueva. *They **are digging** in the cave.*

dive	bucear[1] zambullirse[1]	**Se zambulle** en el agua sin mirar. *He **dives** into the water without looking.*
dribble (soccer)	driblear gambetear regatear[2]	El delantero **dribleó** a tres defensas y marcó un gol. *The striker **dribbled** past three defenders and scored a goal.*
drip	gotear	El grifo **goteaba** mientras estaban dormidos. *The faucet **was dripping** while they were asleep.*
drizzle	lloviznar	**Está lloviznando** ahora mismo. *It **is drizzling** right now.*
drown	ahogar(se)	**Me habría ahogado** sin el salvavidas. *I **would have drowned** without the life jacket.*
embellish	embellecer	Siempre **embellecen** sus historias de aventuras. *They always **embellish** their adventure stories.*
emphasize	enfatizar	Intenté **enfatizar** ese punto. *I tried **to emphasize** that point.*
enlarge extend	ampliar	**Amplió** la habitación al tirar esa pared. *She **extended** the room by knocking down that wall.*
enroll (school)	matricularse	Debo **matricularme** el mes que viene. *I have to **enroll** next month.*
entail implicate	implicar	No sabía lo que **implicaría**. *He didn't know what it **would entail**.*
equate (put on the same level)	equiparar igualar	Lo **equipararon** con su jefe por muchos años. *They **equated** him to his boss for many years.*
evict dislodge	desalojar	**Desalojaron** a la familia entera el mes pasado. *They **evicted** the entire family last month.*
expel	expulsar	Lo **habrían expulsado** si se enteraban. *They **would have expelled** him if they'd found out.*
expose	exponer	**Expondré** toda la tesis. *I **will expose** the entire thesis.*
face confront	afrontar enfrentarse a	Debes **enfrentarte a** tus miedos. *You have to **face** your fears.*
fade	desvanecerse	La mancha **se desvaneció** por completo. *The stain completely **faded** away.*
faint	desmayarse	**Se desmayó** al ver sangre tras el accidente. *He **fainted** when he saw blood after the accident.*
fall behind	atrasarse	Se **atrasará** si no se apura. *He **will fall behind** if he doesn't hurry.*

---

[1] In general, **"bucear"** refers to underwater swimming, whereas **"zambullirse"** refers to the act of jumping into water.

[2] The verb **"regatear"** is often used in Spain.

feed	alimentar	Mi vecina a veces **alimenta** a mi gato. *My neighbor sometimes **feeds** my cat.*
find a girlfriend	ponerse de novio	Quisiera **ponerse de novio**. *He'd like to **find a girlfriend**.*
find out	averiguar enterarse	Sabía que **se enteraría** tarde o temprano. *I knew he **would find out** sooner or later.*
fire dismiss	despedir	Tuvieron que **despedir** a muchos empleados. *They had to **fire** many employees.*
fit	caber	Creo que **cabe** en esa habitación. *I think it **fits** in that room.*
flatter	halagar adular	Halaga al jefe para que le dé un aumento. *He **flatters** the boss to give him a raise.*
flicker	parpadear	La luz **está parpadeando**. *The light **is flickering**.*
foil thwart	frustrar	El mal clima **frustró** sus planes. *The bad weather **thwarted** her plans.*
found	fundar	**Fundarán** una asociación para ayudar a la gente. *They **will found** an association to help people.*
frown	fruncir el ceño	**Frunció el ceño** cuando vio la pintura. *He **frowned** when he saw the painting.*
fume	humear	**Humeaba** cuando se enteró de la noticia. *He **was fuming** when he heard the news.*
get along	llevarse bien	Mis hijas no **se llevan bien**. *My daughters don't **get along**.*
get independence	independizarse	El país **se independizó** hace mucho tiempo. *The country **got independence** a long time ago.*
get involved	involucrarse	Es mejor no **involucrarse** en esos asuntos. *It's best to not **get involved** in those matters.*
get together	juntarse	¿**Nos juntaremos** este sábado? ***Will** we **get together** this Saturday?*
govern	gobernar	Abusaba del poder cuando **gobernaba**. *He abused power when he **governed**.*
grab grasp seize	agarrar	**Agarra** el último antes que alguien más lo haga. ***Grab** the last one before someone else does.*
grind	moler	Debes **moler** bien la pimienta. *You have to **grind** the pepper well.*
hang	colgar	¿Puedes **colgar** la ropa? *Can you **hang** the clothes?*
hang on	aferrarse	No debes **aferrarte** al pasado. *You shouldn't **hang on** to the past.*
harmonize	armonizar	Intenté que **armonizaran** los colores. *I tried to make the colors **harmonize**.*

have to do with	tener que ver con	Eso **tiene que ver con** lo que pasó ayer. *This **has to do with** what happened yesterday.*
hesitate	vacilar dudar	No debes **vacilar** luego de empezar. *You shouldn't **hesitate** after you've started.*
highlight stand out	destacar(se)	Siempre intentaba **destacarse**. *He'd always try to **stand out**.*
hire contract	contratar	**Contrataré** a un carpintero para eso. *I **will hire** a carpenter for that.*
house accommodate	alojar hospedar	**Hospedarán** a toda la familia. *They **will house** the entire family.*
hurry rush	apurar(se) apresurar(se)	¿Puedes **apresurarte**? *Can you **hurry up**?*
hurt	herir(se) lastimar(se)	**Se lastimó** por accidente. *He **hurt himself** by accident.*
hush	callarse acallar	**¡Cállate**, estamos intentando escuchar! ***Hush**, we're trying to listen!*
impose	imponer	**Impusieron** una nueva ley recientemente. *They **imposed** a new law recently.*
imprison	encarcelar	**Encarcelaron** al delincuente que cometió el crimen. *They **imprisoned** the felon who committed the crime.*
inform on rat out	delatar [1]	**Delatará** a sus cómplices para obtener una sentencia reducida. *He **will inform on** his accomplices to get a reduced sentence.*
intend	tener la intención de	**Tengo la intención de** comenzar una dieta. *I **intend** to start a diet.*
iron	planchar	No me gusta **planchar** la ropa. *I don't like to **iron** clothes.*
irrigate water	regar	Si las **hubieran regado**, no se habrían muerto. *If they **had watered** them, they wouldn't have died.*
jump hop	saltar brincar	**Saltábamos** en todos lados cuando éramos niños. *We **would jump** everywhere when we were kids.*
kneel	arrodillarse	**Arrodíllate** para ver debajo de la mesada. ***Kneel down** to see under the counter.*
knock over	volcar	**Volcó** el jarrón el otro día. *He **knocked over** the vase the other day.*

---

[1] The verb **"delatar"** can also mean *"to give away (one's real feeling or intention),"* e.g., **"Su rostro delató su ira"** *(His face gave away his anger)*. It can also be used as a reflexive verb meaning *"to give oneself away,"* e.g., **"Se delató diciendo eso"** *(He gave himself away by saying that)*.

lean on	apoyarse en	Siempre **se apoyaba en** mí cuando tenía trabajo. *She always **leaned on** me when she had work.*
lease	rentar arrendar	Mis padres **están rentando** su casa. *My parents **are leasing** their house.*
light **illuminate**	alumbrar iluminar	Una lámpara allí **iluminaría** toda la habitación. *A lamp there **would light** the entire room.*
load	cargar	¿Me ayudarías a **cargar** el auto? *Would you help me **load** the car?*
make fun of	burlarse de mofarse de	Es desagradable que **te hayas burlado** de él así. *It's unpleasant that you **made fun of** him like this.*
manage **handle**	manejar	Yo siempre **manejaba** el dinero del hogar. *I used to always **handle** the house's money.*
manifest	manifestar(se)	Pensé que un fantasma **se había manifestado**. *I thought a ghost **had manifested**.*
manufacture	fabricar	**Fabrican** autos allí. *They **manufacture** cars there.*
mar **spoil**	estropear(se)	¡Mira! Los tomates **se estropearon** al sol. *Look! The tomatoes **spoiled** in the sun.*
meet up	reunirse	**Nos reuniremos** en el aula. *We **will meet up** in the classroom*
murmur	murmurar	Solo logro **murmurar** cuando tengo sueño. *I only manage to **murmur** when I'm sleepy.*
nail **force in**	clavar	Tuve que **clavar**lo a la pared. *I had to **nail** it to the wall.*
neglect	descuidar	Siempre **descuido** mis plantas sin querer. *I always **neglect** my plants by accident.*
nourish **nurture**	nutrir	Debes **nutrir**te bien. *You should **nourish** yourself well.*
pack	empacar	**Empaqué** todo en cinco minutos. *I **packed** everything in five minutes.*
pamper **spoil**	mimar	Siempre **mimo** a mi mascota. *I always **pamper** my pet.*
pave	pavimentar empedrar	**Están pavimentando** la calle. *They **are paving** the street.*
penalize	penalizar	Tirar basura **se penaliza** con multas. *Throwing trash **is penalized** with fines.*
perceive	percibir	Puedo **percibir** el sarcasmo en su respuesta. *I can **perceive** the sarcasm in his answer.*
pet **stroke** **fondle**	acariciar	A mi gato le encanta que lo **acaricien**. *My cat loves being **petted**.*
pick up **collect**	recoger	¿Puedes ir a **recoger** a tu hermana? *Can you go **pick up** your sister?*

pierce (body)	hacerse agujeros en	Quiere **hacerse agujeros en** la oreja. *She wants to get her ear **pierced**.*
pinch	pellizcar	¡No me **pellizques**! *Don't **pinch** me!*
please pander to	complacer	Él es difícil de **complacer**. *He is hard to **please**.*
point out	señalar	Los lectores **señalaron** que había un error. *The readers **pointed out** that there was a mistake.*
pollute contaminate	contaminar	No debes **contaminar** el ambiente. *You shouldn't **pollute** the environment.*
pop in one's head	cruzarse por la cabeza	**Se me cruzó por la cabeza** la idea de hacerlo. *The idea of doing it **popped into my head**.*
portray	retratar	Creo que **retrataron** muy bien a su persona en la película. *I think they **portrayed** her persona very well in the movie.*
pose (photo)	posar	Ya **están posando** para la foto. *They **are** already **posing** for the photo.*
postpone	posponer	**Pospusieron** el evento por la lluvia. *They **postponed** the event because of the rain.*
praise	alabar	**Alabaron** su actuación en esa película. *They **praised** her acting in that movie.*
pray	orar rezar	**Oraban** todos los días. *They **used to pray** every day.*
predict	pronosticar predecir	Nunca **pronostican** bien el clima. *They never correctly **predict** the weather.*
prescribe	recetar prescribir	Le **recetaron** unas vitaminas para su enfermedad del año pasado. *They **prescribed** him some vitamins for his last year's illness.*
preserve	preservar	La comida **se preserva** mejor en la nevera. *Food **is preserved** best in the fridge.*
press	presionar oprimir pulsar	**Habría oprimido** el botón para entrar. *He **would have pressed** the button to go in.*
pretend	fingir	No **finjas** estar dormido. *Don't **pretend** to be asleep.*
prevail	prevalecer	**Prevalecen** los colores fríos en la pintura. *Cold colors **prevail** in the painting.*
prick	pinchar	Debes **pinchar** el pastel para ver si está listo. *You have to **prick** the cake to see if it's ready.*
prohibit ban	prohibir	El gobierno **prohibió** algunas importaciones el año pasado. *The government **prohibited** certain imports last year.*

promote (advertise)	promocionar	La empresa **promocionó** su producto nuevo durante meses. *The company **promoted** its new product for months.*
promote (raise in rank)	promover	**Promovieron** al escritor el año pasado. *They **promoted** the writer last year.*
provide	proporcionar proveer	Las bananas **proporcionan** mucho potasio. *Bananas **provide** a lot of potassium.*
punch in	fichar	**Fiché** mi hora de salida hace dos horas. *I **punched in** my exit time two hours ago.*
put together	juntar	**Juntó** todos los materiales y comenzó el proyecto. *He **put together** all the materials and started the project.*
quote cite	citar	**Citaron** muchas pruebas en su última investigación. *They **cited** a lot of evidence in their latest research.*
rally behind	reunirse detrás	**Se reunieron detrás** del presidente en su última campaña. *They **rallied behind** the president in his last campaign.*
ransack	saquear	**Saquearon** todo el lugar cuando entraron. *They **ransacked** the entire place when they broke in.*
rape violate	violar	El sospechoso fue acusado de **violar** a alguien. *The suspect was accused of **raping** someone.*
record engrave	grabar	**Grabaron** sus nombres en el anillo antes de la boda. *They **engraved** their names on the ring before the wedding.*
refill	rellenar	**Rellenaré** tu vaso con agua. *I **will refill** your glass with water.*
refine	refinar	Debes **refinar** tu búsqueda en Internet. *You have to **refine** your search on the internet.*
register sign up	registrar(se)	Sabía que habría que **registrarse** para entrar. *I knew you'd need to **register** to get in.*
regret	lamentar sentir arrepentirse de	**Lamentaría** perdérmelo toda mi vida. *I **would regret** missing it all my life.*
rehearse	ensayar	Tuvieron que **ensayar** la obra muchas veces. *They had to **rehearse** the play many times.*
remove	quitar eliminar	Intentaré **quitar** esa mancha enseguida. *I'll try to **remove** that stain immediately.*
replenish	reponer	¡Nunca **repones** el jabón! *You never **replenish** the soap!*
rescue	rescatar salvar	Lo **habrías rescatado**, si hubieras estado allí. *You **would have rescued** him had you been there.*

restart **reboot**	reiniciar	**Reiniciaré** la computadora. *I **will restart** the computer.*
restore **(order or connection)**	restablecer	**Restableceremos** la paz para prevenir conflictos. *We **will restore** peace to prevent conflicts.*
restore **(repair)**	restaurar	**Restauré** los muebles antiguos. *I **restored** the old furniture.*
resume	reanudar(se) reasumir	**Reanudarán** las negociaciones mañana. *They **will resume** the negotiations tomorrow.*
reverberate	reverberar	El ruido **reverbera** por toda la casa. *The noise **reverberates** through the entire house.*
reward	recompensar premiar	Lo **habrían recompensado** por su trabajo. *They **would have rewarded** him for his work.*
rise	subir	Los precios **subieron** mucho el año pasado. *Prices **rose** a lot last year.*
rot **decay**	pudrir(se)	**Se pudrirá** si no lo usas pronto. *It **will rot** if you don't use it soon.*
run out	acabarse quedarse sin	Es difícil **quedarse sin** ahorros. *It's not hard to **run out** of savings.*
run over	atropellar	Lo **habría atropellado** si no hubiera corrido. *It **would have run** him **over** if he hadn't run.*
sacrifice	sacrificar	A veces debes **sacrificar** un poco de tu tiempo. *Sometimes you have to **sacrifice** a bit of your time.*
sadden	entristecer	La noticia de la muerte de su tío lo **entristeció**. *The news of his uncle's death **saddened** him.*
scorn	desdeñar despreciar	Siempre **desdeña** a su nuera. *She always **scorns** her daughter-in-law.*
scrap (car)	desguazar	Allí **desguazan** los autos viejos. *They **scrap** old cars there.*
scribble **doodle**	garabatear borronear	Los niños **garabatean** mucho. *Children **scribble** a lot.*
scrub	fregar	**Fregaré** los platos luego de la cena. *I **will scrub** the dishes after dinner.*
seal	sellar	**Sellarán** el sobre. *They **will seal** the envelope.*
shake	sacudir	**Sacude** la botella muy bien. ***Shake** the bottle very well.*
sharpen	afilar	Debes **afilar** bien tus cuchillos de cocina. *You have to **sharpen** your kitchen knives well.*
shove **tuck**	meter	¿**Meterán** todo eso en la cajuela? *They **will shove** all that into the trunk?*
shovel	palear	Siempre **paleaban** la nieve cuando vivían allí. *They always **shoveled** the snow when they lived there.*

sigh	suspirar	**Suspiro** cada vez que veo a mi abuelo. *I **sigh** every time I see my grandfather.*
sin	pecar	El hombre creyó que **había pecado**. *The man believed that he **had sinned**.*
sketch **outline**	bosquejar esbozar	**Esbozaré** la trama. *I **will outline** the plot.*
skimp	escatimar	**Escatimaron** en la decoración cuando se mudaron. *They **skimped** on the decorations when they moved in.*
skip over	saltarse	Logró **saltarse** un año. *He managed to **skip over** a year.*
slap	abofetear palmear	**Abofeteó** al villano en la escena del crimen. *He **slapped** the villain at the crime scene.*
slash	acuchillar	El asesino **acuchilló** a la víctima en la película. *The murderer **slashed** his victim in the movie.*
slide **slip**	deslizar(se)	**Está deslizándose** como puede. *He **is sliding** the way he can.*
smash **crush**	aplastar	Lo **habría aplastad**o si no se hubiera movido. *It **would have crushed** him if he hadn't moved.*
sneak	colarse	Logramos **colarnos** en el lugar. *We managed to **sneak** into the place.*
snore	roncar	Mi perro **ronca** muy fuerte. *My dog **snores** very loudly.*
soak **drench**	empapar remojar	**Remojé** los frijoles secos por cinco horas. *I **soaked** the dry beans for five hours.*
sow	sembrar	**Sembraré** las semillas en primavera. *I **will sow** the seeds in spring.*
specify	especificar	**Especificó** exactamente qué salón era. *He **specified** exactly what classroom it was.*
spill **shed**	derramar(se)	El té **se habría derramado** si no hubiera tomado la taza. *The tea **would have spilled** if I hadn't stopped the cup.*
splash	salpicar	La tinta **salpicó** la pared por accidente. *The ink **splashed** on the wall by accident.*
sponsor	patrocinar	Me parece excelente idea que los **patrocines**. *I think it's a great idea that you **sponsor** them.*
spread **(extend)**	extender	Debes **extender** las sábanas sobre el colchón. *You have to **spread** the bedsheets over the mattress.*
spread **(propagate)**	propagar(se) difundir	Las enfermedades se **propagan** muy rápido. *Diseases **spread** very quickly.*
squander **fritter**	malgastar desperdiciar	Deja de **malgastar** tu dinero. *Stop **squandering** your money.*

squeeze	apretar exprimir estrujar	Debes **exprimir** bien los limones. *You have to **squeeze** the lemons well.*
stain **taint**	manchar	Siempre **manchaba** la ropa con comida. *I used to always **stain** my clothes with food.*
stammer	balbucear tartamudear	Intenta no **balbucear**. *Try not to **stammer**.*
stamp	estampillar timbrar	Debes **timbrar** el paquete. *You have to **stamp** the package.*
start **(vehicle)**	arrancar [1]	Mientras esperaba allí, el auto no **arrancaba**. *While I was waiting there, the car **wouldn't start**.*
stir	revolver agitar	¿Puedes **revolver** el guisado, por favor? *Can you **stir** the stew, please?*
stray **get lost**	perderse extraviarse	**Se habría perdido** sin el mapa. *He **would have gotten lost** without the map.*
stretch	estirar(se)	Siempre **me estiro** cuando me despierto. *I always **stretch** when I wake up.*
strip **(remove)**	quitar	Le **quitaron** la piel a la naranja y se la comieron. *They **stripped** the skin off the orange and ate it.*
stun	aturdir	El ruido fuerte me **aturdió** mientras leía. *The loud noise **stunned** me as I was reading.*
stutter	tartamudear	**Tartamudeé** mucho durante ese discurso. *I **stuttered** a lot during that speech.*
summarize	resumir	Debo **resumir** los textos en estos libros. *I have to **summarize** the texts in these books.*
support **back up**	apoyar respaldar	¿Puedes **apoyar** a tu hermano? *Can you **support** your brother?*
suppress **cancel**	suprimir	**Suprimieron** muchas temáticas del programa anoche. *They **suppressed** many themes from the show last night.*
surrender **give up**	rendirse	¡**Ríndete** así gano esta ronda! ***Give up** so I win this round!*
surround **encircle**	rodear	Lo **habrían rodeado** si hubieran podido. *They **would have surrounded** him if they could.*
survey **poll**	encuestar	**Encuestaron** a cien individuos la semana pasada. *They **surveyed** a hundred individuals last week.*
swallow	tragar(se)	Debes **tragar** tu medicación. *You have to **swallow** your medication.*

---

[1] The verb "**arrancar**" can also mean *"to pull out," "to uproot,"* or *"to rip out,"* e.g., "**El dentista me arrancó el diente**" *(The dentist pulled out my tooth).*

swell	hinchar(se)	**Se hinchó** muy rápido mi pie después del partido. *My foot **swelled** up really fast after the game.*
take charge of	encargarse de	Mi marido tuvo que **encargarse** de su sobrino. *My husband had **to take charge of** his nephew.*
take for granted	dar por hecho dar por sentado	**Dio por hecho** que ganaría esa carrera. *He **took for granted** that he'd win that race.*
tangle	enmarañar	**Se me enmarañó** el pelo mientras lo peinaba anoche. *My hair **got tangled** while I was styling it last night.*
tear **rip**	rasgar desgarrar	Mi perro **rasgaba** todos los papeles que veía. *My dog **would rip** all the papers he saw.*
terrorize **terrify**	aterrorizar	Cuando era niño, los muñecos me **aterrorizaban**. *When I was a child, dolls **terrified** me.*
thunder	tronar	**Está tronando** ahora. *It **is thundering** now.*
tickle	hacerle cosquillas a	Sus padres solían **hacerles cosquillas a** sus hijos. *His parents used to **tickle** their kids.*
toast	brindar	**¡Brindemos** por tu éxito! *Let's **toast** to your success!*
touch	tocar	Me **habría tocado** la cara si no me hubiera movido. *It **would have touched** my face if I hadn't moved.*
transfer	transferir	Te **transferiré** el dinero directo a tu cuenta. *I **will transfer** the money directly into your account.*
trigger	desencadenar	Ese movimiento **desencadenó** una avalancha. *That movement **triggered** an avalanche.*
turn around	voltearse dar la vuelta	**Se volteará** para ver el auto. *He **will turn around** to see the car.*
twinkle	titilar	Las estrellas **titilan** y los planetas no. *Stars **twinkle** and planets don't.*
uncover	destapar	Alguien **destapará** el misterio algún día. *Someone **will uncover** the mystery one day.*
unleash	desatar	**Desataron** al dragón cuando comenzó la guerra. *They **unleashed** the dragon when the war started.*
waste	derrochar desperdiciar	**Estás desperdiciando** los recursos. *You **are wasting** the resources.*
watch over	vigilar	**Vigila** el horno para que no se queme. ***Watch over** the oven so that it doesn't burn.*
withdraw **retreat**	retirar	La tortuga **se retiró** a su caparazón al verme. *The turtle **withdrew** into its shell upon seeing me.*
withdraw (money)	retirar	**Retirará** dinero del banco. *He **will withdraw** money from the bank.*

| wrinkle | arrugar | Ten cuidado de no **arrugar** tu ropa.
*Be careful not to **wrinkle** your clothes.* |
| **yawn** | bostezar | No **bosteces** en público.
*Don't **yawn** in public.* |

2. ADJECTIVES VI

Below is a list of some important adjectives that we need at this level:

English	Spanish	Examples
abnormal	anormal	Este queso tiene un color **anormal**. *This cheese has an **abnormal** color.*
advocate (supporter)	defensor	Es **defensor** de los derechos de los niños. *He's an **advocate** for children's rights.*
affectionate	cariñoso afectuoso	Mi abuelo es muy **cariñoso**. *My grandfather is very **affectionate**.*
agricultural	agrícola	Se ha interesado mucho en el trabajo **agrícola**. *He's become very interested in **agricultural** work.*
anxious eager	ansioso	Mi gato se pone **ansioso** en el parque. *My cat gets **anxious** in the park.*
appetizing	apetitoso	Ese filete se ve muy **apetitoso**. *That steak looks very **appetizing**.*
arctic	ártico	No me agradan estos fríos **árticos**. *I don't like these **arctic** colds.*
attached (file)	adjunto	Puedes encontrar el archivo **adjunto** al correo. *You can find the file **attached** to the mail.*
audacious	audaz	Resultó ser muy **audaz**. *She ended up being very **audacious**.*
bankrupt	quebrado	Para fin de mes, estoy **quebrado**. *By the end of the month, I'm **bankrupt**.*
bent	doblado	El tenedor quedó **doblado**. *The fork ended up **bent**.*
broken down (vehicle)	averiado roto	Dejé el auto en casa porque se había **averiado**. *I left the car at home because it had **broken down**.*
cheerful	alegre	La maestra es muy **alegre** con los niños. *The teacher is very **cheerful** with the children.*
chemical	químico	Ten cuidado con las reacciones **químicas**. *Be careful with **chemical** reactions.*
civilian	civil	Al renunciar, volvió a ser un **civil**. *When he renounced, he went back to being a **civilian**.*
compassionate	compasivo	Es muy **compasivo** con los animales. *He's very **compassionate** with animals.*

corny	cursi	Me escribió un poema **cursi**. *He wrote me a **corny** poem.*
creepy	escalofriante	Con esa máscara se ve **escalofriante**. *With that mask he looks **creepy**.*
crispy	crocante crujiente	Me gustan las tostadas bien **crocantes**. *I like my toast very **crispy**.*
crowded	concurrido atestado	El cine estaba demasiado **concurrido**. *The cinema was too **crowded**.*
deceased	difunto	Era de mi **difunto** abuelo. *It belonged to my **deceased** grandfather.*
deceptive	engañoso	Ese anuncio fue **engañoso**. *That advertisement was **deceptive**.*
devoid of	desprovisto de	Esta región está **desprovista de** materia prima. *This region is **devoid of** raw material.*
disabled	discapacitado	Ese estacionamiento es para personas **discapacitadas**. *That parking space is for **disabled** people.*
dissatisfied	insatisfecho	Quedé **insatisfecho** con el servicio. *I was **dissatisfied** with the service.*
elementary	elemental	Es **elemental** saber cocinar. *It's **elementary** to know how to cook.*
empty-handed	con las manos vacías	Llegó **con las manos vacías**. *He came **empty-handed**.*
even & odd	par e impar	Ordenaron las cosas en **pares e impares**. *They ordered the things in **evens and odds**.*
expected	esperado	Fue un resultado **esperado**. *It was an **expected** result.*
extra (to-spare)	de sobra	Tengo algunas toallas **de sobra**. *I have a few **extra** towels.*
fierce	feroz	El león del zoológico se ve **feroz**. *The lion at the zoo looks **fierce**.*
giant	gigante	Tienen un elefante **gigante** en este zoológico. *They have a **giant** elephant in this zoo.*
gigantic	gigantesco	La montaña era **gigantesca**. *The mountain was **gigantic**.*
gratifying	gratificante	Es **gratificante** hacer trabajo de caridad. *It is **gratifying** to do charity work.*
greedy	codicioso	Mantente alejado de la gente **codiciosa**. *Stay away from **greedy** people.*
hasty	apresurado	Estaba muy **apresurado** por irse. *He was very **hasty** to leave.*
heartwarming	reconfortante	Es una historia **reconfortante**. *It's a **heartwarming** story.*

hollow	hueco ahuecado	Ese árbol está **ahuecado**. *That tree is **hollow**.*
homeless **roofless**	sin hogar sin techo	Era un joven **sin hogar**. *It was a **homeless** young man.*
hooked	enganchado	Está **enganchado** a la pared. *It's **hooked** to the wall.*
hurt	herido lastimado	Se sintió muy **herida** por el comentario. *She felt very **hurt** by the comment.*
immune	inmune	Hoy nadie es **inmune** a las críticas. *Today no one is **immune**. to criticism.*
impolite	descortés maleducado	El mesero fue un tanto **descortés**. *The waiter was a bit **impolite**.*
in a hurry	apurado	Estaba **apurada** por llegar allí. *She was **in a hurry** to get there.*
in open-air **outdoors**	al aire libre	Está permitido fumar **al aire libre**. *Smoking is allowed **outdoors**.*
in charge	encargado a cargo	Le gusta sentirse **encargado** de todo. *He likes to feel **in charge** of everything.*
indebted	endeudado	Estuvo muy **endeudado** por un año. *He was very **indebted** for a year.*
inebriated	ebrio	Estaba **ebrio** anoche. *He was **inebriated** last night.*
inner **internal**	interior interno	Mi voz **interior** me dice que no lo haga. *My **inner** voice tells me not to do it.*
juristic	jurídico	Le gusta mucho el ámbito **jurídico**. *He really likes the **juristic** scope.*
latter **last**	último	Tomamos el **último** autobús. *We took the **last** bus.*
led by	dirigido por liderado por	Eran **liderados por** el mayor de ellos. *They were **led by** the oldest one of them.*
lower	inferior	Se le hinchó el labio **inferior**. *His **lower** lip got swollen.*
loyal	leal fiel	Tengo muchos amigos **fieles**. *I have a lot of **loyal** friends.*
lurking **stalking**	al acecho	Mi perro está **al acecho** en el patio. *My dog is **lurking** on the patio.*
mature **ripe**	maduro	Ese aguacate todavía no está **maduro**. *That avocado isn't **ripe** yet.*
merciful	misericordioso	Fue muy **misericordioso** con la multa. *He was very **merciful** with the fine.*
needy	necesitado	Hay mucha gente **necesitada** en este barrio. *There are many **needy** people in this neighborhood.*

negligible	despreciable insignificante	La cantidad de azúcar que tiene es **insignificante**. *The amount of sugar it has is **negligible**.*
newcomer	recién llegado	En realidad, es un **recién llegado** a la clase. *Actually, he is a **newcomer** to the class.*
ongoing **in progress**	en curso en desarrollo	La pantalla dice que la descarga está **en curso**. *The screen says the download is **in progress**.*
opponent **adversary**	adversario	Fue un buen **adversario** en el juego. *He was a good **opponent** in the game.*
ostentatious	ostentoso	Esa mansión es muy **ostentosa**. *That mansion is very **ostentatious**.*
outstanding	sobresaliente destacado	Siempre ha sido un alumno **destacado**. *He's always been an **outstanding** student.*
overcrowded	superpoblado atestado	El estadio estaba **superpoblado**. *The stadium was **overcrowded**.*
overlooking **(building)**	con vista a	Me gustan las casas **con vista a** la playa. *I like houses **overlooking** the beach.*
overweight	con sobrepeso	El ejercicio es muy útil para la gente **con sobrepeso**. *Exercise is very useful for **overweight** people.*
overwhelming	abrumador	El aroma era **abrumador**. *The aroma was **overwhelming**.*
pending	pendiente	Sigue en estado **pendiente**. *It's still in **pending** status.*
poisonous	venenoso	¡Esa planta es muy **venenosa**! *That plant is very **poisonous**!*
predicted	predicho previsto	El final estaba **predicho**. *The ending was **predicted**.*
profitable	rentable provechoso	Es un negocio bastante **rentable**. *It's a pretty **profitable** business.*
rear	trasero de atrás	No funciona la luz **trasera**. *The **rear** light isn't working.*
reluctant	reacio renuente	Cocinó aunque era **reacio** a hacerlo. *He cooked, although he was **reluctant** to do so.*
replete with	repleto de	El armario está **repleto de** tazas. *The cabinet is **replete with** mugs.*
reputable	de confianza acreditado	Lo obtuve de un proveedor **de confianza**. *I got it from a **reputable** provider.*
rooted	arraigado	Tiene una cultura profundamente **arraigada**. *He has a deeply-**rooted** culture.*
rotten	podrido	La mitad de los huevos estaban **podridos**. *Half of the eggs were **rotten**.*

rough	áspero bruto	Esa lija es muy **áspera**. *That sandpaper is very **rough**.*
royalty (king)	realeza	Mi vecina dice descender de la **realeza**. *My neighbor says she descends from **royalty**.*
seasonal	estacional	Ese trabajo solo es **estacional**. *That job is just **seasonal**.*
second-hand	de segunda mano	Venden prendas **de segunda mano** aquí. *They sell **second-hand** garments here.*
secure **safe**	seguro	El dinero estará **seguro** aquí. *The money will be **safe** here.*
shallow (water)	poco profundo	La piscina es muy **poco profunda**. *The pool is very **shallow**.*
sharp (knife)	afilado	Se corta con un cuchillo **afilado**. *You cut it with a **sharp** knife.*
slippery	resbaladizo	¡Cuidado! El piso está **resbaladizo** allí. *Be careful! The floor is **slippery** there.*
smooth	liso terso	La superficie quedó bien **lisa**. *The surface came out very **smooth**.*
sold out	agotado	Las entradas estaban **agotadas**. *The tickets were **sold out**.*
stranded	encallado varado	Lo encontraron **encallado** en una isla. *They found him **stranded** on an island.*
stray	extraviado	Encontré un gato **extraviado**. *I found a **stray** cat.*
stubborn	obstinado terco	A veces soy un poco **obstinado**. *Sometimes I'm a bit **stubborn**.*
stuck	atascado atrapado	El perro estaba **atascado** en el agujero. *The dog was **stuck** in the hole.*
subsequent	subsiguiente posterior	Olvidé seguir los pasos **subsiguientes**. *I forgot to follow the **subsequent** steps.*
tanned	bronceado	Volvió **bronceada** de sus vacaciones. *She came back **tanned** from her vacation.*
terrified **terrorized**	aterrorizado	La película me dejó **aterrorizado**. *The movie left me **terrified**.*
tidy	ordenado arreglado	Me gusta mantener el escritorio **ordenado**. *I like to keep my desk **tidy**.*
tied	atado	Las zanahorias vienen **atadas** juntas. *The carrots come **tied** together.*
tiny	minúsculo diminuto	Se compró una casa **minúscula**. *She bought a **tiny** house.*
trustworthy	confiable fidedigno	No sé si ese cheque se ve **confiable**. *I don't know if that check looks **trustworthy**.*

unexpected	inesperado imprevisto	Tuve una visita **inesperada**. *I had an* **unexpected** *visit.*
unpleasant	desagradable	Liberó un olor muy **desagradable**. *It released a very* **unpleasant** *smell.*
unscathed	ileso indemne	Sobrevivió **ileso** al accidente. *He survived the accident* **unscathed**.
upper	superior	Se encuentra en el cajón **superior**. *It's in the* **upper** *drawer.*
upstairs	de arriba	Lo encuentras en el baño **de arriba**. *You can find it in the* **upstairs** *bathroom.*
waterproof	a prueba de agua	La chaqueta era **a prueba de agua**. *The jacket was* **waterproof**.
widespread	generalizado extendido	Ahora es una moda **generalizada**. *Now it's a* **widespread** *trend.*

3. Concepts & Behavior

A more abstract topic is related to *concepts and behavior*, or "**los conceptos y el comportamiento**." The table below covers some related vocabulary:

ability *capacity*	**capacidad**^f	*legacy*	**legado**^m
affection	**cariño**^m **afecto**^m	*legend*	**leyenda**^f
anxiety	**ansiedad**^f	*leisure*	**ocio**^m
apology	**disculpa**^f	*luxury*	**lujo**^m
applause	**aplauso**^m	*mentality*	**mentalidad**^f
aptitude	**aptitud**^f	*mercy*	**misericordia**^f
attitude	**actitud**^f	*mischief*	**travesura**^f
birth	**nacimiento**^m	*mood*	**humor**^m [1]
certainty	**certeza**^f	*motive*	**motivo**^m
chance (accident)	**casualidad**^f	*myth*	**mito**^m
charm	**encanto**^m	*nap*	**siesta**^f
choice	**elección**^f **opción**^f	*nightmare*	**pesadilla**^f
comfort	**comodidad**^f	*novelty*	**novedad**^f
common sense	**sentido común**^m	*nuisance*	**fastidio**^m

---

[1] For instance, "**estar de buen humor**" means *"to be in a good mood"* and "**estar de mal humor**" means *"to be in a bad mood."*

compliment (praise)	**cumplido**[m] **halago**[m]	*objective*	**objetivo**[m]
concern	**inquietud**[f] **preocupación**[f]	*opportunity chance*	**oportunidad**[f]
contrast	**contraste**[m]	*pat*	**palmadita**[f]
courage	**coraje**[m] **valor**[m]	*perspective outlook*	**perspectiva**[f]
courtesy	**cortesía**[f]	*pinch*	**pellizco**[m] **pizca**[f]
craziness	**locura**[f]	*plagiarism*	**plagio**[m]
cycle	**ciclo**[m]	*praise*	**alabanza**[f]
death	**muerte**[f] **fallecimiento**[m]	*prejudice*	**prejuicio**[m]
deception	**engaño**[m]	*pride*	**orgullo**[m]
deterioration	**deterioro**[m]	*privilege*	**privilegio**[m]
difficulty	**dificultad**[f]	*promise*	**promesa**[f]
disrespect	**falta**[f] **de respeto**	*purpose*	**propósito**[m]
dream sleeping	**sueño**[m]	*pursuit of happiness*	**búsqueda**[f] **de la felicidad**
ethnicity	**etnia**[f]	*race (ethnicity)*	**raza**[f]
ease	**facilidad**[f]	*rage*	**furia**[f] **cólera**[f] [1]
encouragement	**ánimo**[m]	*randomness*	**aleatoriedad**[f]
fable	**fábula**[f]	*reach*	**alcance**[m]
failure	**fracaso**[m] **fallo**[m]	*recognition acknowledgment*	**reconocimiento**[m]
fate	**destino**[m]	*refusal*	**rechazo**[m]
focus	**foco**[m]	*renaissance*	**renacimiento**[m]
feeling	**sentimiento**[m]	*respect*	**respeto**[m]
foolishness	**tontería**[f]	*responsibility*	**responsabilidad**[f]
freedom liberty	**libertad**[f]	*rest remainder*	**resto**[m]
friendship	**amistad**[f]	*rhythm*	**ritmo**[m]
gender sex	**sexo**[m]	*scientific research*	**investigación científica**[f]
goal (aim)	**meta**[f]	*self-esteem*	**autoestima**[f]
goodwill	**buena voluntad**[f]	*shadow*	**sombra**[f]
greed	**codicia**[f]	*silence*	**silencio**[m]

---

[1] When used as a masculine noun, the word "**cólera**" refers to the *cholera* disease.

glance *gaze*	**mirada**[f]	*snore*	**ronquido**[m]
habit	**hábito**[m]	*solidarity*	**solidaridad**[f]
hatred	**odio**[m]	*solitude* *loneliness*	**soledad**[f]
heaviness	**pesadez**[f]	*slap*	**bofetada**[f] **cachetada**[f]
hobby	**pasatiempo**[m]	*slavery*	**esclavitud**[f]
homage *tribute*	**homenaje**[m]	*spirit*	**espíritu**[m]
hope *expectation*	**esperanza**[f]	*spite* *grudge*	**rencor**[m]
hunch (feeling)	**corazonada**[f]	*stupidity*	**estupidez**[f]
hypothesis	**hipótesis**[f]	*subtlety*	**sutileza**[f]
idiocy	**idiotez**[f]	*suggestion*	**sugerencia**[f]
impulse	**impulso**[m]	*sympathy*	**simpatía**[f]
inequality	**desigualdad**[f]	*term*	**término**[m]
intelligence	**inteligencia**[f]	*thirst*	**sed**[f]
interchange	**intercambio**[m]	*thought* *thinking*	**pensamiento**[m]
joy	**alegría**[f]	*tip* *gratuity*	**propina**[f]
knowledge	**conocimiento**[m]	*virtue*	**virtud**[f]
language	**idioma**[m] **lenguaje**[m]	*weakness*	**debilidad**[f]
laughter	**risa**[f]	*wisdom*	**sabiduría**[f]
leadership	**liderazgo**[m]	*whisper*	**susurro**[m]
learning	**aprendizaje**[m]	*yawn*	**bostezo**[m]

4. ECONOMY & BUSINESS

The economy is "**la economía**" in Spanish, and *business* is "**el negocio**" which is a plural noun. Some important vocabulary is in the following list:

achievement	**logro**[m]	*index*	**índice**[m]
acquaintance	**conocido**[m]	*industrial waste*	**desechos**[m] **industriales**
advantage	**ventaja**[f]	*installment*	**cuota**[f] **plazo**[m]
agriculture	**agricultura**[f]	*interest*	**interés**[m]

apprenticeship	**aprendizaje**^m	*internship*	**pasantía**^f
asset	**activo**^m **bien**^m	*investment*	**inversión**^f
auction	**subasta**^f	*investor*	**inversor**^m **inversionista**^m
audit	**auditoría**^f	*living standard*	**nivel**^m **de vida**
banking	**banca**^f	*loan*	**préstamo**^m
banknote	**billete**^m	*machine*	**máquina**^f
bankruptcy	**bancarrota**^f **quiebra**^f	*mailing list*	**lista**^f **de correo**
barter	**permuta**^f **trueque**^m	*making decisions*	**tomar decisiones**
benefit	**beneficio**^m	*management* [1]	**gestión**^f **gerencia**^f **dirección**^f
birthrate	**índice**^m **de natalidad** **tasa**^f **de natalidad**	*maternity leave*	**licencia**^f **por maternidad**
brainstorming	**lluvia**^f **de ideas**	*member*	**miembro**^m
branch office	**sucursal**^f	*merchandise*	**mercancía**^f
bubble	**burbuja**^f	*mismanagement*	**mal manejo**^m
budget	**presupuesto**^m	*money exchange*	**cambio**^m
business	**negocio**^m	*mortgage*	**hipoteca**^f
challenge	**reto**^m **desafío**^m	*on my own*	**por mi cuenta**
charity	**caridad**^f	*over-the-counter*	**de venta libre**
chart	**tabla**^f **gráfico**^m	*phase*	**fase**^f
committee	**comité**^m **comisión**^f	*pile*	**montón**^m **pila**^f
commitment	**compromiso**^m	*priority*	**prioridad**^f
company	**empresa**^f	*process*	**proceso**^m
coin	**moneda**^f	*procrastination*	**procrastinación**^f **dilaciones**^f
consumer	**consumidor**^m	*profits*	**ganancias**^f
consumption	**consumo**^m	*progress*	**progreso**^m

---

[1] In general, **"gestión"** refers to the act of managing and controlling the company, whereas **"gerencia"** refers to the organizational body of management in a company. On the other hand, **"dirección"** can be used for both meanings.

contract	**contrato**^m	*public holiday*	**día festivo** **día feriado**
cost-of-living	**costo**^m **de vida**	*quality*	**calidad**^f
credit	**crédito**	*range*	**gama**^f
cubicle	**cubículo**^m	*ratio*	**proporción**^f
currency	**divisa**^f	*reminder*	**recordatorio**^m
customer service	**servicio**^m **al cliente**	*resignation*	**dimisión**^f **renuncia**^f
deadline	**plazo**^m **fecha límite**^f **fecha tope**^f	*resource*	**recurso**^m
dealership	**concesionario**^m	*retail (sales)*	**venta al por menor**
debt	**deuda**^f	*reward*	**recompensa**^f
decline	**disminución**^f	*rise*	**subida**^f **ascenso**^m
development	**desarrollo**^m	*royalty (payment)*	**regalía**^f
digit	**dígito**^m **cifra**^f	*scale*	**escala**^f
dollar	**dólar**^m	*scrap*	**chatarra**^f
done deal	**trato hecho**	*skill*	**habilidad**^f **destreza**^f
employment	**empleo**^m	*sponsor*	**patrocinador**^m
entrepreneurship	**emprendimiento**^m	*staff* *personnel*	**personal**^m
excess	**exceso**^m	*stage* *step*	**etapa**^f
exchange rate	**tipo**^m **de cambio**	*statistics*	**estadística**^f
executive	**ejecutivo**^m	*street value*	**valor**^m **en la calle**
expenses	**gastos**^m	*stress*	**estrés**^m
expertise	**pericia**^f	*strike*	**huelga**^f **paro**^m
exports	**exportaciones**^f	*success*	**éxito**^m
fair (exhibition)	**feria**^f	*supplier*	**proveedor**^m
finances	**finanzas**^f	*supplies*	**suministros**^m
fixed schedule	**horario**^m **fijo**	*supply and demand*	**oferta y demanda**
flea market	**mercado**^m **de pulgas** **mercado callejero**^m	*surplus (goods)*	**excedente**
fortune	**fortuna**^f	*surplus (money)*	**superávit**^m
franchise	**franquicia**^f	*talent*	**talento**^m

fund	**fondo**^m	*tax*	**impuesto**^m
Gross Domestic Product (GDP)	**Producto**^m **Interno Bruto (PIB)**	*trade*	**comercio**^m
growth	**crecimiento**^m	*unemployment*	**desempleo**^m **desocupación**^f
guarantee	**garantía**^f	*unemployment benefits*	**subsidio**^m **por desempleo**
headquarters	**sede**^f	*unfinished business*	**asuntos**^m **pendientes asuntos**^m **inconclusos**
hierarchy	**jerarquía**^f	*wealth*	**riqueza**^f
high season	**temporada alta**^f	*wholesale*	**venta al por mayor**
human development	**desarrollo**^m **humano**	*windmill*	**molino**^m
imports	**importaciones**^f	*workday*	**jornada laboral**^f
income revenue	**ingreso**^m	*workshop*	**taller**^m

5. FAMILY II

We continue to add more to our vocabulary related to the family.

ancestor	**antepasado**^m	*orphan*	**huérfano**^m
brother-in-law	**cuñado**^m	*parents*	**padres**^m
clan	**clan**^m	*single*	**soltero**^m **soltera**^f
cousins	**primos**^m	*sister-in-law*	**cuñada**^f
divorce	**divorcio**^m	*spouse partner*	**cónyuge**^{m,f}
divorced	**divorciado**^m **divorciada**^f	*tribe*	**tribu**^f
engagement	**compromiso**^m **noviazgo**^m	*trouble hardship*	**dificultad**^f **apuro**^m
father-in-law	**suegro**^m	*twins*	**gemelos**^m [1] **mellizos**^m [1]
grandparents	**abuelos**^m	*visitor*	**visitante**^m
link (tie or bond)	**vínculo**^m	*vow (marriage)*	**voto**^m
marital status	**estado civil**^m	*wedding*	**boda**^f

---

[1] We use "**gemelos**" to refer to identical twins, and "**mellizos**" to refer to non-identical twins.

marriage	**matrimonio**[m]	*widow*	**viuda**[f]
married	**casado**[m] **casada**[f]	*widower*	**viudo**[m]
mother-in-law	**suegra**[f]	*will* *testament*	**testamento**[m]

6. PEOPLE III

We add more vocabulary related to people that we encounter in our daily life.

acrobat	**acróbata**[m,f]	*hero*	**héroe**[m]
alien	**alienígena**[m,f]	*homeless people*	**indigentes**[m] **personas sin hogar**
altercation	**altercado**[m]	*interpreter*	**intérprete**[m,f]
aristocrat	**aristócrata**[m,f]	*janitor*	**conserje**[m,f]
astronaut	**astronauta**[m,f]	*knight* *gentleman*	**caballero**[m]
baker	**panadero**[m]	*laborer*	**obrero**[m]
beggar	**mendigo**[m] **pordiosero**[m]	*manager*	**director**[m] **gerente**[m]
blacksmith	**herrero**[m]	*mechanic*	**mecánico**[m]
bully	**matón**	*messenger*	**mensajero**[m]
captain	**capitán**[m]	*miner*	**minero**[m]
caretaker	**cuidador**[m]	*news anchor*	**presentador**[m] **de noticias**
chemist	**químico**[m]	*nurse*	**enfermero**[m] **enfermera**[f]
clown	**payaso**[m]	*painter*	**pintor**[m]
cowboy	**vaquero**[m]	*peasant*	**campesino**[m]
crew (plane)	**tripulación**[f]	*peer*	**par**[m]
dwarf	**enano**[m]	*physiotherapist*	**fisioterapeuta**[m,f]
farmer	**granjero**[m]	*pirate*	**pirata**[m,f]
feature *characteristic*	**característica**[f]	*plumber*[1]	**plomero**[m] **fontanero**[m]
feature *trait*	**rasgo**[m]	*postman*	**cartero**[m]

[1] The word "**plomero**" is more common in Latin America, whereas "**fontanero**" is often used in Spain. Some countries in South America use the alternative word "**gasfitero**[m]."

firefighter	**bombero**[m]	*prisoner*	**prisionero**[m] **preso**[m]
flight attendant	**auxiliar**[m,f] **de vuelo** **aeromozo**[m]	*scholar*	**erudito**[m] **sabio**[m]
freelancer	**trabajador independiente**[m] **trabajador autónomo**[m]	*servant*	**criado**[m] **sirviente**[m]
gesture	**gesto**[m]	*shepherd*	**pastor**[m]
greeting	**saludo**[m]	*slave*	**esclavo**[m]
guard	**guardia**[m,f]	*tailor*	**sastre**[m]
hairdresser	**peluquero**[m]	*witch*	**bruja**[f]

7. WAR

War, or "**la guerra**," is another important topic in any language. Some related vocabulary is presented in the table below:

agreement	**acuerdo**[m]	*marshal*	**mariscal**[m]
ally	**aliado**[m]	*military*	**militar**[m]
ambush	**emboscada**[f]	*morale*	**moral**[f]
armor	**armadura**[f]	*mourning (grief)*	**duelo**[m] **luto**[m]
army	**ejército**[m]	*needs*	**necesidades**[f]
atomic bomb	**bomba atómica**[f]	*order (command)*	**orden**[f]
attack	**ataque**[m] **atentado**[m]	*result* *outcome*	**resultado**[m]
balance *equilibrium*	**equilibrio**[m]	*pact*	**pacto**[m]
barrier	**barrera**[f]	*panic*	**pánico**[m]
battle	**batalla**[f]	*parade*	**desfile**[m] **parada**[f]
blast or gust (air)	**ráfaga**[f]	*peace*	**paz**[f]
bow (weapon)	**arco**[m]	*poison*	**veneno**[m]
bullet	**bala**[f]	*population*	**población**[f]
burden	**carga**[f]	*poverty*	**pobreza**[f]
burial	**entierro**[m]	*prison*	**prisión**[f] **cárcel**[f]
cemetery	**cementerio**[m]	*relief*	**alivio**[m]
chaos *mess*	**caos**[m] **desorden**[m]	*revenge*	**venganza**[f]
circumstances	**circunstancias**[f]	*rocket*	**cohete**[m]

collapse	**colapso**[m] **derrumbe**[m]	*ruins*	**ruinas**[f]
conqueror	**conquistador**[m]	*sacrifice*	**sacrificio**[m]
conquest	**conquista**[f]	*sadness* *sorrow*	**tristeza**[f]
consequences	**consecuencias**[f]	*shelter*	**refugio**[m] **albergue**[m]
control	**control**[m]	*shipwreck*	**naufragio**[m]
corpse	**cadáver**[m]	*shooting*	**tiroteo**[m] **disparo**[m]
crying	**llanto**[m]	*shortage*	**escasez**[f]
dagger	**puñal**[m] **daga**[f]	*siege*	**asedio**[m] **cerco**[m]
damage	**daño**[m] **perjuicio**[m]	*spear*	**lanza**[f]
depletion (resources)	**agotamiento**[m] **merma**[f]	*support*	**apoyo**[m]
despair	**desesperación**[f]	*sword*	**espada**[f]
disaster	**desastre**[m]	*tank*	**tanque**[m]
effort	**esfuerzo**[m]	*tomb* *grave*	**tumba**[f]
enemy	**enemigo**[m]	*theft*	**robo**[m] **hurto**[m]
famine	**hambruna**[f]	*tragedy*	**tragedia**[f]
fatality	**fatalidad**[f]	*trap*	**trampa**[f]
genocide	**genocidio**[m]	*treason*	**traición**[f]
gun	**pistola**[f]	*trigger*	**gatillo**[m]
homeland	**patria**[f]	*triumph*	**triunfo**[m]
hunger	**hambre**[m]	*troop*	**tropa**[f]
infrastructure	**infraestructura**[f]	*veteran*	**veterano**[m]
killing	**matanza**[f]	*victory*	**victoria**[f]
lack of	**falta**[f] **de**	*volunteer*	**voluntario**[m]
loss	**pérdida**[f]	*warrior*	**guerrero**[m]
march	**marcha**[f]	*weapon*	**arma**[f]
marine	**marina**[f]	*zone*	**zona**[f]

8. MEDIA II

More vocabulary related to media and entertainment is in the following table:

art	**arte**[m]	*mainstream*	**corriente dominante**[f]

band (music)	**banda**[f]	*mania*	**manía**[f]
broadcast	**emisión**[f]	*masterpiece*	**obra maestra**[f]
broadcasting station	**emisora**[f]	*maze*	**laberinto**[m]
cards deck	**baraja**[f]	*media coverage*	**cobertura mediática**[f]
cartoon	**caricatura**[f] **dibujos animados**[m]	*New Year's Day*	**el Año Nuevo**
celebrity	**celebridad**[f]	*New Year's Eve*	**la Noche Vieja**
circus	**circo**[m]	*noise*	**ruido**[m]
comment remark	**comentario**[m]	*orchestra*	**orquesta**[f]
concert	**concierto**[m]	*painting*	**pintura**[f]
craftsmanship	**artesanía**[f]	*plot (movie)*	**trama**[f]
criticism	**crítica**[m]	*poem*	**poema**[m]
crossword	**crucigrama**[m]	*poster*	**póster**[m] **cartel**[m] **afiche**[m]
debate	**debate**[m]	*protagonist*	**protagonista**[m,f]
dice	**dado**[m]	*rehearsal*	**ensayo**[m]
drum	**tambor**[m]	*review (movie or book)*	**reseña**[f] **crítica**[f]
entertainment	**entretenimiento**[m]	*riddle*	**acertijo**[m] **adivinanza**[f]
exhibition	**exposición**[f]	*scene (movie)*	**escena**[f]
fairy	**hada**[f 1]	*script (movie)*	**guion**[m]
fame	**fama**[f]	*shock*	**choque**[m]
fantasy	**fantasía**[f]	*show performance*	**espectáculo**[m] **función**[f]
fireworks	**fuegos artificiales**[m]	*spectacle*	**espectáculo**[m]
fun	**diversión**[f]	*stage (platform)*	**escenario**[m]
gazette	**gaceta**[f]	*subtitle*	**subtítulo**[m]
headline	**titular**[m]	*symphony*	**sinfonía**[f]
image	**imagen**[f]	*tattoo*	**tatuaje**[m]
journalism	**periodismo**[m]	*trend*	**tendencia**[f]
magic	**magia**[f]	*tune melody*	**melodía**[f]

---

[1] Even though this is a feminine noun, it takes the definite article "**el**" in the singular form. You can revisit **Level I, Lesson 6** for further review.

9. RELIGION II

We add more vocabulary related to *religion*.

believer	**creyente**^(m,f)	*nun*	**monja**^f
blessing	**bendición**^f	*pilgrim*	**peregrino**^m
Christmas Eve	**la Nochebuena**	*pilgrimage*	**peregrinaje**^m **peregrinación**^f
curse	**maldición**^f	*priest*	**sacerdote**^m **cura**^m
Easter	**la Pascua**	*rabbi*	**rabino**^m
Good Friday	**el Viernes Santo**	*ritual*	**ritual**^m **rito**^m
mass	**misa**^f	*Scripture*	**la Escritura**^f
monk	**monje**^m	*sect*	**secta**^f

10. SPORTS II

More vocabulary related to sports is in the table below. If you are interested in *soccer*, or "**el fútbol**," you can refer to **Appendix D** for a more extensive set of vocabulary. In addition, an extra set of flashcards dedicated to soccer vocabulary is available for readers who purchased this book, for free for a limited time, at https://www.adrosverse.com/books-and-flashcards/ using the same coupon code provided in **Appendix A**.

ball boy	**recogepelotas**^m	*parachute*	**paracaídas**^m
bat (baseball)	**bate**^m	*performance*	**desempeño**^m **rendimiento**^m
betting	**apuesta**^f	*physiotherapy*	**fisioterapia**^f
bullfight	**corrida**^f	*post (soccer)*	**poste**^m **palo**^m
commentator	**comentarista**^(m,f)	*practice*	**práctica**^f
competition	**competencia**^(f 1) **competición**^(f 1)	*prize*	**premio**^m

---

[1] The use of "**competencia**" is more common in Latin America, whereas "**competición**" is often used in Spain.

contest	**concurso**[m]	*rivalry*	**rivalidad**[f]
cycling	**ciclismo**[m]	*running track*	**pista**[f] **de carreras**
defender	**defensor**[m] **defensa**[m,f]	*score*	**puntaje**[m] **marcador**[m]
diving	**buceo**[m][1] **zambullida**[f][1]	*skydiving*	**paracaidismo**[m]
draw (random selection)	**sorteo**[m]	*sled* *sledge*	**trineo**[m]
fencing	**esgrima**[f]	*stretching*	**estiramiento**[m]
friendly match	**partido amistoso**[m]	*team*	**equipo**[m]
header	**cabezazo**[m]	*throw-in (soccer)*	**saque lateral**[m]
helmet	**casco**[m]	*tournament*	**torneo**[m]
horse riding	**equitación**[f]	*trophy*	**trofeo**[m]
midfielder (soccer)	**mediocampista**[m] **centrocampista**[m]	*whistle*	**silbato**[m] **pito**[m]
on the bench	**en el banquillo**	*wrestling*	**lucha**[f]

[1] In general, "**buceo**" refers to underwater swimming, whereas "**zambullida**" refers to the act of jumping into water.

REFERENCES

The following is a list of references that we found useful in writing this book:

Sagar-Fenton, Beth & McNeill, Lizzy (2018). How many words do you need to speak a language? Retrieved from https://www.bbc.com/news/world-44569277

Nation, Paul & Waring, Robert (1997). Vocabulary Size, Text Coverage, and Word Lists, by Paul Nation and Robert Waring. Retrieved from https://www.lextutor.ca/research/nation_waring_97.html

Francis, W. N., Kucera, H., Kučera, H., & Mackie, A. W. (1982). Frequency analysis of English usage: Lexicon and grammar. Houghton Mifflin.

Nation, Paul. (2019). 4000 Essential English Words 1-6. Compass Publishing.

Real Academia Española (RAE)
https://www.rae.es/

Foreign Service Institute (FSI)
https://www.state.gov/foreign-language-training/

Anki Webpage
https://apps.ankiweb.net/

Vermeer, Alex. (2017). Anki Essentials v1.1: The complete guide to remembering anything with Anki [Kindle edition].

Toledano, C. A. (2005). Pitman's Commercial Spanish Grammar (2nd edition). Project Gutenberg.

Madrigal, Margarita (1989). Madrigal's Magic Key to Spanish: A Creative and Proven Approach. Broadway Books.

Bregstein, Barbara (2020). Easy Spanish Step-by-Step (2nd edition). McGraw Hill.

Vilaplana, Cynthia (2017). Argentine Spanish: A Guide to Speaking Like an Argentine: The Complete Lessons [Kindle edition].

SpanishDict dictionary, translation, and learning website.
https://www.spanishdict.com/

Homeschool Spanish Academy (HAS) website.
https://www.spanish.academy/

Lawless Spanish website.
https://www.lawlessspanish.com/

Spanish411 website.
https://spanish411.net/

ThoughtCo website.
https://www.thoughtco.com/

APPENDIX

Appendix A. Coupon Code for Free Flashcards

The Anki flashcards that accompany this book are available for free until December 31, 2023. Once you download the cards and back them up with the Anki account you create, the cards do not expire.

To download the free flashcards that accompany this book:

1. Visit the ADROS VERSE EDUCATION website at:
   https://www.adrosverse.com/books-and-flashcards/
2. Add the product **"Spanish: All-Levels Complete Lessons"** Anki Flashcards to the *Shopping Cart*.
3. Go to the *Shopping Cart* and use the following Coupon Code:

AVEAMZNSP1

4. Proceed to *Checkout* and place your order.
5. Download the flashcards in ".zip" format and extract the ".apkg" files.

Appendix B. Verb Tenses and Conjugation Charts

We provide two useful cheat sheets that give you an overall perspective of most moods and verb tenses in Spanish.

The two sheets are available **in color** in pdf format on the resources page of our website at https://www.adrosverse.com/resources/

The first cheat sheet is the Verb Conjugation Chart which is structured as a comprehensive reference for the reader. The imperative mood is not included in this chart.

Unless mentioned otherwise, the stem that should be added to the conjugation suffixes is assumed to be formed from the infinitive by removing the final "**ar**" from "-**ar**" verbs, the final "**er**" from "-**er**" verbs, and the final "**ir**" from "-**ir**" verbs. The irregular verbs for each tense are summarized for quick referencing.

The second sheet dives deeper into the irregular verbs of each tense, where applicable. Besides the imperative mood, we cover the irregular verbs in four tenses in the indicative: the present, the preterite, the imperfect, the simple future; one in the subjunctive, that is, the present subjunctive, and the past participle irregulars which are used in many tenses including: present perfect, pluperfect, and conditional perfect.

We recommend that you keep these two sheets handy by printing them out or having them available separately on your desk or electronic device.

VERB CONJUGATION CHART

CONDITIONAL

CONDITIONAL PERFECT

Yo habría hablado (I would have spoken)

Irregular: Same past participle irregulars discussed in the indicative present perfect.

Regular:
habría
habrías
había + past participle
habríamos
habríais
habrían

SIMPLE CONDITIONAL

Yo hablaría (I would speak)

Irregular: Same irregular verbs in the simple future: decir, haber, hacer, poder, poner, querer, saber, salir, caber, tener, venir, valer.

Regular:
-ía
-ías
-ía
-íamos
-íais
-ían

*Add one of the above endings to the infinitive

INDICATIVE

FUTURE PERFECT

Yo habré hablado (I will have spoken)

Regular:
habré
habrás
habrá + past participle
habremos
habréis
habrán

Irregular: Same past participle irregulars discussed in the indicative present perfect.

SIMPLE FUTURE

Yo hablaré (I will speak)

Regular:
-é
-ás
-á
-emos
-éis
-án

Irregular:
- decir, haber, hacer, poder, poner, querer, saber, salir, caber, tener, venir, valer.
- One can use conjugated "ir" + "a" + infinitive to express the future in informal speech.

*Add one of the above endings to the infinitive

SUBJUNCTIVE

PRESENT

que yo hable (that I speak) | Yo hablo (I speak)

Irregular verbs:
ir   dar
ser   estar
saber   haber
as well some verbs with orthographic-only changes.

Regular:

	-ar	-er/-ir
	-e	-a
	-es	-as
	-e	-a
	-emos	-amos
	-éis	-áis
	-en	-an

*Stem formed from third-person singular by dropping "-o"

Regular (indicative present):

-ar	-er	-ir
-o	-o	-o
-as	-es	-es
-a	-e	-e
-amos	-emos	-imos
-áis	-éis	-ís
-an	-en	-en

Irregular:
- e → ie, e.g. pensar (pienso)
- o → ue, e.g. poder (puedo)
- e → i, e.g. pedir (pido)
- i → ie, e.g. adquirir (adquiero)
- u → ue, e.g. jugar (juego)
- irregular yo form, e.g. dar (doy)
- others: ir, ser, oler, oír

PRESENT PERFECT

que yo haya hablado (that I have spoken) | Yo he hablado (I have spoken)

Irregular: Some past participle irregulars discussed in the indicative present perfect.

Regular:
haya
hayas
haya + past participle
hayamos
hayáis
hayan

Regular:
he
has
ha + post participle
hemos
habéis
han

Irregular: Regular past participle: -ado (-ar verbs), -ido (-er/-ir verbs). Irregular verbs: abrir, cubrir, decir, escribir, hacer, imprimir, morir, poner, resolver, romper, ver, volver.

PROGRESSIVE TENSES

Progressive tenses are formed by adding the proper conjugation of the verb "estar" to the gerund:

Present Progressive: Yo estoy hablando (I am speaking)
Past Progressive: Yo estaba hablando (I was speaking)
Future Progressive: Yo estaré hablando (I will be speaking)
Conditional Progressive: Yo estaría hablando (I would be speaking)

PRETERITE

Yo hablé (I spoke)

Regular:

-ar	-er/-ir
-é	-í
-aste	-iste
-ó	-ió
-amos	-imos
-asteis	-isteis
-aron	-ieron

Irregular: andar, conducir, dar, decir, estar, hacer, ir, poner, poder, querer, saber, ser, tener, traer, venir, ver, as well as some other verbs with orthographic changes.

IMPERFECT

que yo hablara (that I spoke) or que yo hablase | Yo hablaba (I spoke)

Irregular: No irregular verbs. Either set of verb endings can be used for conjugation.

Regular:

-ra	-se
-ras	-ses
-ra	-se
-ramos	-semos
-rais	-seis
-ran	-sen

*Stem formed from third-person plural by dropping "-ron"

Regular:

-ar	-er/-ir
-aba	-ía
-abas	-ías
-aba	-ía
-ábamos	-íamos
-abais	-íais
-aban	-ían

Irregular: Only three irregular verbs:
ir
ser
ver

PLUPERFECT

que yo hubiera hablado (that I had spoken) or que yo hubiese hablado | Yo había hablado (I had spoken)

Irregular: Same past participle irregulars in the indicative present perfect.

Regular:

hubiera	hubiese
hubieras	hubieses
hubiera	hubiese + past participle
hubiéramos	hubiésemos
hubierais	hubieseis
hubieran	hubiesen

(or)

Regular:
había
habías
había + past participle
habíamos
habíais
habían

Irregular: Same past participle irregulars discussed in the indicative present perfect.

IRREGULAR VERBS

PRESENT INDICATIVE TENSE

1. Irregular in the "yo" form only
"-oy": estar (estoy), dar (doy)
"-go": hacer (hago), poner (pongo), valer (valgo), salir (salgo), traer (traigo), caer (caigo)
"-cer"/"-cir": conocer (conozco), ofrecer (ofrezco), conducir (conduzco), traducir (traduzco)
Completely irregular in the "yo" form:
saber (sé), caber (quepo), ver (veo)

2. Stem change except "nosotros/-as" & "vosotros/-as"
e → ie: corregir, elegir, medir, pedir, reír, repetir, seguir, servir
e → i: advertir, atender, atravesar, calentar, cerrar, comenzar, confesar, convertir, defender, divertir, empezar, encender, entender, enterrar, fregar, herir, hervir, mentir, negar, pensar, perder, preferir, querer, regar, sugerir, temblar, tropezar, verter
o → ue: acordar, almorzar, aprobar, contar, costar, dormir, encontrar, forzar, morder, mostrar, poder, probar, volar, volver
u → ue: jugar
i → ie: adquirir, inquirir

3. Irregular in the "yo" form with "-go" ending + Stem change in all other forms except "nosotros/-as" & "vosotros/-as":
decir (digo, dice), venir (vengo, viene), tener (tengo, tiene)

4. Completely irregular verbs: ser, ir, oler, oír

5. Orthographic changes only:
"-guir" → "-go": e.g., extenguir (extingo), seguir (sigo)
"-ger"/"-gir" → "-jo": e.g., proteger (protejo), exigir (exijo)
"-quir" → "-co": e.g., delinquir (delinco)
"-uir" (excluding "-guir") add "y" between stem & suffix in all forms except "nosotros/-as" & "vosotros/-as":
atribuir (atribuyo, atribuye), construir (construyo, construye), contribuir (contribuyo, contribuye), disminuir (disminuyo, disminuye), distribuir (distribuyo, distribuye), huir (huyo, huye), incluir (incluyo, incluye), sustituir (sutituyo, sustituye)
Some "-iar" & "-uar" ending verbs add an accent to "i" or "u" before conjugation suffix in all forms except "nosotros/-as" & "vosotros/-as":
enviar (envío, envía), fiar (fío, fía), liar (lío, lía), variar (varío, varía), actuar (actúo, actúa), continuar (continúo, continúa), habituar (habitúo, habitúa), situar (sitúo, sitúa)

PRESENT SUBJUNCTIVE TENSE

Only 6 irregular verbs:
ser: sea, seas, sea, seamos, seáis, sean
estar: esté, estés, esté, estemos, estéis, estén
ir: vaya, vayas, vaya, vayamos, vayáis, vayan
haber: haya, hayas, haya, hayamos, hayáis, hayan
saber: sepa, sepas, sepa, sepamos, sepáis, sepan
dar: dé, des, dé, demos, deis, den

GERUND

1. ir → yendo

2. "-iendo" → "-yendo"
"-er" or "-ir" with stem the ending in a vowel
leer → leyendo, atraer → atrayendo, destruir → destruyendo, huir → huyendo

3. e → i: decir → diciendo, pedir → pidiendo

4. o → u: dormir → durmiendo, morir → muriendo

5. "-iendo" → "-endo"
"-er" or "-ir" with stem the ending in "-ll" or "-ñ"
bullir → bullendo, mullir → mullendo, teñir → tiñendo

PRETERITE TENSE

1. Verbs ending in "-ducir" + "decir" & "traer"
"-ducir" → "-duj-": conducir (conduj-), traducir (traduj-), producir (produj-), reducir (reduj-), introducir (introduj-), deducir (deduj-), seducir (seduj-)
"decir" → "dij-" & "traer" → "traj-"

2. Verbs "estar", "tener" & "andar"
"estar" → "estuv-", "tener" → "tuv-", "andar" → "anduv-"
e → ie: corregir, elegir, medir, pedir, reir, repetir, seguir, servir

3. Verbs that change first vowel from "a" or "o" to "u"
a → u: haber (hub-), poder (pud-)
o → u: poner (pus-), saber (sup-), caber (cup-)

4. Verbs that change the stem in the 3rd person
e → i: pedir (pidió), mentir (mintió), sentir (sintió), seguir (siguió), servir (sirvió), hervir (hirvió), preferir (prefirió), convertir (convirtió), despedir (despidió), impedir (impidió), divertir (divirtió), sugerir (sugirió), vestir (vistió), repetir (repitió), reir (rió)
o → u: dormir (durmió), morir (murió)
"final stem vowel" → "y": caer (cayó), leer (leyó), roer (royó), oír (oyó), influir (influyó), concluir (concluyó)

5. Verbs "venir" & "querer"
irregular: "venir" → "vin-", "querer" → "quis-"

6. Verbs "ser", "ir", "dar" & "ver"
Irregular and do not follow a specific rule.
ser/ir (for both verbs): fui, fuiste, fue, fuimos, fuisteis, fueron
dar: di, diste, dio, dimos, disteis, dieron
ver: vi, viste, vio, vimos, visteis, vieron

IMPERFECT TENSE

Only 3 completely irregular verbs:
ser: era, eras, era, éramos, erais, eran
ir: iba, ibas, iba, íbamos, ibais, iban
ver: veía, veías, veía, veíamos, veíais, veían

FUTURE INDICATIVE TENSE

1. Some verbs ending in "-er" and "-ir" drop the "e" or the "i" and add a "d" to the stem:
tener → tendr-, poner → pondr-, valer → valdr-, venir → vendr-, salir → saldr-

2. Some verbs ending in "-er" drop the "e" from the stem:
saber → sabr-, poder → podr-, caber → cabr-, querer → querr-, haber → habr-

3. Verbs "decir" & "hacer"
decir → dir-, hacer → har-

IMPERATIVE

Only 8 completely irregular verbs:
ser (sé), ir (ve), venir (ven), tener (ten), decir (di), hacer (haz), poner (pon), salir (sal)

PAST PARTICIPLE

abrir (abierto), absolver (absuelto), cubrir (cubierto), decir (dicho), escribir (escrito), freír (frito), hacer (hecho), impimir (impreso), morir (muerto), poner (puesto), proveer (provisto), resolver (resuelto), romper (roto), satisfacer (satisfecho), ver (visto), volver (vuelto)

Appendix C. List of English Cognates and False Cognates

The following list contains some of the most common English cognates in Spanish. This list is an extension to the list provided in **Level I, Lesson 2**.

English	Spanish	Examples
-or	-or	actor, benefactor, color, conductor, doctor, error, exterior, favor, honor, horror, interior, inventor, monitor, sector, senador, superior, tractor
-ble	-ble	cable, considerable, flexible, horrible, inevitable, inseparable, noble, notable, posible, probable, susceptible, terrible, variable, viable
-al	-al	animal, canal, casual, central, coral, criminal, digital, fatal, festival, final, formal, gradual, habitual, ideal, industrial, integral, internacional, legal, local, mineral, musical, natural, normal, original, personal, profesional, total, rival, social, terminal, viral, vital, vocal, virtual
-al	-co -ca	crítico, eléctrico, físico, lógico, mágico, mecánico, óptico, político
-ic	-ico -ica	básico, democrático, diabético, fantástico, mecánico, plástico, público, romántico, tóxico
-ant	-ante	abundante, constante, distante, dominante, elegante, ignorante, importante, instante, restaurante, significante, tolerante
-ent	-ente	accidente, agente, aparente, cliente, competente, continente, decente, diferente, diligente, evidente, excelente, incidente, inocente, inteligente, permanente, proponente, prudente, suficiente, urgente
-ment	-mento	complemento, documento, elemento, experimento, instrumento, monumento, parlamento, suplemento, testamento
-ist	-ista	artista, comunista, dentista, especialista, lista, novelista, optimista, pianista, turista
-am	-ama	caligrama, diagrama, programa, radiograma, telegrama
-em	-ema	ecosistema, emblema, poema, problema, sistema
-ous	-oso -osa	curioso, delicioso, fabuloso, famoso, furioso, industrioso, misterioso, nervioso, religioso, victorioso

-ry	-rio -ria	adversario, aniversario, arteria, contrario, culinario, diccionario, extraordinario, imaginario, industria, itinerario, literario, memoria, misterio, notario, ordinario, primario, salario, satisfactorio, voluntario
-tion	-ción	acción, administración, atención, civilización, coalición, concepción, condición, conversación, correlación, creación, descripción, determinación, ecuación, edición, expedición, federación, ficción, fracción, función, fundación, generación, indignación, institución, moción, nación, noción, ocupación, operación, porción, posición, prohibición, publicación, recomendación, revolución, satisfacción, sección, sensación, superstición, tradición, transacción, transición
-tional	-cional	adicional, condicional, institucional, nacional, operacional, racional, tradicional
-tial	-cial	confidencial, esencial, inicial, parcial, potencial, presidencial, residencial
-ce -cy	-cia	agencia, Alicia, aristocracia, deficiencia, democracia, diferencia, distancia, esencia, evidencia, experiencia, farmacia, Francia, gracia, importancia, justicia, licencia, negligencia, permanencia, potencia, presencia, profecía, provincia, referencia, secuencia, subsistencia, urgencia, violencia
-ty	-dad	autoridad , cavidad, comunidad, dignidad, diversidad, electricidad, gravedad, honestidad, hospitalidad, humanidad, identidad, integridad, personalidad, posibilidad, privacidad, proximidad, unidad, universidad, vanidad
-tor	-dor	administrador, colaborador, creador, dictador, elevador, investigador, generador, operador, orador, ventilador
-ly	-mente	exactamente, finalmente, naturalmente, normalmente, personalmente, probablemente, totalmente
-phy	-fía	biografía, cinematografía, filosofía, fotografía, geografía
-ct	-cto -cta	abstracto, acto, adicto, compacto, conflicto, contacto, correcto, directo, efecto, exacto, impacto, insecto, intelecto, perfecto, producto

-sion	-sión	admisión, agresión, comisión, colisión, compasión, conclusión, conversión, decisión, discusión, erosión, expresión, extensión, ilusión, impresión, inclusión, invasión, misión, ocasión, omisión, pasión, profesión, provisión, sesión, versión, visión
-ism	-ismo	astigmatismo, comunismo, despotismo, electromagnetismo, idealismo, mecanismo, metabolismo, organismo
-fy	-ficar	certificar, clarificar, clasificar, dignificar, glorificar, gratificar, identificar, justificar, magnificar, modificar, notificar, unificar, verificar
-id	-ido -ida	ávido, espléndido, fluido, líquido, lúcido, plácido, rápido, rígido, sólido, tímido, válido, vívido
-ile	-il	ágil, automóvil, facsímil, fértil, frágil, hostil, juvenil
-iv	-ivo -iva	activo, adictivo, adhesivo, aditivo, administrativo, atractivo, cognitivo, decisivo, definitivo, efectivo, elusivo, festivo, imperativo, incentivo, informativo, inventivo, masivo, nativo, negativo, positivo, respectivo
ph	f	elefante, filosofía, fonético, foto, teléfono
th	t	auténtico, autor, catedral, católico
st-	est-	estable, estación, estricto, estudiante, estúpido
sp-	esp-	especial, específico, espiritual, esposo

Furthermore, below is an extended list of false English cognates.

Spanish Word	Meaning in English	English Cognate	Meaning of cognate in Spanish
éxito	*success*	exit	**salida**
molestar	*to annoy*	molest	**abusar**
constipado	*cold (illness)*	constipated	**estreñido**
recordar	*to remind or remember*	record	**grabar**
actual	*current*	actual	**real**
red	*network*	red	**rojo**
enviar	*to send*	envy	**envidiar**
carpeta	*folder*	carpet	**alfombra**
grosería	*rudeness*	groceries	**comestibles**
embarazada	*pregnant*	embarrassed	**avergonzado**
fábrica	*factory*	fabric	**tela**
sopa	*soup*	soap	**jabón**

realizar	*to perform or fulfill*	realize	**darse cuenta de**
ropa	*clothes*	rope	**cuerda**
pie	*foot*	pie	**pastel**
introducir	*to insert*	introduce	**presentar**
parientes	*relatives*	parents	**padres**
compromiso	*commitment or engagement*	compromise	**acuerdo**
delito	*crime*	delight	**deleite**
chocar	*to hit or clash*	choke	**estrangular**
contestar	*to answer*	contest (a verdict)	**impugnar**
largo	*long*	large	**grande**
rapista	*shaver barber*	rapist	**violador**
preservativo	*condom*	preservative	**conservante**
grapa	*staple*	grape	**uva**
arma	*weapon*	arm	**brazo**
lectura	*reading*	lecture	**conferencia**
pan	*bread*	pan	**cacerola**
horno	*oven*	horn	**cuerno**
ingenuidad	*naivety*	ingenuity	**ingenio**
salado	*salty*	salad	**ensalada**
envolver	*to wrap*	involve	**involucrar**
familiar	*relative*	familiar	**conocido**
policía	*police*	policy	**política**
soportar	*to put up with*	support	**apoyar**
últimamente	*lately*	ultimately	**por último**
librería	*bookstore*	library	**biblioteca**
codo	*elbow*	code	**código**
bombero	*firefighter*	bomber	**bombardero**
advertencia	*warning*	advertisement	**publicidad**
vaso	*glass (drinking)*	vase	**jarrón**
tarjeta	*card*	target	**objetivo**

Appendix D. Soccer Vocabulary

Football or *soccer* is incredibly popular in Latin America. It is quite useful to familiarize yourself with the vocabulary associated with "**el fútbol**."

armband	**brazalete**^{m} **cinta**^{f}	*manager*	**director técnico**^{m}
assist	**asistencia**^{f}	*midfield*	**mediocampo**^{m} **media cancha**^{f}
assistant referee	**juez**^{m} **de línea**	*midfielder*	**centrocampista**^{m,f} **mediocampista**^{m,f}
bench	**banca**^{f} **banquillo**^{m}	*mistake*	**error**^{m}
bicycle kick	**chilena**^{f} **bicicleta**^{f}	*move*	**jugada**^{f}
central defender	**defensa central**^{m,f}	*nutmeg*	**túnel**^{m}
champion	**campeón**^{m}	*offside*	**fuera**^{m} **de juego** **fuera**^{m} **de lugar**
championship	**campeonato**^{m}	*own goal*	**autogol**^{m}
championship title	**título**^{m} **de campeón**	*pass*	**pase**^{m}
chance	**ocasión**^{f} **remate**^{m}	*penalty*	**penal**^{m} **penalti**^{m}
clearance	**despeje**^{m}	*penalty area*	**área**^{f} **de penal**
coach	**entrenador**^{m}	*penalty shootout*	**penales**^{m} **penaltis**^{m}
comeback	**remontada**^{f}	*playing field*	**campo**^{m} **cancha**^{f} **terreno**^{m}
corner	**tiro**^{m} **de esquina** **córner**^{m}	*possession*	**posesión**^{f}
corner flag	**banderín**^{m}	*post (goal)*	**poste**^{m}
crossbar	**larguero**^{m} **travesaño**^{m}	*red card*	**tarjeta roja**^{f}
cup	**copa**^{f}	*referee*	**árbitro**^{m}
defender	**defensor**^{m}	*right-back*	**lateral derecho**^{m}
defensive wall	**barrera defensiva**^{f}	*score*	**marcador**^{m}
dive	**clavado**^{m} **piscinazo**^{m}	*shin guards*	**canilleras**^{f} **espinilleras**^{f}
dribble	**regate**^{m}	*shot*	**tiro**^{m} **disparo**^{m}

equalizer	**gol**[m] **del empate**	*soccer ball*	**pelota**[f] **balón**[m]
extra time	**prórroga**[f]	*soccer match*	**partido**[m] **de fútbol**
fans	**hinchas**[m,f] **aficionados**[m]	*soccer player*	**futbolista**[m,f] **jugador**[m] **de fútbol**
flag	**bandera**[f]	*soccer shoes*	**botas**[f] **guayos**[m] **botines**[m]
forward	**delantero**[m] **atacante**[m,f]	*soccer team*	**equipo**[m] **de fútbol**
foul	**falta**[f]	*spectacular goal*	**golazo**[m]
free kick	**tiro libre**[m]	*sportsmanship*	**deportividad**[f] **espíritu deportivo**[m]
gloves	**guantes**[m]	*stadium*	**estadio**[m]
goal (score)	**gol**[m] **tanto**[m]	*stands*	**gradas**[f]
goal (structure)	**portería**[f] **arco**[m] **valla**[f]	*stoppage time* *injury time*	**tiempo**[m] **de descuento**
goal kick	**saque**[m] **de meta**	*studs*	**tacos**[m]
goalkeeper	**portero**[m] **arquero**[m] **guardameta**[m,f] **golero**[m]	*substitute player*	**suplente**[m,f]
goalkeeper area	**área**[f] **de meta** **área chica**[f]	*tackle*	**entrada**[f] **tackle**[m]
grass *pitch*	**césped**[m]	*the captain of the team*	**el capitán**[m] **del equipo**
halftime	**medio tiempo**[m]	*throw-in*	**saque lateral**[m]
handball (soccer)	**mano**[f]	*tie*	**empate**[m]
hat trick	**tripleta**[f]	*touchline*	**línea**[f] **de banda**
header	**cabezazo**[m]	*t-shirt* *jersey*	**camiseta**[f]
injury	**lesión**[f]	*victory*	**victoria**[f]
kickoff	**saque inicial**[m]	*volley*	**volea**[f]
kit	**kit**[m]	*whistle*	**pito**[m] **silbato**[m]
left-back	**lateral izquierdo**[m]	*World Cup*	**Mundial**[m]
locker rooms	**vestidores**[m] **camerinos**[m]	*yellow card*	**tarjeta amarilla**[f]

In addition to the vocabulary above, the following verbs come in handy when you want to watch or describe soccer in Spanish.

Verbs:

English	Spanish	Examples
to attack	atacar	El equipo perdió, aunque **atacó** hasta el último minuto. *The team lost, although they **attacked** until the last minute.*
to break	romper	**Rompió** el récord de goles por partido. *He **broke** the record of goals per match.*
to bump into	toparse	**Se topó** contra el otro jugador sin querer. *He **bumped into** the other player by accident.*
to clear	despejar	Despejó el balón fuera del área de penal. *He **cleared** the ball outside the penalty area.*
to defeat	derrotar	El equipo fue **derrotado**. *The team was **defeated**.*
to defend	defender	El arquero **defiende** el arco. *The goalie **defends** the goal.*
to dive (pretend)	tirarse un clavado tirarse a la piscina	No me gustan los jugadores que **se tiran el clavado** todo el tiempo. *I don't like players who **dive** all the time.*
to eliminate	eliminar	**Eliminaron** a muchos equipos fuertes para llegar a la final. *They **eliminated** many strong teams to reach the final.*
to even the score	igualar	Con ese gol, **igualaron** el puntaje. *With that goal, they **evened the score**.*
to fight (quarrel)	pelear	A veces se **pelean** los jugadores. *Players sometimes **fight**.*
to follow	seguir	Los jugadores **siguen** al capitán. *The players **follow** the captain.*
to head	cabecear	**Cabecea** la pelota muy bien. *He **heads** the ball very well.*
to lose	perder	Si siguen jugando así, **perderán**. *If they keep playing that way, they **will lose**.*
to mark	marcar	Este defensor es conocido por **marcar** muy bien a los delanteros. *This defender is known for **marking** strikers very well.*

to play	jugar	Siempre **juegan**, dando todo de sí. *They always **play**, giving it their all.*
to prevail	imponerse	El equipo logró **imponerse** en el último minuto. *The team managed to **prevail** in the last minute.*
to qualify	clasificarse	**Clasificaron** para las semifinales. *They **qualified** for the semifinals.*
to recover	reponerse recuperarse	Se tomará dos semanas para **recuperarse** de la temporada. *He's going to take two weeks to **recover** from the season.*
to referee	arbitrar	Me parece que **arbitró** bien hoy. *I think he **refereed** well today.*
to run	correr	Ese jugador **corre** mucho en el partido. *That player **runs** a lot in the game.*
to score	marcar	Acaban de **marcar** otro tanto. *They've just **scored** another goal.*
to simulate **to feign**	simular	El árbitro le mostró tarjeta amarilla por **simular** una lesión. *The referee showed him a yellow card for **feigning** injury.*
to stretch	estirar(se)	Debes **estirarte** antes de jugar en la cancha. *You have to **stretch** before playing on the field.*
to substitute	sustituir	Va a **sustituir** al jugador titular. *He's going to **substitute** the main player.*
to sweat	sudar	Estaban **sudando** después de ganar el título. *They were **sweating** after winning the title.*
to tackle	entrarle a taclear	Lo **tacleó** sin previo aviso. *He **tackled** him without a warning.*
to tie	empatar	Al final **empataron** el juego. *In the end, they **tied** the game.*
to try	intentar	**Intentaron** ganar pero fue difícil. *They **tried** to win but it was hard.*
to volley	volear	Logró **volear** el balón al delantero. *He managed to **volley** the ball to the striker.*
to warm up	calentar	**Calentarán** antes de jugar. *They **will warm up** before playing.*
to win	ganar	Creo que este año **ganarán** el campeonato. *I think that this year they **will win** the championship.*

Appendix E. Idioms in Spanish

In Spanish, there are a lot of idioms, called "**modismos**," that do not have direct translation in English. Here are some of the most common verbal idioms.

Idioms with "Buscar"

buscar excusas	to make excuses
buscar hacer algo	to try to do something
buscar trabajo	to look for work
buscar pelea	to seek a fight
buscar su dinero	to be after his/her money
buscarla	to look for trouble
ir a buscar algo	to go fetch something
ir a buscar a alguien	to go pick up someone
el más buscado	the most wanted
buscarse	to find oneself
buscarse la vida	to try to make a living
buscársela	to ask for trouble
se busca piso	apartment wanted
Búscate la vida.	Figure it out yourself.

Idioms with "Comer"

comer el coco a alguien	to brainwash someone
comer fuera	to eat out
comer fuerte	to eat a big meal
tan necesario como comer	as necessary as eating
¡Come y calla!	Shut up and eat your food!
comerse el coco	to worry
comerse el mundo	to conquer the world
comerse las palabras	to swallow one's words
comerse las uñas	to bit one's nails
se lo comió todo	he ate it all
¿Cómo se come eso?	What on earth is that?
ser de buen comer	to enjoy one's food
ser muy parco en el comer	to not be a big eater

Idioms with "Dar"

dar a	to be facing

dar a conocer	to introduce or present
dar a luz	to give birth
dar algo por perdido	to give up on something for being lost
dar asco	to disgust
dar calabazas a alguien	to reject or turn someone down
dar carta blanca a alguien	to give carte blanche to someone
dar como	to consider
dar ejemplo	to set an example
dar la bienvenida	to welcome
dar de comer	to feed
dar gritos	to shout
dar las gracias	to thank
dar un paseo dar una vuelta	to take a walk
dar un abrazo	to hug
dar la vuelta	to turn over
dar pena	to feel sad or sorry for
dar permiso	to give permission
dar por sentado/hecho	to take for granted
dar rienda suelta a	to give free rein to
darse a	to take on or devote oneself to
darse a conocer	to make oneself known
darse a creer que	to start thinking that
darse cuenta de	to realize
darse la mano	to shake hands
darse por	to consider oneself
darse por ofendido	to take offense
darse por vencido	to acknowledge defeat
darse prisa	to hurry up
dárselas de	to pretend to be
si se da el caso	in case that happens
lo mismo da	it makes no difference
me da lo mismo me da igual	it's all the same to me
a mí no me la das	you can't fool me

Idioms with "Decir"

decir entre/para sí	to say to oneself
decir la hora	to tell time
decir por decir	to talk for the sake of talking

es decir	that is to say
es mucho decir	that's saying a lot
ni que decir tiene que … no hay que decir que …	it goes without saying that …
no hay más que decir	there's nothing more to say
no sé qué decir	I don't know what to say
o por mejor decir	or in other words
ya es decir	that's saying a lot
¿Cómo diríamos?	How shall I put it?
¿Cómo se dice …?	How do you say …?
Dicho y hecho.	No sooner said than done.
¡Lo dicho, dicho está! ¡Lo que he dicho!	I stand by what I said!
por decirlo así	so to speak
¡Quién lo diría!	Can you believe it?!
tragarse lo dicho	to eat one's words
ya me dirás	tell me your side of it
se diría que	it seems, one would say
se me ha dicho que	I've been told that
y no se diga	not to mention
a decir de todos	by all accounts
es un decir	it's just an expression

Idioms with "Dejar"

dejar de (infinitive)	to stop or give up doing something
dejar aparte	to leave aside
dejar atrás	to leave behind
dejar a uno (infinitive)	to let someone do something
dejar a uno de la mano	to abandon someone
dejar a uno entrar	to let someone in
dejar algo para después	to leave something until later
dejar algo por imposible	to give up something as impossible
dejar así las cosas	to leave things as they are
dejar caer	to drop
dejar de existir	to come to an end
dejar plantado	to jilt or stand someone up
dejar mucho que desear	to leave a lot to be desired
dejar estar	to let it go, to let it be
no puedo dejar de	I can't help but
¡Deja eso!	Stop it! Drop that!

dejarse	to let oneself, to neglect oneself
dejarse decir que	to let slip that
¡Déjate de eso!	Stop it! Cut it out!
¡Déjate de bromas!	Stop joking around!

Idioms with "Echar"

echar de menos	to miss
echar la culpa	to blame
echar flores	to flatter
echar a perder	to ruin
echar a alguien a un lado	to push someone aside
echar abajo	to pull down or demolish
echar la llave	to lock, to turn the key
echar los frenos	to brake
echar maldiciones	to curse
echar pelo	to grow hair
echar sangre	to shed blood
echar una carta	to mail a letter
echar un discurso	to give a speech
echarse a	to start to
echarse a llorar	to burst out crying

Idioms with "Hacer"

hacer caso a	to pay attention to, to heed
hacer daño a	to harm
hacer el bien	to do good
hacer el mal	to do bad
hacer falta	to be lacking
hacer un papel	to play a part
hacer amigos	to make friends
hacer una broma	to play a joke on someone
hacer buenas migas	to hit it off with someone
hacer época	to attract attention
hacer un recado	to run an errand
hacer la vista gorda	to turn a blind eye
hacer un viaje	to take a trip
hacer una visita	to pay a visit
hacer caso omiso de	to ignore or disregard
hacer el mal	to do bad
hacer las paces	to make peace

hacer su agosto	to make a killing
hacer pedazos	to break into pieces
hacer sombra	to provide shade
hacer una pregunta	to ask a question
hacerse el malo	to play the bad guy
hacerse tarde	to get late
hacerse daño	to hurt oneself
hacérsele agua la boca	to make someone's mouth water

Idioms with "Llevar"

llevar a cabo	to carry out
llevar la contraria	to take the opposite side
llevar (time)	to spend
llevar ... años a	to be ... years older than
llevar ... centímetros a	to be ... cm taller than
llevar a cabo	to carry out
llevar a	to lead to
llevar a alguien a creer que	to lead someone to believe that
llevar la casa	to run the household
llevar lo mejor/peor	to get the best/worst of it
llevar una vida tranquila	to lead a quiet life
llevarse	to take away, to remove
llevarse bien	to get along
llevar mal	to not get along

Idioms with "Meter"

meter de contrabando	to smuggle in
meter miedo a alguien	to scare someone
meter la narices	to stick one's nose
meter prisa a alguien	to hurry someone
meter ruido	to cause a stir
meter un lío	to make a fuss
meter la pata	to put one's foot in one's mouth
meterse a (infinitive)	to start
meterse a (job)	to become
meterse con alguien	to provoke someone
meterse en la cama	to get in bed
meterse en peligro	to get into danger
meterse en sí mismo	to withdraw into oneself
meterse en donde no lo llaman	to meddle

Idioms with "Poner"

poner a uno a (hacer algo)	to start someone (doing something)
poner algo aparte	to set something aside
poner algo como ejemplo	to give something as an example
poner algo en duda	to cast doubt on something
poner énfasis en	to stress or emphasize
poner una objeción	to object
poner pleito	to sue
poner el reloj	to set the watch
ponerse a	to begin
ponerse a bien con alguien	to be on good terms with someone
ponerse al teléfono	to get on the phone
ponerse con alguien	to argue or compete with someone
ponerse de	to take a job as
ponerse delante	to get in the way, to intervene
ponerse la piel de gallina	to get goosebumps

Idioms with "Quedar"

quedar boquiabierto	to be speechless
quedar a la espera de	to look forward to
quedar atrapado	to get stuck
quedar en nada	to come to nothing
hacer quedar mal	to make someone look bad
quedarse en blanco	to go blank
quedarse tan ancho	to show no regret
quedarse corto	to fall behind
quedarse dormido	to fall asleep
quedar bien con alguien	to get along with someone
quedar mal con alguien	to not get along with someone
quedarse parado	to stand still
quedarse con el día y la noche	to be left penniless
no queda otra más que …	there is no alternative but …
queda por ver si …	we will see if …

Idioms with "Tomar"

tomar en serio	to take seriously
tomar el pelo	to pull someone's leg
tomarlo con calma	to take it easy
tomar a broma/risa	to take as a joke

tomar aire/un respiro	to take a breath
tomar aliento	to catch one's breath
tomar asiento	to take a seat
tomar un paseo	to take a walk
tomar la palabra	to take the floor, to speak
tomar partido por	to side with
tomar un bocado	to take a bite
tomarla con uno	to pick a fight with someone
tomarse por	to consider oneself to be
Tómate tu tiempo.	Take your time.
Lo tomas o lo dejas.	Take it or leave it.
¿Por quién me tomas?	What do you take me for?
¡Tómate esa!	Take that!
¡Toma ya!	Believe it or not!

Idioms with "Traer"

traerse algo	to be up to a plan or a scheme
traerse bien	to dress well, to behave
traerse mal	to dress poorly, to misbehave

Idioms with "Ver"

A ver	Let's see
ver para creer	seeing is believing
ver venir a alguien	to see what someone is up to
dejarse ver	to show one's face
Eso está por ver.	That remains to be seen.
estar de buen ver	to be good-looking
¡Hay que ver qué listo es!	You wouldn't believe how smart he is!
ni visto ni oído	in the twinkling of an eye
por lo que se ve	apparently
¿Ves lo que quiero decir?	Do you see what I mean?

Appendix F. List of Diminutives and Augmentatives in Spanish

The following are extended lists of diminutives and augmentatives in Spanish:

1. Diminutives

Spanish Word	Meaning in English	Diminutive in Spanish	Meaning in English
abajo	*below*	abajito	*little below*
abuelo/-a	*grandfather/-mother*	abuelito/-a	*grandpa/-ma*
ahora	*now*	ahorita	*right now*
amigo[m]	*friend*	amiguito[m]	*little friend*
amor[m]	*love*	amorcito[m]	*sweetie*
árbol[m]	*tree*	arbolito[m]	*little tree*
avión[m]	*plane*	avioncito[m]	*little plane*
barba[f]	*beard*	barbilla[f]	*chin*
bolso[m]	*bag*	bolsillo[m]	*pouch or pocket*
café[m]	*coffee*	cafecito[m]	*little coffee*
calle[f]	*street*	callecita[f]	*little street*
camión[m]	*truck*	camioncito[m]	*little truck*
casa[f]	*house*	casita[f]	*small house*
cerca	*close*	cerquita	*pretty close*
chica[f]	*small*	chiquita[f]	*little boy*
chico[m]	*small*	chiquito[m]	*tiny*
coche[m]	*car*	cochecito[m]	*baby stroller*
favor[m]	*favor*	favorcito[m]	*little favor*
flor[f]	*flower*	florecita[f] florcita[f]	*small flower*
fuente[f]	*fountain*	fuentecita[f]	*small fountain*
gordo[m]	*fat*	gordito[m]	*chubby*
hermano/-a	*brother/sister*	hermanito/-a	*little brother/sister*
hijo/-a	*son/daughter*	hijito/-a	*little son/daughter*
joven[m,f]	*young*	jovencito/-a	*youngster*
juego[m]	*game*	juguete[m]	*toy*
lago[m]	*lake*	laguito[m]	*small lake*
lápiz[m]	*pencil*	lapicito[m]	*small pencil*
león[m]	*lion*	leoncito[m]	*little lion*
luz[f]	*light*	lucecita[f]	*little light*
mamá[f]	*mom*	mamita[f]	*mommy*
mano[f]	*hand*	manita[f]	*little hand*
manteca[f]	*lard*	mantequilla[f]	*butter*

mañana^f	*morning*	mañanita^f	*early morning*
mesa^f	*table*	mesita^f	*small table*
momento^m	*moment*	momentito^m	*little moment*
niño/-a	*child*	niñito/-a	*little child*
nuevo^m	*new*	nuevecito^m	*brand-new*
pájaro^m	*bird*	pajarito^m	*small bird*
pan^m	*bread*	pancito^m	*bread roll*
papá^m	*dad*	papito^m	*daddy*
pastel^m	*cake*	pastelito^m	*small cake*
patín^m	*skate*	patinete^m	*scooter*
pato^m	*duck*	patito^m	*duckling*
pedazo^m	*piece*	pedacito^m	*small piece*
perro^m	*dog*	perrito^m	*little dog*
pez^m	*fish*	pececito^m	*small fish*
pobre^{m,f}	*poor*	pobrecito^m	*poor thing*
poco^m	*little*	poquito^m	*very little*
pollo^m	*chicken*	pollito^m	*chick*
puñal^m	*dagger*	puñalito^m	*small dagger*
rato^m	*while*	ratito^m	*little while*
reloj^m	*clock*	relojito^m	*small clock*
rincón^m	*corner*	rinconcito^m	*little corner*
segundo^m	*second*	segundito^m	*little second*
silla^f	*chair*	sillita^f	*little chair*
sol^m	*sun*	solecito^m	*little sun*
solo/-a	*alone*	solito/-a	*all alone*
suave^{m,f}	*soft*	suavecito/-a	*very soft*
trago^m	*sip*	traguito^m	*little sip*
torta^f	*cake*	tortilla^f	*tortilla*
Venecia^f	*Venice*	Venezuela^f	*Little Venice*
verde^{m,f}	*green*	verdecito/-a	*greenish*
volcán^m	*volcano*	volcancito^m	*little volcano*
zapato^m	*shoe*	zapatito^m	*little shoe*

2. Augmentatives

Spanish Word	Meaning in English	Augmentative in Spanish	Meaning in English
abrazo[m]	*hug*	abrazote[m]	*big hug*
amigo[m]	*friend*	amigote/-a	*crony or pal*
animal[m]	*animal*	animalote[m]	*big or nasty animal*
barriga[f]	*belly*	barrigón/-ona barrigudo/-a	*paunchy or potbellied*
bofetada[f]	*slap*	bofetón[m]	*big slap*
bueno[m]	*good*	buenazo[m]	*good-natured*
cabeza[f]	*head*	cabezazo[m]	*header (sports) headbutt*
		cabezón/-ona cabezote/-a cabezudo/-a	*big-headed stubborn*
cachete[m]	*cheek*	cachetón/-ona	*plump-cheeked*
caja[f]	*box*	cajón[m]	*drawer*
casa[f]	*house*	casona[f]	*big house*
cintura[f]	*waist*	cinturón[m]	*belt*
coche[m]	*car*	cochazo[m]	*amazing car*
codo[m]	*elbow*	codazo[m]	*elbow jab*
cuerda[f]	*rope or string*	cordón[m]	*shoelace*
éxito[m]	*success*	exitazo[m]	*great success*
favor[m]	*favor*	favorzote[m]	*huge favor*
fiesta[f]	*party*	fiestota[f]	*big party*
foto[f]	*photo*	fotaza[f]	*great photo*
fuerte[m,f]	*strong*	fortachón/-ona	*beefy*
grande[m,f]	*big*	grandote/-a grandullón/-ona	*overgrown big guy/girl*
hombre[m]	*man*	hombrón[m]	*big or strong man*
hotel[m]	*hotel*	hotelazo[m]	*big or fancy hotel*
martillo[m]	*hammer*	martillazo[m]	*hammer blow*
misil[m]	*missile*	misilazo[m]	*missile strike*
papel[m]	*paper*	papelote[m]	*worthless paper*
película[f]	*movie*	peliculón[m]	*blockbuster*
perro[m]	*dog*	perrote[m] perrazo[m]	*big or mean dog*
puerta[f]	*door*	portazo[m]	*door slam*
rata[f]	*rat*	ratón[m]	*mouse*
silla[f]	*chair*	sillón[m]	*armchair*
soltero[m]	*single*	solterón[m]	*old bachelor*

Appendix G. Acronyms and Abbreviations

Acronyms, initialisms, and abbreviations are common in Spanish. Here, we summarize some basic rules and list some common examples.

Acronyms and Initialisms

Acronyms and initialisms are both utilized to shorten a phrase by using the first letter of each word. The difference between an acronym and an initialism is that the former is pronounced as one word, e.g., "NASA" and "LASER," whereas the latter is pronounced as separate letters, e.g., "ATM" and "UN."

In most cases, we follow the same rules to form acronyms and initialisms in Spanish. For example:

United Nations	*UN*	**O**rganización de las **N**aciones **U**nidas	ONU
Organization of American States	*OAS*	**O**rganización de los **E**stados **A**mericanos	OEA
North Atlantic Treaty Organization	*NATO*	**O**rganización del **T**ratado **A**tlántico **N**orte	OTAN
International Monetary Fund	*IMF*	**F**ondo **M**onetario Internacional	FMI
World Health Organization	*WHO*	**O**rganización **M**undial de la **S**alud	OMS
Non-Governmental Organization	*NGO*	**O**rganización **N**o **G**ubernamental	ONG

Abbreviations

An abbreviation is a shortened version of a word or phrase. It uses the initial part of a word or a combination of the initial and final parts, and is often characterized by a period at the end.

Examples of such abbreviations are titles and professions, such as:

Sr./Sra. (or Sr.ª)	señor/señora	*Mr./Mrs.*
Srta.	señorita	*Miss*
D./Dña. (or D.ª)	don/doña	*Sir/Madam*
Dr./Dra. (or Dr.ª)	doctor/doctora	*Dr.*

Prof./Prof.ª	profesor/profesora	*Prof.*
Ing.	ingeniero/ingeniera	*Eng.*

The months of the year are abbreviated as follows:

January	enero	*July*	jul.
February	feb.	*August*	agosto
March	mar.	*September*	set./sept.
April	abr.	*October*	oct.
May	mayo	*November*	nov.
June	jun.	*December*	dic.

Notice that the months of **"enero"** *(January)*, **"mayo"** *(May)*, and **"agosto"** *(August)* are not abbreviated.

The days of the week are often abbreviated using a single letter as follows:

Mon.	*Tue.*	*Wed.*	*Thur.*	*Fri.*	*Sat.*	*Sun.*
lunes	martes	miércoles	jueves	viernes	sábado	domingo
L	M	X	J	V	S	D

Notice that **"X"** is used for **"miércoles"** *(Wednesday)* to differentiate it from **"martes"** *(Tuesday)*.

The units of time are sometimes abbreviated as **"d"** for **"día"** *(day)*, **"h"** for **"hora"** *(hour)*, **"min"** for **"minuto"** *(minute)*, and **"s"** for **"segundo"** *(second)*. The **"a.m."** and **"p.m."** abbreviations are used in Spanish in a similar manner to that in English.

The *Before Christ (BC)* era is referred to as **"antes de Cristo"** or **"antes de Jesucristo,"** and is abbreviated as **"a.C."** or **"a.J.C."** The *Common Era (CE)* is often referred to as **"después de Cristo"** or **"después de Jesucristo,"** and is abbreviated as **"d.C."** or **"d.J.C."**

The four cardinal directions are abbreviated as **"N"** for **"norte"** *(north)*, **"S"** for **"sur"** *(south)*, **"E"** for **"este"** *(east)*, and **"O"** for **"oeste"** *(west)*. The four ordinal directions are abbreviated as **"NE"** for "**noreste**" *(northeast)*, "**NO**" for "**noroeste**" *(northwest)*, "**SE**" for "**sureste**" *(southeast)*, and "**SO**" for "**suroeste**" *(southwest)*.

The capital of Argentina, "**Buenos Aires**," is abbreviated as "**Bs. As.**" The common *"e.g."* abbreviation in English has the equivalent "**ej.**" in Spanish.

Abbreviation of Plural Nouns

One notable exception to abbreviation in Spanish is the doubling of the letters in the abbreviation of plural nouns. Some examples are:

*United **S**tates of **A**merica*	USA	**E**stados **U**nidos	EE. UU.[1]
***H**uman **R**esources*	HR	**R**ecursos **H**umanos	RR. HH.
***P**ublic **R**elations*	PR	**R**elaciones **P**úblicas	RR. PP.

[1] Although "**EE. UU.**" is the correct format according to RAE standards, other variations such as "**EE UU**" and "**EEUU**" are widely accepted.

The doubling of the letters does not usually apply when the abbreviation of a plural word is more than one letter. For example, "**Uds.**" is the abbreviation for "**ustedes**" *("you" in plural form)*, and "**ejs.**" is the abbreviation for "**ejemplos**" *(examples)*.

In addition, the doubling of the letters does not apply when the main noun being described is not in plural form. The most notable example is "**ONU**," the abbreviation for the "**Organización de las Naciones Unidas**," which is translated as the *"Organization of the United Nations,"* simply referred to in English as the *"United Nations,"* or the *"UN"* for short. Notice that the main noun in the Spanish name is "**organización**," which is singular. Thus, the doubling of the letters does not apply.

Appendix H. The Use of "Ojalá" in Spanish

The expression **"ojalá"** is derived from the Arabic influence on the Spanish language and is used to express hope that something would happen or would have happened. **"Ojalá"** is always followed by a verb tense in the subjunctive mood.

In this summary, we will cover the use of **"ojalá"** in the following tenses:

1. The Present Subjunctive

In the present subjunctive, **"ojalá"** can be translated roughly as *"hopefully"* to express hope for something, that is *possible*, to happen in the *present* or the *future*, for example:

Ojalá que **no llueva** esta noche.	*Hopefully, it **won't rain** tonight.*
Ojalá que **venga** mi hermano hoy.	*Hopefully, my brother **will come** today.*

2. The Imperfect Subjunctive

"Ojalá" can also be used along with the imperfect subjunctive to express hope that something, that is *unlikely* or *improbable*, would happen in the *present* or the *future*, for example:

Ojalá que **pudiéramos** ganar mucho dinero en un año.	*I wish we **could** make a lot of money in one year.*
Ojalá que **viniera** mi hermano hoy, pero siempre está ocupado.	*I wish my brother **would come** today, but he is always busy.*

3. The Perfect Subjunctive

The expression **"ojalá"** can also be used with the present perfect to hope that something, that is *possible* to happen, has happened in the *past*, for example:

Ojalá que **haya llegado** mi amigo a pesar del tráfico.	*I hope that my friend **has arrived** despite the traffic.*
Ojalá que ya **hayan arreglado** la tele.	*I hope that they **have** already **fixed** the TV.*

Although less common, "**ojalá**" can also be used with the present perfect to hope that something, that is *possible* to happen, will have happened at some point in the *future*, for example:

Ojalá que **haya llegado** mi amigo para la próxima semana.	*I hope that my friend **will have arrived** by next week.*
Ojalá que ya **hayan arreglado** la tele para mañana.	*I hope that they **will have fixed** the TV by tomorrow.*

4. The Pluperfect Subjunctive

The expression "**ojalá**" can also be used with the pluperfect subjunctive to wish that something, that is *impossible* to happen, would have happened in the *past*, for example:

Ojalá yo **hubiera estudiado** medicina.	*I wish I **had studied** medicine.*
Ojalá mi abuelo **no hubiera muerto**.	*I wish my grandfather **hadn't died**.*

Summary

We can summarize the use cases of "**ojalá**" in the following table with the verb "**ser**" as an example:

	Present or Future	**Past**
Possible or Probable	Present Subjunctive e.g., Ojalá (que) sea …	Perfect Subjunctive e.g., Ojalá (que) haya sido …
Impossible or Improbable	Imperfect Subjunctive e.g., Ojalá (que) fuera …	Pluperfect Subjunctive e.g., Ojalá (que) hubiera sido …

INDEX- SPANISH

INDEX- ENGLISH